ODYSSEY

The
ODYSSEY
of Homer

A New Verse Translation by
Allen Mandelbaum

□

With Twelve Engravings by
Marialuisa de Romans

University of California Press
Berkeley · Los Angeles · New York · Oxford

University of California Press
Berkeley and Los Angeles, California

Copyright © 1990 by Allen Mandelbaum

Library of Congress Cataloging-in-Publication Data

Homer.
[Odyssey. English]
The Odyssey of Homer: a new verse translation
by Allen Mandelbaum; with twelve engravings by Marialuisa de Romans.
p. cm.
ISBN 0-520-07021-6 (alk. paper)
1. Odysseus (Greek mythology)–Poetry. I. Mandelbaum, Allen, 1926-   . II. Title.
PA4025.A5M36   1990
883'.01–dc20   90-34719
Printed in the United States of America   CIP

1 2 3 4 5 6 7 8 9

This translation of the
Odyssey
is inscribed to
Heather Hans and Nicholas Mandelbaum
and their generation

Can men with human speech be here—close by?
But I must try, must see with my own eyes.

VI, 125-126

BOOKS BY ALLEN MANDELBAUM

POETRY

Journeyman, 1967

Leaves of Absence, 1976

Chelmaxioms: The Maxims, Axioms, Maxioms of Chelm, 1978

A Lied of Letterpress, 1980

The Savantasse of Montparnasse, 1988

VERSE TRANSLATIONS/EDITIONS

Life of a Man by Giuseppe Ungaretti, 1958

Selected Writings of Salvatore Quasimodo, 1960

The Aeneid of Virgil, 1972 (National Book Award, 1973), 1981

Selected Poems of Giuseppe Ungaretti, 1975

Inferno of Dante, 1980

Purgatorio of Dante, 1982

Paradiso of Dante, 1984

Ovid in Sicily, 1986

Ungaretti and Palinurus, 1989

The Odyssey of Homer, 1990

Convivio I: From Modern Italian Poetry (in preparation)

CONTENTS

ODYSSEY

BOOK I

To the Muse.

·

The anger of Poseidon.

·

In Poseidon's absence,
a gathering of the gods in Zeus' halls on Olympus.

Athena's plea for help for the stranded Odysseus;
Zeus' consent.

·

Athena in the guise of Méntës visits Ithaca.

Her advice to Telémachus:
he is to confront the Ithacan elders
with the problem of the suitors
and to leave Ithaca to search
for news of his father.

·

Penelope's appearance among the suitors.

Her silencing of Phémius the singer.

Telémachus and the suitors:
their sharp exchange.

·

Nightfall:
Telémachus and his old nurse, Euryclēia.

Muse, tell me of the man of many wiles,
the man who wandered many paths of exile
after he sacked Troy's sacred citadel.
He saw the cities—mapped the minds—of many;
and on the sea, his spirit suffered every
adversity—to keep his life intact,
to bring his comrades back. In that last task,
his will was firm and fast, and yet he failed:
he could not save his comrades. Fools, they foiled
themselves: they ate the oxen of the Sun,
the herd of Hélios Hypérion;
the lord of light requited their transgression—
he took away the day of their return.

Muse, tell us of these matters. Daughter of Zeus,
my starting point is any point you choose.

All other Greeks who had been spared the steep
descent to death had reached their homes—released
from war and waves. One man alone was left,
still longing for his home, his wife, his rest.
For the commanding nymph, the brightest goddess,
Calypso, held him in her hollow grottoes:
she wanted him as husband. Even when
the wheel of years drew near his destined time—
the time the gods designed for his return
to Ithaca—he still could not depend
upon fair fortune or unfailing friends.
While other gods took pity on him, one—
Poseidon—still pursued: he preyed upon
divine Odysseus until the end,
until the exile found his own dear land.

But now Poseidon was away—his hosts,
the Ethiopians, the most remote
of men (they live in two divided parts—
half, where the sun-god sets; half, where he starts).
Poseidon, visiting the east, received

Greek [1-24]

the roasted thighs of bulls and sheep. The feast
delighted him. And there he sat. But all
his fellow gods were gathered in the halls
of Zeus upon Olympus; there the father
of men and gods spoke first. His mind upon
the versatile Aegísthus—whom the son
of Agamemnon, famed Oréstes, killed—
he shared this musing with the deathless ones:

"Men are so quick to blame the gods: they say
that we devise their misery. But they
themselves—in their depravity—design
grief greater than the griefs that fate assigns.
So did Aegísthus act when he transgressed
the boundaries that fate and reason set.
He took the lawful wife of Agamemnon;
and when the son of Átreus had come back,
Aegísthus murdered him—although he knew
how steep was that descent. For we'd sent Hermes,
our swiftest, our most keen-eyed emissary,
to warn against that murder and adultery:
'Oréstes will avenge his father when,
his manhood come, he claims his rightful land.'
Hermes had warned him as one warns a friend.
And yet Aegísthus' will could not be swayed.
Now, in one stroke, all that he owes is paid."

Athena, gray-eyed goddess, answered Zeus:
"Our father, Cronos' son, you, lord of lords,
Aegísthus died the death that he deserved.
May death like his strike all who ape his sins.
But brave Odysseus' fate does break my heart:
long since, in misery he suffers, far
from friends, upon an island in the deep—
a site just at the navel of the sea.
And there, upon that island rich in trees,
a goddess has her home: the fair-haired daughter
of Atlas the malevolent (who knows

Greek [25–52]

the depths of every sea, for he controls
the giant column holding earth and sky
apart). Calypso, Atlas' daughter, keeps
the sad Odysseus there—although he weeps.
Her words are fond and fragrant, sweet and soft—
so she would honey him to cast far off
his Ithaca; but he would rather die
than live the life of one denied the sight
of smoke that rises from his homeland's hearths.
Are you, Olympus' lord, not moved by this?
Was not Odysseus your favorite
when, on the spacious plain of Troy, beside
the Argive ships, he sacrificed to you?
What turned your fondness into malice, Zeus?"

Zeus, shepherd of the clouds, replied: "My daughter,
how can the barrier of your teeth permit
such speech to cross your lips? Can I forget
godlike Odysseus, most astute of men,
whose offerings were so unstinting when
he sacrificed to the undying gods,
the masters of vast heaven? Rest assured.
Only Poseidon, lord whose chariot runs
beneath the earth, is furious—it was
Odysseus who deprived the grandest Cyclops,
the godlike Polyphémus, of his eye.
(Thöósa—nymph whose father, Phórcys, keeps
a close watch on the never-resting deep—
gave birth to that huge Cyclops after she
had lain in her deep sea-cave with Poseidon.)
And ever since his son was gouged, the god
who makes earth tremble, though he does not kill
Odysseus, will not let him end his exile.
But now we all must think of his return—
of how to bring him home again. Poseidon
will set aside his anger; certainly
he cannot have his way, for he is only
one god against us all, and we are many."   □ □ □

Greek [53-79]

Athena, gray-eyed goddess, answered him:
"Our father, Cronos' son, you, lord of lords,
if now the blessed gods indeed would end
the wanderings of Odysseus, let us send
the keen-eyed Hermes to Calypso's isle,
Ogýgia. Let him there at once declare
to her, the goddess with the lovely hair,
our undeniable decree: Steadfast
Odysseus is to find his homeward path.
But I shall make my way to Ithaca
at once, to give his son the strength to summon
the long-haired Ithacans; when they assemble
he can denounce—and scatter—all the suitors:
they are forever slaughtering his sheep,
his shambling oxen with their curving horns.
Then off to sandy Pylos and to Sparta
I'll send him to seek tidings of his father's
return; he may yet hear some hopeful word—
and men will then commend him for his search."

That said, Athena fastened on fine sandals:
these—golden, everlasting—carried her
with swift winds over seas and endless lands.
The goddess took her bronze-tipped battle lance,
heavy and huge and solid; with this shaft,
she—daughter of so great a force—can smash
the ranks of warriors who've earned her wrath.
One leap—and from Olympus' peaks she reached
the land of Ithaca. She stood before
Odysseus' door, the threshold of his court.
She gripped the bronze-tipped shaft, and taking on
the likeness of a stranger, she became
lord Méntës, chieftain of the Táphians.
She found the braggart suitors at the gate.
Delighting in their dicing, they reclined
on hides of oxen they themselves had skinned—
with pages and attendants serving them,
some mixing wine and water in wide bowls,

Greek [80-110]

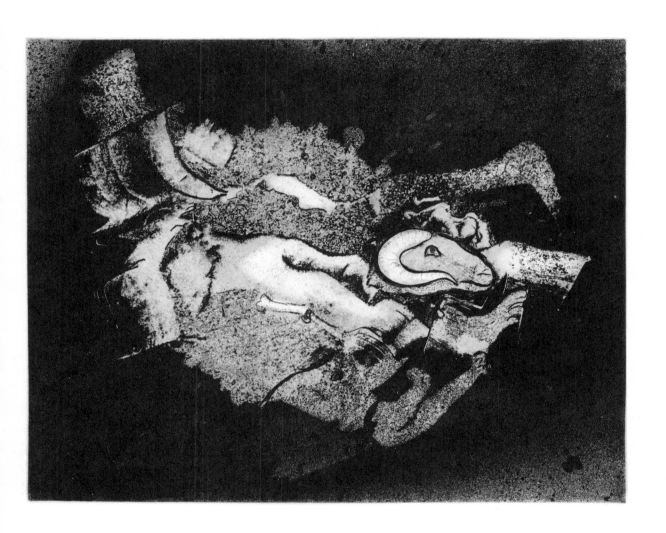

The Feast of the Suitors

while others washed the tables down with sponges
and readied them for food, and others still
stacked meat in heaps on platters—high and full.

The very first to notice Méntës' presence
was young Telémachus. He—sad, morose—
sat with the suitors. In his reverie,
he saw his sturdy father—would that he,
returning suddenly, might banish these
intruders from his palace and restore
the rights and rule that had been his before.
Such was the sadness of Telémachus,
alone among the suitors, till he saw
Athena; he rushed toward the outer door,
ashamed that none had gone to greet the stranger.
He drew near, clasped her right hand, even as
his left relieved her of the heavy lance.
And when he spoke, his words were like winged shafts:
"My greetings, stranger. Welcome to our feast.
Eat first—and then do tell us what you seek."

He led the way; Athena followed him.
Once they were in the high-roofed hall, he placed
her lance against a column at whose base
a polished rack, with slots for spears, was set;
within that rack there stood still other shafts,
the many spears that brave Odysseus left.
He led the stranger to a tall chair, wrought
with care; across its frame he spread rich cloth.
There he invited her to sit and rest
her feet upon a stool; and he himself
sat nearby, on another well-carved chair,
set far off from the suitors, lest his guest,
in all that brouhaha, might look askance
at feasting with such overbearing men—
and, too, because he wanted so to gather
what news he could about his distant father.
That they might wash their hands, a servant poured

Greek [111-136]

fresh water from a lovely golden jug
into a silver basin; at their side
she placed a polished table. The old housewife
was generous: she drew on lavish stores;
to each of them she offered much and more.
The carver offered meats of every sort,
and for their wine he set out golden cups;
and these—again, again—a page filled up.

But then the suitors swaggered in; they sat,
in order, on low seats and high-backed chairs.
The pages poured fresh water for their hands,
and servants brought them baskets heaped with bread.
The suitors' hands reached out. The feast was theirs.

When they had had their fill of food and drink,
the feasters felt the need for chant and dance—
at banquets, these are pleasing ornaments.
A steward now consigned a handsome harp
into the hands of Phémius, who was forced,
from time to time, to entertain those lords.
He struck the strings, and music graced his words.

Then, as Telémachus turned toward his guest,
lest he be overheard, he held his head
close to the gray-eyed goddess—and he said:

"Dear guest, will you be vexed at what I say?
This harping and this chant delight these men,
for all these goods come easily to them:
they feed—but never need to recompense.
They feast at the expense of one whose white
bones, surely, either rot beneath the rain,
unburied and abandoned on the land,
or else are preyed upon by churning waves.
Yet, were Odysseus to return, were they
to see him here again, they would not pray
for gold or richer clothes—just faster feet.

Greek [137-165]

But he has died by now, died wretchedly;
and nothing can console us now, not even
if some man on this earth should say my father
will yet return. The day of his homecoming
is lost: it is a day we'll never see.
But tell me one thing—tell me honestly:
Who are you? Of what father were you born?
Where is your city, where your family?
On what ship did you sail? Why did that crew
bring you to Ithaca? And who were they?
For surely you did not come here on foot!
And also tell me truthfully—is this
the first time you have come to Ithaca,
or have you been my father's guest before?
For many other foreigners have come
to visit us—like you, my father knew
the ways of many men and many lands."

Athena, gray-eyed goddess, answered him:
"My words to you are true: I'm Méntës, son
of wise Anchíalus; the Táphians,
tenacious oarsmen, are the men I rule.
Now I have landed here with ship and crew;
we cross the winedark sea toward Témesë—
all this in search of copper. What we stow
is gleaming iron, which we're set to barter.
Outside the city, moored in Rheīthron's harbor,
close to the fields, beneath Mount Néion's forest,
my ship is waiting. Years ago, your father
and mine were guests and friends. (Just ask the brave
Laértës—though they say he shuns the city;
it seems that now he much prefers to grieve
far off, alone, except for one old servant.
She, when his body aches from the hard climb
he makes, from slope to slope, to tend his vines,
still carries food and drink right to his side.)

□   □   □

Greek [166-193]

"Now I have come—for I had heard indeed
that he, your father, had returned. Surely
it is the gods who now obstruct his journey.
For bright Odysseus has not died upon
this earth: he is alive somewhere, delayed
upon an island set among vast waves,
held by harsh savages, against his will.
I am no augur or interpreter
of flights of birds, but now I shall foretell—
even as the immortals prompt my soul—
events my mind can see: Your father will
not be kept back from his dear land much longer,
though they may bind him fast in iron chains;
he is a man of many wiles, who can
contrive the way to reach his home again.
But you—do tell me now with honesty:
Are you, so tall, indeed Odysseus' son?
Your head and handsome eyes resemble his
extraordinarily; we two had met
quite often in the days before he left
for Troy, where others, too—the Argives' best—
sailed in their hollow ships. But since then I
have not seen him, and he has not seen me."

Telémachus' reply was keen and wise:
"Dear friend, I cannot be more frank than this.
My mother says I am his son, but none
can know for sure the seed from which he's sprung.
In any case, would I had been the son
of one so blessed that he grew old among
his own belongings. I, instead, am born—
or so they say—of one who surely was
the most forsaken man, the most forlorn.
Now you have had and heard my full response."

Athena, gray-eyed goddess, answered him:
"Despite misfortune now, your family
can count on future fame: Penelope

Greek [194-222]

is mother of a son who is most worthy.
But tell me truthfully: What sort of feast
is this? A banquet? Or a wedding party?
This surely is no meal where each has brought
his share. Why did this crowd seek out your house?
These guzzlers seem to me no better than
a pack of swaggerers—too rude, too coarse.
Seeing their shameful doings, any man
of sense would feel both anger and contempt."

Telemachus' response was wise, precise:
"Dear guest, to all you ask, I now reply.
I tell you that as long as he, my father,
was in his native land, this house was rich
and great. But then the gods willed otherwise—
they made my father vanish: they devised
oblivion for him—much deeper than
oblivion known by any other man.
And though he's dead, my grief would be less deep
if he had fallen in the land of Troy,
among his fellow warriors, or else—
once he had wound up all the threads of war—
had died at home, among his very own.
Then all of the Achæans would have built
a tomb for him; and, too, he would have won
much glory for his son in days to come.
Instead, the spirit-winds—the stormy Harpies—
snatched him away ingloriously: he
was banished into black obscurity.
And I am left with grief and misery.
I sigh not only over him: the gods
have given me still more calamities.
All lords with power in these isles—who rule
Dulíchium and Samos and Zacýnthus,
the wooded isle, and those who now presume
to rule in rocky Ithaca—continue
to woo my mother and consume my goods.
She'll not reject the hateful wedding or

Greek [223-249]

accept it. Meanwhile all their gluttony
lays waste my house; they soon will ruin me."

Pallas Athena, now incensed, replied:
"The absent one, Odysseus, is indeed
the man whom you, unhappy son, could use:
he'd break the back of this marauding band.
Would he—returned—were now to take his stand
upon the threshold with his helmet, shield,
and pair of spears—the mighty man that I
first saw on his way back from Éphyrë,
the land of Ílus, son of Mérmerus;
along his homeward way, he stayed with us—
I saw him drinking, feasting, in our house.
(He'd sailed in his fast ship to visit Ílus,
to seek a fatal venom he could smear
on his bronze arrow-tips; but in his fear
of the undying gods' displeasure, Ílus
refused to give Odysseus that dread drug.
My father gave it to him, for he loved
your father so extraordinarily.)
For if Odysseus were to show himself
among this pack of suitors with the same
strength he showed then, they all would meet quick death
and bitter wooing. But of things like these—
whether or not your father, on returning,
will take revenge within his palace—we
know nothing; such things lie upon the knees
of gods. But for yourself, you must consider
the way in which to rid your house of suitors.
Now hear my words and think on them with care.
Tomorrow ask the lords of Ithaca
to gather here; then speak to all, and let
the gods be witnesses. Command the suitors
to scatter, each on his own way; and order
your mother, should she be inclined to wed,
to go back to her mighty father's house.
Let him prepare his daughter's wedding and

Greek [250–276]

the gifts—appropriately rich—she merits.
As for yourself, the path I urge is this,
if you would listen: Find the fittest ship
and, with a crew of twenty oarsmen, seek
some word of your long-absent father—for
a mortal may have heard about him, or
your ears may chance to hear the voice that Zeus
so often uses when he brings men news.
Sail first to Pylos: question noble Nestor.
Then visit Sparta's king, blond Meneláus:
of all Achæans clad in bronze, he was
the last to reach his home. If you should hear
word that your father is still alive and steers
a homeward path, then—though you are much tried—
you surely can hold out for one more year.
But if you learn that he has died, return
to your dear land and raise a mound for him;
complete a just, unstinting funeral,
then marry off your mother to some man:
you will have done all that you should—and can.
But then weigh carefully in mind and soul
how best to kill the suitors in your halls—
by way of open combat or of guile.
Forget the pastimes of a child: you are
a boy no longer. Or have you not heard
what fame Oréstes gained when he avenged
the murder of his father? Everyone
knows how he killed that master of deceptions,
Aegísthus, slayer of great Agamemnon.
You, too, my friend—I see you tall, robust—
must never flinch or falter if you want
to win the praise of men in time to come.
But now I must return to my swift ship;
this long delay may make my comrades fret.
Consider carefully—heed what I've said."

□ □ □

Greek [277-305]

Telémachus' reply was keen and wise:
"My guest, your words come from a friendly mind—
words like a father's to a son—and I
shall not forget them. But why not extend
your stay? Although your voyage presses, bathe—
refresh your spirit; then, fine gift in hand,
you can with satisfaction sail away.
That gift will be a precious, handsome thing,
a keepsake such as dear friends give to friends."

Athena, gray-eyed goddess, answered him:
"Do not delay me now. I truly wish
to leave; whatever gift your heart would give—
you'll choose a handsome one, I'm sure—can be
consigned when I stop here again, on my
return, that I may bear it home. And it
will earn for you a gift of equal merit."

When that was said, gray-eyed Athena left,
quick as a bird. Within his heart she'd set
resolve and strength and memories more intense—
more bent upon his father—than before.
And he was pensive, marveling, aware
that he had had some god as visitor.

At once he went among the suitors—he,
a mortal like a god. The flawless bard
was chanting still; the suitors sat in silent
astonishment. He sang of the Achæans:
their sad return from Troy, the penalty
Athena made them pay. Penelope,
within her rooms above, hung on his words;
she grasped the wondrous sense of every verse.
The pensive daughter of Icárius
descended the steep stairs, escorted by
two of her maids: she did not come alone.
And when that lovely woman reached the hall,
beside a pillar that sustained the roof,

Greek [306-333]

she stopped—a glowing shawl before her face,
and, to each side, there stood a faithful maid.
In tears, Penelope implored the singer:

"You, Phémius, know many other deeds
of men and gods—exploits that bring delight
to mortals, acts that singers celebrate.
Then, seated here among these suitors sing
of such things—while they drink their wine in silence.
But stop this dismal chant, for it consumes
the heart within my breast, since I have been
struck by a loss that cannot be forgotten.
Indeed, such was the man for whom I grieve
with endless memory, a man whose glory
is known through Hellas, Argos—all of Greece."

This was Telémachus' astute reply:
"My mother, why not let the faithful singer
delight us as his heart impels? The singer
is not to blame; this grief was brought by Zeus,
he who assigns to those who feed on bread
the good or evil he alone decrees.
Do not fault Phémius if he would sing
the Dánaans' sorry doom: men hold most dear
whatever song is newest to their ears.
Allow your heart and soul to listen, for
Odysseus was not the only one
to lose in Troy the day of his return:
there many other warriors met their death.
But go now to your room; tend to your tasks,
the distaff and the loom; your women can
complete the work that they began. Leave speech
to men: to all those here and—most—to me;
within this house, I have authority."

Amazed, while going to her room, she laid
to heart her son's wise words. Then, with her maids,
she reached the upper floor, and wept and wept

Greek [334-363]

for her dear husband, her Odysseus,
until Athena, gray-eyed goddess, shed
sweet sleep upon her eyelids.

But the suitors
began to clamor in the shadowed hall:
each hoped that he might lie in bed with her.
For them Telémachus had these sharp words:

"How arrogant you are—beyond all measure—
you who would win my mother. Feast with pleasure
for now, but let there be no brouhaha:
to hear the song of one whose voice is like
the gods'—that is most fine. There will be time
tomorrow to assemble, one and all;
within that council I shall frankly call
on every one of you to quit my halls.
Just hold your future revels someplace else;
consume your own fine goods; let each for each
prepare, in turn—in his own house—a feast.
Or if you think it easier—or better—
to eat your unpaid way through one man's wealth,
feast here indeed. But I shall then implore
the gods, who live forever, asking Zeus
to grant me my requital: all of you
would then die unavenged within these halls."

The angry suitors bit their lips, amazed
to hear Telémachus speak words so brave.
Antínoüs, Eupeīthes' son, replied:

"Telémachus, the gods indeed may teach
brash blustering to you and braggart speech.
But let us hope that they'll not intervene,
that Cronos' son will not make you the king
of seagirt Ithaca, whatever claim
your birth might bring."
□ □ □

Greek [364–387]

To this, Telémachus'
reply was keen and wise: "Antínoüs,
though what I say may well incite your wrath,
I would be king were Zeus to grant me that.
I want that honor: do you really think
that kingship is a sorry destiny?
To be a king does not mean misery:
a ruler's house grows rich at once; his name
gains glory everywhere. In any case,
our seagirt Ithaca has many lords—
other Achæan chiefs both young and old;
and since the firm Odysseus now is dead,
one of these princes may succeed him. Yet
I still shall rule in my own hall and keep
the servants that Odysseus won for me."

Eurýmachus, the son of Pólybus,
replied: "This matter rests on the gods' knees—
which lord of the Achæans will be king
in seagirt Ithaca. But do be sure,
your house has you as lord, your goods are yours.
As long as there are men in Ithaca,
no one—whoever he may be—can come
and seize your wealth by force, against your will.
But, dear friend, tell me now about the stranger:
Where does he come from? Did he say what country
he can call home? Where is his family?
Where are his native fields? Did he bring word
about Odysseus' coming home? Or was
he traveling on his own affairs? He left
so quickly, suddenly; he did not wait
to meet us—but his aspect was not base."

Telémachus' reply was careful, weighed:
"Eurýmachus, that day is lost—the day
on which my father would return. And thus,
no news that men may bring can win my trust:
I pay no heed to any prophecy,

Greek [388-414]

to any seer my mother may have called
into this hall. That stranger is a friend
whom I inherited. He comes from Taphos:
Méntës, the son of wise Anchíalus—
so he announced himself. And he commands
those men who love to row, the Táphians.”

Though he said this, his heart knew he had met
the deathless goddess: she had been his guest.

The suitors, charmed by dance, entranced by song,
rejoicing, waited for the night to come.
And then dark evening fell as they caroused,
and each—to sleep—went back to his own house.
Telémachus walked toward the fair courtyard:
there stood the high-walled room, set well apart,
where he would spend the night. But as he walked,
not sleep but hope and worry filled his thoughts.
Beside him, blazing torches in her hands
to light his way, went careful Euryclēīa,
daughter of Ops, who was Peisénor's son.
(Long years ago, when she had just been touched
by loveliness, Laértës purchased her:
he paid as much as twenty oxen cost.
And even as he honored his dear wife,
so had he honored her. But he had never
brought her to bed with him: he took much care
never to wound his wife or stir her anger.)
And it was she who led him to his door,
who bore bright torches as they crossed the court,
for none among the handmaids loved him more—
she was the one who'd nursed Telémachus.

Once he'd unlatched the door of his fine room,
he sat down on the bed, shed his soft tunic,
and handed it to the astute old woman.
She smoothed and folded it, then hung it on
a peg beside the bedstead. When she left,

Greek [415-440]

she shut the door, drew to the silver knob,
then pulled the drop-strap fast. Telémachus—
night long, and covered by a wool-fleece wrap—
thought on the trip his goddess-guest had mapped.

BOOK II

Dawn.

.

A public appeal in vain:
Telémachus before the elders of Ithaca;
his complaint against the suitors.

The omen of the eagles:
an augur's prediction of Odysseus' return
and his vengeance on the suitors.

.

Telémachus and Athena, as Mentor, by the shore:
the goddess' plan for Telémachus' departure.

Their secret preparations;
a swift ship and a sturdy crew.

An evening sailing—
off to Pylos.

Firstlight: when Dawn's rose fingers touched the sky,
the dear son of Odysseus—quick to rise
and dress—soon set within his shoulder strap
his sharp blade; to his feet—anointed, sleek—
he tied fine sandals. As he crossed the threshold,
he seemed a god. At once he told his heralds—
with voices clarion-clear—to call a council.
The long-haired Ithacans were soon assembled.
Then he, his lance of bronze held fast, advanced—
but not alone: behind, two brisk hounds paced.
On him Athena shed a deathless grace,
and all the people marveled as he came
to the assembly ground. He took his place:
his father's seat. The elders all gave way.

The first to speak was lord Aegýptius,
one bent with age, astute in all life's ways.
The spearman Ántiphus was his dear son,
the good Odysseus' close companion, one
who'd sailed in hollow ships to Ílion,
where many fine foals graze. But in the cave
of brutal Cyclops, when that savage ate
the Ithacans, his final meal was made
of Ántiphus. Three other sons were born
of lord Aegýptius; and although one,
Eurýnomus, had joined the suitors' band,
the last two farmed their aged father's lands.
And yet Aegýptius did not forget
his absent son: his grief was long and deep.
Now, even as he wept, he urged the chiefs:

"Do listen, Ithacans, to what I say.
This is our first assembly since the day
when hollow ships bore bright Odysseus
away. But who is he who summons us?
Who needed so to see us gather here—
a younger man or one well on in years?
Did he hear word of an approaching force

Greek [1-30]

and want to share that first alert with us?
Or did he need to rally this assembly
for other public matters he'll discuss?
In any case, he seems to me courageous,
blessed by the gods: may Zeus be generous—
and let this man fulfill what his heart wills."

His words were done. Odysseus' dear son
delighted in the presage he had heard.
He sat no longer but prepared to speak.
He stood among the Ithacans. Peisénor,
the herald, wise in counsel, set the scepter
into his hands. And then Telémachus
spoke words meant—chiefly—for Aegýptius:

"Old man, as you yourself are soon to hear,
the one who called this council is at hand.
I am the man who wanted us to meet,
the man who—more than any here—must grieve.
I have no news of an invading fleet,
no urgent warning I must now repeat
to every Ithacan—nor would I speak
of other public things. All that I plead
is my own sorry case: A double curse
has fallen on my house. For I have lost
a most courageous father, he who once
ruled you who gather here—a man most gentle.
And still another evil threatens me:
The ruin of my house will be complete;
all that we own will be consumed. The suitors—
dear sons of those who are the noblest here—
against her will, besiege my mother now.
They are afraid to seek her father's house—
though it's Icárius who should endow
his daughter with a dowry, then bestow
her hand upon that man he favors most.
Instead, they crowd into our house. They slaughter
oxen and rams and fat goats; there they guzzle

Greek [31-56]

our glowing wine: their stupid rite, their revel.
They waste our wealth away: there's no defense—
no man who, as Odysseus could, might end
this pestilence. I am too weak to check
their insolence; yes—even if I tried,
I lack warcraft, the power that defies.
Had I the force, I certainly would fight:
their acts are unendurable—my house
has gone to ruin—a disastrous course.
You, too, should scorn their ways and feel the force
of shame for what your neighbors here have wrought:
beware—the gods, grown angry for these acts
of malice, may assault you in their wrath.
I call upon Olympian Zeus and Themis,
she who disperses and convenes men's meetings:
my friends, let each of you go his own way;
leave me to my despair. Or can it be
that brave Odysseus' hate brought injury
to the Achæans with their sturdy greaves,
and you, revenging that, would harass me,
inciting those who court Penelope?
If that is so, it would indeed be better
were you—and not the suitors—to consume
my herds and treasures: then I could at least
receive fair recompense. We would persist,
would press our claim throughout the town, insist
on payment for our goods, until their worth
was given back in full. But now you cast
despair into my heart—a sorrow past
all care and cure."

       These were his bitter words.
Throwing his scepter to the ground, he wept;
and pity overcame the people. All
the rest were motionless; and no one dared
to answer him with harsh words—none, except
Antínoüs, who, in replying, said:
□ □ □

Greek [57-83]

"Telémachus, with roaring words, unchecked,
your anger blames, defames us. But be sure,
if anyone's to blame, it's not the suitors,
but that supreme deceiver—your dear mother.
Three years have passed—the fourth will soon be gone:
she still continues to connive, to thwart
the hearts of the Achæans. She would sport:
she offers every suitor hope and promise—
meanwhile her mind is bent on something else.
Her heart devised this guile: Within her room
Penelope set up a spacious loom.
The web was wide, the threads were fine, and she
assured us all—unhesitatingly:
'Young men, since bright Odysseus now is dead,
be patient; though you're keen to marry me,
wait till the cloth is done, lest any thread
unravel. This is lord Laértës' shroud—
the robe he'll wear when dark death strikes him down.
I weave it now, lest some Achæan women
condemn me for neglect, for having let
a man who'd won such wealth lie at his death
without a shroud.' These were her words—and we,
with manly hearts, agreed. So she would weave
that mighty web by day—but then, by night,
by torchlight, she undid what she had done.
She hoodwinked all of us for three long years;
but when, as spring returned, the fourth was here,
one of her women servants—well aware
of how your mother had connived—told all.
We caught Penelope as she unraveled
that lovely web. So she—against her will—
completed it. This is our just retort
to you—that you may know it in your heart
and the Achæans all may know it, too:
Send off your mother now, and order her
to wed the suitor chosen by her father—
and pleasing to herself. And should she vex
the sons of the Achæans any longer,

Greek [84-115]

should she consider nothing but the gifts
Athena gave to her (and, I admit,
no woman can surpass her handiwork,
discerning mind, and subtle craftiness;
not even those of ancient days could match
your mother—even the Achǽan women
with their thick tresses, in the distant past:
Mycénë of the lovely crown, Alcménë,
and Tyro—none has ever had her wits),
then will her calculations be—this once—
mistaken. For as long as she intends
to keep the stubborn counsel that some god
has planted in her heart, so long shall we
consume your goods, your wealth. That may bring glory
to her, but it means poverty for you.
Be sure of this: We will not tend our fields
or leave your halls until your mother shall
have chosen one of us and married him."

Telémachus' reply was thoughtful, wise:
"Antínoüs, there is no way in which
I can expel—against her will—the one
who gave me life, who raised me. Now my father—
alive or dead—is elsewhere on this earth.
And should I choose to send my mother off,
then I alone would bear the bitter cost
of having to repay Icárius
the price of all her dowry brought to us.
So would I suffer at her father's hand,
and to those sufferings the gods would add
still others; for my mother, as she left
this house, would call upon the dread Avengers;
men, too, would blame me. Thus, I never shall
send off my mother. But if you can feel
remorse within your heart, then leave my halls;
just hold your future revels someplace else:
consume your own fine goods: let each for each
prepare, in turn—in his own house—a feast.

Greek [116-140]

Or if you think it easier—or better—
to eat your unpaid way through one man's wealth,
then prey on me. But I shall then implore
the gods who live forever, asking Zeus
to grant me my requital: each and all,
you'd then die unavenged within my halls."

Telémachus had spoken. Zeus, whose voice
is heard across wide earth, sent down to him
a pair of eagles from the mountain's peak.
Their wings outstretched, they glided, side by side,
on currents of the wind; but when they reached
a point above the raucous suitors, each
wheeled round and—furiously—flapped its wings.
They stared at those below; their gaze spelled death.
Then, having clawed each other's cheeks and neck,
they flew off to the right, across the roofs,
across the city. All of the assembled
had seen the eagles; all in wonder pondered
what was to be. Then old lord Halithérses,
who was the son of Mastor, spoke; no augur
in those days was a more discerning reader
of birds in flight as omens of the future.
His words of prophecy were wise, well meant:

"Ithacans, listen to my words. The suitors—
above all—are the ones who need to hear:
it's they who face the wave of dark disaster;
their end is near; Odysseus won't delay,
won't stay away from those he holds most dear;
he is already near; and he has planted
the seed of death and slaughter for the suitors—
for each and all of them. And he will bring
calamity to others of us here
in Ithaca, the island bright with sunlight.
But let us think in time how we can check
these men. Or let them all consent to end
their revels: they would profit from that course.

Greek [141-169]

I am no neophyte who prophesies:
I know with certainty. And I affirm
that, for Odysseus, his time is come:
even as I predicted when the man
of stratagems first sailed to Ílion,
a lord among the Argives. Then I said
that, after suffering many trials and woes,
the loss of all his comrades, he—unknown
to everyone—at last would reach his home
twenty years later. This is surely so."

Eurýmachus, the son of Pólybus,
replied: "Old man, go back to your hearthside.
There you can play the prophet for your sons—
lest they encounter harm in days to come.
But in this matter, I'm the wiser one.
For certain, many birds beneath the sun
fly back and forth—but not all flights forewarn.
As for Odysseus, he is far-off—dead—
and would that you had died with him instead
of babbling—fast and free—of auguries,
inciting in Telémachus more deep
resentment—even as you hope to see
the gift that he will bring to your house if
you please him with convenient prophecies.
But I shall tell you something sure: Take heed—
if you, who know so many ancient things,
beguile that boy with prophecies and spur
his acts of anger, he will only suffer
more grievously; and, too, the penalty
that we shall make you pay will be so heavy—
enough to make you brood most bitterly.
To you, Telémachus, this is my counsel:
Send back your mother to her father's house.
Let him prepare the wedding feast and offer
abundant gifts—the sort that are most proper
for any man who marries off a daughter.
Until that wedding day has come, the sons

Greek [170-198]

of the Achæans will persist in courting;
there is no thing, no one, we fear—not even
Telémachus, for all his blustering
harangues, nor all the empty auguries
that you, old man, dispense, becoming still
more hateful as you rattle on. As long
as she postpones that wedding, wearying
her suitors, for so long will we abuse,
with no repayment ever, any goods
Telémachus possesses. Day by day
we wait upon her word. Penelope,
and only she, sets us against each other,
competing for a matchless bride; and we
will seek no other, even those—not few—
well suited to us should we choose to woo."

Telémachus' reply was prudent, shrewd:
"As for this matter, I now ask no more
of you, Eurýmachus, and all the rest
of your fine company; the deathless gods
and all the Ithacans have heard my words.
Just give me twenty comrades and a ship—
a swift ship for a voyage out and back.
Then I shall make my way to sandy Pylos
and Sparta, seeking tidings of my father,
who left so long ago. I want to hear
if he is coming home. Perhaps some mortal
will share such word with me, or it may be
the voice of Zeus that reaches me—for he
often divulges news to men. If I
should hear that my dear father is alive
and may return, then I, however tried
my strength may be, shall wait another year.
But if I hear that he no longer lives,
then I, returning to my own dear land,
to honor him will heap a death-mound high
and offer to his memory rich rites—
and give my mother to another husband."   □ □ □

Greek [199-223]

Such were his words. He sat. In that assembly,
rose Mentor, comrade of the good Odysseus.
Odysseus, when he sailed away, confided
his house to Mentor—ordering his kin
to do as his friend bid—to see that all
his goods were kept intact. And what was urged
by Mentor now were wisdom's very words:

"Ithacans, listen well to what I say.
From this time on, no sceptered king need be
benign and kind, a man of righteous mind:
let kings be cruel and corrupt, malign—
for none among his people now recall
divine Odysseus, though his rule was gentle
and fatherly. But I am not incensed
by all the suitors' plots and violence;
for they, in plundering Odysseus' wealth,
have put their lives at risk (though they insist
that he will not come back). Instead, my wrath
indicts the rest of you, who sit in silence,
who speak no word to block their arrogance,
though you are many and the suitors few."

Evénor's son, Leócritus, replied:
"You, Mentor, are a rabble-rousing lout.
How dare you urge the Ithacans to block
our suit? What fighting men can you recruit
with nothing but a banquet in dispute?
We are too many, and for certain you
and yours are far too feeble and too few.
If Ithacan Odysseus himself
were to appear, intent on driving out
the noble suitors feasting in his house,
then even she—his wife—who longs to see
the day of his return, would only grieve.
For he would meet a squalid destiny
were he to face so many. How absurd—
your words! But now, you Ithacans, be off;

Greek [224–252]

let each of you go back to till his farm.
Let Mentor with the help of Halithérses
(they both are old friends of this fellow's father)
encourage him to travel, though I think
he'll linger long in Ithaca, awaiting
some word: he's not a man for journeying."

That said, he quickly broke up the assembly.
And while the other Ithacans returned
to their own homes, the road the suitors chose
was that which led to good Odysseus' house.

Telémachus went off alone, along
the shore. He bathed his hands in the gray waves
and to Athena, gray-eyed goddess, prayed:

"Do hear me: As a goddess, yesterday
you came to us, commanding me to sail
across the shadowed sea, that I might learn
about my long-gone father's coming home.
But the Achǽans thwart my plan—that band
of suitors, in their brutal arrogance."

So did he pray; and in the guise of Mentor—
in both his aspect and his voice—Athena
drew closer as she offered him winged words:

"Telémachus, you will not be a fool
or cringing coward; if it's true that you
have drawn upon your father's force and worth
(for he was one whose acts fulfilled his words),
your journey will not go to waste. But if
you're not his son, and not Penelope's,
the speech you speak will never lead to deeds.
Do what your plan demands. Ignore the senseless
proposals and desires of the suitors,
who are not wise or just. They do not know
how death and darkest fate draw closer now:

Greek [252-283]

they all will die together in one day.
The journey you would take is now at hand.
In me your father's house has one true friend:
for you I shall equip a rapid ship,
and I shall share your voyage. On your part,
prepare your stores, and stow them well: the wine
in jars, and grain—the marrow of all mortals—
in sturdy leather sacks. Now let me choose
those Ithacans who'll serve as willing crew.
This seagirt island has so many ships—
both new and old. I'll pick the craft most fit.
We'll ready her without delay; then we
shall launch her on her way, across the deep."

So did Athena, Zeus's daughter, speak.
Telémachus, who'd heard her voice, took heed.
He did not linger. But his heart was filled
with sadness when he found the suitors still
within his house, where in the courtyard they
were skinning goats and roasting hogs. Smiling,
Antínoüs approached Telémachus
and clasped his hand and spoke these words to him:

"Telémachus—so grand, impetuous
an orator—it's time to set aside
the hostile speech and deeds your thoughts devise.
But let us eat and drink as we have done.
Be sure, all the Achæans will provide
a boat and the best oarsmen, then you can
sail off at once to sacred Pylos and
seek word of your fine father in that land."

Telémachus' reply was sharp, precise:
"Antínoüs, I cannot feast in peace
or be content with men so arrogant.
What more do you require? Through all those years
when I was still a boy, you suitors squandered
the riches that were mine. But I am grown;

Greek [284-314]

and listening to the words of others, I
can understand; my spirit gains new force;
I'll try to set harsh fates on a dark course
against you—as I journey now to Pylos
or on returning to my house. For I
do go—and know my journey won't be wasted,
although I leave as passenger, not master:
I own no ship and am without a crew;
but this, it seems, is just as you would choose."

That said—as if indifferent—he withdrew
his hand: the hand Antínoüs had clasped.
The suitors saw—and as they skinned his goats
and roasted hogs for that day's feast, they mocked
Telémachus. They jeered and fleered. And one
young suitor—swaggering—announced with scorn:

"He really means to murder us. He'll bring
avengers from the land of sandy Pylos—
even from Sparta—he is that obsessed.
Or is it fatal drugs he wants to fetch
from Éphyrë's rich fields—the poisons he
can cast into our wine—and utterly
annihilate us?"

                And another chimed:
"Who knows? While sailing in his hollow ship,
he may die—distant from his dear ones—just
as did Odysseus. And in that case he
adds one more chore, a thing most difficult:
We'd have to share his wealth between us, but
we'd surely give this palace to his mother
and to the one who weds her."

                                So they scoffed.

But he went down into his father's vast
storeroom, where heaps of gold and bronze were massed

Greek [315-338]

and clothes in chests and flasks of fragrant oil.
And in that room stood giant jars of wine—
a wine most sweet, well aged, unmixed, divine.
These, jar on jar, were ranged along the walls
against the day when, after many trials,
Odysseus might end his long exile.
The double doors were shut; their fit was close.
There, night and day, a knowing woman watched
over those treasures. She—daughter of Ops,
Peisénor's son—was faithful Eurycleīa.
Telémachus led her inside and said:

"Dear nurse, do pour from large to smaller jars
sweet wine, the tastiest you can provide—
except for that which you have set aside
for the return of one who fills your mind—
unfortunate Odysseus (yes, you hope
that he, escaping death and fate, might find
his own dear home again). Fill up twelve jars;
make sure their lids are sealed, secure. Then store
choice grain, ground fine, in tight-stitched leather skins—
some twenty measures. None must hear of this.
Place all those jars and skins in one large heap.
And then at evening, when, inclined to sleep,
my mother climbs the stairs to her own rooms,
I'll come to fetch what you've prepared. For I
will sail to sandy Pylos, then to Sparta,
to gather any news of my dear father."

His speech was done. The dear nurse, Eurycleīa,
cried out in grief, then, weeping, spoke winged words:
"Dear child, why did your mind concoct this plan?
Why do you want to journey through broad lands,
you who are so well loved, an only son?
Divine Odysseus died far from his home,
in some strange land, among those we don't know.
These suitors here, as soon as you have left,
behind your back will plot your death, a trap

Greek [338–367]

to kill you, then your riches will be theirs;
each of those plunderers will take his share.
Watch over what is here: what need is there
to suffer risk and sadness? Do not stray
across the never-resting sea's harsh ways."

Telémachus' reply was wise and sharp:
"Forget your fears, old nurse: my plan was not
devised without the counsel of a god.
But swear that you will not reveal my plot
until eleven days or twelve have passed—
or till my mother, asking for me, hears
that I have gone—for otherwise the tears
that she will shed may mar her loveliness."

Then, having sworn, at once she drew the wine
into the ample jars and poured the flour
into the tight-sewn skins. Telémachus,
returning to the hall, mixed with the suitors.
And then Athena, gray-eyed goddess, thought
of still another measure. Taking on
the likeness of Telémachus, she went
throughout the city; to each man she met,
she spoke directly, asking all to group
at dusk to board a swift ship. Then she asked
Noémon, far-famed son of Phrónius,
to let her use his ship. And that request
was promptly met.

                    And when the sun sank low
and shadows thickened on the roads, the goddess
was quick to draw that swift ship down to sea.
She furnished it with all a fine craft needs.
She moored it at the harbor mouth; and when
the stout crew gathered, she encouraged them.
Then she returned to good Odysseus' house
and overcame the suitors with sweet sleep:
she soon cut short their guzzling ways and cast

Greek [368-396]

their cups down from their hands. They did not stay
much longer now, but, straggling, went their way
across the city, back to bed; sleep lay
heavy upon their lids. At this, Athena
(whose voice and guise were now like Mentor's) called
Telémachus to leave the spacious hall:

"Telémachus, your comrades—at the oars—
are waiting for your signal. Let us go;
there is no need to linger on the road."

That said, Pallas Athena moved ahead.
He followed where her rapid footsteps led.
They found his long-haired comrades on the shore.
Telémachus told them with sacred force:

"Friends, come now, let us go to fetch the stores:
all that we need is heaped within the house.
My mother does not know what we have done;
no handmaid's heard our plan—except for one."

That said, he led the way. His shipmates came
along, and once they'd carried back the stores,
they stowed them in the stout hull, in accord
with everything Odysseus' son had urged.
Athena boarded, then Telémachus;
they sat together at the stern. The rest
cast off and took their places on the thwarts.
But now Athena blessed them with a brisk
west wind that sang across the winedark sea.
At that, Telémachus spurred on his men:
their sail was needed now. He wanted them
to raise the mast of fir and step it in
the socket of its box. They did just this.
And then, with firm forestays, they fastened it.
With twisted oxhide thongs, they hoisted high
the sail; it swelled beneath the windswept sky.
The foaming wave was loud along the keel.

Greek [397–428]

Headway was brisk. And having angled, fixed,
each piece of rigging on that swift black ship,
the Ithacans were free at last to lift
their brimming bowls: they poured libations for
the deathless gods, the everlasting force—
above all, for the gray-eyed daughter of Zeus.
All night and through firstlight, their keel held course.

Greek [429-434]

BOOK III

Arrival in Pylos:
seaside sacrifices to Poseidon.

·

Telémachus as Nestor's guest:
his plea for news of his father.

The aged warrior's tale:
the concluding events of the Trojan War;
the departure from Troy;
the later fates of some of the Achǽan chiefs—
but not of Odysseus.

·

Athena's departure.

Nestor's sacrifice of a heifer to the goddess.

·

Peisístratus—Nestor's son—and Telémachus
off by chariot to Sparta,
to Meneláus and Helen.

The sun had left the splendid sea: it climbed
into the bronze of heaven, bringing light
to the immortals and to those who die
on earth, the giver of the gift of grain.
The Ithacans had reached the coast of Pylos,
the sturdy fortress-city built by Néleus.
Along the shore, the men of Pylos stood,
offering sacrifices—jet black bulls—
to please the dark-haired god who shakes the land:
Poseidon, lord of quakes and shifting sands.
Nine sectors had been traced along the beach;
five hundred men had been assigned to each,
and every sector sacrificed nine bulls.
Now, after tasting of the inner parts,
the men of Pylos, with their feast in course,
were offering burnt thighbones to the god,
when, heading straight for shore, the visitors
hauled in and furled the sail of their lithe ship.
They moored. They disembarked. Athena stepped
onto the shore; Telémachus came next.
Then, turning first to him, the goddess said:

"There is no need to be at all ashamed,
for you have crossed this sea with but one aim:
to find what fate your father suffered—where
the earth has hidden him. But now it's Nestor,
the master horseman, whom you must seek out;
let him reveal the riches of his mind.
Nestor knows much—and he will not tell lies."

Telémachus' reply was careful, wise:
"Mentor, how shall I meet, how shall I greet him?
I'm still unskilled at subtle turns of speech.
When one is young, he may indeed be blamed
for questioning his elder. I'm ashamed."

This was the gray-eyed goddess's reply:
"Telémachus, your mind will prompt some words;

Greek [1-26]

others will come to you—a god will urge.
I do not think that you were born and raised
without the gods' attentive tutelage."

That said, Pallas Athena moved ahead;
he followed where her rapid footsteps led.
They reached the center of the sacred feast.
There Nestor sat together with his sons,
surrounded by his people; some were roasting
already-skewered meats and some preparing
still other slabs on spits. But when they saw
the strangers, all the men of Pylos rushed
to welcome them with hands outstretched; they asked
the visitors to join the celebrants.
First, Nestor's son, Peisístratus, drew near.
He took them by the hand. He had them sit,
as members of the feast, upon soft fleece
spread on the sands, beside his father and
his brother, Thrasymédës. And he fetched
choice shares of vitals for the newfound guests.
Then he poured wine into a golden cup;
and with the words that welcomed them, he pledged
Athena, daughter of aegis-bearing Zeus:

"Pray now to lord Poseidon, stranger: we
would honor him with this festivity.
And after you have poured libations and
offered your prayer—just as the gods command—
pass on this cup of sweet wine to your friend,
that he may pour his proper share. I'm sure
he, too, would pray to the immortals: all
men need the gods. But since your friend is young—
no older than I am—indeed you must
be first to take from me this golden cup."

When that was said, he set the cup of honey-
sweet wine into her hand. And she was pleased—
delighted with his tact and courtesy,

Greek [27-52]

content that she was chosen to receive
the gold cup first. At once—and fervently—
the gray-eyed goddess prayed to lord Poseidon:

"Listen, Poseidon, lord who holds earth fast;
do not prevent completion of the tasks
that we have undertaken—we who pray
to you. Above all, grant to Nestor glory,
and to his sons; and to the others—all
the men of Pylos—grant a just requital,
a recompense for their fine hecatomb.
And let Telémachus and me sail home
in safety, once we've reached our visit's goal."

So did she pray—her task well under way.
Then to Telémachus she gave the handsome
two-handled cup; and just as she had done,
Odysseus' dear son prayed to lord Poseidon.
The backs and flanks were roasted now; with this,
the men of Pylos slid them off the spits.
Each took his share of that abundant feast.
Now, with their need for food and drink appeased,
the horseman Nestor was the first to speak:

"It surely is more proper to inquire—
to ask our guests to tell us who they are—
after and not before we've shared this feast.
Who are you, strangers? And what is the land
from which you sailed the seaways to these sands?
Are you just traders? Or a prowling crew
that preys at random, pirates on the loose,
who risk their lives, but plunder others' goods?"

Telémachus' reply was keen and wise;
he did not cloak his goal in weak disguise;
Athena had endowed his heart with force,
that he might ask about his far-off father:

□ □ □

Greek [53-77]

"O Nestor, Néleus' son, the Greeks' great pride,
you ask what is our home—I'll tell no lies.
We come from Ithaca, the sunlit city
beneath Mount Néion; but what brings me here
is nothing public—this is my affair.
I've come in search of word about my father—
the famous, the unfaltering, Odysseus.
They say that he, while fighting at your side,
destroyed the citadel of Troy, its might.
We have been told how other chiefs who went
to war against the Trojans met sad death.
But of his death nothing is known—such is
the will of Cronos' son; and now no one
can say if he was killed by enemies
upon dry land, or lost upon the seas
when storm winds struck the waves of Amphitrítë.
Thus, I am at your knees. I must beseech:
Tell me of his sad death. Were you at hand
or have you heard some word of that doomed man?
She who gave birth to him gave birth to grief.
You need not sweeten anything for me.
Forget discretion; set aside your pity:
tell me completely—all you chanced to see.
I plead with you: Recall the words and deeds
with which the firm Odysseus faithfully
fulfilled his promises to you in Troy,
the land of the Achæans' misery.
With that in mind, speak truthfully to me."

The horseman, Nestor of Gerénia, answered:
"O friend, you have recalled to me the griefs
we sons of the Achæans had to meet
when, there in Troy, we fought unstintingly.
I can recall our many miseries
as in our ships we roamed the misty sea
in search of booty, following Achilles,
and our long struggle for the citadel
of Priam—there our best, our bravest, fell.

Greek [79-108]

There lies the warlike Ajax, there Achilles,
and there Patróclus, he whose counsel matched
the gods'; and there, Antílochus, my own
dear son, unflinching, strong—a man so fast
of foot and bold in battle. And these deaths
were not the only sorrows that we met.
What mortal man could tell our trials in full?
And even if you asked to hear them all—
and stayed some five or six years here with me
to listen to that dark and dreary story—
before the tale was done, you would grow weary
and make your way back to your own dear country.
For nine years—unrelentingly—we tried
with wile on wile, device upon device,
to ruin Troy—until, at last, the son
of Cronos crowned our plotting with that prize.
Astute Odysseus had no equal there;
no one can vie with what is past compare—
your father so outstripped us all in guile.
(Your father—if you are indeed his child.
Yet as I watch your ways I am amazed:
your words are so like his; no man would think
that one so young could mime Odysseus' speech.)
And there, in all that time, I and divine
Odysseus never differed: of one mind,
whether in council or assemblies, his
and my good sense and shrewdness would advise
the best course for the Greeks. But after high
Troy had been sacked, the heart of Zeus devised
a dismal homeward journey for the Argives.
Not all the Greeks had been both just and wise;
thus, many met a sorry death; the gray-
eyed goddess' fatal anger doomed their way.
She—daughter of so powerful a father—
incited Átreus' two sons to quarrel.
These two had asked the Argives to assemble
at sunset (so, when answering that call—
a summons without sanction, sense, or rule—

Greek [109-138]

the sons of the Achæans were all dull
with wine). But when they tried to justify
their calling for this meeting, there was strife.
For Meneláus urged them all to think
of their return across the sea's broad back.
But Agamemnon was not pleased by that.
Instead, he felt the Argives must not leave:
it surely was more urgent to appease
the goddess and her terrifying wrath
by offering holy hecatombs to her.
That fool ignored this truth: that he could never
reverse Athena's anger—for the minds
of gods, who live forever, don't incline
to sudden shifts. And so, with words of spite,
two brothers stood and clashed; the armored Argives
rose up and, brawling bitterly, took sides.
And all night long, each side conspired against
the other: they had violence in mind—
while dark calamity was Zeus' design.
But some of us at daybreak launched our ships
across the glowing sea; on board we stored
our goods and the low-girdled Trojan women.
One half of the Achæans stayed behind
with Agamemnon, shepherd of his people;
the other half embarked and left. Their ships
moved swiftly on the waters' vast abyss:
a clement god had smoothed the sea's rough surface.
When we touched Ténedos, the gods received
our sacrifices: we were keen to reach
our homes. But cruel Zeus refused to heed
our longing. He—again—incited strife.
Some, shifting back to Agamemnon's plan,
now turned their ships around: they headed back.
Odysseus, wise and crafty lord, did that.
But I, together with the fleet I led,
fled straight ahead. I knew that Zeus was bent
upon disaster. Diomédës went
my way; he spurred his men. Blond Meneláus

Greek [139-168]

sailed later, overtaking us at Lesbos.
There we were studying which route was best,
whether to keep steep Chios to our left,
heading toward Psýria, or else—as we
debated our long journey—to proceed
landward of Chios, past the windswept cliffs
of Mímas. Then we asked the god to send
an omen; he showed us a sign—commanded
our ships to cleave the sea directly, head
straight for Eubœa—if we wished to flee
most quickly from the threat of tragedy.
A shrill wind started up, the ships ran swiftly
across the seaways rich with fish; that night
we landed at Geræstus. There we honored
Poseidon, offering upon his altar
the roast thighbones of many bulls, for we
had crossed the open sea.

                         "On the fourth day,
Diomédës and his comrades chose to stay
their ships in Argos. I sailed straight to Pylos.
The wind that favored me maintained its course:
the god who sent it never sapped its force.

"So, my dear child, I came back knowing nothing—
and still know little—of the others who
stayed on at Troy or went back with Odysseus—
who of those Argives has been saved, who lost.
But I shall share with you all I have heard
since my returning home—for it is just
that nothing be concealed from friends. They say
that safe return has blessed the Mýrmidons,
consummate spearmen, whom the famous son
of generous Achilles guided home.
And Philoctétës, son of noble Póīas,
made safe return; so did Idómeneus
bring all his men who had survived the war
to their own Cretan shores—the sea stole none.

Greek [169-192]

As for the son of Átreus, though your home
is far from his, you've surely heard how he
returned and met a wretched fate—the death
he met, the trap Aegísthus had devised.
But then the killer paid a horrid price.
How good a thing it is for one who dies
to leave a son behind: it was Oréstes
who took revenge upon the murderer
Aegísthus, master of deceptions. Friend,
may you, too (I can see that you are handsome
and sturdy), be courageous, that your name
among men still unborn may merit fame."

Telémachus' reply was keen and wise:
"O Nestor, Néleus' son, the Greeks' great glory,
Oréstes was indeed a fine avenger:
the Greeks will surely grant him ample fame,
and song, in time to come, will sing his name.
Would that the gods gave me Oréstes' force,
that I might crush the suitors' insolence.
Yet, for my father and for me, the gods
have not spun much good fortune. But I must—
for now—submit and suffer: I've no choice."

The horseman, Nestor of Gerénia, answered:
"O friend, you speak of this and I remember:
they say that many suitors of your mother,
in your own halls, are bent on treachery.
Or have you given way to them most freely?
Or did your fellow Ithacans—spurred on
by some god's voice—become your enemies?
Perhaps on your return you may strike down
the sinful suitors—either on your own
or even with the help of all the Argives.
For if Athena, gray-eyed goddess, chose
to love you with the care that she bestowed
on excellent Odysseus in the land
of Troy, the site of the Achæans' sorrows

Greek [193-220]

(for I have never seen the gods declare
a love as open as the love she shared—
Pallas Athena at your father's side),
were you to be a man Athena prized
and favored as she did your father, then
the suitors would forget all marriage plans."

Telémachus' reply was cautious, wise:
"I do not think that this will come to pass,
dear lord; what you have said is too immense—
I am amazed! Although I hope for this,
I know it's not to be, not even if
the gods should will it so."

       The gray-eyed goddess
replied to him: "Telémachus, what speech
dares to escape the barrier of your teeth!
A god, if he is pleased to bring a man
home safely—even from a distant land—
can do that easily. Were I that man,
I'd rather face the harshest trials along
my way before the day of my return,
than to have easy passage back but find
death right at my hearthside—like Agamemnon,
trapped by Aegísthus and by his own wife.
And yet we must admit, the gods have limits:
not even they can free a man most dear
from death's hard clasp—the doom that all men share."

Telémachus' reply was wise, discreet:
"Mentor, despite our grief let us not speak
of these things any longer. For my father,
there will be no return. The deathless gods
already have decided on his lot:
death and dark desolation. Now, instead,
I would ask Nestor something else, for he
surpasses all men in sagacity.
O Nestor, Néleus' son, tell me the truth:

Greek [221-247]

How was the ruler of such spacious lands,
the son of Átreus, Agamemnon, killed?
Where then was Meneláus? And what plan
allowed Aegísthus' wiles to strike a man
more mighty than himself? Was Meneláus
elsewhere, far-off from his Achǽan Argos?
And did his absence, even as he wandered,
permit Aegísthus to transgress—to murder?"

The horseman Nestor then replied: "My son,
I'll tell you everything. This—on your own—
you've seen: you know just how things would have been
if, on return from Troy, blond Meneláus
had found Aegísthus living in that palace.
Even in death they'd never have heaped up
a burial mound: they would have let the dogs
and birds tear him apart—Aegísthus, cast
along the plain outside the city. None
of the Achǽan women would have mourned
for one who had contrived so much corruption.
We were at Troy—at work, at war—while he,
at ease in Argos, land where horses pasture,
connived with his beguiling words to capture
the wife of Agamemnon. And at first
bright Clytemnéstra scorned indecency:
her sentiments were just. Moreover, she
was in the company of an attendant,
a poet whom the son of Átreus,
when he set out for Troy, had strictly charged
to serve as Clytemnéstra's watchful guard.
But when the gods' design had so enmeshed
her will that she was ready to submit,
Aegísthus tricked her guardian: he led
that poet to a barren isle and there
left him to rot—a prey and prize for birds.
His will was now at one with hers: Aegísthus
took Clytemnéstra into his own house.
Then, on the holy altars of the gods,

Greek [248-273]

he roasted many thighs, and he hung high
both woven cloths and gold: beyond all hopes
his heart had harbored, he had gained his goal.

"On my return from Troy, I sailed together
with Meneláus—we were friends. But when
we neared the cape of Athens, Súnium,
the sacred headland, with his gentle shafts
Phoebus Apollo struck and killed the helmsman
of Meneláus while his hand held fast
the steering rudder: he, son of Onétor,
was Phróntis, whom no man has yet surpassed
in piloting a ship when storm winds blast.
So Meneláus, although he was keen
to journey on, stopped then at Súnium
to bury and to honor his companion.

"But then, while voyaging the winedark sea
in hollow ships, on rapid course he reached—
now, in his turn—steep Cape Maléa's peak.
There the commanding voice of Zeus decreed
a wretched path for him: he poured shrill blasts
and swollen combers, mountainous and vast.
Lord Zeus split Meneláus' fleet in two.
Half of the ships were thrust to Crete. And there,
where the Cydónians have their home, along
the Iárdanus, a smooth cliff plunges, sheer,
down to the fogbound sea, beside the boundary
of Gortyn. And against that headland, west
of Phæstus, the libeccio drives a mass
of breakers; but that sharp rock holds them back.
Just at that point, five ships struck. Though the men
were able—barely—to escape life's end,
all of those boats were battered on the reefs.
Meanwhile five other ships in that same fleet—
dark-prowed—were thrust by wind and wave to Egypt.
There, as he wandered—harbor after harbor—
. . .

Greek [274-301]

among strange peoples, Meneláus gathered
abundant gold and many other treasures.

"Meanwhile, at home, the web Aegísthus wove
had won the woman. After that he killed
the son of Átreus and forced his will
upon the people. Seven years he ruled
Mycénae rich with gold; but in the eighth,
he was undone: from Athens bright Oréstes
returned: he killed his father's murderer.
That done, Oréstes offered to the Argives
a funeral feast for both his hated mother
and cowardly Aegísthus. That same day
the lord of the great war-cry, Meneláus,
returned to Argos, bearing his rich trove,
all of the goods and gold his ships could stow.

"So do not wander long, far from your house—
my friend—if you have left behind your wealth,
with men so arrogant within your gates.
Should they divide and then devour your goods,
your journey would have been of little use.
Yet you must go to see lord Meneláus.
His safe return is recent: he's come back
from lands that lie beyond a sea so vast
that any man who, driven off his course
by storm winds, reached those coasts would have small hope
of sailing home again: even the birds
can cross such waters only once a year—
that unremitting stretch of sea and fear.
So go now with your comrades and your ship.
Or if you want to go by land, there are
horses and chariot at hand: my sons
will guide you into sunlit Lacedæmon,
blond Meneláus' home. There, face-to-face,
you can implore, insist—and he will state
the truth. He is too wise to tell you lies."

□ □ □

Greek [302–328]

His words were done. The sun sank. Darkness won.
Among the guests, the gray-eyed goddess said:
"Old man, your words have urged the wisest course.
But now cut out bulls' tongues and mix the wine.
Once we complete the offerings we owe
Poseidon and the other deathless gods,
we can give thought to sleep. For it is time.
The light has left; beneath the dark it hides.
It is not right to linger overlong
where gods are feasting. We had best be gone."

These were Athena's words. They heeded her.
Each guest refreshed his hands with water poured
by pages; and young servants brimmed the bowls
with wine and poured the portion of the gods—
the first drops—into every feaster's cup.
Bulls' tongues were cast upon the flames; then each
guest stood and doused them, sizzling, with his share
of wine. That done, each feaster drank his fill.
And now Athena and Telémachus
were ready to return to their quick ship.
But Nestor held them back—he would insist:

"Not Zeus nor any other deathless god
would ever let you take your leave like this:
as if, when you sailed off in your lithe ship,
you left a man in rags, a pauper—one
who had no cloaks or blankets in his house,
that he and those who are his guests might sleep
in peace. I do have handsome blankets, cloaks.
The son of such a man—Odysseus' own—
will never lie down on a ship's bare deck
as long as I'm alive or am survived
by sons who, after me, within my halls
will welcome any guest who seeks my house."

Athena, gray-eyed goddess, answered him:
"Old friend, your words make sense. Telémachus

Greek [329-357]

does well if he obeys your better way.
He, then, will go with you, sleep in your halls—
while I return to our black ship to bring
courage to all and news of everything.
I am the only older man among them:
the others are the friends who followed us—
all the same age as strong Telémachus.
Tonight, beside the hollow black ship, I
shall lie along the sands. But at firstlight,
I'll make my way to the Caucónians,
greathearted men, who owe a debt to me—
a debt that's neither new nor small. But send
this man (since he has come to be your guest)
along his way to Sparta with a chariot
and one of your dear sons; and see that he
has horses fast and strong, untiring."

When that was said, gray-eyed Athena sped
away, as swift as a sea eagle: wonder
gripped everyone who saw her swift departure.
The sight astonished Nestor. The old man
held fast Telémachus as they clasped hands.
These were the words he offered then:

                                        "O friend,
I do not think that you will prove to be
a coward or a clod, if you—so young—
can count upon the gods as your companions.
Of those who claim Olympus as their home,
your comrade is not any other than
Zeus' daughter, rich with spoils, Tritogenía.
And it was your brave father whom she honored
among the Argives. Favor us, Athena:
grant bright renown to me and to my sons
and to my honored wife. I'll sacrifice
to you a broad-browed heifer, one year old,
unbroken, not yet subject to the yoke,
and I shall overlay her horns with gold."   □ □ □

Greek [358–384]

Athena

This was his prayer. Athena heard his words.
Then Nestor of Gerénia led them all,
his sons and sons-in-law, to his bright halls.
Once they had reached his handsome palace, all
sat down in rows on chairs and high-backed thrones.
Then, for his guests, the old man mixed a bowl
of sweet wine that was more than ten years old—
wine from a jar whose leather lid had been
loosened by the housekeeper. From that jar
he also drew the bowl of the libation
he poured as he prayed long and fervently
to Athena, daughter of aegis-bearing Zeus.
Libations had been poured and, bowl on bowl,
each guest had drunk as much as pleased his soul.
Then for the night, each went to his own home.
But Nestor had Telémachus, the dear
son of divine Odysseus, sleep there,
upon a corded bedstead set beneath
the echoing arcade. Next to him slept
Peisístratus, fine spearman, sturdy captain,
the youngest—still unmarried—son of Nestor.
But Nestor slept within the high-roofed house.
The queen, his wife, prepared and shared his couch.

As soon as Dawn's rose fingers touched the sky
with her first light, the horseman Nestor woke,
went out, and sat on the smooth seats of stone
that—white and gleaming, oil-anointed—stood
at his high doors. These were the seats where Néleus,
whose counsel matched the gods', once sat; but he,
defeated by his fate, had gone to Hades.
The one who sat there now, scepter in hand,
was Nestor, the Achæans' guardian.
Now, come from their own rooms, the old man's sons
assembled: Pérseus, Strátius, and Echéphron,
Arétus, and the godlike Thrasymédës.
And when the sixth, Peisístratus, arrived,

· · ·

Greek [385-415]

they had Telémachus sit at his side.
The horseman Nestor was the first to speak:

"May what I will, my sons, be briskly done;
for at this rich feast for a deity,
Athena showed herself to me so plainly
that in my offerings to the gods, it's she—
above all—whom I'd ask to favor me.

"Come now; let one of you select a heifer
along the plain, and have a herdsman drive her,
so that we don't lose time. And let another
go back to brave Telémachus' black ship
and fetch his crew; leave only two as watchmen.
Let someone else among you find Laércës,
the goldsmith, for we need him urgently:
he has to coat the heifer's horns with gold.
The rest of you must stay together here
and see the servants work: they must prepare
a feast in our great halls and, round the altar,
set seats and logs as well as limpid water."

So Nestor spoke. His sons set right to work.
The herdsman brought the heifer from the plain.
And brave Telémachus' companions came
from their brisk, shapely ship. The smith was here
with hammer, anvil, tough tongs: with his gear,
his tools of bronze, he gave to gold his forms.
Unseen, the gray-eyed goddess watched the rite.

Old Nestor, master charioteer, brought gold.
The smith so thinned it down that it might coat
the heifer's horns—and fill with deep delight
Athena when she saw the sacrifice.
Then Strátius and Echéphron gripped the heifer;
they tugged her to the altar by the horns.
And, from within the house, Arétus brought
a basin that was bossed with floral forms—

Greek [417-441]

a basin filled with lustral water—while
the basket in his other hand held barley.
And Thrasymédës, stubborn warrior,
stood by, with his sharp ax, ready to strike,
while Pérseus held a bowl to catch the blood.
Then Nestor, master charioteer, began
the rite: he washed his hands and sprinkled barley,
prayed to Athena fervently and cast
hairs from the heifer's head into the flames.

When they had prayed and sprinkled barley grains,
stout Thrasymédës, Nestor's son, who stood
beside the heifer, struck: the ax blade cut
the sinews of the neck; the heifer lost
her force. The women raised the sacred shout:
his daughters and the wives of Nestor's sons
and his dear wife, Eurýdicë, the eldest
daughter of Clýmenus. At that, the men
hauled up the forepart of the heifer's body;
they lifted her and pulled her head back tight;
Peisístratus, commanding captain, sliced
her throat. When the black blood had flowed and life
had left the bones, they quickly cut the carcass,
hacked out the thighs and, as is proper, wrapped
those portions in a double layer of fat;
and then they set raw meat on top of that.
Old Nestor seared these parts on burning logs.
But then, to coat the chunks, he splashed dark wine.
The young stood by with spits—forks with five tines.
And when the roasted thighs, Athena's share,
had been consigned and all the celebrants
had tasted of the heifer's vital parts,
they sliced the rest and skewered it on spits;
their pointed forks in hand, they roasted it.

Meanwhile the youngest daughter of Néleus' son,
Nestor, the lovely Polycástë, bathed
Telémachus. And after she had washed

Greek [441-467]

and—with unstinting oil—anointed him,
she wrapped him in a tunic and rich cloak.
Fresh from the bath, the dear son of Odysseus
was handsome as a god. The seat he took
was next to Nestor, shepherd of his people.

And when the outer meats were done and drawn
off from the spits, then, served by noble men,
who poured wine into golden cups, they feasted.
And with their need for food and drink appeased,
the horseman Nestor was the first to speak:

"Now yoke the horses with the handsome manes
beneath the chariot of Telémachus.
My sons, the time for journeying has come."

This, Nestor said. They listened. They obeyed.
They quickly yoked brisk horses to the staves.
Within the chariot box, the housewife set
bread, wine, and dishes held to be the best
for kings whom Zeus has nurtured. Then they stepped
onto the chariot: Telémachus
was first, then Nestor's son, Peisístratus—
captain of men—and it was he who took
the reins and cracked the whip. The horses raced
across the fields; the towering fort of Pylos
was soon behind them. All day long the horses
shook hard the yoke they carried on their necks.
The sun sank; all the roads were dark with shadows.
They came to Phérae. There they spent the night
as guests of Díoclës, whose father was
Ortílochus, Alphéus' son. And he
received his guests with every courtesy.

As soon as Dawn's rose fingers touched the sky,
they yoked their team of horses. Quick to mount
their many-colored chariot, they rode out,
the son of Nestor starting up the swift

Greek [468-494]

horses. They reached the fertile fields of grain.
Their journey soon would end, beyond that plain—
so quickly had their horses carried them.
The sun sank; all the roads were dark with shadows.

BOOK IV

A land of valleys ringed by deep ravines—
such was that part of Sparta they had reached.
They drove to Meneláus' house, where he
was offering his many kin a feast
to celebrate a double wedding: both
his son and flawless daughter were betrothed.
Long since—in Troy—he'd pledged Hermíonë
to Neoptólemus, son of Achilles,
the man who breaks the ranks of enemies.
The gods had brought to pass that marriage vow;
and so, with horses, chariots, he now
was sending to the Mýrmidons' bright city—
where Neoptólemus, her lord, was king—
his dear Hermíonë. And he had brought
Aléctor's daughter as the bride he'd sought—
a Spartan girl—for his beloved son,
strong Megapénthës, born of a slave woman.
(The gods had granted Helen no more children
after the birth of her Hermíonë,
a girl as fair as golden Aphrodítë.)
So, in the high-roofed hall of Sparta's king,
his family and friends were reveling
in joy. A godlike singer graced his chant
with notes upon the harp. Two acrobats—
among them all—began their whirling dance.

The travelers brought their horses to a halt
before the palace walls. Telémachus
and Nestor's son, the bright Peisístratus,
now waited at the gate. There Etëóneus,
the busy chamberlain of Meneláus,
was going out—but he turned back at once
to tell the people's shepherd what he'd seen.
With these winged words, he drew close to the king:

"O Meneláus, visitors have come—
two strangers—men like those descended from
the seed of mighty Zeus, who nurtured you.

Greek [1-28]

Shall we unhitch their horses here or send
these visitors to one who is more free
to offer them his hospitality?"

Blond Meneláus answered with contempt:
"Before this I had never known that you,
Boéthus' son, could be a babbling fool.
We two, on our way home from Troy, have surely—
hoping that Zeus would end our misery—
shared to the full the hospitality
of others. Now unhitch their horses: lead
our guests into the house, to share our feast."

Then Etëóneus hurried through the hall:
in need of help, he called on other lords.
They tied the sweating horses to the stalls,
once they'd unhitched the yokes; they poured out wheat
together with white barley; then they propped
the chariot against the polished wall
and led the guests into the gleaming halls.
The young men were astonished when they saw
the radiance inside those high-roofed rooms,
a brightness like the light of sun or moon.
But when their eyes had feasted to the full,
the guests went to the polished baths, where they
were washed by handmaids and smoothed down with oil,
then clothed in tunics and soft cloaks. That done,
they took their places next to Átreus' son.
That they might wash their hands, a servant poured
fresh water from a lovely golden jug
into a silver basin; at their side
she placed a polished table. The old housewife
was generous: she drew on lavish stores;
the visitors were offered much and more.

Blond Meneláus spoke these words of welcome:
"Eat of this feast; enjoy it; when you're done,
we'll ask you who you are. Your fathers' stock

Greek [29-63]

has not been lost, for you are surely born
of sceptered kings whom Zeus had bred; no one
who is a common man can claim such sons."

That said, he offered them the fat ox-flanks—
the choicest parts, for men of highest rank.
Their fare was ready now; their hands reached out.
Then, with their need for food and drink appeased,
Telémachus—his head held close, that none
might overhear—said this to Nestor's son:

"Now, Nestor's son, dear to my heart, look hard:
in these resounding halls, there's gleaming bronze
and gold, electrum, silver, ivory.
Inside, the court of Zeus on high Olympus
must look like this: these riches are prodigious.
I gaze upon such wealth—and am amazed."

He spoke, but Meneláus overheard;
and when he answered, these were his winged words:
"Dear sons, no mortal man can vie with Zeus:
his halls are everlasting—and his goods.
As for my wealth, there may be other men
to match me, or there may, by chance, be none.
But it has cost me many wanderings
and many griefs to bring these treasures here,
stowed in my ships; for more than seven years
I traveled till at last I reached my home.
Through Cyprus and Phoenicia I have roamed,
through Egypt. I have seen Sidónians,
Erémbians, and Ethiopians;
I saw the land of Libya, where the lambs
grow horns as soon as they are born, and dams
give birth three times a year; no shepherd there,
no master, can complain—they never lack
sweet milk or meat or cheese. Their year is one
long milking-time. But even as I roamed,
amassing treasures there, a traitor killed

Greek [64-91]

my brother, stealthily surprising him—
with the connivance of a faithless wife.
For me, in all this wealth, there's no delight.
Whoever they may be, your fathers must
have told you of the trials that I endured
and how, while I was gone, my precious goods
and handsome house fell into ruin. Would
that I still had that house with but a third
part of my riches, and the gods had saved
the lives of those who died on Troy's wide plains,
so far from Argos, land where horses graze!
Indeed, I often weep for all the Greeks;
for seated in my hall, at times I ease
my heart with tears, but then again, I stop—
the chill of endless sadness is too much.
Yet, though I grieve for all of them, there's none
of the Achæans whom I mourn as much
as I lament Odysseus: the mere thought
of him can make me shun both food and drink;
there's none of us who did or suffered more
than lord Odysseus. Sorrow was his lot,
and I am fated never to forget
his trials: he has been gone so long, and we
know nothing—whether he's alive or dead.
I'm sure that he is mourned by old Laértes
and wise Penelope and by the son
he left behind—just born—within his house,
Telémachus."

> These were his words. They stirred
Telémachus to weep. And so he let
a tear fall from his eyelids to the ground
on hearing of his father; but his hands
held up his purple cloak before his eyes.
Aware of what had happened, Meneláus
debated in his heart and mind: Should he
await some word Telémachus might speak
or should he take the lead and test the son.   □ □ □

Greek [92-119]

He pondered long, but he was still uncertain
when from her fragrant, high-roofed room came Helen—
like Ártemis, whose bow and shafts are golden.
Her handmaids, too, were there: Adrástë placed
a well-wrought chair for her; Alcíppë brought
a soft wool rug; and Phylo carried out
a silver basket, gift to Helen from
Alcándrë, wife of Pólybus, who lived
in Egypt, where the opulence of Thebes
filled homes with treasures rich beyond belief.
There, Pólybus had given Meneláus
a pair of silver bathing tubs, two tripods,
and ten gold talents. And Alcándrë added
these other gracious gifts: a golden distaff
for Helen, and a basket set on wheels—
a silver basket trimmed with golden rims.
Now, next to Helen, Phylo set this gift,
the basket filled with lovely yarn; across it
there lay the distaff wound with violet wool.
So Helen sat, feet resting on a stool,
and asked—for she was eager to hear all:

"Zeus-nurtured Meneláus, do we know
the names of these men visiting our home?
Shall I disguise my thoughts or speak the truth?
But guile is not the course to choose. I swear
I've never seen two women or two men
as similar as are the brave Odysseus
and this young visitor who stands before us.
He has to be Telémachus, the son
Odysseus left behind—the boy just born—
when for my shameless sake you all sailed off—
Achæans set to wage a savage war."

The fair-haired Meneláus then replied:
"Wife, I can see what you describe: you're right.
Such were his feet, his hands, such was his gaze,
his head, his hair. And just before, when I

Greek [120–151]

recalled Odysseus, telling of his pain
and of the trials he suffered for my sake,
this young one here held up his purple cloak
to shield his eyes as he shed tears: he cried."

Peisístratus, the son of Nestor, spoke:
"O Meneláus, son of Átreus,
Zeus-nurtured chief of men, just as you say,
this is indeed Odysseus' son. But he
is too discreet and shy of heart to speak
on his first visit here, that openly
before a man whose voice brings both of us
the joy we'd take in hearing from a god.
The horseman Nestor of Gerénia
has sent me here with him—I am his guide.
He wants to seek your counsel now, to find
what word or act could serve as his best course.
Yes, when a father leaves, the son will meet
much grief if others do not offer help;
just so, Telémachus—his father's left;
there's no one now to keep distress in check."

The fair-haired Meneláus answered him:
"Ah, now into my house has come the son
of one whom I loved much, who suffered pain
to serve my cause; if he returned, I planned
to favor him beyond all other Dánaans.
Would Zeus the thunderer had only let
the two of us return in our swift ships,
for then I would have handed him a town
in Argos—I'd have built a house for him
and led him here from his dear Ithaca
with all his goods, his son, and all his people;
I would have cleared out an entire town
and given it to him and his—a town
among those round about, where I am lord.
Then, here in Argos, we'd have often met
in love and gladness, two as friends and guests,

Greek [152-178]

with nothing that could ever part our paths
till, wrapped in blackest clouds, we met our death.
A god must have been envious of that,
for he has destined him—a fate not known
by any other—never to come home."

Such were his words; they all were stirred to tears.
The Argive Helen, Zeus's daughter, wept;
Telémachus and Meneláus wept;
and Nestor's son could not hold back his tears—
his heart recalled the great Antílochus,
his brother, killed by bright Dawn's splendid son.
Remembering him, he called upon winged words:

"Old Nestor always used to say that you,
the son of Átreus, were the most astute
of men: he told us this whenever we
would ask about you in our house. And now,
if you can only do so, hear me out.
I don't delight in weeping at a feast;
there will be time for tears at Dawn's first light—
I'm sure there's nothing wrong in mourning one
who's met his fate: the only honor we
bestow on mortals in their misery
is this: we crop our hair and we shed tears.
My brother, too, has died. He hardly was
the least of Argives; you yourself may well
have known Antílochus. I never met
or saw him, but they say that few could match
his speed as runner and his stout warcraft."

The fair-haired Meneláus answered him:
"Dear friend, you've spoken with as much good sense
as older men's wise words and acts reflect:
you are indeed your father's son—you speak
with wisdom. One can tell quite easily
that you're the seed of one whom Cronos' son
blessed twice—when he was born and when he wed.

Greek [179–208]

Zeus gave and gives these gifts throughout each day
to Nestor, that he may grow old at ease
within his halls, and that his sons may be
wise counselors and never-flinching spearmen.
But now, enough lament; let's feast again;
let them pour water, and we'll wash our hands.
When morning comes, Telémachus and I
will have much time to question and reply."

When that was said, Asphálion, the zealous
attendant lord of noble Meneláus,
poured water, and the feasters washed their hands.
Their fare was ready now; their hands reached out.

Then Zeus-born Helen hit upon this plan:
Into the wine that they were drinking, she
now cast a drug that undid every grief
and rage, obliterating any memory
of misery. Whoever drinks of this,
once it is mixed within his bowl, forgets.
On that day he will never let a tear
fall down his cheek, not even if his mother
and father die, not even if his brother
or son is killed by bronze before his eyes.
For Zeus's daughter had such cunning potions,
the healing drugs that she'd received in Egypt,
the gifts of Polydámna, wife of Thon.
(The soil of Egypt, giver of much grain,
provides a wealth of drugs; some, when concocted,
are helpful, some are harmful. There each man
is an expert physician. None can match
Egyptians; they belong to Pæon's clan.)
Now, when she'd spiced the wine bowls with this drug,
she had that brew poured out into the cups,
then spoke again:

      "God-nurtured Meneláus,
you, son of Átreus, and all other sons

Greek [209–235]

of worthy warriors gathered here, remember:
The god who portions good, who portions evil,
to this man, then to that, is Zeus; in truth
his power rules all things. Yet here and now,
while seated in this hall, come feast, delight
in talk. I have a tale that suits this hour.
I cannot list—much less recount in full—
the labors of the stout Odysseus, but
I'll tell you something he was staunch enough
to dare and do in Troy, that land where you
Achæans suffered much. As his disguise,
he first impaired his body with harsh blows,
and then across his shoulders drew a cloak
in tatters; hidden in a beggar's guise—
so different from the man who stood beside
Achæan ships—Odysseus made his way
up from the plain into the town of Troy.
The Trojans took no notice; all his foes
were calm. I was the only one to know
that it was he, however much disguised.
I questioned him; he gave some shrewd replies.
But when I bathed him, rubbed him down with oil,
gave him fresh clothes, and swore a sacred oath
not to reveal his visit to the Trojans
before he'd reached his own swift ships and tents,
he told me the Achæan stratagem.
And after he had slaughtered many Trojans
with his sharp bronze, he went back to the Dánaans
with much that he had learned in Troy. The women
of Troy were wailing loud, but I was glad;
by now my heart was longing to return;
and, too, I mourned the folly Aphrodítë
inflicted on me, when she led me there
from my beloved land—when I deserted
my daughter, bridal chamber, and my husband—
a match for any man in mind and form."

□ □ □

Greek [236-264]

The fair-haired Meneláus then replied:
"Indeed, dear wife, all you have said is right.
I've come to know the stratagems and minds
of many warriors; I've traveled far;
but I have never seen a man to match
Odysseus' never-flinching heart. How much
he did and suffered in the well-carved horse!
There all we Argive chieftains sat, intent
on death and doom for Troy. There, too, you came—
you must have been incited by some god
who wanted to give glory to the Trojans.
Handsome Dëíphobus had followed you.
Three times you circled round that hollow trap;
you touched the wood, you felt it out; you called
upon the Dánaan chieftains, naming each;
you mimed in turn the voice of all the wives
of Argives in that horse. And Týdeus' son
and I and good Odysseus heard you cry
our names aloud. Both I and Diomédës
were eager to leap up and hurry out
or, still inside, to answer you at once.
Odysseus held us back; he blocked that course,
however keen we were. By now the rest
of the Achǽans' sons kept still, except
for Ánticlus, who longed to answer you.
But stout of hand, Odysseus closed his mouth
until Athena led you off; his grip
was firm. He never flinched. He saved us all."

Telémachus' reply was thoughtful, wise:
"Zeus-nurtured Meneláus, son of Átreus,
there's little comfort in what you have said;
all that Odysseus did within the horse
did not prevent his sorry death; not even
a heart of iron could have saved his life.
But send us off to bed; once we are wrapped
in sleep, we might find sweet forgetfulness."
□ □ □

Greek [265–295]

That said, the Argive Helen told her maids
to set out beds beneath the portico,
to cover them with handsome crimson rugs,
and top these, too, with blankets and soft fleece.
The maids, each with a torch in hand, went off;
and they prepared the beds. A herald led
the guests out to the portico. They slept
within the outer court—while Meneláus
found rest apart, inside; beside him lay
the loveliest of women, long-robed Helen.

Firstlight. As Dawn's rose fingers touched the sky,
lord Meneláus of the loud war-cry
awoke. He dressed, set in his shoulder strap
his sharp blade. To his feet—anointed, sleek—
he tied fine sandals. As he crossed the threshold,
he seemed a god. Then he sat down beside
Telémachus and asked:

                         "What brought you here,
Telémachus, across the sea's broad back
to lovely Lacedǽmon? Public matters
or something else? But do tell me the truth."

Telémachus' reply was wise, astute:
"Zeus-nurtured Meneláus, son of Átreus,
it's tidings of my father that I seek.
My home is close to ruin, my rich lands
laid waste; my house is full of enemies;
they're always butchering my crowds of sheep,
my herds of shambling oxen with curved horns—
my mother's suitors, men who know no bounds.
Thus, I am at your knees, I now implore:
Tell me of his sad death. Did you yourself
see how he died, or was it someone else
who brought you word of his sad wanderings?
She who gave birth to him gave birth to grief.
You need not sweeten anything for me

Greek [296–326]

by way of your discretion or your pity:
tell me completely—all you chanced to see.
I plead with you—recall the words and deeds
with which the firm Odysseus faithfully
fulfilled his promises to you in Troy,
the land of the Achæans' misery.
With that in mind, do speak the truth to me."

Then Meneláus said: "How cowardly
they are! So keen to occupy the bed
of such a stalwart man. As when a hind
has laid her pair of newborn, suckling fawns
to sleep within a mighty lion's lair
and gone to roam and graze the mountain spurs
and grassy hollows, and the lion returns
to find that pair of fawns within his den
and slaughters them ferociously, so will
Odysseus kill the suitors savagely.
O father Zeus, Athena, and Apollo,
would that Odysseus might assault the suitors
with that same strength he showed when, long ago
in well-built Lesbos, in a wrestling match,
he faced Philomeleīdes, throwing him
with force: how all Achæans then rejoiced!
Could he regain that strength, his foes would meet
swift death and bitter wooing. What you need
to know, I'll tell you now; I won't deceive—
I won't use shifty or evasive speech.
I heard about your father from the Old
Man of the Sea, who speaks unerringly.
I'll tell you now all that he told to me.

"Though I was eager to go home, the gods
still held me there in Egypt: I had not
fulfilled their will, not offered what they want,
not sacrificed unblemished hecatombs.
Now, in the surging sea that fronts the coast
of Egypt, lies an island known as Pharos.

Greek [327-355]

If favored by shrill winds, a hollow ship
has need of but one day to make that trip.
And Pharos offers timely anchorage;
there, men can draw deep water from the wells,
and launch their shapely ships across the swell.
The gods becalmed me there for twenty days;
none of those kindly winds that can conduct
a crew across the sea's broad back sprang up.
My stores and my men's strength all would have been
consumed if one among the gods had not
been merciful to me: Eidóthëa,
the daughter of the Old Man of the Sea,
the mighty Próteus. I touched her heart
as I had touched no other's; she met me
while I was wandering alone, apart
from my whole crew; as always, they had gone
with their bent hooks to fish around the shore,
for hunger gnawed their bellies. She drew near:
'Stranger, are you so much the fool, so stripped
of wits, or is it that you relish this
distress—are you a man who thrives on trials?
You have been stalled so long upon this isle;
you can't find home; your comrades' will is sapped.'

"These were her words, and this was my reply:
'Whatever goddess you may be, I'll speak
with honesty: it's not my will that keeps
me here; I must have sinned against the gods,
the rulers of vast heaven. Tell me now—
since gods know all—which one of the immortals
impedes my journey home; and tell me how
I can sail out across the fish-rich sea.'

"These were my words. The lovely goddess answered:
'Stranger, I tell you truly—hiding nothing.
This island's often visited by one
who never errs—the Old Man of the Sea,
the deathless Próteus of Egypt; he

Greek [356-385]

knows each and every secret of the deep;
he is Poseidon's servant. And they say
it's he who fathered me. If you can lie
in wait and catch that Old Man by surprise,
he'll tell you of the passage you must take,
and just how long, across the fish-rich sea,
your journey home will be. And if you wish,
he'll tell you, whom Zeus nurtured, every good
and evil that's been done within your halls
while you were gone upon your long, hard way.'

"These were her words, and this was my reply:
'Then tell me *how* I am to lay my snare,
lest that divine Old Man detect my plan
and so escape. It's hard for those-who-die
to get the better of a deity.'

"These were my words. The lovely goddess answered:
'The never-erring Old Man of the Sea
comes from the depths just when the sun has reached
the sky's midpoint—the time when Zephyr breathes
and screens him with the dark and ruffled waves.
He sleeps encircled by the sleeping herds
of seals, whom lovely Amphitrítë raised;
up from the bitter brine, the same gray swell,
these seals emerge; they bear a bitter smell.
At break of day I'll lead you to those caves
and have you lie in wait; and you must take
three of your crew along with you—but choose
the best of those who man your stalwart ships.
I'll tell you all that Old Man's traps and tricks.
First, one by one, he'll count those seals—and when
he's finished tallying and scanning them,
he'll lie among them as a shepherd would
among his flocks. When he lies down to rest,
be quick: attack with daring, spare no strength.
Grab him and hold him fast, however hard
he strives and writhes. He'll try to take the shape

Greek [386–416]

of every animal upon this earth,
as well as water forms and dazzling shapes
that blazing fire takes. Don't let your grasp
fall slack; just grip him harder still—hold fast.
But when, as his own self—the very shape
he had when he laid down to rest—he pleads
to have you speak, then, warrior, do not press;
release your grip on the Old Man and ask
what god it was who blocked your homeward path
and how you are to cross the fish-rich sea.'

"That said, she plunged into the surging deep,
and I went back to where my ships were beached
along the sands. I walked; the many thoughts
within my heart were dark. But when I reached
the ship and shore, we had our supper, saw
night—gift of gods—descend, and then we went
to sleep beside the sea. As soon as Dawn's
rose fingers touched the sky, I went to pray
with fervor to the gods. I took with me
three men I trusted most in any test.
Meanwhile Eidóthëa had left the shore
and, after plunging down, came back with four
sealskins; she drew them up out of the sea,
four skins from the broad bosom of the deep,
all freshly flayed—prepared—to snare her father.
She scooped out hiding places in the sand;
there she awaited us. We drew up close;
she had us lie down in a row, then cast
a sealskin over each of us—perhaps
no hiding place can be more foul than that:
around those seals who had been bred in brine,
the stench was deadly. Who could lie beside
those monsters of the sea? But she devised
a way to save us: she'd brought sweet ambrosia—
its fragrance was delicious. Placing it
where each of us might smell it, she undid
the stench of seals. Through all that morning, we

Greek [417-447]

just waited patiently—until that crowd
of beasts came from the waves; and then they lay
along the shoreline in a row. At midday
the Old Man rose out from the sea; he found
his plump seals, and he scanned them, took his count.
We were the first among his tallied beasts;
yet having caught no sign of our deceit,
he, too, lay down. Then we assaulted him;
we shouted, held him fast. But that Old Man
did not forget his guiles and wiles. At first
he turned into a thick-maned lion, then
into a snake, a leopard, a huge boar;
then he was flowing water, then a tree
that towered with its leaves. We did not let
our grasp fall slack. But when he tired at last,
that connoisseur of craft and cunning asked:
'O Átreus' son, tell me what god it was
who planned this trap with you? What do you want?'

"These were his words, and this was my reply:
'Old Man, why do you question me? Why try
to put me off? You must know well enough
just what I want. For so long I've been blocked,
held on this isle; I can't go home; my heart
lacks strength. But tell me—since the gods know all—
which one among the deathless ones has stalled
my trip. How can I cross the fish-rich sea?'

"These were my words, and his reply was quick:
'You should have brought unblemished hecatombs
to Zeus and to the other gods before
you had embarked; then you'd have sailed across
the winedark sea and reached your native shores.
It's not your fate to see your friends again,
to reach your sturdy home in your own land,
before you've reached the river Nile once more,
the sacred stream of Zeus; there you must offer
your holy hecatombs to the immortals,

Greek [448-479]

the rulers of vast heaven. Only then
will they restore your longed-for homeward path.'

"These were his words. My heart was broken: he
would have me face a long and weary trial,
across the misty sea to reach the Nile.
Yet I replied: 'Old Man, just as you bid,
so shall I do. But come now, tell me this—
and tell me truthfully: Of the Achǽans,
did all return intact within their ships—
all those whom I and Nestor left behind
when we sailed out from Troy? Did any die
a harsh death on his ship or in the arms
of friends, when threads of war had reached their end?'

"These were my words. His answer came at once:
'Why ask me this, o son of Átreus?
Why do you probe my mind? Why try to find
all I might know? For when you make me speak
such truth, what you will learn will bring you grief.
So many died and many are alive.
There is no need for me to list the chiefs
who fell at Troy, for you were there. But two
among the captains of the bronze-clad Greeks
met death along their homeward path. A third
still lives, pent somewhere on the spacious sea.

"'One, Ajax, with his long-oared fleet, was wrecked.
Poseidon first had dashed his ships against
the giant rocks of Gýrae, but he let
Ajax escape the sea; and he indeed
would have evaded fate (despite the hate
Athena had for him), had he not bragged
with blinded heart. He said that he'd escaped
the sea's abyss despite the gods: Poseidon
heard Ajax rave; at once he gripped his trident
in giant hands; he struck the rock of Gýrae
and cracked it. One half stayed in place, but one

Greek [480–508]

split off, plunged down into the sea; that part
was where the maddened, blustering Ajax sat;
it bore him down into the boundless tide.
And there, when he had drunk much brine, he died.

"'The second was your brother. He indeed
escaped the fates and, unlike Ajax, saved
his hollow ships—he had great Hera's aid.
But when he neared Maléa's promontory,
a storm wind drove him over fish-rich seas;
and groaning heavily, off course, he reached
the coast of what was once Thyéstës' land,
where now Thyéstës' son, Aegísthus, lived.
Yet here, too, he could hope for safe return:
the gods made that wind change; it now blew fair;
and glad, he disembarked on his own shore.
He touched the soil; he kissed it; many tears
were his—warm tears he shed upon the ground;
at long last he could see the land he'd left.
But from a lookout point, he had been seen.
Aegísthus, master of deceit, had set
a sentry; two gold talents were his prize.
For one whole year he'd watched and waited there,
lest Agamemnon might slip by unseen
and summon all the fighting strength he'd need.
That sentry hurried to Aegísthus' house
to tell of what he'd witnessed from his perch.
Aegísthus hit upon this cunning plot
at once: He posted twenty chosen men—
the city's best—at one side of the hall
to lie in wait. Along the other side,
he had a feast prepared. Then he rode out
with chariot and horses to invite
the shepherd of the people, Agamemnon—
a guest suspecting nothing of his fate—
to feast. And thus he slaughtered Átreus' son
just as one kills an ox within its stall.

. . .

Greek [509–535]

Of Agamemnon's followers, not one
was left: they all died in Aegísthus' halls.'

"His words were done. My spirit now was broken.
Seated upon the sands, I cried: my soul
had lost its will to live beneath the sun.
But when my need to weep and writhe was done,
the never-erring Old Man of the Sea
said this to me: 'Enough. These endless tears
can't help us, son of Átreus. It is time
to reach your land as quickly as you can.
Either you'll find Aegísthus still alive,
or else—anticipating you—Oréstes
already will have killed that pest; perhaps
the funeral feast will have you, too, as guest.'

"He said no more. My heart and mind again,
despite my grief, were comforted. Winged words
were mine as I replied: 'Now I have heard
about these two; but tell me of the third,
the one who lives—a prisoner somewhere
on the vast sea—unless he, too, is dead.'

"These were my words and his reply was quick:
'It is Laértës' son, the one who lived
in Ithaca. I saw him as he wept
so many tears. Against his will, he's kept
a captive in the grottoes of Calypso—
her island home, where he can only sorrow.
And he cannot return to his own land:
he has no ships at hand, no oars, no friends
to carry him across the sea's broad back.
And as for you, Zeus-nurtured Meneláus,
your destiny is not to die in Argos,
the land where horses pasture. The immortals
will send you to the farthest edge of earth,
to the Elysian Fields, where Rhadamánthus,
the fair-haired, has his home. That land provides

Greek [536-565]

the easiest of lives: it never rains
or storms, it never snows along that plain;
the Ocean always sends the West Wind's breath,
the singing breeze that brings fresh life to men.
The gods will give you this for Helen's sake;
you are the man Zeus' daughter chose as mate.'

"That said, he plunged into the surging sea.
And I, together with my godlike men,
went to my ships. I walked; the many thoughts
within my heart were dark. But when we reached
the ships and shore, we took our supper, saw
night—gift of gods—descend, and then we went
to sleep beside the sea. As soon as Dawn's
rose fingers touched the sky, we first drew down
our ships onto the glowing sea, then stepped
our masts and set our sails. My crews embarked;
each took his proper place along the thwarts,
and then they beat the gray sea with their oars.

"We sailed back to the sacred stream of Zeus,
the Nile; we moored within the river mouth
and offered up unblemished hecatombs.
When I'd appeased the anger of the gods,
the everliving ones, I raised a mound
for Agamemnon—so that his renown
might never die. That done, I sailed back home;
the deathless ones sent out a kindly wind
and brought me back with speed to my dear land.

"But now, don't leave just yet, stay here as guests
till the eleventh or the twelfth day comes.
When you go off, I'll give you handsome gifts,
three horses and a gleaming chariot;
and, too, a lovely cup, that you may pour
libations to the never-dying gods
and so remember me through all your days."
□   □   □

Greek [566-592]

Telémachus' reply was tactful, wise:
"O son of Átreus, do not keep me here
too long. I'd gladly stay for one whole year
within your house—and with no longing for
my mother and my home. I'm pleased indeed
to hear your tales, to listen as you speak.
But I have been your guest for some time now;
and there, in sacred Pylos, all my friends
wait anxiously for me. Whatever gift
you choose to offer, let it be a treasure
that's suited to me. Ithaca's not right
for horses—keep them for your own delight.
Your land has ample plains; it's rich in clover
and galingale, wheat, spelt, broad-eared white barley.
But Ithaca has neither racing space
nor meadows: it is good for grazing goats.
No isle that rests upon the sea is fit
for driving chariots along, or rich
in meadows—least of all, my Ithaca,
yet it's more dear than land where horses pasture."

His words were done. And Meneláus smiled.
He stroked him with his hand, and then replied:
"Dear child, the way you speak is a sure sign
that you're the scion of a noble line.
I'll change my gift—indeed I can. Instead
I'll give the fairest, richest thing I have:
a mixing bowl designed with care and craft;
it is of silver, and its rim, of gold—
Hephæstus' work. This bowl was given me
by gallant Phædimus, Sidónian king,
when, on my homeward way, he welcomed me.
And now I mean for you to take this gift."

Such were the words they shared with one another.

Meanwhile, before the palace of Odysseus,
the suitors sported on the leveled field—

Greek [593–626]

as in the past—with all their arrogance:
they threw the discus, tossed the javelin.
There sat Antínoüs and, at his side,
godlike Eurýmachus, the two who led
the suitors; of that crowd, they were the best.
Noémon, son of Phrónius, drew close;
and turning to Antínoüs, he probed:

"Antínoüs, do we or don't we know
when we shall see Telémachus return
from sandy Pylos? When he sailed, he took
a ship of mine. And now I need it back:
I have to cross to spacious Elis—there
I have twelve mares with stout mules at the teat,
not broken in as yet. I want to lead
some suckling off and break him in."

                        That stunned
the suitors: they were sure he'd never gone
to Pylos, but was still at home, among
the flocks or with the swineherd on his own
farmlands in Ithaca. Antínoüs,
Eupeīthes' son, said:

                        "Tell me honestly:
When did he leave? What young men followed him?
Were they the sons of chiefs or were they just
his hired men or slaves? He has enough
of these to man a ship. And tell me, too,
in truth—I want to know it well, in full:
Did you give him that ship against your will?
Or did you give it freely, when his plea
persuaded you?"

              Noémon answered: "Freely.
Could anyone do otherwise when he
hears such a man—in deep distress—entreat?
To hold back such a gift is hard indeed.

Greek [627-651]

His crew has those who are the best young men
in all of Ithaca—except for us.
Their captain, whom I saw when they embarked,
was either Mentor or, if not, a god
who seemed the very image of that lord.
Yet something puzzles me: Just yesterday,
at early dawn I saw good Mentor here;
yet he, some days before, embarked for Pylos!"

That said, he went back to his father's house.
His words had troubled those two lords; at once
they made their fellow suitors stop their sports
and had them sit. Enraged, Antínoüs—
with fury filling his black heart—spoke out:

"Ah yes, Telémachus indeed has won:
where we were sure he'd fail, he's dared and done.
Despite us all, a young man hauls a ship
down to the sea. He sets out on a trip—
his crew, a company of men most fit.
The worst is yet to come; may Zeus cut down
his stamina before his youth is done.
But come, give me a swift ship and a score
of comrades; as he sails back to these shores,
I'll wait along the straits that separate
this isle and rocky Samos. Yes, he went
to find his father—but he will find death."

That said, they all were stirred and urged him on.
They rose and went into Odysseus' home.

Penelope was not to waste much time
before she learned that crime was on their minds.
The herald Medon was to tell her all,
for even as he stood outside the yard,
he'd overheard their scheme. He hurried through
the hall to bring Penelope the news.
He stepped across the threshold, and she asked: □ □ □

"Why did the noble suitors send you here?
Is it to have divine Odysseus' maids
set their own tasks aside and tend instead
to readying a banquet for that band?
Would they might end their wooing and their feasts—
were this the final meal they'd ever see!
You who, forever banqueting, exhaust
the wealth and goods of my Telémachus!
When you were boys, you surely paid no heed:
long since, you could have heard your fathers speak
about Odysseus, how his words and deeds
had never wronged a man within this land;
divine kings often treat one man with hate
and one with love—but that was not his way;
his rule brought harm to none. But your vile thoughts
are plain enough to see: there's nothing just
within your minds and acts. Men never do
remember one's good deeds with gratitude."

This was the prudent Medon's wise reply:
"I wish that this were their worst enterprise.
There's something still more vicious on their minds;
I pray that Zeus not let it come to pass.
For they intend to kill Telémachus
with their sharp bronze along his homeward path;
to seek news of his father, he has gone
to holy Pylos and fair Lacedæmon."

His words were done. Her knees, her heart, went weak.
In tears, she lost the flow and force of speech.
But then, at last, her voice returned. She said:

"Why has my son sailed off? He had no need
to board swift ships, those horses of the sea
that carry men across the waves. Did he
want to erase his name from memory?"

□   □   □

Greek [680–710]

This was the prudent Medon's wise reply:
"I do not know if he was driven by
some god, or if his own heart urged him on
to Pylos—in the hope that he might learn
about his father's coming back or else
about the fate that checked his homeward course."

That said, he went back through Odysseus' house.
But she was wrapped in devastating grief;
she could not bear to sit on any seat,
though there were many in her room; she slumped
down on the threshold, moaning wretchedly;
around her all the handmaids in her halls
were sobbing quietly—the young, the old.
These were the words of sad Penelope:

"Hear me, dear friends; for the Olympian
has burdened me with greater misery
than any woman born and bred with me.
Long since I lost a lionhearted husband,
unmatched among the Dánaans, one whose fame
has spread through Hellas, Argos—all of Greece.
And storm winds now have carried from this house
my own dear son; and he has left without
one word to me. Not even you gave thought—
my cruel friends—to wake me from my sleep,
though you knew well enough that he'd gone off
to board his black and hollow ship. Had I
but known that he was planning to depart,
then he, however anxious to embark,
would have stayed here or, if he sailed away,
left me, his mother, dead within these halls.
But now let one of you be quick to call
the servant whom my father gave to me
when I came here as bride: old Dólius,
the man who tends my orchard's many trees.
I'll have him go and sit beside Laértës
at once, to tell him all that's happened here;

Greek [711–738]

perhaps his mind can then devise a plan—
he might yet plead before the Ithacans,
denouncing their desire to destroy
both his and the divine Odysseus' line."

Her dear nurse, Eurycleia, then replied:
"Whatever you may choose to do, dear bride—
to kill me with cruel bronze or let me live
within your house—there is no word I'll hide.
I knew his plans; I gave him his supplies,
all that he'd asked of me: bread and sweet wine.
And then he had me swear a solemn oath
that I'd not let you learn of this before
the twelfth day came—unless you missed your son
and heard that he had gone: he did not want
to have you mar your lovely face with tears.
But now, once you have bathed, put on fresh clothes,
do go upstairs with your own maids and pray
to Zeus's gray-eyed daughter: she can save
your son from death. Don't trouble old Laértes;
he has enough distress. The blessed gods
do not—I think—detest Arceisius' race;
these high-roofed halls, these fields that stretch so far
will be your son's; he will survive this trial."

Her words had lulled Penelope's laments,
had checked her tears. And now her mistress went
to bathe; then she put on fresh clothes and climbed
upstairs together with her maids. She placed
some barley for Athena in a tray
and to the gray-eyed goddess prayed:

                              "May you,
untiring daughter of aegis-bearing Zeus,
hear what I now beseech: If the astute
Odysseus in his halls has ever burned
fat thighs of oxen or of sheep for you,
remember now those sacrifices: save

Greek [739-765]

my son; be shield and shelter; keep him from
the suitors' savagery and insolence."

That said, she cried aloud—the sacred shout;
the goddess heard her prayers. The suitors now
began to clamor in the shadowed hall.
And one of those young braggarts then cried out:

"The queen whom we all courted surely means
to marry one of us: she cannot guess
that for her son we've schemed a rapid death."

These were his words, but none among that crowd
knew what would come to pass. Antínoüs
turned to that band of suitors, saying this:

"Be still, you fools; don't bray and boast aloud,
lest someone carry word of what we plot
to those inside the house. Come, let's get up
in silence and complete the plan that pleased
the hearts of all of us; we are agreed."

That said, he chose their finest men—a score.
They rushed to their swift ship along the shore.
They drew their black boat to a deeper spot,
then stepped the mast and set the sail and strapped
the oars in leather thongs. Their sturdy squires
brought them their fighting gear. They moored their ship
well out, where it might ride, then disembarked.
They had their meal while waiting for the dark.

Meanwhile, within her upper room, astute
Penelope, not touching drink or food,
lay wondering: Would her blameless son elude
his death or would the suitors cut him down?
Just as a lion is beset by doubt
and fear when he's surrounded by a crowd
of hunters closing in—a cunning ring—

Greek [766-792]

so was Penelope, while pondering,
beset, until sweet sleep came suddenly.
Then she lay back, at rest; her limbs fell slack.

And now Athena thought of something else.
She made a phantom in a woman's shape:
Iphthímë, daughter of Icárius
the brave. That sister of Penelope
had wed Eumélus; now she lived in Phérae.
Athena sent that phantom to the house
of the divine Odysseus; it would tell
Penelope to end her tears, to wail
no more. It glided through the bolted door
by way of the latch-thong. Beside the bed
the phantom stood and said:

                              "Penelope,
the sleep you sleep is sad—the sleep of grief.
But listen: Now the gods who live at ease
would have you weep no more; you need not be
distressed; your son is coming back—in him
the gods have not found any fault or sin."

This was the wise Penelope's reply
as she slept sweetly at the gate of dreams:
"Why, sister, are you here? Your home is far;
you've never come to visit me before.
And you would have me set my pain apart,
the many griefs that grip my mind and heart.
Long since, I lost a lionhearted husband,
unmatched among the Dánaans, one whose fame
has spread through Hellas, Argos—all of Greece.
And now my own dear son, embarked upon
a hollow ship, has sailed away—so young,
he does not know what trials he'll meet; his speech
cannot keep pace when older men debate.
I mourn his father with a grief so great,
yet I weep more for him; I am afraid
. . .

Greek [793-820]

that men within the land to which he's gone
may strike him down—or he may die at sea.
So many plot against him; they are keen
to kill him; they don't want him here back home."

To this, the shadowed phantom then replied:
"Take heart; don't fear too much. He has a guide
to whom so many men have prayed for aid:
Pallas Athena—one whose force is great.
And she takes pity on your wretchedness.
It's she who sent me here to tell you this."

Again the wise Penelope replied:
"If you're a god yourself or if you come
commanded by a god, I beg of you:
Tell me the fate of that unhappy one.
Is he alive somewhere beneath the sun
or is he dead by now in Hades' halls?"

To this, the shadowed phantom then replied:
"I will not tell the truth to you in full,
not let you know if he's alive or dead.
Words empty as the wind are best unsaid."

That said, the phantom glided through the door,
along the latch-thong path it used before;
it joined the breath of winds. Penelope
leaped up from sleep. Her heart was warmed—she'd seen,
within the dark of night, so clear a dream.

The crew of suitors soon embarked, set sail
across the watery paths; their minds were set
on murder—on Telémachus' quick death.

There is a stony isle that looms mid-sea
between the shores of Ithaca and Samos:
its name is Ásteris. It is not wide,
and yet it has twin bays where ships can lie.
There the Achæans lay in wait for him.

Greek [821-847]

BOOK V

Hermes, emissary of the gods:
his mission to Calypso;
Odysseus to be freed from Calypso's hold.

·

Odysseus fashioning his sailing craft.

His departure from Ogýgia.

·

Calm sailing—
then, Poseidon's angry tempest;
Odysseus' wreck and scramble in high waves and storm.

The saving shawl of the sea-nymph Ino.

The landing on Schería's shore.

Shelter in a heap of fallen leaves;
sweet sleep for Odysseus.

Now Dawn had left her lord Tithónus' side:
she rose from their shared couch, bringing her light
to the immortals and to those who die.
The gods, convened in council, sat with Zeus,
the thunder lord, whose force is absolute.
To them, Athena, as she called to mind
Odysseus' many miseries, defined
the threats that lay in wait, the troubling fate
he faced as captive in Calypso's cave:

"You, father Zeus, and all of this assembly
of blessed, never-dying gods, hear me:
From this time on, no sceptered king need be
benign and kind, a man of righteous mind:
let kings be cruel and corrupt, malign—
for none among his people now recall
divine Odysseus, though his rule was gentle
and fatherly. And now, against his will,
Calypso keeps him captive in her grotto,
her island home, where he can only sorrow.
And he cannot return to his own land:
he has no ships at hand, no oars, no friends
to carry him across the sea's broad back.
Now, too, they mean to ambush his dear son,
to murder him along his homeward run;
for news of his dear father, he has gone
to sacred Pylos and bright Lacedæmon."

Zeus, shepherd of the clouds, replied: "My daughter,
how can the barrier of your teeth permit
such words to cross your lips? For surely this
delay—to keep Odysseus far away
until on his return he takes revenge
against the suitors—is the scheme you planned.
As for Telémachus, your cunning can
return him to his land on safe sea paths,
and you can thwart the suitors' plot, so that
those baffled men retreat with empty hands." ☐ ☐ ☐

Greek [1–27]

That said, he turned to Hermes, his dear son:
"Yes, you have served us well on many missions.
Go now, and tell the nymph with lovely hair
that this is our infallible decree:
Odysseus is to reach his home, though he
must sail alone, without the company
of gods or men. His craft will be makeshift,
planks bound by many thongs; in such a ship,
his crossing will be trying, tiring, yet
when twenty days have passed, that man of wiles
will reach Schería's fertile soil, the isle
of the Phaeácians, men the gods befriend.
There they will honor him with willing hearts,
as if he were a god. They will escort
Odysseus to his homeland in their ship,
with bronze and gold and clothes—so many gifts:
after the sack of Troy, had he sailed back
directly, with his share of spoils intact,
not even then would he have been that rich.
Such is the destined way in which he'll come
to his own land, his friends, his high-roofed home."

That said, the keen-eyed messenger was quick.
First, to his feet he fastened handsome sandals:
these, golden, everlasting, carried him
with swift winds over seas and endless land.
He took the wand that charms the eyes of men:
some, he enchants with sleep, just as he can,
at will, awaken others. Wand in hand,
Hermes took flight. He passed Piéria's peaks
and, from the upper air, swooped toward the waves;
then, like a bird, he skimmed—a tern that bathes
its thick wings in the brine as it hunts fish
in surge that never rests—the dread abyss.
So Hermes rode the countless troughs and crests.

At last he reached landfall, the distant isle.
He quit the violet waves. He made his way

Calypso's Grotto

on land and found the fair-haired nymph's deep cave.
She was at home. A splendid fire blazed
upon her hearth; its fragrance wafted far
across the isle—the scent of burning logs
of juniper and tender thuja boughs.
Inside that grotto, with her golden shuttle,
the nymph was weaving; moving back and forth
before her loom, she sang—her voice was graceful.
The grotto was surrounded by rich forests:
alder and poplar trees and pungent cypress.
There broad-winged birds built nests: owls, cormorants,
and chattering sea crows, who ply their tasks
among the waves. The grotto's entranceway
was ringed by robust vines with clustered grapes.
Pure water rose from four springs in a row,
but then, meandering, the four streams flowed
through gentle fields of violets and parsley.

Even a god who chanced to see that site
would feel the force of wonder and delight.
But when his mind had marveled at it all,
he went at once into the spacious cave.
Calypso, brightest goddess, seeing Hermes,
did not have any doubts: the deathless gods
can recognize each other, even when
their dwelling places lie so far apart.
Yet generous Odysseus was not there,
but where he always sat, along the shore,
sighing and weeping, grieving as he tore
his heart and watched the restless sea. Calypso
sat Hermes on a gleaming chair, then asked:

"Hermes, my honored guest—a welcome one—
what matter brings you here with your gold wand?
You've hardly been a frequent visitor.
Tell me the thoughts you want to share. If I
can answer your request, and my heart finds

. . .

Greek [57-89]

it seemly, I shall help you willingly.
But first—a time for friendship, courtesy."

That said, the goddess showed him to a table
heaped with ambrosia, and she poured red nectar.
So Hermes ate and drank, and when his soul
had been refreshed with food, this was his answer:

"You ask—as goddess to a god—why I
am here, and you do not want me to lie.
Zeus ordered me to come, against my will:
who'd want to cross an endless stretch of brine?
Who'd want to find no mortals' town nearby
where men, to please a god, may sacrifice
choice hecatombs, roast thighs that so delight?
And yet there is no god that can elude
or slight the will of aegis-bearing Zeus.
He says there is a man with you, a man
most miserable, one of those who fought
nine years for Priam's citadel, then sacked
that stronghold in the tenth year and sailed back.
But since his men had sinned against Athena,
she sent harsh winds, harsh seas, as punishment.
Then all of his brave comrades died, but he,
impelled by wind and wave, has reached your realm.
Now Zeus would have you send him home at once:
his fate is not to die here, far from friends—
he is to see his dear ones, find again
his high-roofed house, return to his own land."

These were his words. The lovely goddess shuddered,
then answered Hermes with her own winged words:
"You gods are cruel and more jealous than
all others: if a goddess beds a man
and wants him—openly—as her dear husband,
then you begrudge her that. Your envy punished
rose-fingered Dawn when she embraced Oríon:
you gods, at ease, your least desire appeased,

Greek [90-122]

sent down chaste Ártemis of the gold throne,
and she, in Delos, killed him with her shafts.
And when fair-haired Deméter dared to clasp
Iásion (they mingled, breast to breast,
upon a field where plows had worked three furrows),
Zeus did not wait too long to find that out,
to kill him with a blazing thunderbolt.
So now, you gods resent my having chosen
a mortal. But when flashing lightning sent
by Zeus had smashed his ship and sunk his men,
and there, alone along the winedark sea,
he clutched the keel until the waves and wind
had cast him on my coast, I welcomed him:
it's I who fed him, I who took him in—
I hoped to give him immortality,
an endless life and yet without old age.
But since there is no god who can elude
or slight the will of aegis-bearing Zeus,
let this man meet his fate on restless seas.
But there's no way that I can help him leave:
I have no ships at hand, no oars, no crew
to carry him across the sea's broad back.
Yet I am fully ready to advise him,
keep nothing hidden from him, so that he
may make his way back to his own land—safely."

Stout Hermes said: "However this may be,
take care to send him off at once. Beware
of Zeus's wrath, lest in the future he
become your unforgiving enemy."

Then sturdy Hermes left. And having heard
the message sent by Zeus, the bright nymph went
to generous Odysseus. He was seated
along the shore; his eyes were never dry,
and his sweet life was squandered as he wept
for his dear home; he now took no delight
in her: the nymph no longer pleased his sight.

Greek [123-153]

By night, indeed, within Calypso's cave,
he slept with her: so side by side they lay,
the willing and unwilling. But by day,
his heart was rent by torment as he sat
along the sands or on the rocks; he watched
the never-resting sea and, watching, wept.
Standing beside him there, the fair nymph said:

"Unhappy man, don't stay—in tears—with me:
do not destroy your life. Most willingly
I set you free. Come now, with your bronze ax
chop down stout trunks and build a broad-beamed craft.
Let cross-planks serve as sides for those base beams,
to carry you across the fog-dark sea.
Within that hull I'll stow much bread and water
and red wine—you'll not suffer thirst or hunger—
and I shall clothe you and provide fair winds
to carry you unharmed to your own land,
if that is what wide heaven's gods demand—
I must give way before their powers and plans."

The patient, bright Odysseus, shuddering,
replied to what he'd heard with these winged words:
"Goddess, I know you've something else in mind—
something beyond my being free to leave—
in urging me to cross the dreadful deep,
the dismal, dour abyss, aboard a craft
so makeshift: even quick and agile ships,
blessed with the favoring wind of Zeus, would fail.
I shall not board these fragile planks unless
you, goddess, swear to set aside all thought
of harming me with new, pernicious plots."

He spoke. Calypso, lovely goddess, smiled.
Her hand caressed him. Her reply was this:
"You are indeed astute, not short on wits:
what cunning urged you on to this request?
I call as witnesses the spacious sky

Greek [154-184]

and earth and waves of Styx that flow below—
the most exacting, the most awesome oath
the blessed gods can swear—that I forgo
all thought of any future harm to you.
My thoughts, my plans for you, are only such
as I myself might seek were I to be
in your own place: within my breast I keep
no heart of iron—I feel for you, your needs."

That said, the lovely goddess led. He followed
her quick footsteps. Together, man and goddess,
they reached the hollow grotto. There he sat
on the same chair that Hermes had just left.
Calypso set before him food and drink
of every sort that suits a mortal's needs.
Then she sat opposite the bright Odysseus.
Her handmaids offered her ambrosia and nectar.
Their fare was ready now. Their hands reached out.
And when their thirst and hunger were appeased,
the lovely goddess was the first to speak:

"Are you, Odysseus, man of many wiles,
Laértës' godly son, still keen to leave
straightway? Is it your native land you need,
your dear home? Though you go, I wish you well.
But if your mind were to divine the trials
that fate will have you meet before you reach
your country, you would choose to stay, to keep
this house with me—and live immortally.
This you would do despite your longing for
your wife, for whom you yearn each day. And yet
I'm sure that I am not inferior
to her in form or stature: it's not right
for mortal women to contend or vie
with goddesses in loveliness or height."

Odysseus, man of many wiles, replied:
"Great goddess, don't be angered over this.

Greek [185-215]

I'm well aware that you are right: I, too,
know that Penelope, however wise,
cannot compete with you in grace or stature:
she is not more than mortal, whereas you
are deathless, ageless. Even so, each day
I hope and hunger for my house: I long
to see the day of my returning home.
If once again, upon the winedark sea,
a god attacks, I shall survive that loss:
the heart within my chest is used to patience.
I've suffered much and labored much in many
ordeals among the waves and in the wars;
to those afflictions I can add one more."

These were his words. The sun sank. Darkness came.
And they, within the hollow of the cave,
taking delight in love, together lay.

Firstlight: when Dawn's rose fingers touched the sky,
Odysseus readied for his enterprise.
He put on cloak and tunic, while the nymph
put on a long and gleaming, gracious robe
woven of subtle threads, then bound a belt
of gold around her waist and veiled her head.
Now she began to plan for his departure.
She gave him a stout ax, the kind one grasps
with two hands: its bronze head had both blades honed;
its haft of olive-wood was tight and fast.
And then she handed him a polished adze.
She led him toward the island's rim—a stand
of tall trees: alder, poplar, and the high,
sky-seeking fir: well-seasoned timber, dry,
aged wood that would float lightly on the sea.
When she had shown him where those tall trees rose,
the fair Calypso turned back to her home.
He started cutting trunks. He worked with speed.
He chopped down all of twenty. With the bronze
axhead, he trimmed them; then, with skill, he smoothed

Greek [216-245]

the timbers and aligned them, straight and sure.
Meanwhile the fairest goddess fetched the augers.
With these he bored each plank. With bolts and pins
he fitted piece to piece, and then he hammered
his hull together. As a carpenter
employs his skill—whenever he must build
freight ships—to trace a spacious hull, so did
the stout Odysseus give his boat due width.
He set deck beams in place and bolted them
with close-set ribs, then added long gunwales.
He hewed a mast and then attached a yard
and shaped a steering oar, to keep on course.
To fend the waves, he fenced his craft from stem
to stern with willow withes; along the deck
he strewed brushwood. Meanwhile the fairest nymph,
Calypso, brought him cloth from which to trim
a sail; and he was also skilled at that.
Sheets, braces, halyards—all were soon made fast.
On rollers, to the sea, he hauled his craft.
The fourth day now was come. His work was done.

The next day, fair Calypso let him go—
but only after she had bathed Odysseus
and seen that he had fresh and fragrant clothes.
On deck she placed a skin of deep-red wine
together with a giant skin of water
and then a haversack of food—with many
succulent provisions. As his guide,
she sent a clement, tutelary wind.
The good Odysseus gladly spread his sail:
seated, he steered—a man most versatile.
Sleep did not overtake his lids: he watched
the Pleiades, the Plowman, slow to set,
and the Great Bear—known also as the Wain—
which circles round one point and spies Oríon
and is the only set of stars that never
bathes in the Ocean's waves. The gracious goddess,
Calypso, had instructed him to keep

Greek [245-276]

the Great Bear on his left along the deep.
Seventeen days he sailed across the sea;
on the eighteenth he saw that he'd drawn close
to shadowed peaks: he now was near the coast
of the Phaeácians' island; in the mist
that land took on the likeness of a shield.

But now Poseidon, lord of quakes and tremors,
returning from the Ethiopians,
could see—down from the Sólymi's steep peaks—
Odysseus sailing on the sea. Incensed,
he shook his head in this soliloquy:

"Skulduggery! While I was visiting
my Ethiopians, the gods gave way:
they turned; they mean to help the Ithacan.
And now he nears the land of the Phaeácians,
where he is fated to escape the trap
of trials that held him fast. This is my task:
to drive him back into his misery."

That said, he massed the clouds and, as he gripped
his trident, whipped the surge and urged all winds
to whirl at will. He hid the land, the sea.
Night scudded from the sky down to the deep.
Eurus and Notus and voracious Zephyr
and Bórëas, who's born in the bright ether,
attacked together; a prodigious breaker
rolled up along their path. The wanderer
felt weak; his knees and heart gone slack, he cried
in anguish to his unrelenting mind:

"Poor man, what end awaits me? I'm afraid
Calypso's words were true: she said I'd face
my worst ordeal before I ever reached
my homeland: on the sea I was to meet
disaster. Everything is now complete.
How many clouds Zeus gathers now to crowd

Greek [277-303]

the vast sky to its limits! He provokes
the sea; the force of all winds crushes me.
The steep descent to death cannot be checked.
Three and four times more blessed were all the Greeks
who died in the vast land of Troy to please
the sons of Átreus. Would that I had met
a death like theirs, had shared their destiny
upon the day when crowds of Trojans cast
bronze shafts at me, while battling round the body
of Péleus' slaughtered son. I would have gained
funeral rites; I would have earned much fame
from the Achǽans. Now instead I find
myself a prey: I face a squalid death."

As he said this, a giant comber crashed
down on Odysseus with force so fierce
it whirled his craft around. He lost his grip:
the steering oar fell slack. Far from the deck
he plunged; rapacious gusts had rushed a vortex
that sheared the mast in half; into the sea
the sail yard and the sail fell—distantly;
that comber held him fast within the deep;
he could not surface quickly in the rage
of that great wave; his clothes—Calypso's gifts—
were hampering and heavy. But at last
he surfaced. It was bitter brine he spat—
the brine that streamed and splattered from his head.

Yet even then, half drowned, Odysseus
did not forget his battered craft: he thrust
across the waves until he gripped the planks.
He huddled in the center to escape
his fate, his death. A great wave took his craft
along its course, this way and that—just as,
across the plains in autumn, Bórëas
drives thistle-tufts that hold each other fast.
Now Notus cast the craft toward Bórëas,

. . .

Greek [304-331]

who drove it on; and Eurus now again
gave it to Zephyr—he became its master.

But Ino, Cadmus' daughter, saw that scene—
she, nymph with lovely ankles, once had been
a mortal, one who spoke with human speech;
but, honored by the gods, she then became
Leucóthëa, a goddess of white waves.
She now took pity on the suffering
of wandering Odysseus. From the sea,
she rose up like a gull upon the wing
and sat down on his battered craft, saying:

"Poor man, why does such spite still drive Poseidon?
Why does he hate you with such bitter passion,
inflicting trial on trial? Yet surely he
can never ruin you, however deep
his need to see you grieve. But you do this—
you seem to be no fool: Strip off your clothes;
abandon to the winds your craft and try
to swim with your own arms and reach the land
of the Phaeácians: there you'll find escape
at last—such is your fate. Come, spread this shawl—
it is immortal—underneath your chest;
and have no fear of suffering or death.
But just as soon as you have touched that shore,
release the shawl; be sure to fling it far
into the winedark sea; then head for land."

That said, the goddess handed him a shawl
and then plunged back at once—much like a gull—
into the billow. That dark wave hid Ino.
But he was hesitant. The patient, bright
Odysseus, troubled, spoke to his own mind:

"Ah me! Let it not be that, once again,
someone immortal has devised a plan
to trap me, urging me to leave this craft.

Greek [332-357]

But I shall set aside the nymph's advice;
my eyes have seen how far away it lies—
the land that, so she says, will set me free.
The better course is this: As long as these
planks are not loosened from their fastenings,
I shall stay here, and although suffering,
I shall resist. But if the combers wreck
my boat completely, I shall swim—for then
I cannot call on any other plan."

But while Odysseus' mind and spirit pondered,
Poseidon, lord of quakes and tremors, stirred
a giant surge, an awesome arch, a curve
the god drove hard against the wanderer;
as gusts grown fierce, impetuous, will toss
a heap of dry straw, scattering some here,
some there, so that wave tossed the boards about.
Odysseus gripped a floating plank; as if
to ride astride a horse, he straddled it;
then he stripped off his clothes—Calypso's gift—
and wrapped the shawl around his waist. Headlong,
he dived into the sea; his hands outstretched,
he swam like one possessed. Just then, Poseidon
saw him; he shook his head and, turning toward
his spirit, murmured this soliloquy:

"Then, after undergoing many griefs,
wander across this sea until you reach
the people Zeus has nurtured; but I think
that even then your present suffering
will not appear to you as some slight thing."

That said, he lashed his fair-maned horses, sped
to Ægae, where he has his palaces.

But now Athena had her counterplan.
She curbed the course of all the other winds;
the goddess ordered them to cease, to rest,

Greek [358-384]

except for Bórëas—impetuous—
whom she incited now to clear the path
of waves that lay along Odysseus' way,
that he, escaping death and fate, might reach
the land of eager oarsmen, the Phaeácians.
Two nights, two days, delivered to the waves,
the Ithacan was driven; many times
his heart foresaw his death. But when the skies
revealed the third day born of fair-haired Dawn,
at last the wind fell still; the air was calm;
the wanderer caught sight of land nearby
as, lifted on the surge, he strained his eyes.
And like the joy of children when they see
new life within a father who lay ill,
bearing atrocious pain, wasting away
(invaded by a demon's curse), until
the gods had healed his horrid misery,
bringing rejoicing—such was the delight
Odysseus felt with land and trees in sight.

But when the wanderer had come in close
to shore, he heard the surge; against the shoals
it hammered hard; the wailing combers rolled
and thundered all along the dry land's coast.
Sea-spume enveloped every thing in sight.
There were no harbors where a ship might ride,
no havens and no coves, just jagged reefs
and jutting crags. Odysseus' knees went weak;
his heart was hesitant; he had to speak
these troubled words to his tenacious soul:

"When Zeus at last has let me see the land
that lay beyond my hopes, when I have cleared
a path across this deep abyss, nowhere
is there an exit place, the least escape
from this gray sea. Just jagged crags—that's all
that waits for me: the rocks are sheer; waves wail;
the water close to shore is deep; my feet

Greek [385–413]

can find no footing; there is no way out.
Were I to seek the land, I might be caught,
be dashed against the rocks—have tried, but lost.
And were I to swim on and try to reach
some harbor of the sea, or sheltered beach,
I fear that once again the tempest might
drive me far off, across the fish-rich seas,
even as I moan deeply—or some god
may send some giant monster of the deep
against me (many such are known to be
nurtured and raised among the waves, the breed
of famous Amphitrítë). I indeed
know how much hate Poseidon has for me."

But while Odysseus' mind and spirit pondered,
a comber hurled him toward the stony shore.
His skin would have been flayed, his bones been smashed,
had not Athena spurred his wits to act:
he rushed to seize a rock with both his hands
and, groaning, gripped it till the surge had passed.
So he escaped the wave; but its backwash
caught him; it pounded hard; it hurled him far
into the open sea. And even as
the suckers of an octopus that's dragged
out from its hole show pebbles clinging fast
and thick; so did that rock display the skin
stripped from his hands—from his tenacious grip.

And trapped within that backwash of the brine,
Odysseus would have died before his time
had not gray-eyed Athena counseled him.
Emerging from the surge that now rolled shoreward,
he swam, his eyes upon the land, to see
if he could find a sheltered bay or beach
that met the sea aslant. But when he reached
a river mouth, a friendly estuary,
he chose that as his landing: it was free
of reefs and offered shelter from the wind.

Greek [414-443]

He knew that there must be a tutelary
river-god, and in his heart he prayed:

"Whoever you may be, o lord, hear me!
In my escape from pitiless Poseidon,
I've now reached you, whom many call upon.
Deserving mercy even in the eyes
of deathless gods is any man who comes—
even as I have come—a wanderer:
after long suffering, at last I reach
your current and your knees. I now beseech
your pity, lord; I am your suppliant."

These were his words. The river-god straightway
restrained his current, curbed his waves, and gave
the gift of calm. He brought the wanderer safe
into the river mouth. The sea's attack
had overcome Odysseus; he collapsed;
his knees went weak; his sturdy hands fell slack.
All of his flesh was swollen; from his mouth
and nose, the bitter brine gushed down in spurts.
Deprived of breath and speech and strength, he lay—
the prey of an atrocious weariness.
When he'd found breath again and in his chest
his heart had found fresh force, Odysseus tossed
away the shawl the nymph had given him:
into the stream that mingled with the sea,
he threw it. When the river current reached
great waves, a billow brought it back to Ino;
the course was quick—straightway her hands received it.
Odysseus, as he clambered from the stream,
sank down among the reeds and kissed the earth,
giver of grain. And in his grief these were
the words he spoke to his tenacious soul:

"What misery is mine? What lies in wait?
If, through the sorry night, I stay awake
here on this riverside, I am afraid

Greek [444-467]

that, breathless, weak, my spirit will fall prey
to bitter frost, chill dew; at break of day
a biting wind will strike. But if I try
to climb the slope and, where the undergrowth
is thick, lie down in the dark wood, I fear
that once fatigue and cold have disappeared
and I am gathered in by gentle sleep
I will become a prize for some wild beast."

But as he pondered, this plan seemed the best:
He headed for the woods and reached the trees
that flanked a clearing not far from the stream.
Between two bushes born in one same spot,
one bush of olives, one of thorns, he crept.
Those bushes grew so twined together that
no harsh, damp winds could penetrate their dense
branches, nor could the scorching sunrays strike,
and even downpours found it hard to pass.
It was beneath these branches that he crept;
and with his hands he gathered a broad bed
at once, for fallen leaves lay there in heaps,
enough to shelter two men—even three—
in wintertime, however cold it be.

The man of many trials was glad indeed
to see this shelter. In the middle, he
lay down. Over his body he heaped leaves.
Just as a man will hide a brand beneath
dark ashes on a lonely farm—to keep
the seed of flame alive and not have need
to trudge far off for fire to feed his hearth—
so did Odysseus wrap himself in leaves.
And on his eyes Athena poured sweet sleep:
she freed the man of trials from harsh fatigue.
The goddess closed the eyelids she held dear.

Greek [467–495]

BOOK VI

Athena's
pre-dawn visit to Nausícaa,
daughter of the king of the Phaeácians,
inspiring her to wash the family's fine clothes
by the riverside,
near Odysseus' thicket.

.

The washing, the meal, the games of the girls.

Odysseus awakened by their shouts.

The meeting of Odysseus and Nausícaa:
food, drink, and a bath for Odysseus.

Her return to town;
his waiting in the grove.

So did the man of many trials give way
to weariness and sleep. But while he lay
along the riverbank, Athena went
to visit the Phaeácians' town and lands.
Wide Hyperēïa once had been their home,
but there they faced a domineering race,
the Cyclops, at their borders: to escape
such neighbors, the Phaeácians sailed away.
Led by godlike Nausíthoüs, they found
an island far from all whose life is toil;
and there they settled—on Scheria's shores.
About the city he had built a wall,
and he constructed homes, and for the gods
built shrines, and gave each man his share of land.
By now Nausíthoüs, struck down by fate,
had gone to Hades' house. And in his place
Alcínoüs was king; the gods had given
to him the gift of counseling with wisdom.
Athena reached his house. In her concern
for brave Odysseus and his safe return,
she headed for a chamber—rich, adorned—
in which a young girl slept, a girl whose form
and loveliness were worthy of a goddess:
Nausícaa, daughter of Alcínoüs.
Nearby, one to each side of the doorposts,
two handmaids slept: the Graces gave to both
the gift of beauty. The bright doors were shut.
But like a gust of air the goddess rushed
to reach the girl's bedside. And when she stood
close to Nausícaa and spoke, she took
the form of Dymas' daughter (he was famed—
a master sailor; she, about the same
age as Nausícaa, was her dear friend).
And in that guise, the gray-eyed goddess said:

"Nausícaa, why did your mother bear
a girl so indolent? Although you near
your wedding day, you—heedless—do not care

Greek [1-27]

for the resplendent clothes that you will wear
and those that are to be your escorts' share.
Rich things can help you gain a name and fame;
a handsome wedding day will bring delight
to both your father and his honored wife.
So just as soon as day breaks let us go
to wash those wedding garments; and I, too,
shall come, a friend to urge you on. Remember,
you will not stay unwed for that much longer.
For some time now, you have been sought by suitors
who are the finest men of the Phaeácians,
of families whose forebears are your own.
But come, at dawn persuade your noble father
to ready mules for you, provide a wagon
to carry robes and sashes and bright woolens.
And it is far more fitting, too, for you
to ride than to go there on foot: the basins
for washing are so distant from the city."

That said, gray-eyed Athena made her way
back to Olympus, which is said to be
the gods' own dwelling place, always serene:
untroubled by the winds, untouched by rain,
and free of snows; within that cloudless sky,
the limpid air extends, bright light presides;
there all the days of blessed gods are spent
in joy. And there the gray-eyed goddess went
after she gave the girl encouragement.

Now Dawn, the flowered one, was quick to come.
She woke Nausícaa of the fine robes.
The girl, astonished by her dream, went through
the rooms, to find her parents. They were home.
Her mother, with her women, sat beside
the hearth; there she spun yarn whose purple dye
was taken from the sea. Alcínoüs
was standing at the threshold, just about
to leave the house and join the noble lords,

Greek [28-55]

famous Phaeácians, at the council ground.
His daughter, drawing closer to him, said:

"Papà, can't you prepare a wagon—high,
with sturdy wheels—a cart to carry my
fine clothes for washing at the riverside?
I have neglected all my finery.
And surely your own clothes for the assembly
of noble chiefs should be immaculate.
And you have five sons living in these halls:
though two are wed, the other three are still
unwed, young men with zest—when they go dancing,
they want their clothing to be clean and fresh.
And I'm the one who should attend to this."

These were her words. Before her father, she
was too ashamed to speak of her own wedding.
But understanding everything, he answered:

"Dear child, I'd not deny you anything.
You'll have your mules. Your wagon will be ready
for you to leave at once—a wagon set
on solid wheels and with a storage chest."

That said, he called the servants; they obeyed.
They readied the mule-wagon, and they led
and yoked the mules to it. Nausícaa
brought out the splendid garments from her room.
She set them in the wagon; and her mother
set every sort of food abundantly
within a basket, tempting offerings,
and then, into a goatskin flask, poured wine.
And now Nausícaa climbed onto the cart.
Her mother gave her flowing olive oil
within a golden flask, that she and her
handmaids might smooth their bodies when they'd bathed.
She took the whip and the bright reins; she struck
the mules to start them up. As they surged forward,

Greek [55-82]

they clattered. And the young girl and her garments
were on their way. Nausícaa was not
alone; her handmaids went along as escort.

When they had reached the handsome river's stream,
where washing trenches never failed, where clothes,
however soiled and stained, were cleansed, for so
fresh and abundant was the waters' flow,
the girls unyoked the mules and drove them on,
beside the eddies where the river churned,
to graze the sweet grass on the banks. They took
the clothes down from the wagon, in their arms,
then plunged them down into the stream's deep flow;
without delay they trampled them again,
again, within the washing trenches; each
young girl competing with her friend, they beat
those clothes to cleanliness. That done, they spread
the stainless garments on the seaside beach
where dashing waters washed the pebbles clean.

And after they had bathed and oiled themselves,
they took their meal along the riverbank
while waiting for the sun to dry the wash.
When she and her handmaids were satisfied
with their delightful food, each set aside
the veil she wore: the young girls now played ball;
and as they tossed the ball, it was white-armed
Nausícaa who led their cadenced chant.
And even as the archer Ártemis
moves on the cliffs of tall Täýgetus
or Erymánthus, glad in her pursuit
of boars and speeding deer, and with her sport
the nymphs of field and forest, daughters of Zeus;
and in her heart, Latóna then rejoices:
her Ártemis stands tall among all others,
her head and brow held high, identified
with ease, though all her comrades there are fair:
. . .

Greek [83-108]

just so, among her band of lovely friends,
the chaste Nausícaa stood out, unwed.

But when the girl was ready to go home—
about to yoke the mules and fold the clothes—
gray-eyed Athena set her mind on still
another stratagem, so that Odysseus
might come to see the gracious girl who then
could lead him to the town of the Phaeácians.
The daughter of the king, as she was tossing
the ball to one of her companions, missed
her throw; the ball fell into a deep pool.
The girls cried out. Their shout was loud. They woke
Odysseus. And as he sat up, he thought:

"What misery is mine? What mortals must
I meet in this new land that I now touch?
Are they unfeeling beings—wild, unjust?
Or do they welcome strangers—does their thought
include fear of the gods? That cry I heard,
the cry that captured me, was tender—like
the voice of young girls—voice of nymphs who haunt
the steepest mountain peaks, the springs that feed
the rivers, and the green of grazing lands.
Can men with human speech be here—close by?
But I must try—must see with my own eyes."

And now he burst out of the underbrush;
with his stout hand he tore a leafy branch
from that thick wood, to hide his nakedness.
He moved out as a mountain lion would
when—sure of his own strength, his eyes ablaze—
through driving wind and rain, he stalks his prey,
wild deer or sheep or oxen; he'll attack
a cattle-fold, however tight the fence
that pens the herd—his hunger's so intense.
So did Odysseus seem as he prepared
to burst into the band of fair-haired girls,

Greek [109-135]

though he was naked; he was ravenous.
But he—his form was filthy, fouled with brine—
struck them as horrible; and terrified,
they scattered on the shore, one here, one there,
along the sandspits jutting out to sea.
The daughter of Alcínoüs was left
alone: her spirit had received the gift
of courage from Athena, who had freed
the limbs of the young girl from fear and trembling.

She did not flinch or flee. She faced him firmly.
He wondered what was best: Was he to clasp
her knees, beseeching help from her, or keep
his distance and, from there, present his plea
with gentle words, entreating her to clothe
his nakedness and guide him to the city?
As he considered this, it seemed more seemly,
more wise, to speak soft words but stay apart—
and not to clasp her knees, lest her young heart
be angry with him. And at once he used
these words that were both gentle and astute:

"O Queen, I do implore: Are you divine
or mortal? If you are a goddess—one
of those who have vast heaven as their home—
then I should liken you most closely to
the daughter of great Zeus: you surely are
an Ártemis in form and face and stature.
But if you are a mortal, an earth-dweller,
then both your father and your noble mother
are three times blessed, and three times blessed, your brothers:
their hearts are surely always glad to see
so fair a blossom entering the dance.
But one whose heart is blessed above the rest
is he who, wooing you with comely gifts,
will lead you to his house, for I confess,
my eyes have never seen so fair a mortal—
neither a man nor woman: as I look

Greek [136-161]

Odysseus

at you, I am amazed. Just once, at Delos,
beside Apollo's altar, have I seen
a tender palm-shoot rise so gracefully
(for I have gone to Delos, too—and many
fine followers were with me on that journey,
the start of so much misery for me).
And just as, when I saw that palm, my wonder
was piercing, lasting, for no trunk has ever
grown from the earth to match that tree, so, lady,
I marvel at you, am amazed; my fear
is deep—I plead but dare not clasp your knees.
Yet I am crushed beneath a heavy grief.
The winedark sea held me for nineteen days;
but on the twentieth, just yesterday,
I was at last set free from brutal waves—
waves whipped by swift storm winds that carried me
out from Ogýgia, island in far seas,
for all that time. A god has cast me here,
that I might suffer still more misadventures:
I do not think my trials are done; before
the end, the gods will surely send still more.
But, lady, pity me; I've suffered much;
I come, a suppliant; you are the first
with whom I plead; I know no others who
can claim this land and city as their home.
Show me your city, and give me some rag
to throw about me—you may chance to have
a wrapping from the clothes you carried here.
And may the gods grant you what your heart wants most,
a husband and a home, and may there be
accord between you both: there is no gift
more solid and more precious than such trust:
a man and woman who conduct their house
with minds in deep accord, to enemies
bring grief, but to their friends bring gladness, and—
above all—gain a good name for themselves."

□   □   □

Greek [162-185]

This was white-armed Nausícaa's reply:
"You, stranger, since you do not seem to be
mad or malicious, know that only he—
Olympian Zeus—allots felicity
to men, to both the noble and the base,
just as he wills. To you he gave this fate,
and you must suffer it—in any case.
But now, since you have come into our land,
into our city, you'll have clothing and
whatever else befits a suppliant
who, after much misfortune, found our shores.
I'll show our city to you, and you'll hear
the name our people bear: this town and land
belong to the Phaeácians. I am
the daughter of King Alcínoüs; on him
the power of the Phaeácians depends."

That said, she urged the band of her fair friends:
"Where are you rushing to? This is a man.
Or do you think he is an enemy?
There is not now, nor can there ever be,
a mortal man so strong that he can reach
our land as the Phaeácians' adversary:
we live apart from all, where strong seas foam—
the very farthest limits of the world;
no other mortals ever touch our soil.
But this man is a luckless fellow, one
who wandered here, and he deserves our care;
the stranger and the beggar—both are sent
by Zeus; and even small gifts win their thanks.
Friends, give the stranger food and give him drink
and bathe him in the stream where winds fall off,
a sheltered stretch along the river's course."

These were her words. The young girls stopped their flight.
Encouraging each other, they led on
Odysseus, as Nausícaa had asked,
down to a sheltered spot. They set fresh clothes

Greek [186-214]

beside him there—a tunic and a cloak—
and flowing oil within a flask of gold,
inviting him to bathe in river water.
Then good Odysseus spoke to the young girls:

"Do stand apart and wait for me, that I
myself may scrub my shoulders free of brine
and smooth my skin with oil; by now, some time
has passed since any oil has touched my flesh.
I do not want to bathe before your eyes,
to be a naked man encircled by
a band of girls so young with such fair hair."

So did Odysseus ask. Her young friends left
to tell Nausícaa of his request.
Then in the waters of the river, bright
Odysseus scrubbed his body free of brine
that soiled his sturdy shoulders and his spine.
And from his head he wiped away the crust
left by the restless sea. When he had washed
all of his body and smoothed down his flesh
with ample olive oil, Odysseus dressed.
And after he put on the clothing she—
the unwed girl—had given him, Athena,
the gray-eyed goddess, made him more robust
and taller; and she gave him thicker hair,
which flowed down from his head in curls and clusters
that seemed much like the hyacinth in flower.
Just as a craftsman who has learned his secrets
from both the gray-eyed goddess and Hephæstus
frames silver with fine gold and thus creates
a work with greater plenitude and grace,
so did the goddess now enhance with grace
the head and shoulders of Odysseus.
Then by the sea he sat apart, a man
handsome and radiant. Nausícaa
admired him. She told her fair-haired friends:
□ □ □

Greek [215-238]

"Listen to what I say. Without the will
of all the gods whose home is high Olympus,
this man would not have come to the Phaeácians.
Before he seemed to me so mean, so shabby;
but now wide heaven's gods could be his kin.
Would that my husband were a man like him,
who lived—and would remain—here in Schería.
But come, friends, bring the stranger food and drink."

They heard her words. They did not make him wait:
the man of many trials now drank and ate.
And when he broke his fast, had his first taste
of food in so long, he was ravenous.

Nausícaa now had something else in mind.
She stowed the folded clothes within the cart,
then yoked the stout-hoofed mules. And—quick to mount—
she put Odysseus on the alert:

"Stand ready, stranger: I'm about to drive
back to my town, my home. I'll be your guide
to my wise father's house; there you will find
the finest men of the Phaeácians.
But you—I know you'll understand—might best
do this: As long as we are passing through
the meadows and the fields that farmers till,
walk quickly with my handmaids, right behind
my mules and wagon. I shall lead and drive.
But let us, just as soon as we draw near
the city, separate. To either side
of that tall wall which rings the city lies
a splendid port. A narrow entrance strip
runs near the sea; along that road, curved ships
are drawn up: every shipman has his spot.
There, too, around Poseidon's handsome shrine,
is an assembly place, a space marked off
by stones, hauled there and set into the ground.
And there, in those ship-berths, our men repair

Greek [239-268]

cables and sails and tackle for black ships,
and there the oars are shaped and filed and thinned.
For the Phaeácians need no bows or quivers:
they care for masts and oars and shapely ships;
with these they cross the gray sea joyously.
Along the road men gather. Many chatter
insidiously. I'd avoid such talk.
I want no one to scoff: among the crowd,
some men are truly insolent—and thus,
I fear that some rude fellow, meeting us,
might say: 'This stranger whom Nausícaa's brought,
this man so grand, so handsome—who is he?
Where did she find him? He will surely be
her husband! She may well have gathered in
some castaway whose ship has gone astray,
whose people live far off—for there are none
whose home is close to us. Or he may be
a god whom she implored so fervently
that he, in answer to her pleas, came down
from heaven—and he's hers forever now.
At least she's found a husband, even if
it is a foreigner that she sought out:
better that way, for she has surely scorned
the many men—so noble—who have been
her suitors here, her own Phaeácians.'
So they will talk. And I shall be ashamed.
And were another in my place, I'd blame
her, too, and cast my shafts in the same way:
a girl who, though her father and her mother
are living, has not asked for their consent
and walks with one whom she has yet to wed.
Stranger, if you would gain a crew and ship
to take you home again and need the quick
assistance of my father, then do this:
Beside the road, you'll find Athena's forest,
a splendid grove of poplars. Set inside it,
a spring, surrounded by a meadow, surges.
My father's park and fruitful vineyard lie

Greek [269-293]

nearby, in hailing distance of the city.
Sit there and wait—just long enough for me
to enter town and reach my father's house.
And when you judge I'm well inside, set out,
walk into town, and ask what way is best
to reach the house of good Alcínoüs.
You'll recognize it easily enough
(even a child could guide you there), for none
of the Phaeácians' homes can match that palace.
Once you are there and past the courtyard, cross
the great hall quickly, till you reach my mother.
She sits before the hearth by firelight,
leaning against a pillar, spinning yarn
whose purple dye, drawn from the sea, is quite
astonishing. Her handmaids sit behind her;
and next to her, at that same pillar, leans
my father's throne. Like an immortal, he
sits, drinking wine. But pass beyond his seat
and throw your arms around my mother's knees,
for she can speed the day of your return.
For if her heart inclines to favor you,
then you indeed may hope to see your friends
and reach your well-built home, your fathers' land."

That said, she struck the mules with her bright whip;
and they were quick to leave the riverbank.
Their trot and run were smooth, and she kept check
upon their pace: she reined them in, so that
Odysseus and her maids might find it easy
to follow her on foot; she plied the lash
with good sense, sparingly. As the sun set,
they reached the fair grove sacred to Athena.
Odysseus halted there. At once he prayed
to her, the daughter of aegis-bearing Zeus:

"May you—Athena Atritóna—hear me.
If, before this, you did not hear my pleas
when I was shipwrecked—battered by the mighty

Greek [294–326]

Poseidon—may you hear me now. Allow
this stranger here on the Phaeácians' isle
to find compassion, to be welcomed well."

This was his prayer. Athena heard his pleas.
And yet she did not show herself directly:
her father's brother had to be respected—
and he did not relent: he raged against
divine Odysseus until the end,
until the exile found his own dear land.

Greek [327-331]

BOOK VII

Odysseus wrapped in mist by Athena.

His arrival
at the palace of Alcínoüs and Arétë:
their kind reception.

Odysseus' tale:
Calypso, shipwreck, reaching Schería.

·

Alcínoüs' promise
to escort Odysseus safely to his homeland.

·

Nightfall.

The man of many trials prayed in the grove.
Meanwhile the mules had brought the young girl home.
And when she reached her father's handsome halls,
she halted at the outer court; as tall
and fair as gods, her brothers hurried out,
unyoked the mules, and carried in the clothes.
She went to her own room, where her old nurse,
Eurymedúsa, lit a fire for her.
One day, long since, Eurymedúsa, caught
among the booty the Phaeácians brought
back from Apēīrë in their shapely ships,
was chosen from the captives as a gift
for King Alcínoüs, a man so wise
that people prized his counsel as godlike.
She was the one who, in those halls, had reared
white-armed Nausícaa. And it was she
who lit the fire and saw to supper now.

Odysseus, roused and ready, was by then
along the road that led to town. His friend,
Athena, hit upon this stratagem:
She wrapped him in a mist so thick that none
among the spirited Phaeácians
who came across the stranger might insult
or mock his ways and ask him who he was.
And just when he was entering the fair town,
the goddess came to meet him, taking on
the likeness of a girl—and in her arms
she bore a pitcher. There across his path,
she stood, and good Odysseus asked:

                       "Dear child,
could you not guide me to the home of one
who rules these people as their king—I mean
the palace of Alcínoüs? For I
have come here as a stranger—sorely tried—
from far, a distant land. I know no one
among the men who rule these lands, this town."   □ □ □

Greek [1–26]

This was the gray-eyed goddess's reply:
"I surely can point out to you, a stranger,
the palace you are looking for: our king
lives near my worthy father's house. So I
will lead the way, while you move quietly.
But do not stare at any man or ask
these people anything. They do not care
too much for strangers; they do not befriend
men who have wandered here from other lands.
They trust the pointed prows of their brisk ships;
with these they cross the sea's immense abyss.
This is their privilege, the special gift
Poseidon gave my countrymen: as swift
as birds in flight, as thoughts—such are their ships."

That said, Athena led; her pace was brisk.
And as he followed, walking through the town
among the famed Phaeácian seamen, none
could see him: he was wrapped within a thick,
prodigious mist—Athena's cunning trick.
Amazed, Odysseus saw the harbors and
the shapely ships, the public squares where men
of standing gathered, and the massive walls—
towering, topped by palisades—a marvel.
And once they reached the palace of the king,
the gray-eyed goddess was the first to speak:

"Sir stranger, we are here: these are the halls
you asked about. Here you will find the lords
whom Zeus has nurtured. They are banqueting.
When you go in, forget your fear: far better
to be a bold man, though a stranger here.
Above all, reach the queen in the great hall:
Arétë is her name; she shares the same
forefathers that Alcínoüs can claim.
Poseidon chose to lie with Períbœa,
who, comeliest of women, was the youngest
girl born of generous Eurýmedon

Greek [27-58]

(in days gone by, he ruled the haughty Giants;
but he led them, in all their arrogance,
to ruin, and he died in their downfall).
The son she bore was bold Nausíthoüs,
who came to be the king of the Phaeácians.
He had Rhexénor and Alcínoüs
as sons; but with his silver bow, Apollo
killed young Rhexénor, who, not married long,
had left behind no son within his halls—
only one child, a daughter called Arétë.
Alcínoüs took Arétë as his wife
and honored her beyond the measure known
by any other woman now on earth—
by all who, subject to their husbands, hold
a house together. She has always been
a mother whom her children have revered,
just as her husband has; and all our people,
as she goes through the city, celebrate
her presence. So profound is her good sense
that—for those men and women she esteems—
she acts as judge in feuds and bickerings.
If she is well disposed to ease your fate,
then you need not wait long to see your friends
and reach your high-roofed halls, your fathers' land."

That said, Athena left the lovely isle.
She crossed the restless sea to Marathon
and then to Athens, where the roads are spacious,
for there she shares an altar with Eréctheus.

Meanwhile Odysseus reached Alcínoüs'
bright palace. But he stopped to ponder long
before he crossed the threshold wrought in bronze.
That high-roofed palace was a realm of light,
of brightness as of sun or moon; the sides,
in from the threshold to the halls, were lined
by a resplendent frieze in azurite;
within, the robust house had doors of gold;

Greek [59–88]

and from bronze thresholds, silver doorposts rose.
Flanking the door were dogs Hephæstus wrought
in gold and silver with bewitching art;
Alcínoüs' palace had these dogs as guards—
undying dogs exempt from age and change.
Then on both sides, aligned along the walls,
in from the threshold to the inner halls,
were thrones, and over them were draped soft cloth—
well-fashioned fabrics, women's handiwork.
Phaeácian chiefs would sit upon those chairs
to eat and drink; rich stores were always there.
And there, on shapely pedestals, were set
statues of golden youths; each statue held
a flaming torch to light the night for guests.
And fifty women served Alcínoüs:
some grind the yellow corn, their mills in hand;
and others weave their webs or, while they sit,
twist their swift spindles as their fingers glint
like leaves of poplar trees swayed by the wind.
Down from the linen on the loom, there dripped
a flow of olive oil, which smoothed the fabric.
As the Phaeácians are the most expert
of men in sailing brisk ships over seas,
so are their women peerless when they weave.
To them, the gray-eyed goddess gave this gift:
consummate art and understanding hearts.

Outside the courtyard, near the doorway, stretches
an orchard large as four-days' plowing covers.
The trees are tall and generous: their branches
bear pears, bright apples, sweet figs, pomegranates,
plump olives. And the fruit they bear is endless;
it never withers, never falters, whether
in summer or in winter. Faithful Zephyr
quickens some fruit and brings full bloom to others.
There pear on pear, apple on apple, cluster
on cluster, fig on fig, can reach rich measure.
There his unstinting vineyard has been planted;

Greek [89–123]

one sector stretches over warm, flat ground;
there vines dry in the sun, while other grapes
are gathered and still others pressed and crushed.
In front are unripe grapes, some just about
to shed their bloom and some just growing dark.
And past the vineyard's final aisle, in rows
well ordered, varied vegetables grow,
blooming throughout the year. There are two springs.
The first spring feeds the garden with fresh water;
the other issues near the courtyard door,
in toward the palace: from this second spring,
the townsfolk draw their water. With such gifts
the gods enriched the king's tall edifice.

Odysseus stopped. He stared, amazed. But once
his thoughts had touched on every point, he crossed
the threshold quickly. In the halls he found
Phaeácian chiefs and elders pouring out
wine offerings to Hermes, keen-eyed god,
who should receive the final offering
whenever men have turned their minds toward sleep.
Still hidden by the mist Athena had sent,
Odysseus moved ahead until he reached
Arétë and the king, Alcínoüs.
He cast his arms around Arétë's knees.
The mist dissolved; Odysseus now was seen.
As he appeared, they all—astonished—gazed
in silence. And Odysseus prayed:

                              "Arétë,
divine Rhexénor's daughter, I beseech:
after so many trials, I now have reached
your husband and your guests. I clasp your knees:
may each of those who feast with you receive
long life, the gods' approval, and bequeath
his riches to his sons, together with
the place and privileges that were his—
the things he merited. And I ask this

Greek [124–150]

of you: a crew to take me home with speed.
These years far from my own have meant much grief."

These were his words. Then, at the hearth, he sat
upon the ashes, near the flame. The guests
were silent, motionless, until at last
old Echenéus, venerable man
whose words were keen, whose understanding spanned
so many things of time gone by, began
to speak. And what he said was rich with sense:

"Alcínoüs, it is not kind or just
to let a stranger sit upon the hearth,
among the ashes on the ground. Clear word
from you is what they all are waiting for.
Come, help the guest to rise: seat him upon
a chair with silver studs, and have the heralds
mix bowls of wine, that we may also pour
wine offerings to Zeus the thunder lord,
since suppliants are always in his care.
And let the housewife offer to the stranger
a supper from whatever she has stored."

As soon as he heard this, Alcínoüs,
exerting sacred force, took by the hand
Odysseus, that astute and prudent man.
He drew him from the hearth and sat him down
upon a chair that stood beside his own—
a gleaming chair from which he asked the son
he loved so much, the brave Laódamas,
to rise. That he might wash his hands, a maid
poured water from a lovely golden jug
into a silver basin; at his side
she placed a polished table. The old housewife
was generous: she drew on lavish stores;
the visitor was offered much and more.
The patient, bright Odysseus drank and ate.
Then vigorous Alcínoüs told a page: □ □ □

Greek [151-178]

"Now mix the bowl, Pontónoüs; let all
within the hall have wine, that we may pour
wine offerings to Zeus the thunder lord,
since suppliants are always in his care."

That said, the herald mixed the honeyed wine;
into the cups of all, he poured the first
drops—these would serve to quench the thirst of gods.
Then, when each man had offered his libation
and, after, drunk as much as he might wish,
Alcínoüs, among the guests, said this:

"Listen, Phaeácian counselors and chiefs,
for what I say is what my heart would speak.
Now that you've banqueted, go home to rest.
Once dawn has come and we have called upon
more elders, we can entertain the stranger
and offer to the gods fine sacrifices.
Then we shall turn our minds to readying
a crew to escort him, so that our guest,
however far away his home may be,
can reach it easily, with no mischance—
a crossing free from grief until his path
lets him set foot on his own land at last.
Once home, he'll have to suffer what his fate
and the relentless Weavers may have spun
for him when he was born. But if he is
one of the deathless ones, who has come down
from heaven, then the gods may have a plan
beyond the measure we can understand.
The gods have always shown themselves to us
true in their likenesses whenever we
have offered them our famous hecatombs;
they sit beside us, sharing in our feasts.
And when we meet the gods upon the road,
even if one of us is all alone,
they do not hide their likenesses; for we
. . .

Greek [179-205]

can claim close kinship with the gods, as can
the Cyclops or the savage Giants' clan."

Odysseus, man of many wiles, replied:
"Alcínoüs, there is no need to wonder.
I certainly am not—in shape or stature—
like the immortals who possess wide heaven;
I am like those who die. If you know men
who have endured much suffering, you can
see me as one of them. And I could tell
of still more trials and griefs the gods have willed.
But let me, even in my sorrow, eat.
There is no thing more shameless than the belly;
however tried we are, whatever pain
assails our heart, the hateful stomach claims
its right to be remembered: it constrains
us always, forcing us to eat and drink,
even as I, though sick at heart, am now
compelled to set aside my long ordeal:
my belly bids me see that it be filled.
But do be quick; at daybreak, carry me,
a man of sorrows, back to my own land,
however hard my homeward way has been.
Once I have seen my goods, my servants, my
own high-roofed house, I'm quite content to die."

These were his words, and all gave their assent:
they urged the king to offer to this guest
both ship and crew—his plan made such good sense.
And after offering libations, each
Phaeácian went to his own house to sleep.
But bright Odysseus stayed within the hall,
and with him sat Arétë and her lord.
Maids cleared away the dishes of the feast.
White-armed Arétë was the first to speak,
for she had recognized his handsome cloak
and tunic: these were her own handiwork—
. . .

Greek [206-234]

clothes woven by her women and her self.
She turned to him, and these were her winged words:

"Stranger, I'll be the first to question you:
Who are you? To what land do you belong?
Who gave these clothes to you? Did you not say
that you had wandered on the waves, astray?"

Odysseus, man of many wiles, replied:
"O Queen, how hard it is to tell you all
my tale from start to finish; many trials
were mine, assigned by the Olympians.
But I can answer what you ask of me.
There is a distant island in the sea:
Ogýgia, home of Atlas' daughter, crafty
Calypso of the lovely hair, dread goddess.
No god or mortal ever visits her.
But in my misery, some god brought me—
alone—to her hearthside; for Zeus had struck
my swift ship with a blazing thunderbolt:
my boat was shattered in the winedark sea.
Then all my worthy shipmates died, but I,
gripping the keel of my curved ship, survived;
for nine days I was dragged along, but in
the dark night of the tenth, the gods cast me
upon Calypso's island. Generously
she welcomed me, took care of me; she fed me;
to me she promised immortality
and never-aging days; but she could not
persuade the heart within my breast. And when
the wheel of years had brought the eighth year near,
she urged me on—to seek my home again,
either because of Zeus and his commands
or else because her mind had some new plan.
She sent me on my way within a craft
that was well made and tightly joined, equipped
with much; Calypso had provided me
with food and sweet wine and with clothing fit

Greek [235-265]

for the immortals. And to speed me on,
she sent a light, warm wind. Across the waves
I sailed for seventeen propitious days;
on the eighteenth, I saw the shadowed peaks
of your own country. And my heart was happy.
I did not know what heavy misery
awaited me. For now it was Poseidon,
the shaker of the earth, who, urging on
the winds, blocked my advance; in the immense
sea-swells he spurred, I lost my every chance
of making headway with my sturdy craft,
which—as I shouted, howled—the tempest smashed.
And then I had to swim across the depths,
until the wind and waves had carried me
close to your shores. But had I tried to land,
waves would have dashed me hard against great crags
on a grim coast. But after drawing back
into the ebb, again I swam until
I reached a river mouth, a friendly place—
beach free of reefs and sheltered from the wind.
I staggered landward, taking heart: divine
night fell. Beyond the river fed by Zeus,
hid by the bushes, I stretched out to sleep;
around me I had gathered heaps of leaves.
I slept through all that night and through sunrise,
till noon. But when the sun had passed its peak,
sweet sleep abandoned me. I woke to see
your daughter's handmaids playing on the shore.
When she, as lovely as a goddess, came
to join their game, I made my plea to her.
She had good sense, more wits than one can hope
to meet in most young people (for the young
are often thoughtless). And she offered me
abundant food and dark wine, had me bathe
within the waters of that stream, and gave
these clothes to me. Despite my sorrowing,
I tell the truth in telling you these things."

□ □ □

Greek [266-297]

Sea Tempest

It was Alcínoüs who answered him:
"Stranger, my daughter was mistaken when
she failed to bring you back with her companions
when they returned to us. For, after all,
she heard you ask to join us in these halls."

Odysseus, man of many wiles, replied:
"For this, your seemly daughter bears no blame:
she asked me to return with her dear maids,
but I refused; I was afraid, ashamed,
lest you, on seeing me, might have grown angry.
We men on earth are prone to jealousy."

This was the answer of Alcínoüs:
"Stranger, the heart within my breast is not
so made as to be angry without cause:
in all things, the best course is moderate.
May father Zeus, Athena, and Apollo
now be my witnesses: I would that you,
a man so worthy, might agree to be
my son-in-law, wedding my daughter and
remaining here. If you should want to stay,
I would provide you with a house and goods.
Though none of the Phaeácians, if you should
will otherwise, would hold you back—for Zeus,
our father, would condemn us for such acts.
Thus I, that you may be assured, have fixed
tomorrow as the day of your departure.
You, overcome by sleep, will take your rest
while our Phaeácian oarsmen take you back
to your own home or else to any shore
for which your heart may long, however far—
even beyond Eubœa, which is said
to be the farthest place by those of us
who saw that land when they brought Rhadamánthus
to visit Títyus, the son of Gǽa.
Yet even there they voyaged out and back
in just one day—and without strain. You, too,

Greek [298-326]

will see just how the oar blades of our crews
lift waves, and why our ships are prized and praised."

Odysseus, when he heard these words, rejoiced.
As his reply, this was the prayer he voiced:
"Our father Zeus, now may Alcínoüs
perform what he has pledged. And may his fame
remain unquenched on earth, giver of grain,
and may I see my native land again."

Such were the words that they exchanged. Arété
of the white arms then bade her women go
to set a couch beneath the portico,
to cover it with purple tapestry,
to add still other wrappings, and on these
to place warm cloaks of fleece. At that command,
her handmaids left the hall, torches in hand.
They soon returned (the bed was firmed and ready)
and, at his side, invited him most gently:
"Stranger, your bed has been prepared: do rest."

And rest was what he wanted. There he slept—
the man of many trials—upon a bed
whose frame had bores through which were strung taut cords,
beneath the echoing arcade. Meanwhile
Alcínoüs slept in the high-roofed house—
its inmost room. His lady shared his couch.

Greek [327–347]

BOOK VIII

Dawn.

The council of Phaeácians:
a ship and crew for Odysseus' homeward journey.

The feast of the Phaeácians:
blind Demódocus, the matchless singer;
the tears of Odysseus.

·

Diversion for Odysseus:
the tournament of the young Phaeácian lords.

Provocation by the rude Eurýalus:
Odysseus' amazing stone-throw.

·

Back to the banquet:
Demódocus' song of the adulterous love
of Árës and Aphrodítë, wife of Hephǽstus;
the dance of the young Phaeácians.

Gifts for Odysseus.

The song of the wooden horse;
Odysseus' tears.

The curiosity of the king:
questions for Odysseus.

As soon as Dawn's rose fingers touched the sky,
Alcínoüs awoke with sacred might,
as did the ravager of towns, Zeus-born
Odysseus. The Phaeácian was his guide;
he led him to the council ground, set by
the ships. When they arrived, they sat beside
each other on the seats of polished stone.
Meanwhile Athena, who was so intent
on safe return for firm Odysseus, went
throughout the town; she'd taken on the guise
of wise Alcínoüs' herald; at the side
of every man the goddess met, she cried:

"Come now, Phaeácian lords and counselors:
at the assembly ground you'll learn about
the stranger newly come into the house
of brave Alcínoüs—he sailed across
wide seas, and he is like the deathless gods."

Her words provoked the eagerness of all;
soon every seat was filled. And many marveled,
seeing Laértës' splendid son. The grace
he wore was godlike, shed upon his face
and shoulders by Athena; and she made
Odysseus taller and more vigorous,
that his Phaeácian hosts might welcome him
with honor and respect—that he might win
his way among the many tests and feats
in which he'd be invited to compete.

And when they all had gathered eagerly,
Alcínoüs spoke first. This was his speech:
"Listen, Phaeácian counselors and chiefs,
for what I say is what my heart must speak.
This guest—I do not know who he may be—
this stranger, from a country that lies east
or west, amid his wanderings has reached
my house. And there is but one thing he seeks:

He asks us for an escort that would speed
his way to his own land. He pleads, he needs
our pledge. And just as strangers have received
our help in days gone by, let us provide
what he requests; for I have not denied—
or ever made to wait and grieve—a man
who came to me and sought a kindly hand.
Come, launch a black ship on the brilliant sea,
a ship prepared for her first voyaging.
And from our people let us choose a crew
of fifty-two young men, those who have proved
that they are best. When you have lashed—hard, fast—
the oarlocks and the oars, then leave the ship
and come back to my halls. And do not wait:
prepare a feast; we all must celebrate;
I'll see that there's abundance for my guests.
For you young men, such is the task I set.
But I ask all the rest, the sceptered chiefs,
to come to my fair palace and to greet
the visitor within my halls—and may
no man refuse me. Call Demódocus
to join us, for his chants are heavenly:
a god gave him this gift in matchless measure:
whatever way his song may take brings pleasure."

That said, he led the way; the sceptered chiefs
all followed him. The heralds went to seek
the godlike singer. And the fifty-two
select young men, obeying his command,
went to the shoreline of the restless sea.
And when that crew had reached the ship and shore,
they drew the black boat down to the deep waters
and set up mast and canvas; with fine craft,
they fitted oars into the leather straps,
then spread the white sail. Having moored the ship
well out into the roadstead, they went back
to brave Alcínoüs' imposing palace.

□ □ □

Greek [30-56]

Now many men had gathered, young and old;
they filled the halls, the courts, the porticoes.
For them Alcínoüs had killed twelve sheep,
two shambling oxen, and eight white-tusked boars;
all these they flayed and dressed for the rich feast.

The herald came; he led the lord of song,
a man for whom the Muse had matchless love:
to him she'd given blessing and affliction—
she took his sight away, but granted him
the gift of sweetest song. Pontónoüs,
the herald, set a silver-studded chair
against a pillar that rose high, just at
the center of the feast; and from a peg
above the singer's head, he hung the harp
and showed him how to reach it with his hands.
And at the singer's side he placed a basket,
a handsome table, and a cup of wine
to drink whenever he was so inclined.

The feast was ready now. Their hands reached out.
But when they had their fill of food and drink,
the poet was persuaded by the Muse
to sing of men of glory, men whose deeds
were chanted in a song whose fame had reached
vast heaven: it recounted the dispute
between Odysseus and the son of Péleus,
Achilles: at the gods' rich feast, those two,
with words of rampant rage and spite, had dueled.
And Agamemnon, lord of men, on seeing
the best of his Achǽans quarrel, was glad,
for he had learned that this would come to pass
(such was the prophecy that he had heard
Apollo speak aloud—in measured verse—
in holy Pytho, where the king had crossed
the stone threshold to seek the oracle).
So did the wave of sorrow start its course,
· · ·

Greek [57-81]

descending on the Trojans and the Greeks—
as mighty Zeus had willed—with grief on grief.

These things the famous singer sang. Odysseus
held fast his purple cloak with sturdy hands;
he drew its great folds over his bent head
and hid his handsome features out of shame,
lest the Phaeácians see the tears he shed.
But when the singer stopped his song, Odysseus,
after he dried his tears, drew back the cloak
and, lifting his two-handled cup, poured out
libations to the gods. Yet once the poet,
urged on by the Phaeácian chiefs, again
began to chant, the Ithacan, concealing
his head, began to sob again. No one
knew of his tears—except Alcínoüs.
He, seated near Odysseus, had heard
his dismal moan. He did not wait. He spoke
to his Phaeácian lords, lovers of oars:

"Listen, Phaeácian counselors and chiefs.
Our hearts are now at peace: we've shared this feast
and heard the harp, whose lovely sounds complete
this rich festivity. But now let's test
our talents out of doors in feats and trials
that show our gifts. Our guest will then be able,
when he goes home, to tell his own dear people
that we have skills no other men can equal
when we are asked to box, jump, race, or wrestle."

That said, he led the way, and they all followed.
The herald hung the resonating harp
upon a peg, then helped Demódocus:
he took his hand and guided him along
the path on which the other lords had gone.
And on that road to the assembly place,
a countless crowd had joined them—all intent
on watching the amazing tournament.

Greek [82–108]

And many young men were already set
to join the contests: Pónteus, Próreus, Prýmneus,
Erétmus, Thóön, Nāuteus, Élatreus,
and Acronéus and Ocýalus,
Anchíalus and Anabásinéus,
and Polynéus' son—grandson of Tecton—
Amphíalus. And just as ready stood
Eurýalus—the son of Nāubolus—
who matched the might of man-destroying Árës:
he was in form and comeliness the best
of all of the Phaeácian youths except
for the incomparable Laódamas.
And now Laódamas, together with
his brothers—Clytonéus, Hálius—
stood up: three sons of lord Alcínoüs.

The footrace was the first contest they faced.
And from the starting point, the pace was fast:
they all flew off with speed; the dust rose up
along the plain. And it was Clytonéus
who won that race—ahead by the same space
that, when they span a furrow, two mules take.
The wrestling tests—most strenuous—were next:
the winner was Eurýalus. The best
at jumping was Amphíalus. The discus
was won by Élatreus. The champion
in boxing was Alcínoüs' stout son,
Laódamas; when they had all been stirred—
delighted by the games—these were his words:

"Come, friends, let's ask the stranger to select
one test at which he is adept. His body
is not to be disprized: his legs, his thighs,
and then, on high, his arms and thick-set neck
and sinewed chest. Yes, he has youthful strength.
Of course, his long ordeal has sapped his force:
I'd say the sea wears out the toughest man—
no thing can pound and punish as it can."   □ □ □

Eurýalus replied: "Your words are just;
and now it is for you, Laódamas,
to go and ask our guest to challenge us."

And when Alcínoüs' fine son heard this,
he came, stood in the center, told Odysseus:
"Come, stranger, be our rival in these tests,
if there's a trial at which you are adept.
You, too, must surely have some sporting skill:
a man can lay no claim to greater fame—
as long as he's alive—than strength and speed
that he displays with his own hands and feet.
Join us and banish worries from your heart.
Your journey will not be delayed by this:
your crew is ready—they have launched your ship."

Odysseus, man of many wiles, replied:
"Laódamas, why must you goad me so?
My heart is held by sorrow, not by sport.
I sit here in your council, but my soul
longs for my home. I've asked your king, your people,
for this one thing alone: to end my exile."

Eurýalus could only taunt: "In truth,
stranger, you hardly seem like one well used
to sport: the talents others have, you lack.
I'd say that you were better suited for
sharp trafficking in ships with many oars:
the captain of a cargo-bearing crew,
a merchant most intent on freight and goods
and greed—no agile athlete, to be sure."

The man of many wiles, Odysseus, eyed
Eurýalus with scorn: "Yes, you are blind
and foolish, stranger—and your words are wild.
The gods distinguish what they give to each:
not form or judgment or persuasive speech
is set before all men in equal reach.

Greek [140-168]

A man may not seem handsome, yet his words
were given beauty's garland by a god;
others delight in seeing him, and he
is modest, clear, convincing when he speaks;
he is conspicuous in all assemblies,
and when he makes his way across the city,
men look at him as at a deity.
Another man is handsome as the gods,
but what he says has not been crowned with grace.
That is your case: a flawless form and face—
even a god could not improve your shape—
and yet your head is empty. I resent
your words: they are impertinent; they vex
the soul within my chest. I am in fact—
despite your ranting—not that ignorant
of sport; indeed I was among the best
as long as I could count on youth and strength.
But now mischance and grief have ground me down.
Along the way I went, I had to face
the wars men wage, then battle bitter waves.
Yet, though I've known misfortune, I shall try
my luck, take up your challenge. I have heard
your words: they wound my heart—now I am stirred . . . "

That said, not bothering to shed his cloak,
he leaped up; and he seized a large, thick stone,
a discus heavier than any thrown
by the Phaeácian men. He whirled that stone,
then hurled it from his sturdy hand. It hummed.
And as it rushed, they crouched down on the ground—
those lovers of long oars, those men renowned
as navigators, the Phaeácians.

That stone, as it sped lightly from his hand,
flew past the points that all the rest had reached.
And taking on the likeness of a man,
Athena measured off the marks and said:

□ □ □

Greek [169-194]

"Stranger, even a blind man, if he groped
and felt these stakes, would know which marked your throw,
for it lies far beyond where others' crowd.
It is ahead. Be sure of this contest
at least, for no Phaeácian here can best
your toss or even match the mark you set."

These were her words. Odysseus—patient, bright—
was glad: he had a friend who took his side.
His spirits high, he challenged, he defied:

"Now you, young men, just try to match that mark;
though soon I'll fling another just as far
or even farther. As for other tests,
if any of the rest of you have heart
and spirit that incite you to contend,
let him come here and try my skill and strength.
You've angered me too much: I'll not hold back—
I'll box and wrestle, even race. I speak
to all of you Phaeácians, barring none
except Laódamas. He is my host;
he welcomed me to this strange land. What guest—
unless he be a fool or utter wretch—
would ever challenge his own host? Who wants
to see the welcome he received cut short?
As for the rest of you, I'll face you all
and scorn no one; I mean to try your mettle.
In any game where men display their skills,
I'm not inept. I know the polished bow;
I wield it well; and when I faced a foe,
I always was the first whose arrow struck
its man—though many comrades stood beside me
and aimed their shafts against the enemy.
At Troy, when we Achæans shot, the only
bowman who bettered me was Philoctétës.
Of all the rest, I say that I am best
by far—I mean the men still on this earth,
who feed on bread. But I cannot compete

Greek [195-223]

with men of ancient days, with Héraclës
or Eurytus of Œchalía, men
who could contend with gods in archery.
(In fact, great Eurytus died just for that;
within his halls he never reached old age.
Apollo—whom he'd challenged—in his rage,
killed him.) And I can cast a lance as far
as others shoot an arrow. But I fear
that some of you Phaeácians here are better
at running: many waves have battered me;
my boat ran short of stores; my legs lack force."

All who had heard were silent: no one stirred—
except Alcínoüs. These were his words:
"Dear guest, you did not answer out of spite.
You wanted us to see your worth and rights.
That man had angered you; where men compete,
he came to you and taunted. Seemly speech
would not allow a man to mock your feats
and prowess. But that's over. Listen now
to what I say, so that when you return
and feast with wife and children in your home,
you then can tell some other chieftain—even
as you recall the skills of the Phaeácians—
the excellences granted us by Zeus
from our forefathers' day until our own.
At wrestling, boxing, we are not the best;
but we're swift runners, and we're unsurpassed
in seamanship; we take delight in banquets,
the harp, a change of dress, warm baths, and bed.

"Come now, Phaeácian masters of the dance,
perform, so that, when he goes home, our guest
can tell his dear ones that we are the best
in sailing and footracing, dance and chant.
And let someone go quickly now to fetch
Demódocus the harp that has been left
within my house—its tones are clear and sharp."   □ □ □

Greek [224–255]

So said godlike Alcínoüs; the herald
went off to fetch the harp from the king's house.
Then nine officials chosen by the people,
masters of games and ceremonials,
took charge. They cleared a level space for dancing
and had the crowd move back to free the field.
The herald had retrieved the clear-toned harp,
and now Demódocus moved toward the center.
Around him in a dance that was divine,
those dancers in their prime—young boys—beat time.
Amazed, Odysseus watched their flashing feet.

The poet's chant was prefaced by the harp,
and then he sang with captivating art
of Aphrodítë of the lovely crown
and Árës: how these lovers lay in secret,
embracing in the house of lord Hephæstus.
And Árës gave his mistress many gifts
after he had disgraced her husband's bed.
But there had been a witness: Hélios.
He did not wait: he rushed straight to Hephæstus,
to tell him of the dalliance in his house.
As soon as he had heard that sorry tale,
Hephæstus hurried to his forge; his heart
was bent on harm; across the block he laid
his mighty anvil, forging strong, tight chains—
unbreakable—to hold those lovers fast.
And when he finished fashioning that trap,
the snare that served his wrath, Hephæstus sought
the room where his bed stood. Once there, he wrapped
those chains around the bed-legs; overhead,
down from the roof, he hung that same strong mesh,
as fine as spiders' webs—made with such craft
and subtlety that it could not be seen,
not even by the gods themselves. That net
in place around the bed, Hephæstus feigned
a journey, just as if he meant to go
to Lemnos, fortress city he loves so.

Greek [256–284]

Once Árës of the golden reins—not blind,
but keen-eyed—saw the master craftsman leave,
he hurried to renowned Hephǽstus' house,
hot for the love of fair-crowned Cytheréa.
She'd just come from the home of Cronos' son,
her mighty father. And she had sat down,
when Árës entered, clasped her hand, and urged:

"Love, let us lie together, take our joy.
Hephǽstus is not here; he's left for Lemnos,
home of the Síntians with their strange speech."

These were his words. She seconded his urge.
But having gone to bed, seeking sweet rest,
they found themselves surrounded by the threads
that shrewd Hephǽstus forged: they could not budge
or lift their limbs. They understood at last
that there was no escaping from this trap.
And now Hephǽstus, ambidextrous lord,
having turned back before he reached the shores
of Lemnos, headed homeward—toward the traitors.
With troubled heart, he hurried to his house.
And at the portico, he stopped; held fast
by savage wrath, he howled to all the gods
a cry that was enough to terrify:

"O father Zeus, and you, the other gods,
blessed and everlasting, do come now
to see this scene—ridiculous, obscene.
Because I limp, Zeus' daughter, Aphrodítë,
scorns me and loves instead destructive Árës:
while he is swift and handsome, I am lame.
And yet the only ones who are to blame
for this are my two parents: they should not
have given birth to me. And now just see
my wife climb into my own bed—with Árës.
To share that sight is more than I can bear.
But none the less, despite their tenderness,

Greek [285-316]

I doubt they'll want to linger thus: quite soon
they will have had enough of their bedroom.
And yet this mesh, this trap, will hold them fast
until her father's given back to me
all that I gave to him—unstinting gifts—
that I might take as bride this shameless bitch:
his daughter's fair, but cannot curb her itch."

These were his words. The gods were quick to reach
the house whose threshold glowed with brass: Poseidon,
whose seas embrace the earth; and that swift runner,
Hermes; and then Apollo, lord whose shafts
strike at a distance. But the goddesses
stayed, each in her own household, out of shame.
The gods, those givers of good things, stopped short,
just at the portico; but they could see
astute Hephæstus' artistry and craft:
when they saw that, nothing could quench their laughs.
And turning toward his fellows, someone said:

"There is no profit in foul deeds. The slow
outstrips the swift; so now Hephæstus, though
he has no speed, has overtaken Árës,
the swiftest of the gods who hold Olympus.
And since he limps, he gains his goal through craft,
and the adulterer must pay for that."

So did the gods, each to the other, speak.
Apollo, son of Zeus, then said to Hermes:
"Gift-giver, son of Zeus—you, messenger
Hermes—would you, though crushed by chains, still be
content to lie with golden Aphrodítë?"

To this, Hermes the messenger replied:
"Apollo, archer-lord who strikes afar,
although I might be held by chains that are
three times more numerous, more tight, than these,
then—even if you gods should watch the sight,

Greek [317-340]

and all the goddesses—I'd find delight
in lying with the golden Aphrodítë."

At that, the deathless gods laughed. But Poseidon
kept pleading with the formidable craftsman,
Hephæstus, to set Árës free. He said:

"Release him, and I promise that he will,
even as you demand, pay out in full,
before the deathless gods, the debt he owes."

The ambidextrous artisan replied:
"Poseidon, you whose seas embrace the earth,
do not ask this of me. No guarantee
that's given for a cur can reassure me.
How could I shackle you before the gods
if Árës should rush off, once he is free
of my tough chains, evading what he owes me?"

Poseidon, who enfolds the earth, replied:
"Even if Árës flees and so reneges
his debt, then I myself will pay that pledge."

The ambidextrous one said: "Your request
is one I neither can nor should reject."

With that, Hephæstus' force released the net.
When the tight chains fell slack, those two leaped up.
Lord Árës fled to Thrace, while off to Cyprus
went smiling Aphrodítë. There, at Páphos,
she had her sacred shrine, her fragrant altar.
And there the Graces bathed her and anointed
her form with the immortal oil appointed
for gods' undying bodies. Then they clothed her
in splendor: to see her was to feel wonder.

This was the tale the famous singer sang.
And hearing him, Odysseus felt the same

Greek [341-367]

delight that touched the hearts of the far-famed
Phaeácian seamen, lovers of long oars.

Alcínoüs then asked Laódamas
and Hálius alone to dance, for none
could match their skill. The brothers took in hand
the splendid purple sphere that Pólybus
had fashioned just for them: the one leaned backward
and tossed it toward the shadowed clouds; the other,
as he leaped high into the air, would catch
that ball before his feet touched earth again.
But after they had showed their skill aloft
and tossing high, they then displayed their art
in dance close to the fruitful soil—they threw
the ball directly back and forth. The other
youths ringed the dance and beat the time; their clamor
pounded louder, louder. Bright Odysseus
then told Alcínoüs:

                    "O man of might,
Alcínoüs, whose fame no man can match,
you said your men were masters of the dance.
Your words were true. I watch and am entranced."

His words delighted great Alcínoüs,
who straightway told his people, fervent oarsmen:
"Listen, Phaeácian counselors and chiefs;
I think our guest has much good sense. Let us
give him a proper sign of our friendship.
Twelve men of note are rulers in this land,
and I am the thirteenth. Let each of us
give him a tunic and a deep-dyed cloak
and add to these a talent of fine gold.
And let's bring all these things together quickly
so that our guest can have in hand his gifts
and, when he feasts with us, be glad in spirit.
And let Euryalus make peace with him,
. . .

Greek [368–396]

offering words and offering a gift—
for what he said before was most unfit."

These were his words. They all agreed and urged
much speed. And heralds went, sent by each chief,
to fetch the gifts. Eurýalus replied:

"Alcínoüs, with whom no man can vie,
even as you would have me do, I wish
to make peace with our guest. To him I give
this sword of heavy bronze: it has a hilt
of silver and a scabbard newly carved
of ivory. He'll find this gift most rich."

That said, he handed to Odysseus
the silver-studded sword, and then he added
winged words:

                    "Good fortune to you, cherished guest.
If any word of spite was spoken, may
the storm winds snatch it up, bear it away.
And may the gods allow your eyes to see
your wife again, to reach your own dear land;
far from your loved ones, you have suffered long."

Odysseus, man of many wiles, replied:
"Friend, I return your greetings: may the gods
allow you happiness. In future days
may you not miss this sword, your gift to me
that comes with words of gentle amity."

That said, he strapped the silver-studded sword
about his shoulders. When the sun went down,
he had in hand the splendid gifts. The heralds
took them to King Alcínoüs' great house;
and there his sons set all that had been offered—
those gracious gifts—before their honored mother.
Led by Alcínoüs, the others gathered.

Greek [397–421]

They sat on high-backed thrones. And he, the king
whose force was holy, said to his Árétë:

"Dear wife, bring out a splendid chest—our best.
Within it, stow a tunic and clean cloak.
And heat a brazen caldron on the flames
and warm the water so that, having bathed
and seen these gifts arrayed and well displayed—
the offerings the fine Phaeácians gave—
our guest may take delight in feasting and
in listening to the poems we shall chant.
I, too, shall give a gift: my fine gold cup—
so that, for all his days, in his great house,
he may remember me as he pours out
wine offerings to Zeus or other gods."

That said, Árétë asked for no delay:
over the fire—the flames already blazed—
her maids must put in place a great tripod.
As soon as that was done, they set the caldron,
poured water that would fill his bath, and heaped
fresh logs to feed the flames. The fire rose;
it wrapped the belly of the caldron, warmed
the water. And meanwhile Árétë brought
a handsome coffer from her inner chamber:
into this chest she set the precious gifts,
the clothes and gold just given to the guest
by the Phaeácians. Then the queen herself
added a lovely tunic and a cloak
and offered him these winged words as she spoke:

"The lid is something you yourself must lock.
Tie fast a knot so that no one may rob
your gifts when, after boarding the black ship,
you lie in sweet sleep on your homeward trip."

When patient, bright Odysseus heard all this,
he quickly shut the lid, then fastened it:

Greek [422–447]

he used a knot most intricate—a trick
he'd learned from queenly Círcë so long since.
The housewife urged him on to bathe at once.
When he saw that warm bath, his heart was glad,
for care and comfort had not been his lot
since he had left fair-haired Calypso's house
(though while he stayed with her, his every need
was met—as if he were indeed a god).
Once they had bathed and rubbed him down, the maids
then wrapped him in a tunic and fine cloak.
Come from the bath, he went to join the men,
who then were drinking wine. Nausícaa—
her beauty was god-given—stood beside
a pillar that sustained the sturdy roof;
seeing Odysseus, she was struck with wonder,
and these were the winged words he heard from her:

"I greet you, guest, as you take leave, so that—
when you've gone back to your homeland—you may
remember me and keep in mind how I,
more than all others, worked to save your life."

Odysseus, man of many wiles, replied:
"Nausícaa, daughter of the generous
Alcínoüs, may Hera's husband, Zeus
the thunderer, now guide me to my house
and let me see the day of my return.
There I shall pray forever and each day
to you as to a goddess. Dearest girl,
to you I owe my life."

                    With that reply,
he sat down on a chair that stood beside
Alcínoüs'. They mixed the wine with care
and portioned out and served the banquet fare.
The herald guided in the worthy singer,
Demódocus, a man the people honored.
He seated him among the banqueters:

Greek [448-472]

there, at the center, propped by a tall pillar,
the poet sat. The man of many wiles,
Odysseus, after he had carved a portion
out of the fat chine of a white-tusked boar
(though, on the backbone, he had left much more)
called to the herald:

              "Go and give this meat
to good Demódocus, that he may eat,
and tell him that I want—despite my grief—
to greet him as a friend. It's only right
that poets win from every man alive
esteem and honor; for the Muse holds dear
the tribe of singers, and to them she's taught
her rules of song—the way to weave a plot."

These were his words. The herald fetched that piece
and offered it to lord Demódocus.
The poet, taking it, was glad. The feast
was served and ready; every hand reached out.
When each had had his fill of food and drink,
Odysseus, man of many wiles, turning
directly to Demódocus, said this:

"Demódocus, I do indeed praise you
above all other men: your teacher was
perhaps the Muse, daughter of Zeus, perhaps
Apollo. You have sung with style and truth
the fate of the Achæans: what they did
and what was done to them, their many griefs.
You sang as if you had been there yourself
or heard this tale from one who shared those trials.
But now, do sing of other things: tell how
the wooden horse was built, the thing of guile
Epēïus made; tell how Athena helped
and how that horse could reach the citadel,
led there by bright Odysseus, whose wiles
had stuffed that horse with warriors who then

Greek [473-495]

sacked Troy. If you can chant this tale to me
with artistry, at once I'll tell all men
that from a gracious god you have received
a gift of song supremely sweet, complete."

These were his words. And when a god had urged
the singer, he began. To start his chant
he chose to tell the tale from that point when,
after they had set fire to their sheds,
the Greeks embarked on their stout ships and then
sailed off. Meanwhile the few men left behind,
led by renowned Odysseus, crouched inside
the horse, on the assembly place of Troy.
The Trojans—by themselves—had hauled that horse
up to the citadel. And there it stood;
for though they were prepared to act, they sat—
unable to decide on what was best.
Indeed, the choices that they faced were three:
either to smash the hollow wooden beast
with ruthless bronze, or else to drag that steed
high up the cliffside and to hurl it down
along the rocks, or else to let it stand
(as if it were a splendid gift that then
would gain for Troy the gods' benevolence).
This third choice was the plan that came to pass.
For it was fated so: the city must
be doomed to its annihilation just
as soon as it enclosed the massive horse
of wood in which the bravest Argives sat,
bringing the Trojans darkness, slaughter, death.
And then he told how the Achæans' sons
burst from their hollow ambush in the horse
and sacked the city, devastating—one
at this point, one at that—the towering fort;
how, like the god of war, Odysseus rushed
to force the doorway of Dëíphobus;
with godlike Meneláus at his side,

. . .

he faced the fiercest fighting, but there, too,
with generous Athena's help, came through.

These things the famous singer sang. Odysseus
was moved; beneath his eyelids, tears ran down
his cheeks. And even as a woman weeps,
flinging herself across the fallen body
of her dear husband where he lies, before
his city and his fellow warriors,
a man who tried to keep the day of doom
far from his children and beloved home;
she, clinging to him, wails; and lance on lance,
the enemies behind her strike her back
and shoulders, then they carry her away
to slavery and trials and misery;
her cheeks are wasted with the pain, the grief:
just so, Odysseus, from beneath his brows,
let fall the tears of sorrow. But no one
knew of his tears—except Alcínoüs.
He, seated near Odysseus, had heard
his dismal moan. He did not wait. He spoke
to his Phaeácians, men who love to row:

"Hear me, Phaeácian counselors and chiefs.
Demódocus must stop at once. His harp
is clear and sharp, but what he sings does not
please everyone. Even as we began
to banquet, he began his godlike chant.
Since then our guest has moaned unceasingly:
his mind must be besieged by misery.
Then let the poet stay his song, that we,
the hosts, and he who is our guest may share
our joy together. That is surely best.
All this is for the sake of our dear guest:
the crew to escort him, the friendly gifts
we give out of affection. Anyone
who has the slightest bit of sense knows this:
The stranger and the suppliant are just

Greek [519-546]

as dear to us as our own brothers. Thus,
do not deny, not hide with cunning thoughts,
what I shall ask of you. The wisest course
is candor. Tell me now what is your name—
the name your mother, father, and the others
who lived in your own city or close-by
would use to call you. There's no man alive
who, whether he is noble or lowborn,
can claim no name at all: as soon as we
are born, our parents name us. Tell me, too,
the people, land, and city that are yours,
so that our ships, with goal well known and sure,
can take you home. Phaeácians have no pilots;
our ships, unlike all other craft, are not
equipped with steering oars; for of themselves
they understand the minds and plans of men.
They know all peoples' cities and rich fields,
and though the sea's abyss be wrapped in mist
and cloud, their course across the sea is swift;
they fear no wreck and no distress, though once—
I now recall—I heard Nausíthoüs,
my father, speak about Poseidon: he
said that the god was furious with us
because we served all men as safe escort.
He warned that someday, as a sturdy ship
of the Phaeácians crossed the fogbound sea
while sailing homeward after convoying,
Poseidon—fierce—would smash that hull to bits,
then fling a mountain-mass around our city
and cut us off forever from the sea.
So did the old man speak; and this the god
can, as he pleases, bring to pass or not
fulfill. But tell me now—and speak with all
frankness: How did you come to stray off course?
Where did you wander? What shores did you touch?
Tell me of mighty cities, many men:
of those who are unfeeling, wild, unjust,
and those who welcome strangers—those whose thought

Greek [547–576]

includes fear of the gods. And tell me why
you weep and why you moan within your heart
when you hear of the doom of Ílion
and of the Greeks. The gods brought this about:
for men they wove the web of suffering,
that men to come might have a theme to sing.
Or did one of your kinsmen die at Troy,
the father of your wife, your daughter's husband:
a steadfast man, a man most dear—of those
who, next to our own blood kin, stand most close?
Or was it, after all, a faithful friend,
a man whom you had cherished? Such a comrade
is not less precious than a brother when
that comrade has a heart that understands."

Greek [577-586]

BOOK IX

Odysseus' tale of trials,
his wanderings since Troy.

·

His fleet of twelve ships;
the sack of the Cíconës.

·

Tempest-driven
to the distant land of the Lotus-Eaters.

·

The land of the Cyclops:
prisoners in Polyphémus' cave,
a meal for their captor.

Potent wine—
and the Achæans' cunning escape.

·

The Cyclops menacing
Odysseus' men and ship.

Polyphémus' curse and bitter prayer
to his father, Poseidon.

Odysseus, man of many wiles, replied:
"Alcínoüs, the king all men revere,
it surely is a pleasant thing to hear
a singer like Demódocus, a man
whose voice is like the gods'. I say we reach
the deepest of delights when, at a feast,
beside the tables heaped with bread and meat,
men, seated in due order, fill the hall
and listen to a harper: joy takes all,
and the cupbearer draws wine from the bowl
and brings it round and brims the cups: my soul
finds nothing on this earth more beautiful.

"But now your heart is set: you want to have
the tale of all my trials—and I must add
more tears to those I have already shed.
What should I tell you first? What should be last?
I've had so many griefs at heaven's hands.
Let me begin by telling you my name,
so that you, too, may know it; for I may—
when I've escaped from fate's most cruel day—
receive you, though my home is far away.

"I am Odysseus, Laértës' son.
Men know me for my many stratagems.
My fame has reached the heavens. And my home
is Ithaca, an island bright with sun.
My homeland has a steep peak, Nériton,
whose woods are rich with rustling leaves. Around
my island many other islands crowd:
Dulíchium and Samos and Zacýnthus,
so thick with woods. But Ithaca itself
lies low along the sea, and farther west
than any other island there; the rest
lie in a separate cluster, facing east.
My home is rough and rocky, but it breeds
robust young men. I know no thing more sweet,
more fair for any man than his own land.

Greek [1-28]

Indeed, Calypso, fairest goddess, tried
to keep me in her cavern, at her side;
she wanted me as husband. So did Círcë,
Aeǽa's cunning woman: she, too, held me
within her halls—she wanted me to be
her mate. Both failed. They never could persuade
the soul within my breast; for if a man
is far from his own home and parents, then
even if he is housed in opulence
within that foreign land, no thing he finds
can be more sweet than what he left behind.

"Enough. My tale would tell you now instead
the trials that, when I sailed from Troy, beset
my journey homeward: sorrows that Zeus sent.

"The wind that carried me from Ílion
brought me to Ísmarus, the Cíconës.
I sacked their city, massacred their men.
We took much treasure and we took their wives—
and shared it all, that none might be deprived
of what was his by right. I urged us then
to hurry back to shore, just as I'd planned.
But no one cared to follow my command:
stupid, they took their time; they guzzled wine
and butchered many sheep along the shore,
and shambling oxen with their curving horns.
Meanwhile the Cíconës who had escaped
called on their fellows, those who lived inland,
neighbors more numerous and strong, adept
at fighting from their chariots or else
on foot, if any skirmish called for that.
They came—as thick as leaves and flowers in spring—
at sunrise. And we faced the punishment
that Zeus had sent: the fate of luckless men.
Arrayed in battle order, they attacked
alongside our swift ships; with bronze-tipped shafts,
both we and they struck hard. All morning long,

Greek [29–55]

while sacred day was still in its ascent,
we stood our ground although we were outmanned.
But once the sun had reached the hour when oxen
must be unyoked, the Cíconës broke through
and we Achæans fled. In each ship's crew,
six of my well-greaved comrades died. The rest
of us escaped that fate, that bitter death.

"Heartsick, we sailed away: we were content
to be alive, but we had lost dear friends;
nor did I let our lithe ships sail ahead
until we'd called three times on each of those
unfortunates the Cíconës had killed
upon the battlefield. But Bórëas—
provoked by Zeus, who summons clouds—now swept
against us: a ferocious tempest wrapped
both land and sea; night scudded down from heaven.
Wind struck our ships aslant; the sails were ripped
and tattered—three and then four strips. In fear
of death, we stowed our sails within the hold,
then rowed and reached the coast. There we remained
two days, two nights—fatigued and tried, afraid.
But when, with fair-haired Dawn, the third day came,
we stepped our masts and set white sails, then sat:
the wind and helmsmen kept us on our path.
I would have reached my Ithaca intact,
if, as I rounded Cape Maléa, combers
and currents had not joined with Bórëas
and driven me off course, beyond Cythéra.

"For nine days I was thrust by savage winds
across the fish-rich sea. And on the tenth
we reached the Lotus-Eaters' land, those men
who feed upon a flower. We went ashore,
drew water, and straightway my crewmen ate
their meal beside our ships. But once that need
for food and drink was set to rest, I sent
two crewmen and a third, who served as herald,

Greek [56–90]

to see what sort of mortals held this land.
Those three were quick to find the Lotus-Eaters,
who did not think of slaughtering my men:
in fact, they shared their lotus food with them.
Those three who feasted on the honey-sweet,
enticing lotus fruit had not the least
desire to bring back word or soon return
at all: they wanted only to stay there,
to feed upon that food and disremember
their homeward path. I had to force them back,
in tears, to their own ships; there, they were dragged
beneath the rowing benches and bound fast.
And I had all my other firm companions
embark with speed upon our rapid ships,
that no one—tasting lotus—might forget
his homeward way. They came on board at once;
each took his proper place along the thwarts;
and then they struck the gray sea with their oars.

"From there we sailed away with troubled hearts.
At last our ships approached the Cyclops' coast.
That race is arrogant: they have no laws;
and trusting in the never-dying gods,
their hands plant nothing and they ply no plows.
The Cyclops do not need to sow their seeds;
for them all things, untouched, spring up: from wheat
to barley and to vines that yield fine wine.
The rain Zeus sends attends to all their crops.
Nor do they meet in council, those Cyclops,
nor hand down laws; they live on mountaintops,
in deep caves; each one rules his wife and children,
and every family ignores its neighbors.

"Outside the harbor, off the Cyclops' coast,
an island lies—not far, yet not too close.
And on that flat and wooded isle, wild goats
form countless herds; for here no men disturb,
no one will scare them off. Elsewhere, across

Greek [91-119]

The Cyclops' Coast

hilltops and woods, the hunters toil; but here
they do not come. Nor are there sheep or cows;
and that land always stays unsown, unplowed—
it knows no men, just flocks of bleating goats.
The Cyclops have no ships with crimson bows,
no shipwrights who might fashion sturdy hulls
that answer to the call, that sail across
to other peoples' towns that men might want
to visit. And such artisans might well
have built a proper place for men to settle.
In fact, the land's not poor; it could yield fruit
in season; soft, well-watered meadows lie
along the gray sea's shores; unfailing vines
could flourish; it has level land for plowing,
and every season would provide fat harvests
because the undersoil is black indeed.
The harbor has safe landings: there's no need
for mooring-tackle or for anchoring
or tying cables hard and fast to shore;
once he has beached, a sailor stays until
his heart decides it's time to go, to follow
fair winds offshore. At harbor head there flows
clear water from a spring within a grotto;
around it poplars grow. Through foggy night,
some god—though he himself stayed out of sight—
had been our guide: we sailed into that harbor.
There was no light; the ships were wrapped in mist;
cloud banks closed off the moon; the sky was black.
We did not see that isle, nor even see
the long waves rolling shoreward, till we beached
our sturdy ships. We lowered all the sails,
and then we disembarked along the sands.
We waited for bright Dawn: sleep held us fast.

"As soon as Dawn's rose fingers touched the sky,
astonished, we explored the island. Nymphs,
daughters of aegis-bearing Zeus, stirred up
the mountain goats so that my men might hunt

Greek [120-155]

and make a meal. We hurried to our ships
to fetch curved bows and lances with long tips.
We formed three bands, and each group cast its shafts;
the god soon gave us all that we could ask.

"I had twelve ships; and each crew caught nine goats;
a tenth was given to my crew alone.
So, through that day we sat until sunset;
we had much meat; our wine was honey-sweet,
red wine my men had taken when we sacked
the sacred high-point of the Cíconës—
the jars we'd stowed away were not yet empty.
Our eyes turned toward the Cyclops' nearby coast:
toward smoke, the sounds of men—and sheep and goats.
But when the sun had gone and darkness won,
we stretched out on the shore. But at firstlight,
when Dawn's rose fingers touched the sky, I called
my men together and informed them all:

"'My faithful comrades, wait for me: I'll take
my ship and crew to see who these may be—
are they unfeeling people, wild, unjust,
or do they welcome strangers, does their thought
include fear of the gods?'

                    "When that was said,
I boarded first; and then I told my comrades
to board and loose the hawsers at the stern.
And they were quick to board. They manned the thwarts,
and then they struck the gray sea with their oars.
When we had reached the nearby shore, we saw—
along the sea—a high cave roofed with laurels:
there many flocks, both sheep and goats, would sleep
by night; the wall that ringed that cave was steep,
a ring of rocks, set deep into the ground,
with tall pine trunks and oaks with towering boughs.
A massive man slept there; alone, far-off,
he shepherded his flocks. One set apart

Greek [156–188]

from other men, he had a lawless heart.
That monster was unlike a man who feeds
on bread: in size, he seemed a wooded peak,
a summit that, apart from all the rest,
is seen alone, a solitary crest.

"I told my other faithful men to stay,
to keep watch on our ship, as I went off
with twelve of my best men. With me I brought
a goatskin, full of honey-sweet dark wine,
a gift that had been given me by Maron,
Evánthës' son, the priest who served Apollo,
the tutelary god of Ísmarus.
For when we sacked that site, our reverence
spared Maron and his wife and son: his home
was in Apollo's shadowed sacred grove.
And he rewarded me with splendid gifts:
he gave me seven talents of wrought gold,
a mixing bowl, all silver, and a wine
that he poured into jars—twelve jars in all—
wine honey-sweet, unmixed, fit for the gods.
No servant—man or woman—shared this secret:
just Maron and his wife and one housekeeper
knew of this wine. And when they drank that red,
sweet, honeyed brew, he'd pour no more than one
cup into twenty measures of pure water;
and from the mixing bowl a fragrance rose
so sweet and so enticing that in truth
no one would stand aside from such a brew.
I filled, then brought, one great skin of this wine,
and food within a basket; my proud soul
foresaw that I was soon to meet a man
most wild and powerful—and ignorant
of righteous thoughts and reverence for laws.
We quickly reached the cavern; he had gone
to pasture his plump flocks. And when we turned
into the cave, the sight left us amazed;
the crates were stuffed with cheeses, and the pens

Greek [189-219]

with sheep and goats: these were in separate folds—
the firstlings, then the yearlings, then the just-born.
And all the well-wrought bowls and pails that served
for milking swam with whey. My comrades urged
our quick departure—though they wanted me
to take the cheeses, above all, and then
drive from the fold those sheep and goats and stow
those stores on our swift ship. That done—they said—
we should be off, to sail across the sea.
But I ignored their counsel, though that course
would have avoided many griefs for us.
Instead I had to wait to see that man,
to find out if he'd welcome me. But then
the courtesy he showed my friends was scant.

"We lit a fire, then burned a sacrifice,
and, taking cheeses, fed ourselves: we sat
and waited in the cave. Then he came back
with all his flocks. He bore a massive pack
of dry wood he would use at suppertime.
That pack—he threw it to the ground—crashed loud.
Afraid, we scrambled, huddling in the back.
Then he spurred on the plump herds that he milked
into the massive cave; he left the males,
the rams and he-goats, in the outer pens.
He lifted high a rock, then set it down
in place: that heavy doorstone closed his cave.
And two-and-twenty sturdy four-wheeled carts
could not have budged that boulder from the ground—
the towering mass that barred the entranceway.
He sat and milked his ewes and bleating goats
in turn; beneath each dam he placed her young.
At once he curdled half of the white milk,
then set the gathered curd in plaited bins.
The other half he set aside in bowls,
to have it ready to be drunk for supper.
Now that his tasks were quickly done, he lit
the fire, noticed us at last, and said: □ □ □

Greek [220-251]

"'Who are you, strangers? And what was the land
you left when you sailed out on water paths?
Are you just traders? Or a prowling crew
that preys at random, pirates on the loose,
who risk their lives, but plunder others' goods?'

"His voice was thunder, and his form a monster's.
We shuddered. Yet I found the words to answer:
'We are Achæans homeward bound from Troy.
Across the sea's great gulf we have been thrust
off course. Winds battered us. On our way home,
strange paths and places are what we have known;
but it is surely Zeus who willed it so.
We're proud to be the men of Agamemnon;
beneath the heavens, he, a son of Átreus,
is now most famous: he has sacked so great
a city, slain so many men indeed.
We hope you'll welcome us; we hope to get
some gift, as custom bids host give to guest.
May you, o mighty one, revere the gods:
we're at your mercy now. The god of guests
is Zeus; for he protects the suppliant—
he watches over honored visitors.'

"That said, his ruthless heart replied at once:
'You are a fool—or just a foreigner
from very far—if you would have me fear
the gods or warn me to beware. The Cyclops
do not pay heed to aegis-bearing Zeus
or other blessed gods, weaker than us.
Be sure, I'd never spare your friends or you
in order to avoid the wrath of Zeus:
my soul alone will bid me what to do.
But tell me where you moored your sturdy ship
when you came here. Is it far off? Or near?
That's something I should like to have made clear.'

☐ ☐ ☐

Greek [252-280]

"He meant to snare me. But my craft matched his.
My strategy was still evasiveness:
'Poseidon, the earth-shaker, smashed my ship;
he cast her on the rocks that line your shores,
against a promontory—for the winds
had driven her toward land. But I and these,
my men, escaped the steep descent to death.'

"These were my words, but no words answered mine:
his heart was pitiless. And springing up,
he stretched his hands and snatched two of my men
at once and smashed them to the ground like pups:
their brains gushed out and wet the earth. He cut
those comrades limb from limb, and then he supped—
and like a mountain lion, left no shred:
he ate the flesh and innards, chewed the bones
down to the marrow. Lifting hands to Zeus,
we wept at this obscenity—helpless.
But when his maw was stuffed with human flesh,
as well as pure milk he then gulped, the Cyclops
stretched out within the cave, among his flocks.
My firm will planned a close approach, that I
might draw out the sharp sword that flanked my thigh
and strike his chest and midriff, holding fast
his liver—with my hand I'd grope for that.
But then I stopped, held back by second thoughts.
His death, in fact, would doom us all: our hands
would never have been able to shove back
the massive stone he'd set in the high entrance.
So, as we sighed, we waited for bright Dawn.

"As soon as Dawn's rose fingers touched the sky,
again he lit the fire and milked his flocks
in turn; beneath each dam, he placed her young.
That work was quickly done. Then he snatched up
two more of mine and dined on them. And when
his meal was done, he drove out his plump flocks:
to leave the cave, he thrust aside the rock.

Greek [281–313]

But then, with ease, he slipped it back in place,
as one might close a quiver with its top.
Next, whistling loud, the Cyclops turned those flocks
up toward the mountains. I was left to plot,
devising ways to foil him; for my heart
wanted to punish him—for this I'd win
much glory from Athena. As I thought,
this plan seemed best. Beside a pen there stood
a cutoff trunk of still-green olive-wood:
once seasoned, that would be the Cyclops' staff.
And it was huge enough to serve as mast
for a black ship of twenty oars—a ship
that carries freight across the deep abyss;
it was that long and thick. Approaching it,
I cut off two arm's-lengths of wood and asked
my men to pare it down. They planed it smooth.
Then I, standing nearby, sharpened its point
and hardened it at once in the fierce fire.
And for that stake I found a hiding place
beneath the dung—for great heaps filled that cave.
I asked my comrades to cast lots to see
which men would dare to lift that stake with me
and grind it into the great Cyclops' eye
when sweet sleep overtook him. And the lots
chose those I would have chosen: they were four;
I was the fifth. When night fell, he returned—
his woolly flocks behind him. Straight away
he drove all his plump beasts into the cave:
not one was left within the outdoor pens.
All this, because he felt some slight suspicion—
or else some god inclined to favor us.
He lifted up and set in place the great
doorstone. And then he sat and milked his ewes
and bleating goats in turn; beneath each dam
he set her young. His work was quickly done.
Again he snatched two men and supped on them.
Then I, a bowl of our dark wine in hand,
drew near the Cyclops. And I spoke to him: □ □ □

Greek [314-346]

"'Cyclops, after your feast of human flesh,
do take and drain this bowl, that you may know
what kind of wine our ship had stowed. For I
was bringing this to you as a libation,
hoping that, moved by mercy, you might help
to send me home. But you are furious—
intolerably mad. And after this,
who'd visit anyone so pitiless?
Why take the way that has no law, no justice?'

"These were my words. He took the bowl. He drained it.
The drink delighted him. He asked for more:
'Come now, good fellow, fill it up again.
And do tell me straightway what your name is:
I'll give you, as my guest, a pleasing gift.
Surely the earth, giver of grain, provides
the Cyclops with fine wine, and rain from Zeus
does swell our clustered vines. But this is better—
a wine as fragrant as ambrosia and nectar.'

"These were his words. Again I poured dark wine.
Three times I offered it and—stupidly—
three times he drank it down. But when it wound
its way around his wits, I said most gently:

"'Cyclops, you ask me for my noted name;
I'll tell it to you if in recompense
you keep your promise and I get that present.
My name is No-one; No-one—so I'm called
by both my mother and my father, and all
my comrades.'

                    "This I said. And he replied:
'No-one, your friends come first; I'll eat you last.
This is the gift I give to you, my guest.'

"That said, the Cyclops reeled, his hulk collapsed;
he fell upon his back, with his thick neck

Greek [347-372]

aslant; sleep, lord of all, now held him fast.
Up from his gullet, bits of human flesh
and wine were gushing: in his drunken sleep,
he'd vomited. Now it was time to thrust
the stake into heaped cinders: it grew hot.
I spurred on all my men with words of hope,
that none might flinch with fear. And when that stake
of olive-wood, though green, was glowing, just
about to blaze, I drew it from the flames.
My men stood round me; into us a god
breathed daring. And they clasped that pointed stake,
then drove the olive-wood into his eye.
I, reaching high, my weight thrown from above,
now whirled that stake around, as one whose bore
drills deep into the timber of a ship,
while those below him twirl it with a thong
they grasp at either end; the drill whirls round
and never rests. So did we twirl that hot
point in his eye; around the glowing wood,
blood flowed. And both his eyelids and his brow
were singed by fire as his eyeball burned;
his eye-roots hissed. Even as, when a smith
plunges an ax or adze into cold water,
the metal hisses as he quenches it
to give that iron strength, so did that eye
hiss round the olive stake's sharp tip. His howl
was terrifying; all the rocks rang out.
Fear drove us back. The stake, which he tugged out,
was fouled with blood. And—crazed—he threw it far;
and then he shouted to the other Cyclops,
who lived in nearby caves on windswept hilltops.
They heard his call and, coming from all sides,
stood near his cave and asked what was awry:

"'What struck you, Polyphémus? Why do you
disturb the godlike night and spoil our sleep?
What mortal can, against your will, drive off
. . .

Greek [373-405]

your flocks or try with treachery or force
to kill you?'

         "Polyphémus, from the cave,
replied: 'My friends, no force can damage me;
No-one, No-one is using treachery.'

"They answered: 'If no one is harming you,
and you are all alone, it surely is
some sickness sent by Zeus; you can't elude
that kind of malady. Pray to Poseidon,
your father: he's the one to call upon.'

"That said, they left. And my heart laughed: my name,
a perfect snare, had trapped him. Racked by pain,
the Cyclops moaned and groped for that great stone,
then shoved it from the entranceway and sat
with hands outstretched in hope that he might catch
the men who, with the sheep, came from the cave—
he must have thought my wits were dim and slack.
But I was seeking a decisive plan,
a scheme to save both me and all my men:
I wove a web of every guile and wile,
as one will do when life's at stake—so great
a menace threatened us. This plot seemed best.
That cave held well-fed rams; and heavy fleece,
dark wool, enfolded those fine, robust beasts.
Now silently I took the twisted withes
of willow, those on which the Cyclops—he
whose heart was set on evil—liked to sleep.
With these I bound the sheep together, three
by three. I tied one comrade fast beneath
the belly of each middle sheep, while two
sheep—one to each side—served to guard my friend.
Three sheep for each of them, but I instead
picked out the largest ram. I grabbed his back
and curled beneath his belly. There I grasped
. . .

Greek [406–434]

his splendid fleece; faceup, I held it tight.
So, anxiously we waited for firstlight.

"As soon as Dawn's rose fingers touched the sky,
he drove the he-goats and the rams outside
to pasture. In the fold, the unmilked dams,
their udders bursting, bleated. Although racked
by pain, their master now felt out the backs
of all the beasts that stood before him, but
that fool did not suspect that all my men
were hid beneath the bellies of the rams.
The last to leave the cave was my great ram,
bearing the weight of his own fleece and me—
with my thick plots. Huge Polyphémus probed
and felt about his back. And then he asked:

"'Dear ram, why are you last to leave this cave?
You never lagged behind the other sheep;
you always were the very first to leave,
always the first to hurry out to feed,
to pasture on the tender grass, to leap
with long strides toward the riverside, to seek
the fold with longing when the sun had set.
But now you are the last to go. I'm sure
that you are grieving for your master's eye;
a coward and his crew first dimmed my mind
with their damned wine. That done, they left me blind.
I don't think death has caught that No-one yet.
Would you could think and speak and tell me where
he's hiding from my fury! I would dash
his brains across this cave: to smash him so
would free me from this No-one pest, these woes.'

"That said, he sent the ram out. When we'd gone
a brief way past the cave and outer pens,
I left the belly of the ram to set
my comrades free. That done, we quickly drove
the fat sheep with long shanks until we reached

Greek [435-464]

our ship; and we turned round again, again,
to see if he was after us. And though
our comrades welcomed our escape from death,
they wept for those of us who now were lost.
But I restrained their tears; my frown forbade
such open grief. For now we had to speed—
to board the many sheep with their rich fleece,
then sail the salty sea. They rushed aboard;
each rower manned his place along the thwarts,
and then they struck the gray sea with their oars.
But when we'd gone as far as shouting distance,
I bellowed these sharp words to Polyphémus:

"'Cyclops, the men you snatched with brutal force
and ate within your cave were surely not
the comrades of a coward. You have caused
much grief; and it returns to haunt you now:
you did not hesitate; hard heart, you ate
your guests within your house; therefore lord Zeus
has joined with other gods to batter you.'

"My words incensed him more. He ripped the top
of a huge peak, then hurled a chunk at us;
that mass fell just beyond our ship's dark prow.
The sea surged as the mass dropped; and the wash
thrust our ship backward, closer to the coast.
But grabbing a long pole, I pushed us off
and signaled with my head: I spurred my men
to fall hard on the oars, to fend against
shipwreck; and they rowed hard—they strained, they bent.
When we were twice as distant as we'd been,
I shouted to the Cyclops, though my men
on all sides curbed me with these cautious words:

"'Why must you goad that savage so? Just now,
the mass that monster cast into the sea
drove back our ship to shore: we thought we'd reached
our end. And if he'd heard us breathe or speak

Greek [465-497]

even the slightest word, he would have hurled
one more rough rock and smashed our heads and hull.
That brute has force to spare: he can throw far.'

"These were their words. But my firm heart was not
convinced. Again my anger had to taunt:
'Cyclops, if any mortal man should ask
about the shameful blinding of your eye,
then tell him that the man who gouged you was
Odysseus, ravager of cities: one
who lives in Ithaca—Laértës' son.'

"I spoke. As he replied, he groaned and sighed:
'I hear again an ancient prophecy.
An augur once lived here, a man most worthy,
excelling all in seeing what would come,
a seer grown old among us: Télemus,
great son of Eurymus. What he foretold
is now fulfilled. He said that I would be
a victim of Odysseus: he would blind me.
But I was always watching out for one
handsome and grand, a formidable man;
instead, one small and insignificant,
a weakling, now has gouged my eye—he won
his way by overcoming me with wine.
But come, Odysseus, you'll receive the gift
I owe to you, my guest; and I'll convince
the great earth-shaker to escort your ship;
I am his son—he says he is my father.
He is the one to heal me, if he would:
no other can—no blessed god, no man.'

"These were his words. And I replied: 'Would I
might just as surely rob you of your life
and breath and hurl you down to Hades' house,
as I am sure that even great Poseidon
will never give you back the eye you lost.'
□ □ □

Greek [498-525]

"These were my words. He prayed to lord Poseidon,
lifting his hands up to the starry heaven:
'Listen, Poseidon, dark-haired lord who clasps
the earth hard fast, if I'm indeed your son
and you declare yourself my father, then
don't let this ravager of towns, Odysseus,
Laértës' son, who lives in Ithaca,
return to his own land. But if his fate
must have him see his dear ones once again
and reach his sturdy home, his native land,
then let him struggle back—a battered man,
with all his comrades lost, and on a ship
of strangers. In his house, let him meet grief.'

"His prayer was done. The dark-haired god took heed.
Again the Cyclops lifted up a stone,
even more staggering than the one he'd thrown
before. He whirled it round; and when he hurled,
fierce force was in that toss. The stone fell just
behind our dark-prowed ship: it barely missed
the steering oar. And as that rough rock fell,
the sea surged high astern—but that wave helped:
its thrust drove our ship toward the island's shore.

"There, on that isle, our other sturdy ships
awaited us; our sighing shipmates sat,
in fear. We beached our boat along the sands,
then disembarked. Out of the hollow hull
we took the Cyclops' flocks, dividing all
in equal shares: what each received was just.
One sheep alone—my ram—was set apart;
my well-greaved crew assigned that gift to me.
Along the sands I sacrificed that ram
to Cronos' son, who gathers thunderclouds,
Zeus, lord of all; for him I roasted thighs.
But he did not accept that sacrifice:
instead his mind was set—he meant to wreck
all of my sturdy ships and faithful friends.   □ □ □

Greek [526–555]

"All through that day we sat, until sunset:
we had much meat; our wine was honey-sweet.
But once the sun had gone and darkness won,
we stretched out on the shore. Then, at firstlight,
when Dawn's rose fingers touched the sky, I called
upon my shipmates to embark, to loose
the hawsers at the stern. They rushed aboard;
each rower manned his place along the thwarts,
and then they struck the gray sea with their oars.

"Heartsick, we sailed away: we were content
to be alive, but we had lost dear friends."

Greek [556-566]

BOOK X

Odysseus' tale continues.

Æolus, warden of the winds;
his gift in a bag for Odysseus.

Ten days of gentle sailing, nearing Ithaca;
Odysseus' slumber, his comrades' jealousy and greed.

The bag unloosed; the tempest.

Back out to sea—and back to Æolus: rejection.

·

The man-eating Laestrygónians:
the loss of eleven ships and their crews.

·

Círcë's isle, Aeǽa.

The enchantress' spell: men into swine.

Hermes' saving herb—*moly*—and advice for Odysseus.

A year with Círcë.

Preparation for the journey to Hades' halls.

Elpénor's misfortune.

"Aeólia, the home of Æolus,
the son of Híppotas, was our landfall.
He, cherished by the deathless ones, held all
that isle, which—floating on a sheer rock base—
is ringed by walls of bronze, unbreakable.
He has a dozen children in his halls:
six daughters and six sturdy sons—and each
is wed, for every brother has received
a sister as his wife. They always feast
together in the house of their fine father
and stately mother: there the food is endless.
By day the smoke of fragrant fat pours out
into the courtyard; and by night each son
sleeps richly swaddled with his trusted wife
upon a corded couch. We reached that isle:
we saw that city, saw the handsome halls.
For one full month we were his guests; he asked
to hear so much—of Troy, the Argive ships,
and the return of the Achæans; I
withheld no thing; my telling was complete.
And when, in turn, I asked to leave and spoke
of help that we might need to see us home,
he did not stint; he offered me a sack
of hide he'd flayed from a nine-year-old ox.
Into that sack he stuffed the howling winds
of every sort or course: for Æolus—
so Zeus had said—was warden of the winds,
to spur or curb just as he willed. He stowed
that sack within my hollow ship and tied
its neck hard fast with shining silver cord,
lest any breeze, however slight, slip out.
He left just one wind—Zephyr—free, to speed
my fleet, my men. And yet his careful plan
failed, for our folly had the upper hand.

"Nine days we sailed, by night and day alike,
and on the tenth our homeland came in sight,
so near that we could see men tending fires.

But sweet sleep overtook me—I was tired:
I'd held the steering oar without a let;
I'd not entrusted it to any comrade;
I wanted our return home to be quick.
Meanwhile my crewmen had begun to speak,
telling each other that I'd had as gifts
from Æolus, fine son of Híppotas,
silver and gold that I was bringing home.
So, turning to his shipmate, someone spoke:

"'Just see what love, what honor he commands
from any man he meets in any land
or town! Just see what booty, splendid spoils,
he carries back from Troy, while we, who toiled
beside him, must return with empty hands.
To this, he now can add the friendly gift
of Æolus. Let's see what's in that sack—
see how much gold and silver he has packed.'

"That's what they urged—and their disastrous plan
prevailed. They opened up the sack. The band
of winds leaped out. The hurricane was quick
to whirl my men away from their own land:
thrust back to sea, they wept. When I awoke,
my staunch soul hesitated: should I leap
off from the deck and die, or should I keep
silent and stay among the living? But
I did not yield: I stayed, covered my face
and lay along the deck. The fierce gale swept
our ships back to Aeólia. My men wept.
We went ashore, drew water, and straightway
my crewmen ate their meal beside our ships.
But when we'd had our fill of food and drink,
together with two comrades I had picked—
one spearman, and another who could serve
as herald—I went back to Æolus.
I found him feasting with his wife and children.
We entered, sitting down along the sill,

Greek [31–62]

close to the posts that flanked the door. They all,
astonished, asked:

            "'Odysseus, why have you
come back? Are you in some dark demon's grip?
We took such care in giving you a gift
to bring you to your homeland and your house
or any other place that you hold dear.'

"These were their words. Dejected, I replied:
'My coward comrades did me in—and, too,
that traitor, sleep. But help me, friends: you can.'

"So did I speak—my words beguiling, sweet.
They stared in silence—till their father said:
'Be quick to leave this isle. No living thing
can match your villainy. It's surely wrong
to welcome or to escort anyone
the blessed gods abhor. Now quit our shores:
you came as one who carries heaven's scorn.'

"That said, despite my tears, he drove me out.
From there we sailed away with bitter hearts.
Our folly, which had lost us the support
and favor of the winds, made rowing hard;
it sapped our force. And yet, without a stop,
for six days and six nights we kept on course.

"Then, on the seventh day, we saw the fort
that crowns the high point of Telépylus,
the city of the Laestrygónians,
founded by Lamus. In that land, the shepherd
returning in the evening with his flock
can greet the herdsman who is going out.
A sleepless man could earn a double wage:
one wage for herding cattle, one for sheep
he led to grazing land: there, two times meet;
the paths of light traverse both day and night.   □ □ □

Greek [63–86]

"We'd reached the famous harbor. On two sides,
we saw the steep rock walls with their sheer rise;
the narrow entranceway was flanked by two
long juts of land. Within that curving cove,
my comrades moored their shapely ships close by
each other: there no wave is ever vexed,
not surging or receding—a bright calm.

"But I held back and moored outside. I tied
my cable to a rock; my black ship stood
beyond one headland's edge. And then I climbed
a rugged slope; I stood at that lookout;
I saw no oxen's furrows and no men—
just puffs of smoke that rose up from the land.
I chose two comrades and a third as herald,
and then I sent those shipmates out to see
what sort of men—bread eaters—held this land.
They disembarked and took a well-tried way
that wagons used for bringing wood to town
down from the mountains. Just outside the town,
they met a stalwart girl beside a spring:
she was the daughter of Antíphatës
the Laestrygónian. The spring where she
was drawing limpid water was Artácia—
a well that served the Laestrygónians.
My men drew near; they asked what king ruled here
and who were those he ruled. She pointed out
her father's high-roofed house. When they went in,
they found his wife; but she stood mountain-high,
and they were horrified. At once she called
for firm Antíphatës; she brought him back
from the assembly place. But all he planned
was sad death for my men. He did not wait:
he grabbed one of my crew and swallowed him;
the other two were able to escape—
they reached our ships. But now it was too late:
the loud alarm had sounded; from all sides
stout Laestrygónians, a countless crowd,

Greek [87–119]

rushed out—and they were not like men but Giants.
The boulders that they hurled down from the cliffs
were huge—the size a man could scarcely lift.
The clamor from the ships was sinister,
the sound of dying men and shattered decks;
they speared my comrades, carried them like fish—
an obscene meal.

                            "While they were slaughtering
my crews in the deep harbor, I drew out
the sharp blade from beside my thigh: I cut
the cables of my dark-prowed ship. I spurred
my men to hurry to their oars: their heart
and haste were needed to escape this trap;
the fear of death pressed all to row as one.
With luck I reached the open sea, far from
the sheer cliffs. But the other ships were lost.

"We sailed away—hearts sick and sad—set free
at last, but with our dear companions dead.
We reached Aeæa, isle of fair-haired Círcë,
the awesome goddess with a human voice,
twin sister of the sinister Aeétës:
they both were born of Hélios—who brought
his light to men—and Pérsë, Ocean's daughter.
In silence we put in to shore; the harbor
seemed safe; some gracious god had been our guide.
We stayed two days, two nights—fatigued and tried.

"But when, with fair-haired Dawn, the third day came,
with spear and sharpened sword in hand I climbed
up from the ship. I reached a rise from which
I hoped to see the signs of human work
and hear the sounds of men. And as I stood
upon that lookout point, up from wide fields
and through the forest and the underbrush,
smoke rose: it came from Círcë's house. The sight
of that black smoke inclined my heart and mind

Greek [120-152]

to seek the source. But as I thought again,
another plan seemed best: I'd first go back
to my swift ship along the shore, find food
to feed my men, and then have them explore.

"But when I had already neared my ship,
some god took pity on my loneliness:
across my path he sent a tall-horned stag.
Down from his pasture in the forest, he—
responding to the sun's oppressive fury—
was heading to the riverbank to drink.
When he had quit the stream, I struck his back;
and right through his mid-spine, my bronze shaft passed.
He moaned; he fell into the dust; his life
took flight. I straddled him and tugged the shaft
out from the wound, then left it on the ground
and gathered lengths of brush and willow withes
to weave a rope two arm's-lengths long, twisted
from end to end. I tied that huge beast's feet
and slung him round my neck, then, trudging, leaned
my weight upon the spear that I'd retrieved.
That way I brought him back to the black ship:
one hand across one shoulder never could
have carried him—that stag was so immense.
I threw him down in front of our lithe ship
and gently urged my comrades, one by one:

"'O friends, however sad, let's not descend
to Hades' halls before our destined day.
No, just as long as there is food and drink
in our swift ship, forget your fears of starving.'

"These were my words. My men did not delay.
They'd hid their heads with cloaks in their despair,
but now they threw those wrappings off and stared:
they saw the stag along the shore: indeed
that beast was huge. And with their eyes appeased,
they washed their hands and readied the fine feast.

Greek [153-182]

All through that day we sat, until sunset:
we had much meat; the wine was honey-sweet.
But when the sun sank and the dark arrived,
we all stretched out and slept on the seaside.

"As soon as Dawn's rose fingers touched the sky,
I called my crew together, and I said:
'Despite your long ordeal, do hear me out:
my friends, we've lost all sense of where we are;
this island may lie east, it may lie west—
where sun, which brings men light, sinks to its rest
or where it's born again. Let's try at once
to see if we can find some better course.
I doubt it, for I climbed a rugged lookout:
we're on an island that is ringed about
by endless seas; so crowned, the isle lies low,
and at its center I saw curling smoke
that rose up through the forest and thick brush.'

"My words were done. And their dear hearts were torn,
recalling the fierce Laestrygónian,
Antíphatës, and the man-eating Cyclops.
Their groans were loud, their tears were many—yet
nothing was gained by weeping. So I split
my well-greaved men into two squads: each band
had its own chief. I headed one; the second
was led by the godlike Eurýlochus.
Within a casque of bronze we mixed our lots
to see who would go off and spy the land.
The choice fell on the firm Eurýlochus.
And he went off with two-and-twenty men;
both they who left and we who stayed then wept.

"Within a forest glen, they found the home
of Círcë: it was built of polished stone
and lay within a clearing. Round it roamed
the mountain wolves and lions she'd bewitched
with evil drugs. But they did not attack

Greek [183-213]

my men; they circled them; their long tails wagged.
And just as dogs will fawn about their master
when he returns from feasts—they know that he
will offer them choice bits—just so, did these
lions and sharp-clawed wolves fawn on my men.
And yet those tough beasts terrified my friends.
They halted at the fair-haired Círcë's door;
within they heard the goddess' sweet voice sing
as she moved back and forth before her web—
imperishable, flawless, subtly-woven—
such work as only goddesses can fashion.

"Polítës, sturdy captain, the most dear
and trusted of my men, now told his friends:
'Someone inside is singing gracefully
as she weaves her great web. And what she sings
echoes throughout the house. Let's call to her.'

"These were his words. They did what he had asked.
She came at once. She opened her bright doors,
inviting them within; and—fools—they followed.
Eurýlochus alone did not go in;
he had foreseen some snare. She led the way
and seated them on chairs and high-backed thrones.
She mixed cheese, barley meal, and yellow honey
with wine from Prámnos; and she then combined
malign drugs in that dish so they'd forget
all thoughts of their own homes. When they had drunk,
she struck them with her wand, then drove them off
to pen them in her sties. They'd taken on
the bodies—bristles, snouts—and grunts of hogs,
yet kept the human minds they had before.
So they were penned, in tears; and Círcë cast
before them acorns, dogwood berries, mast—
food fit for swine who wallow on the ground.

"Meanwhile Eurýlochus rushed back to us
to let us know our comrades' shameful fate.

Greek [214-245]

But he was speechless; though he longed for words,
his heart was struck with pain, tears filled his eyes;
nothing but lamentation filled his mind.
But when we—baffled—questioned him, at last
he told us what had happened to our friends:

"'Odysseus, we did follow your commands:
we crossed the underbrush and reached the glen.
We found a sheltered house with smooth stone walls.
And there, intent on her great web, a goddess
or woman could be heard distinctly singing.
My comrades called to her; she opened wide
the gleaming doors, inviting them to enter.
They, unsuspecting, trailed along. But I
held back; I felt this was a trap. They dropped
from sight together. Though I kept close watch—
I waited long—no comrade reappeared.'

"These were his words. Across my back I cast
my massive sword of bronze with silver studs,
and then I slung my bow; I ordered him
to lead me back along the path he'd taken.
But he, his arms about my knees, implored:

"'May you, whom Zeus has nurtured, leave me here;
don't force me to retrace my path. I know
that you will not return and not bring back
our men. With those we have let's sail away,
for we may still escape the evil day.'

"These were his words. I was compelled to say:
'Eurýlochus, you can stay here and eat
and drink beside the hollow black ship; I
must go, however; I cannot forgo
a task so necessary—this I owe.'

"That said, I left the sea and ship behind.
But after I had crossed the sacred glades

Greek [246-275]

and was about to reach the halls of Círcë,
the connoisseur of potions, I saw Hermes,
who bears the golden wand, approaching me.
He'd taken on the likeness of a youth
just come of age, blessed with a young man's grace.
He clasped my hands. These were his words to me:

"'Where are you wandering still, unlucky man,
alone along these slopes and ignorant
of this strange land? Círcë has locked your friends
like swine behind the tight fence of her pens.
And have you come to free them? On your own,
be sure, you never will return; you'll stay
together with the others in her sties.
But come, I'll save you from her snares, I'll thwart
her plans. Now, when you enter Círcë's halls,
don't leave behind this tutelary herb.
I'll tell you all her fatal stratagems:
She'll mix a potion for you; she'll add drugs
into that drink; but even with their force,
she can't bewitch you; for the noble herb
I'll give you now will baffle all her plots.
When Círcë touches you with her long wand,
draw out the sharp sword at your thigh, and head
for her as if you meant to strike her dead.
Shrinking, she'll ask you then to share her bed.
And do not, then or later, turn her down,
for she will free your friends and be of help
to you, her guest. But first force her to swear
the blessed gods' great, massive oath: She must
forgo all thought of any other plots—
when you are stripped and naked, she must not
deceive you, leave you feeble, impotent.'

"When that was said, he gave his herb to me;
he plucked it from the ground and showed what sort
of plant it was. Its root was black; its flower
was white as milk. It's *moly* for the gods;

Greek [276-305]

for mortal men, the mandrake—very hard
to pluck; but nothing holds against the gods.

"Then Hermes crossed the wooded isle and left
for steep Olympus. And I took the path
to Círcë's house—most anxious as I went.
I stopped before the fair-haired goddess' door;
I halted, called aloud; she heard my voice.
At once she opened her bright doors and then
invited me to follow her. I went
with troubled heart. She led me to a chair,
robust and handsome, graced with silver studs;
a footrest stood below. And she poured out
an ample drink into a golden bowl.
With her conniving mind, she mixed her drugs
within that bowl, then offered it to me.
I drank it down. But I was not bewitched.
She struck me with her long wand. Then she said:
'Now to the sty, to wallow with your friends!'

"At that, out from its sheath along my thigh,
I drew my sword as if to have her die.
She howled. She clasped my knees and, as she wept,
with these winged words, made her appeal to me:

"'Who are you? From what family? What city?
You drank my drugs, but you were not entranced.
No other man has ever passed that test;
for once that potion's passed their teeth, the rest
have fallen prey: you have within your chest
a heart that can defeat my sorcery.
You surely are the man of many wiles,
Odysseus, he whom I was warned against
by Hermes of the golden wand: he said
that you would come from Troy in a black ship.
But now put back your blade within that sheath
and let us lie together on my bed:
in loving, we'll learn trust and confidence.' □ □ □

Greek [306-335]

"These were her words. And this was my reply:
'Círcë, how can you ask for tenderness,
you who have turned my comrades into swine
and now, insidiously, try to bind
me, too—for once I'm naked on your bed,
you'll snare me, leave me weak and impotent?
I will not share your bed unless you swear
the mighty oath, o goddess—to insure
that you'll forgo all thoughts of further plots.'

"These were my words. As I had asked, she swore
at once. And after that great oath was pledged,
I then climbed onto Círcë's lovely bed.

"Meanwhile four girls were busy in the halls;
these maids were once dear daughters of the woods
and springs and seaward-flowing sacred streams.
Across the high-backed chairs, one handmaid first
draped linen cloth and then threw purple rugs.
The second drew up silver tables set
with golden baskets, while the third maid mixed
smooth honeyed wine in silver bowls and brought
fair golden cups. The fourth maid filled a tripod
with water and, beneath it, lit a fire;
and when it bubbled in the glowing bronze
caldron, she set me down inside a tub.
Over my head and shoulders she poured water—
gradually tempering its heat—
to free my limbs and soul from long fatigue.
And when that maid had bathed and, with rich oil,
had smoothed my body and about me cast
a tunic and a handsome cloak, she led
the way and sat me on a high-backed chair,
robust and handsome, graced with silver studs;
a footrest stood below. A servant brought
a lovely golden jug from which she poured
fresh water out into a silver bowl,
so I might wash my hands; then at my side

Greek [336-370]

she placed a polished table. The old housewife
was generous; she drew on lavish stores,
inviting me to eat. But I was not
inclined to feed my frame: I sat and thought
of other things; my soul foresaw the worst.
Círcë, who saw me seated there denying
all food and filled with dark despair, drew near.
And, at my side, she called on these winged words:

"'Odysseus, do not sit there like some mute,
with tattered heart, not touching drink or food.
Do you suspect another trap? Forget
your fears. I swore the strongest oath there is.'

"These were her words. And this was my reply:
'Círcë, what man with justice in his mind
would think of food and drink before he freed
his comrades and could see them with his eyes?
If you indeed would have me drink and eat,
release my men: bring back my faithful friends.'

"These were my words. And Círcë—wand in hand—
now left the hall and, opening the pens,
drove out my men; they had the shape of fat
nine-year-old hogs. They faced her. She drew close.
Upon the flesh of each of them, she spread
another herb. At that, their bodies shed
the bristles that had grown when they'd gulped down
the deadly brew she'd offered them at first.
Now they were men again—and younger than
they were before, more handsome and more grand.
They knew me quickly; each man clasped my hand.
Their cries of joy were long and loud; throughout
the house a clamor rose. And Círcë, too,
was moved. Then she—the lovely goddess—urged:

"'Odysseus, man of many wiles, divine
son of Laértës, go to your swift ship

Greek [371-402]

along the shore and beach it on dry land.
First store your goods and all your gear in caves,
but then return with all your faithful friends.'

"These were her words. My proud soul was convinced:
I hurried to the shore and my swift ship.
And there I found my faithful crew in tears.
Even as calves upon a farm are glad
when cows return from pasture, having had
their fill of grass, and come back to their stalls;
and all the calves frisk round unchecked; no pen
can hold them as they race around their dams,
lowing again, again—so did my men,
when they caught sight of me, weep tears of joy:
they felt as if they'd touched their native land,
their rugged Ithaca, where they were bred
and born. In tears, they uttered these winged words:

"'You, whom Zeus nurtured, have come back; for us
this joy is like the joy that would erupt
on our return to Ithaca, our home.
But tell us now the fate of all the rest.'

"These were their words. I quietly replied:
'Come, let us beach our ship along dry land
and stow our goods and all our gear in caves.
Then, all of you be quick to follow me;
in Círcë's sacred halls you soon will see
your comrades eating, drinking; they can count
on never-ending stores.'

                              "My words were done.
At once they answered my commands. But one—
Eurýlochus—did try to check their course:

"'My sorry friends, where are we heading now?
Why court catastrophe in Círcë's house?
She'll turn us into lions, wolves, or hogs—

Greek [403–433]

and we'll be forced to guard her massive halls.
So did the Cyclops catch and trap our friends—
then, too, the rash Odysseus was with them.
They, too, died through the madness of this man.'

"I heard his words. I had a mind to draw
the sharp blade sheathed beside my sturdy thigh.
I'd have sliced off his head and flung it down
upon the ground—although Eurýlochus
was kin of mine by marriage. But my men
drew near and checked me with these gentle words:

"'If you—one sprung from Zeus—prefer it so,
he can stay here and watch the ship. We'll go
with you: lead us to Círcë's sacred house.'

"That said, they left the ship and shore behind.
Eurýlochus came, too. He did not stay:
my rage was ominous—he was afraid.

"Meanwhile, with kindness, Círcë, in her halls,
cared for my other men: she bathed them all,
and then she smoothed their skins with gleaming oil
and wrapped them in fine tunics and soft cloaks.
We found them feasting on abundant stores.
But when they all had recognized each other,
their tears and wails were loud throughout the halls.
Bright Círcë, standing at my side, advised:

"'Odysseus, man of many wiles, divine
son of Laértës, do not urge more tears.
I know indeed the many miseries
you have endured upon the fish-rich sea
and how, on land, you faced fierce enemies.
But eat this food and drink this wine—and find
the force you had when you first left behind
your homeland, rugged Ithaca. Your minds
can only think of bitter wanderings;

Greek [434-463]

you're worn and weary, without joy or ease;
you've lived too long—too much—with grinding griefs.'

"These were her words. And our proud hearts agreed.
Day after day we stayed for one whole year:
we ate much meat; the wine was honey-sweet.

"But when the months that fill a year had passed,
and seasons had revolved, and once again
the long days reached their end, my comrades said:

"'Wake from your trance, remember your own land,
if fate is yet to save you, if you can
still reach your high-walled house, your native isle.'

"These were their words. And my proud heart agreed.
Through all that day we sat, until sunset:
the meat was fine; the wine was honey-sweet.
But once the sun had gone and darkness won,
within the shadowed halls, my comrades slept.

"And I went off to Círcë's splendid bed.
I clasped her knees. She heard as I beseeched:
'Círcë, fulfill the promise made to me:
do let me leave for home. My men entreat,
and my own heart wants that. Whenever you
are out of hearing, all my men implore
again, again: they long to leave these shores.'

"The lovely goddess gave this quick reply:
'Odysseus, man of many wiles, divine
son of Laértës, do not spend more time
within my house if you will otherwise.
But you cannot reach home till you complete
another journey—to the house of Hades
and fierce Perséphonë. There you must seek
the soul of that blind seer, Tirésias
the Theban: he alone among the dead

Greek [464–492]

preserves his wits and sober sense: this gift
Perséphonë has granted just to him,
for all the other dead are wandering shades.'

"My heart was broken as I heard her words.
Seated upon that bed, I cried: my soul
had lost its will to live, to see the light.
But when my need to weep and writhe was done,
these were the words with which I answered her:

"'Círcë, who'll serve as pilot on that way?
No man has ever sailed in his black ship
to Hades' halls.'

              "And her reply was quick:
'Odysseus, man of many wiles, divine
son of Laértës, there's no need to fret
about a helmsman. After you have stepped
the mast and spread your white sail, you can sit:
the breath of Bórëas will guide your ship.
But when you've crossed the Ocean, you will see
the shore and forests of Perséphonë—
the towering poplars and the willow trees
whose fruits fall prematurely. Beach your ship
on that flat shore which lies on the abyss
of Ocean. Make your way on foot to Hades.
In those dank halls, the Pýriphlégethon
together with a branch of Styx, Cocýtus—
two roaring rivers—form one course and join
the Ácheron. Just there you'll find a rock.
Draw near that spot and, as I tell you, dig
a squared-off ditch—along each side, one cubit.
Three times pour offerings around that pit
for all the dead: pour milk and honey first,
then pour sweet wine; let water be the third.
And scatter over these white barley meal.
Then give the helpless dead your fervent pledge
that, when you come to Ithaca, you'll offer

Greek [493–522]

as sacrifice your finest barren heifer
and heap her pyre high with handsome gifts.
But to Tirésias alone pledge this:
the finest jet black ram that you possess.
And after you have called upon the famed
tribes of the dead, do sacrifice a ram
and black ewe: bend their heads toward Érebus,
but you must turn toward Ocean's streams. That done,
so many souls of men now dead will come.
For them, command your crew to flay and burn
the slaughtered sheep, throats slit by ruthless bronze;
and pray unto the gods, to mighty Hades
and fierce Perséphonë. Draw your sharp sword
out from the sheath that lies along your thigh:
keep close watch on the blood of sacrifice,
lest any of the helpless dead draw near
that pit before you meet Tirésias.
Soon he, the seer, leader of men, will come
to tell you what will be your path, how long
your homeward journey is to take, and how
you'll make your way across the fish-rich sea.'

"So Círcë said. Upon the throne of gold,
Dawn came straightway. The goddess Círcë clothed
my frame in cloak and tunic; she herself
put on a long and gleaming, gracious robe
of subtly-woven threads. She bound a belt
of gold around her waist; she veiled her head.
And I went through the house; with gentle words
I spurred my comrades, one by one. I urged:
'You've had enough sweet sleep. It's time to go.
Great Círcë told me all that we must know.'

"These were my words. And their proud hearts agreed.
But I was not to lead all of my men
away from Círcë's isle. One of my band,
our youngest man, Elpénor—not too brave
nor too alert—had lain alone, stretched out

Greek [523-553]

along the roof of Círcë's house to find
some cooler air: he'd taken too much wine.
Then, when he heard the noise of our departure,
he jumped up suddenly, and so—forgetting
the long way down by ladder—off the roof
headfirst he fell. And from his spine, his neck
was broken off; his spirit went to Hades.

"But I, to those who followed me, now said:
'Though you may think that you are going home,
back to your own dear land, another road
is ours, for Círcë said we first must see
the halls of Hades and Perséphonë;
there we must meet Tirésias of Thebes.'

"My words broke their dear hearts. They sat and wept;
they tore their hair; but all of that lament
gained nothing for us. Still in tears, we went
back to the shore; alongside our black ship,
Círcë had tied a ram and jet black ewe,
but none of us had seen her go or come;
she passed us by so easily. How can
a man detect a god who comes and goes
if gods refuse to have their movements known?"

Greek [554-569]

BOOK XI

Odysseus' tale continues.

Ocean's end; Odysseus' descent to Hades.

Libation, barley meal, and sheep's blood
for the soul of the Theban seer Tirésias and the other souls.

The meeting with the shade of Elpénor.

Tirésias' prophecy
and warnings for Odysseus' homeward journey.

The souls taste from the pit of dark blood.

Odysseus' meeting with his mother, Anticleīa,
and with the wives and daughters of great lords:
Tyro, Antíopë, Alcménë, Mégara, Epicástë, Chlóris,
Leda, Iphimedeīa, and others.

·

Odysseus and Arétë.

·

Odysseus' tale of Hades resumes.

Encounters with Agamemnon,
Achilles, Ajax, Minos, Oríon, Héraclës,
and with the sufferers in Hades:
Títyus, Tántalus, Sísyphus.

The terrifying outcry from the assembly of the dead—
Odysseus' departure from Ocean's shore.

"We reached the shore and ship. We drew our craft
down to the gleaming sea. We stepped the mast
and set our sail, embarked our sheep; downcast,
in tears, we went aboard. Then fair-haired Círcë,
the awesome goddess with a human voice,
sent forth a friend who favored us, a wind
that swelled our sail and spurred our ship's dark prow.
Once we'd secured our gear, we settled down;
the wind and helmsman kept us on our course.
The sail held taut; all day we sped along.
The sun sank; all sea roads were darkened now.

"We sailed by night to find deep Ocean's end;
we sailed until we reached the limit-land,
the shadowed home of the Cimmérians.
Their city wears a shroud of mist and clouds;
the lord of light can never gaze at them—
not when he climbs the starry sky nor when
he wheels and then descends to earth again:
drear night enfolds those melancholy men.

"We landed, beached our ship, and drove ashore
our sheep, then made our way at Ocean's side;
we reached the place that Círcë had described.
Here Perimédës and Eurýlochus
held fast the ram and ewe we'd sacrifice.
I drew the sharp blade from beside my thigh
and dug a ditch one cubit on each side;
around that pit, for all the dead, I poured
libations: offering milk and honey first,
then sweet wine, then pure water. Over these
I scattered—properly—white barley meal.
Then to the lifeless, listless dead I pledged
that when I had returned to Ithaca
I'd sacrifice a splendid barren heifer
and heap her pyre high with precious gifts;
and for Tirésias I pledged the best
black ram in all the flocks that I possess.

Greek [1-33]

And after I'd implored with vows and prayers
the tribes of those dead souls, I seized the sheep
and slit their throats above the pit; cloud-dark
blood ran. From Érebus there came a crowd
of dead souls: girls, young bachelors, and old men
much tried by grief, and tender brides still new
to sorrow. Many fighting-men came, too;
they'd died in battle, pierced by bronze-tipped spears;
and they still wore their bloodstained battle gear.
These crowded round the pit upon all sides;
they uttered strange outcries. I paled with fear.
At that, I spurred my men to flay and roast
the sheep we'd sacrificed, whose throats I'd cut
with ruthless bronze; and we prayed to the gods,
to Hades' force and fierce Perséphonë.
With my sharp sword again unsheathed, I watched
over the pit of sacrificial blood,
lest any of the fragile dead draw near
that blood before I met Tirésias.

"The first dead soul to come was young Elpénor,
my comrade: one who'd yet to find a grave
beneath the earth's wide ways; we'd left his corpse
unwept, unburied, there in Círcë's house;
we had another task—and hurried off.
The sight of him provoked my tears and pity;
and when I spoke to him, my words were winged:
'Elpénor, you on foot were faster than
my ship. How did you reach this shadowed land?'

"These were my words; this was his sad reply:
'Odysseus, man of many wiles, divine
son of Laértës, my undoing lay
in some god sending down my dismal fate
and in too much sweet wine. I lay stretched out
on Círcë's roof; too stupefied to think
of taking the long ladder down, I fell
headfirst, down to the ground. My neck was cracked,

Greek [34-64]

split from my spine; my spirit went to Hades.
Now I beseech you in the name of those
you left behind, the absent ones: your wife
and he who reared you when you were a child,
your father, and Telémachus, the son
you left alone at home. I know that you,
on leaving Hades' halls, will find landfall
with your stout ship at the Aeǽan isle.
There, lord, I ask you to remember me.
Do not abandon me, unwept, unburied,
lest you provoke the anger of the gods.
Burn me and any armor that is mine,
and on the shore of the gray sea, heap high
a mound for this unhappy man. Do this
for me, and set upon that mound the oar
I used when I, alive, rowed with my friends.'

"And then the shade of my dead mother came:
she, Anticleīa, child of generous
Autólycus, had been alive when I
had left for holy Ílion. I wept—
that sight had touched my soul with pity—yet,
even within my grief, I did not let
my mother's spirit near the blood before
Tirésias had heard all I would ask.

"Theban Tirésias came next. He grasped
his golden staff. He knew me, and he said:
'Odysseus, man of many wiles, divine
son of Laértës, why have you, sad man,
abandoning the sunlight, cared to come
to see the dead and this dejected realm?
But now it's time to stand aside: leave free
the pit and sheathe your sharpened blade, that I
may taste this blood and tell you words of truth.'

□ □ □

Greek [65-96]

"He spoke. I sheathed my silver-studded sword.
As soon as he had tasted that dark blood,
the prince of prophets offered me these words:

"'You, bright Odysseus, seek a honey-sweet
homecoming, but a god will make it harsh.
I do not think you can elude the lord
who makes earth tremble, for his heart has stored
much fury since you blinded his dear son.
But even so—though sadly tried—you can
return to your own home if you would check
your will and your dear comrades' once you've left
behind the violet sea and your stout ship
has touched Thrinácia, the island where
you'll find the grazing cattle, splendid flocks
of Hélios, who sees and hears all things.
If you leave his rich herds untouched and turn
your mind to going home, then you can still
reach Ithaca, though after grim ordeals.
And even if your solitary self
escapes, your coming home will be delayed
and sad: with all your comrades lost, you'll make
that journey on a ship that's not your own;
and in your house you will meet griefs, a pack
of overbearing men, who would devour
your goods; they woo your godlike wife with gifts.
But you, returned, will crush their impudence;
and when, within your halls, you've killed them all
either through guile or else in open war
with your sharp bronze, then take a shapely oar
and visit many cities till you reach
a land where men know nothing of the sea
and don't use salt to season what they eat;
they're ignorant of boats with purple cheeks
and shapely oars that are the wings of ships.
I give you this clear sign—it can't be missed.
When, on the road, you come upon a man
who calls the oar you carry on your back

Greek [97-128]

a fan for winnowing, you can be sure:
that place is where you are to plant your oar.
That done, present Poseidon with fine gifts:
a ram, a bull, a boar that mates with sows.
Then, once you have returned to Ithaca,
take care to offer holy hecatombs
to the undying gods, wide heaven's lords—
to each in turn. You will not die at sea:
the death that reaches you will be serene.
You will grow old—a man of wealth and ease—
surrounded by a people rich, at peace.
All I have said will surely come to be.'

"These were his words, and this was my reply:
'Tirésias, gods wove this destiny.
But tell me one thing—tell me honestly.
I see the soul of my dear mother; she
sits near the pit of blood, but does not speak
to her own son, nor does she look at me.
How can I let her know that I am he?'

"These were my words; this was his quick reply:
'The answer's easy; set it in your mind.
Those whom you let approach the pit of blood
will speak the truth to you, and those dead souls
whom you refuse will surely move away.'

"That said, the soul of lord Tirésias,
now he had given me his prophecy,
went back to Hades' halls. But I sat still
until my mother came to drink the blood
dark as a cloud. And she knew who I was
at once; I saw her tears, heard her winged words:

"'Son, how have you, despite the mist and fog,
come here alive? The living find it hard
to reach this realm: it lies so far beyond
great rivers and dread deeps and, most of all,

Greek [129-157]

the Ocean none can cross on foot; it takes
stout ships to face that journey. Have you come
with ship and comrades, after wandering long,
from Troy? Have you been back to Ithaca?
And have you seen your wife within your halls?'

"These were her words, and this was my reply:
'Mother, it is necessity that brought me
to Hades' house, to hear the prophecy
the spirit of Tirésias the Theban
would offer me. I've yet to near the shore
of dear Achǽa; I've not touched our isle.
I've wandered without joy, in deep dejection,
from that day when, behind bright Agamemnon,
I left for Ílion, where fine foals graze,
to fight against the Trojans. But I need
to hear one thing—and tell me honestly:
How did fierce death defeat you? With long sickness?
Or did the archer-goddess Ártemis,
whose arrows are more gentle, find the mark?
Tell me about my father and the son
I left in Ithaca. Are they still seen
as kin of one who's king? Or does another
possess my scepter now, since many say
that I will not return? Reveal to me
the mind and intent of the wife I wed.
Does she stand by my son and keep all things
just as they've always been? Or was she taken
as wife by some illustrious Achǽan?'

"My honored mother answered me at once:
'Indeed steadfast, within your house she stays.
Her dreary nights and days are wept away.
No one's usurped your kingship; and your lands
are held in peace by your Telémachus.
As suits a guardian of justice, he
shares in his people's festive gatherings:
men want his counsel; he's a precious guest.

Greek [158-187]

Your father keeps to his own farm; he never
comes down into the town. To ease his rest
he has no bed, no cloak, and no bright blankets;
he sleeps, in winter, where the servants sleep,
in ashes by the fire; his clothes are ragged.
But when the summer and rich autumn come,
then all about the slopes of his vineyards
lie heaps of scattered fallen leaves; and there
he lies in sorrow, tending his great grief;
over your fate he weeps. A harsh old age
has overtaken him. So, too, my fate
was sadness, and my last years bore that weight.
The expert archer-goddess' gentle shafts
did not strike me within my house; no sickness
mined me, the sort that often saps life's force,
that wears away the body hatefully;
it was lament for you—your gentleness
and wisdom—o my radiant Odysseus—
that robbed me of the honey-sweet of life.'

"She'd spoken. And despite my doubts, I longed
to clasp my mother's shade within my arms.
Three times—my heart kept urging me—I tried;
and three times she escaped my hands, much like
a shadow or a dream. The pain grew sharp
and sharper in my heart. My winged words said:

"'Dear mother, why do you shrink back when I
want so to hold you fast? Can't we embrace
and, with our arms around each other, take
our fill of this chill grief in Hades' house?
Or are you just a phantom sent to me
by great Perséphonë, that she might add
still other tears to those that I have shed?'

"That said, my honored mother answered quickly:
'Poor child, most tried of men, Perséphonë,
daughter of Zeus, is not deceiving you

Greek [188-217]

in any way: this is the law that rules
all mortals at their death. For just as soon
as life has left the white bones, and the sinews
no longer hold together bones and flesh,
when the erupting force of blazing fire
undoes the body, then the spirit wanders:
much like a dream, it flits away and hovers,
now here, now there. But hurry back to light;
and may your mind remember my reply,
so that you can reveal it to your wife.'

"Such were the words we shared. Then all the wives
and daughters of great lords came forward, sent
by famed Perséphonë. Those women thronged
around the pit of blood; and since I longed
to question each of them, I weighed the ways
in which that might be done. This plan seemed best.
Unsheathing the sharp sword along my thigh,
I did not let them all draw near at once.
But one by one they came; and each described
her lineage and, when I asked, replied.

"The first I saw was Tyro: she declared
herself to be the daughter of Salmóneus
and wife of Crétheus, son of Æolus.
When she was still a girl, her heart was set
on the divine Enípeus, handsomest
of all earth's rivers. Wild with love, she watched
his lovely current. But the god who shakes
and clasps the earth took on Enípeus' shape;
and at the churning river mouth, he lay
with her. Above them rose a huge dark wave;
arching, it hid them: god and mortal girl.
Poseidon loosened Tyro's virgin girdle;
then, shedding sleep on her, he did love's work.
At that, he clasped her hand and spoke soft words:

▢ ▢ ▢

Greek [218-247]

"'You can be happy, woman, in our love:
even as this year turns, you will give birth
to splendid children: matings of the gods
are never barren. Care for—tend—your sons.
Go home, keep silent, tell no one; but know—
your lover was Poseidon, god of tremors.'

"That said, Poseidon plunged beneath sea-surge.
Conceiving, she bore Pélias and Néleus;
and both became firm servants of great Zeus.
And Pélias, lord of great herds, lived in spacious
Iólcus; Néleus' home was sandy Pylos.
The queenly woman's other sons were born
of Crétheus: Æson, Phérës, Amytháon,
adept at fighting from his chariot.

"And after her I saw Antíopë,
Asópus' daughter, she who claimed the glory
of having slept within the arms of Zeus,
to whom she bore two sons: Amphíon, Zéthus,
the pair who founded seven-gated Thebes
and walled it round with towers; without these,
despite that city's strength, it would have been
too hard to keep a place so spacious safe
from enemies.

      "And then I saw Alcménë,
wife of Amphítryon. After she lay
in mighty Zeus's arms, she bore a son:
the dauntless, lionhearted Héraclës.

"And I saw Mégara, bold Creon's daughter,
wife of Alcménë's never-yielding son.

"I also saw the lovely Epicástë,
mother of Oedipus; unknowingly,
she'd shared in a monstrosity: she married
. . .

Greek [248-272]

her own son. And she wed him after he
had killed his father. But the gods did not
wait long to let men know what had been wrought.
Yet since they had devised dark misery,
the gods let him remain in handsome Thebes;
and there, despite his dismal sufferings,
he stayed with the Cadméans as their king.
But she went down into the house where Hades
is sturdy guardian of the gates; for she,
gripped by her grief, had tied to a high beam
her noose. But when she died, she left behind
calamities for Oedipus—as many
as the Avengers of a mother carry.

"And I saw fairest Chlóris, she whose beauty
caught Néleus; with his countless gifts, he won
as wife the youngest daughter of Amphíon,
the son of Íasus, whose power had once
possessed the Mínyae's town, Orchómenus.
And to her husband, Chlóris, queen of Pylos,
bore splendid sons: Nestor and Chrómius
and Periclýmenus. Then she gave birth
to Pero, gifted with amazing beauty.
All of the nearby chieftains sought her hand,
but Néleus had decreed that any man
who wanted her as wife must first bring back
the cattle with broad brows and curving horns
that Íphiclës of Phýlacë had stolen
from Tyro, Néleus' mother. Íphiclës
was powerful; the trial was hard; and only
the seer, Melámpus—acting on behalf
of his dear brother—dared to face that task.
But he was blocked when Zeus devised a plot:
the herdsmen caught him, bound him fast in chains.
But when the old year's months and days were done,
and seasons started their new rounds, the force
of Íphiclës relented: after he
. . .

Greek [273-296]

had heard Melámpus' many prophecies,
he set him free. Zeus' will was now complete.

"And I saw Leda, she who bore her husband,
Tyndáreüs, two stalwart sons: Castor,
horse-tamer, and the boxer Polydēuces.
The earth, giver of grain, now covers both.
But Zeus gave them a special dignity;
for each of them, though under earth, is dead
one day but lives the next, in turn. Those brothers
were gifted by their fate with godlike honor.

"And after them I saw Iphimedēīa,
Alœus' wife, who claimed that she had lain
with lord Poseidon. Famous Ephiáltës
and godlike Otus were the sons she bore,
but both were fated to a life cut short.
Grain-giving earth had made those two more handsome
and tall than any other man except Oríon.
Even at nine, they were nine cubits wide;
as for their height, it matched nine stretched arm's-lengths.
They even threatened the undying gods'
Olympus with confusion and assault;
upon its peak they planned to heap Mount Ossa
and then, on top of that, Mount Pélion,
whose woods are loud with leaves; from there they'd climb
to heaven. They'd have done what they designed
if they had reached their manhood. But the son
of Zeus, whom fair-haired Leto bore, killed both
before the hair beneath their temples showed
enough to beard their chins with ample growth.

"And I saw Phædra, Procris, and Ariádnë—
malicious Minos' lovely daughter—she
whom Théseus tried to carry off from Crete
to holy Athens' hill. But their escape
brought no delight to him: along the way,
. . .

Greek [297–324]

in seagirt Día, Ártemis was swayed
by Dionysus; she killed Ariádnë.

"Then I saw Clýmenë and Mǽra and
the obscene Eriphýlë, she who sold
her husband's life: she bartered him for gold.

"But I cannot recount or name them all:
the many wives and daughters of the brave.
Immortal night would end before I did.
But now the time for sleep has come, and I
must either meet the crew on your swift ship
or else rest here. Should I begin my trip?
You and the gods must now decide on this."

These were his words. And all were silent, still—
held in the shadowed hall by some deep spell.
White-armed Arétë was the first to speak:

"Phaeácians, how does he persuade you now—
his face and frame and his astute good sense?
He is my honored guest, though all of you
received him, too. Then do not send him off
in haste and do not grudge the many gifts
he needs; for each of you, within his house,
has ample wealth—just as the gods have willed."

Then Echenéus, the old warrior, spoke:
"Dear friends, the words of our wise queen seem just.
Do as she says—though on Alcínoüs
our final words and actions must depend."

This was Alcínoüs' reply: "Her plan
has my consent as surely as I am
alive—and king of the Phaeácians.
And though he longs to see his home, our guest
can wait until tomorrow dawns; by then
I shall have gathered all the gifts at last.

Greek [325-351]

While all of us must plan his trip, that task
is mainly mine: it's I who rule this land."

Odysseus, man of many wiles, replied:
"Alcínoüs, all peoples know your fame;
and even if you spoke for a delay
of one full year, while you prepared my way
with shipmates and fine gifts, I'd gladly wait.
Indeed, if I returned to my own land
with riches in my hands, I'd surely win
much more respect, a warmer welcoming
by all who saw me back in Ithaca."

This was the answer of Alcínoüs:
"Odysseus, you don't seem to be a cheat
or liar—though we know that dark earth breeds
so many who, in every land, deceive
with tales of things that no man's ever seen.
But you have grace and wisdom in your speech.
You've told with skill—as would a poet sing—
your own and all the Argives' sufferings.
But tell me this—and tell me honestly:
Did you lay eyes on any of the men
who went with you to Ílion and met
their fate along that plain? The night is long—
a length beyond foretelling. It is not
yet time to sleep within this hall. I want
more things of wonder and astonishment.
I could stay here until divine Dawn wakes
if you'd resume your tale of trials and pains."

Odysseus, man of many wiles, replied:
"Alcínoüs, most notable of men,
it's true that there's still time for tales and talk,
yet there is, too, a time for sleep. But if
you want to hear still more, I should not wish
to keep from you the tale of other griefs
more bitter still, the sad ordeals of friends

Greek [352-382]

who had escaped the Trojans' ominous
war-cries but then, returning home, were killed—
the victims of an evil woman's will.

"As soon as pure Perséphonë had scattered
the women—weaker spirits—here and there,
the saddened soul of Agamemnon, son
of Átreus, came forward. And a crowd
surrounded him: within Aegísthus' halls
these men had died alongside Agamemnon.
As soon as he caught sight of me, he knew
just who I was. His moan was loud, his tears
were many; he stretched out his arms; he longed
to hold me fast, but all his force was gone;
the power of his agile limbs was lost.
I looked, I wept, and pity filled my heart.
And when I spoke, I offered these winged words:

"'O Agamemnon, Átreus' famed son,
how did dour death defeat so great a captain?
Was it Poseidon, hurling his harsh storms
against your ships, who finally won out?
Or did you die on land, when fighting-men
destroyed you as you raided herds and flocks
or tried to win their women and their town?'

"These were my words. This was his quick reply:
'Odysseus, man of many wiles, divine
son of Laértës, I was not undone
by lord Poseidon: none of his harsh storms
attacked my ships. Nor did I meet my end
on land, struck down by fighting-men. My fate
was readied by Aegísthus with the aid
of my conniving wife: inviting me
to feast within his halls, he butchered me
just as one kills an ox within a stall.
And so the death I died was mean and small:
around me, without let, they killed us all

Greek [383-413]

as, in the house of one with power and wealth,
for wedding feasts or banquets jointly set
or revels, servants slaughter white-tusked hogs.
You surely have set eyes on many men
destroyed in single combat or the clash
of frenzied ranks, but you'd have been still more
distraught if you had seen, in that great hall,
our bodies round the wine bowl and the food
heaped high; our warm blood streamed across the floor.
I heard Cassandra, Priam's daughter, wail
even as—clinging to me—she was killed
by Clytemnéstra, mistress of dark guile.
Face down, along the ground, my chest pierced through,
lifting my fists, dying, I beat the earth,
and my bitch-wife moved off. She had no heart:
I left for Hades, but she did not shut
my eyes nor did she move to close my mouth.
Nothing is more obscene, more bestial, than
a woman's mind when it is all intent
on dregs—the filth my wife concocted when
she killed her own true husband. Coming home,
it was my children's and my servants' welcome
I'd hoped for; but that artist of corruption
heaped shame upon herself and on all women
in time to come, even the upright ones.'

"These were his words, and this was my reply:
'Long since, the bitter hate of thundering Zeus
against the sons of Átreus has used
conniving women as its instruments:
how many of us died through Helen's fault;
and Clytemnéstra, while you were far off,
devised her plot.'

                "These were my words—and he
was quick to answer: 'Therefore do not be
too open with your wife: do not disclose
all that you know; tell her one thing and keep

Greek [414–443]

another hidden—though you'll never meet
death at the hands of your Penelope,
a prudent wife, whose heart has understanding.
When we set off for war, Penelope
was still a young bride: at her breast she held
an infant son, who now must sit among
the ranks of men—a happy son, for he
will see the father whom he loves come home;
and as is right, he'll hold his father close.
But I was not allowed to sate my eyes,
to see my own beloved son: my wife
denied that sight to me—she killed me first.
And I should add this warning: Don't forget
to moor in secret when you bring your ship
to your dear shores: no woman merits trust.
But tell me one thing—tell me honestly:
Have you heard word of where my son now lives?
Has sandy Pylos or Orchómenus
or Meneláus' Spartan plain become
my son's new home? For certainly the bright
Oréstes has not died upon the earth.'

"These were his words, and this was my reply:
'Why, Agamemnon, do you ask me that?
I do not know if he's alive or dead.
Words empty as the wind are best unsaid.'

"So did we two shed tears and share sad talk.
And then Achilles, Péleus' son, approached;
and with the son of Péleus came Patróclus,
flawless Antílochus, and Ajax—he
whose form and stature outdid all the Dánaans'
except for the incomparable Achilles.
The shade of Æacus' swift-footed grandson
knew me. In tears he offered these winged words:

"'Odysseus, man of many wiles, divine
son of Laértës, will your spirit find

Achilles in Hades

new tasks still more audacious than this quest?
How did you dare to come to Hades, home
of shades of faded men, the helpless dead?'

"These were his words, and this was my reply:
'Achilles, Péleus' son, the bravest Dánaan,
I've come to seek Tirésias, to listen
to any counsel he might have: a plan
to help me reach my rocky Ithaca.
I've not yet neared the coasts of the Achǽans;
I have not touched our soil. I've met sad trials.
Achilles, neither past nor future holds
a man more blessed than you. In life indeed
we Argives honored you as deity;
and now, among the dead, you are supreme.
In death you have no need to grieve, Achilles.'

"These were my words. He did not wait to answer:
'Odysseus, don't embellish death for me.
I'd rather be another's hired hand,
working for some poor man who owns no land
but pays his rent from what scant gains he gets,
than to rule over all whom death has crushed.
But tell me something of my worthy son:
Has he, a lord of men, gone off to war,
become a chieftain? And what have you heard
of stalwart Péleus? Does he still preserve
his place of honor with the Mýrmidons,
or is he scorned in Hellas and in Phthía
because old age has slowed his hands and feet?
I do not rise beneath the rays of sun
to take the form I had in Troy's broad land
when, to defend the Argives, my attacks
killed stalwart men: if I could only stand
beside my father for the briefest hour,
I'd make my force and formidable hands
the hated scourge of those whose savage acts
deprive him of due honor and respect.'   □ □ □

Greek [474–503]

"These were his words, and this was my reply:
'Of your fine father, Péleus, I've heard nothing;
but of your dear son, Neoptólemus,
just as you wish, I'll tell you everything.
For I myself brought him in my lithe ship
to Scyros, where he joined the well-greaved Greeks.
And when our council met to plan attacks
against the Trojans, he was always first
to speak; in what he said, he never erred.
The only ones more subtle than your son
were godlike Nestor and myself. And when
Achæans fought along the plain of Troy,
your son did not draw back into the ranks
and ruck; he thrust ahead. No one could stand
against his fury: fierce, he killed and maimed
so many—I can't tell or list the names
of every warrior that he, defending
the Argives, killed. But I will tell you this:
Your son's bronze shaft struck down Eurýpylus,
the son of Télephus—the handsomest
man I had ever seen except for Memnon,
who was the son of gods. And the Cetēīans
who crowded round Eurýpylus were slaughtered—
all died because a woman had been bribed.
And, too, when we, the finest of the Argives,
were entering the horse Epēīus built,
and it was I who led, who would decide
to shut our ambush or to open wide,
then all the other Dánaan lords and chiefs
wiped tears away, their every limb was weak;
but not once did I see your son's fair face
grow pale or see him dry his cheek. Again,
again, he asked to leave the horse; he gripped
his sword-hilt and his massive bronze-tipped shaft,
longing to smash the Trojans. Once we'd sacked
the towering town of Priam, he went back—
bearing his share of spoils and one fine prize—
to board his ship; he was unscathed, intact;

Greek [504–535]

no sharp speartip had struck him; no close fight
had left the wounds that war so often brings—
for Árës' fury strikes haphazardly.'

"That said, across the Field of Asphodels,
with long strides swift Achilles' spirit left;
my tale of his son's fame had made him glad.

"The other dead souls stood in sadness, each
shade speaking to me of his griefs. Just Ajax,
the son of Télamon, stood off, apart,
still angry with me for my victory
when I, not he, beside our ships, received
the prize Achilles' mother had adjudged:
the arms and armor of her son. Would I
had never won that prize, for Ajax died
at his own hands because of that: earth closed
above a flawless man, one who surpassed
in feats and features all the Greeks except
for Péleus' son. I spoke with gentleness:

"'Ajax, son of great Télamon, even
in death can't you forget your bitterness
against me for the fatal arms I won?
Those arms allowed the gods to heap disaster
upon the Argives: when you fell we lost
a bulwark. We Achǽans always mourn
your death as we do that of Péleus' son.
And Zeus alone must bear the blame: his venom,
his hatred for the ranks of Dánaan spearmen,
decreed your doom. My lord, dismiss your wrath;
come, hear my words; do not be obstinate.'

"So did I plead. He did not answer me.
He went back into Érebus; he joined
the other dead souls. Even in his wrath,
he might have spoken to me then, or I

. . .

Greek [536–565]

to him. But now the heart within my chest
wanted to see the shades of the other dead.

"There I saw Minos—famous son of Zeus—
who, seated, holding fast his golden scepter,
delivered judgments on the dead; they gathered,
seated or standing, at the spacious gates
of Hades; they beseeched, and he passed sentence.

"And then I saw immense Oríon, driving
across the Field of Asphodels a throng
of savage beasts, those he had killed upon
the lonely mountain slopes. Within his hands
he gripped a club of bronze that cannot crack.

"I saw the son of splendid Gǽa, Títyus,
stretched on the ground for some six hundred cubits.
Two vultures sat, one to each side, and tore
his liver; their beaks plunged into his bowels,
he could not ward them off; for Títyus
had violated Leto, splendid mistress
of Zeus, as she was walking through the fields
of lovely Pánopeus, heading toward Pytho.

"And I saw Tántalus in deep torment;
he stood upright within a pool, his chin
just touched by water. But despite his thirst,
he could not drink: as soon as that old man
bent over, seeking water, all that pool—
dried by a demon—shrank; and Tántalus
saw black earth at his feet. Above his head,
trees—leafy, high—bore fruit: from pomegranates
to pears, sweet figs, bright apples, and plump olives.
But just as soon as he reached out to touch,
winds blew that fruit up toward the shadowed clouds.

"And I saw Sísyphus' atrocious pain:
he tried to push a huge stone with his hands.

Greek [566-594]

He'd brace his hands and feet and thrust it up
a slope, but just when he had neared the top,
its weight reversed its course; and once again
that bestial stone rolled back onto the plain.
Sweat drenched his straining limbs: again he thrust,
and dust rose from the head of Sísyphus.

"And I caught sight of mighty Héraclës
(that is to say, his shade; for he himself
rejoices in the feats of deathless gods
and has as wife the lovely-ankled Hébë,
daughter of Zeus and golden-sandaled Hera).
Around him rose the tumult of the dead,
like birds that scatter everywhere in terror;
and he, like dark night, gripping his bare bow
and with an arrow on his bowstring, glared
menacingly, like one about to shoot.
Around his chest he had a giant belt
of gold embossed with horrifying things:
lions with massive manes, wild boars, and bears;
duels and battles, massacres and murders.
May he whose craft conceived that baldric never
devise a second one. As soon as he
returned my gaze, he knew just who I was.
And as he wept he offered these winged words:

"'Odysseus, man of many wiles, divine
son of Laértës, you are saddened by
the fate you bear, a destiny like mine
when underneath the sun I lived my life.
I was the son of Zeus, the son of Cronos,
and yet the trials that I endured were countless;
for I was made to serve a man by far
inferior to me: he set hard tests.
He even sent me here to fetch the hound
of Hades—he was sure there was no task
more dangerous. And yet I brought it back
. . .

Greek [595–625]

from Hades' house, because I had the help
of Hermes and Athena, gray-eyed goddess.'

"His words were done. But when he had gone back,
I, lest still others come, stood there steadfast,
waiting for more dead heroes of the past.
And I'd have seen those warriors as I wished,
had crowds of dead souls not assembled then
with such a strange outcry that, terrified
and pale, I feared that fierce Perséphonë
might, from the halls of Hades, menace me
with Gorgon's head, that grim monstrosity.

"At that, I hurried to my ship and ordered
my comrades to embark and loose the hawsers.
They came on board at once and manned the thwarts.
The current took our ship on Ocean's course.
At first we rowed, but then a fair wind rose."

Greek [626–640]

BOOK XII

Odysseus' tale continues.

Return to Círcë's isle.

A burial mound for the corpse of Elpénor.

Círcë's warnings and instructions.

.

The Sirens' isle and their enticing song;
Odysseus bound to the mast.

The vortex of Charýbdis; voracious Scylla.

.

The landing on Thrinácia, isle of Hélios.

Odysseus' comrades' forbidden feast
on the sun-god's precious cattle.

Hélios' appeal to Zeus for vengeance:
a doomed crew, the destruction of the ship,
and the death of all but Odysseus.

Nine days on the sea, adrift;
safe haven on Calypso's shore.

The end of Odysseus' tale.

"After our ship had slipped the Ocean's stream,
we coursed along the sea's broad surge and reached
the island of Aeǽa, home of Dawn's
firstlight, her space for dancing, and the site
of sunrise. There, along the sands, we beached
our sturdy ship, and then we disembarked.
We waited for bright Dawn; sleep held us fast.

"As soon as Dawn's rose fingers touched the sky,
I sent my comrades off to Círcë's house
to carry back the dead Elpénor's corpse.
Then we cut firewood; and as we stood
beside his pyre along a promontory,
the tears we shed were many. When his body
and armor had burned down, we heaped a mound,
and at the top we placed his shapely oar.

"We spoke of all we'd done, each thing in turn.
Círcë—not unaware that we'd come back
from Hades' house—had soon dressed handsomely.
She hurried to our side; her handmaids bore
abundant bread and meat and dark red wine.
She, brightest goddess, stood among us, saying:

"'Undaunted, you have gone—alive—to see
the house of Hades; you are twice-made men—
all other mortals die but once. Yet come,
devote this day to food and drink; and when
Dawn rises, set your sail. And I'll describe
the sea paths you must take; I shall not hide
a single thing—so that you meet no snares
at sea and no misfortunes on the land.'

"These were her words, and our proud hearts agreed.
All through that day we sat, until sunset:
we had much meat; the wine was honey-sweet.
But once the sun had gone and darkness won,
my men lay near the cables at the stern;

Greek [1-32]

then Círcë took my hand—she led me far
from my dear comrades. And she sat me down
beside her, asking me to tell her all.
I told her what we'd done, each thing in turn.
Then mighty Círcë spoke these things to me:

"'Now all has been fulfilled. But you must hear
and do all that I say. A god will, too,
remind you. It will be the Sirens you
meet first—and they entrance all visitors.
Whoever, unaware, comes close and hears
the Sirens' voice will nevermore draw near
his wife, his home, his infants: he'll not share
such joys again: the Sirens' lucid song
will so enchant him as they lie along
their meadow. Round about them lie heaped bones
and shriveled skin of putrefying men.
But row beyond the Sirens. Knead sweet wax
and stop your shipmates' ears so none of them
will hear the Sirens sing. But if you wish
to listen to their song, just stand erect
before the mast and have your men tie fast
your hands and feet, and wind the ends around
the mast itself; then with your back against
the mast, you can delight in that sweet chant.
But don't forget to tell your crew that if
you plead with them to loose those bonds, they must
add still more ropes and knots. When they have rowed
beyond the Sirens, you will have to choose
between two sea roads. But I'll not advise
which way you are to take; I'll just describe
what each is like, and you must then decide.

"'One sea road runs among steep crags; the waves
of azure Amphitrítë pound their base:
the blessed gods call these the Wandering Rocks.
Even the birds can't make their way above
such cliffs—and they repel the trembling doves

Greek [33-62]

that bring ambrosia to our father Zeus:
at times the sheer cliff snatches one of these,
and Zeus sends down another to complete
their ranks. And past those cliffs no mortals' ship
has ever sailed intact. There vicious blasts
of fire join the sea-surge in attack:
the sailors' bodies and the vessels' planks—
one vortex churns them all. And just one craft
alone—as all men know—has ever passed
those crags: the *Argo,* Jason's ship, when he
sailed homeward from Aeétes' coast. She, too,
would have been smashed against the rocks had not
Hera, for love of Jason, steered her through.

"'The other sea road runs along two cliffs.
The first crag has a heaven-high sharp peak:
a never-fading cloud envelops it—
so dark that, round it, air is never limpid,
neither in summer nor in fall. No man
could ever scale that cliff or stand upon
its top, though he had twenty feet and hands;
it is as sheer as if it had been burnished.
Midway on that cliffside, a dark cave lies.
It faces west, toward Érebus. Famous
Odysseus, you will head your ship toward that.
The cave is set so high on that cliffside
that even the most stalwart man who shot
an arrow upward from his ship could not
strike such a target. Scylla lives inside.
There she barks fearfully. Her voice is like
a newborn whelp, but she is murderous—
a monster who can only bring despair—
even a god would shun the sight of her.
She has twelve feet—and all of them deformed—
and six long necks: on each a vicious head
with three rows of abundant, close-set teeth,
replete with black death. Half her body's kept
deep in that cavern, but she thrusts her heads

Greek [63-93]

out of her horrid home. She searches round
the rocks; she looks for dolphins and sea dogs
and any larger creatures she may chance
to catch, for wailing Amphitrítë breeds
a multitude of such enormous beasts.
No sailor yet can boast of sailing past
her cliff with ship intact: each of her mouths
snatches a man from every passing prow.
The second of the twin cliffs—so you'll see—
is near the first, but it is not as steep;
even an arrow can outreach that peak.
Upon that cliff there grows with ample leaves
a great fig tree. Beneath its boughs Charýbdis
sucks up black water. And three times a day
she vomits out the brine, and then three times
she sucks it back ferociously. Don't let
your ship draw near when she is gulping brine;
no one—not even he who makes earth tremble—
could save you then. Hold closer to the cliff
of Scylla: better far to mourn six men
than to lament the loss of all of them.'

"These were her words, and this was my reply:
'Come, tell me: Is there any stratagem,
goddess, through which I can escape the grim
Charýbdis, yet ward off the other when
she preys upon my men?'

                              "These were my words.
The goddess answered quickly: 'Can't you curb
your zeal for torments, war, ordeals—and yield
even to the immortal gods? This Scylla
is not a mortal, but a deathless horror:
atrocious, savage, and invincible.
The one defense against her is retreat.
For if you were to stop at her cliffside
to arm yourself, I fear that she would strike
again; again she'd stretch six heads and snatch

Greek [94–123]

Scylla

another six. Instead, sail straight ahead:
at full speed pass her and beseech Cratǽis,
her mother—she who, giving birth to Scylla,
brought men calamity. Cratǽis will
prevent her reaching out to prey again.
And then you'll reach the island of Thrinácia:
there, Hélios' many cows and plump flocks graze;
for he has seven herds of cattle, seven
fair flocks of sheep—and each has fifty beasts.
They never do give birth and never die.
Their guards are Phaëthúsa and Lampétië,
the fair-haired nymphs whom bright Neǽra bore
to Hélios Hypérion. And after
she'd given birth and reared them both, their mother
sent them to the fair island of Thrinácia,
to watch their father's sheep and curved-horn cows.
If you leave his rich herds untouched and turn
your mind to going home, then you can still
reach Ithaca, though after dour ordeals.
And even if your solitary self
escapes, your coming home will be delayed
and sad: you will have lost all your shipmates.'

"So Círcë spoke. Upon the throne of gold,
Dawn came straightway. Then Círcë left the beach.
At that, I hurried to my ship and ordered
my comrades to embark and loose the hawsers.
They came aboard at once. The fair-haired Círcë,
the awesome goddess with a human voice,
sent forth a friend who favored us, a wind
that swelled our sail and spurred our ship's dark prow.
Once we'd secured our gear, we settled down;
the wind and helmsman kept us on our course.
With an uneasy heart, I told my men:

"'The prophecies of Círcë are not meant
for one or two of us; they must be shared,
my friends: beforehand, know we may meet death

Greek [124–156]

or may, escaping destiny, be spared.
Above all, Círcë urges us to flee
the song of the beguiling Sirens and
their flowered meadow. I alone—she says—
may hear their voices. Tie me then hard fast—
use knots I can't undo. I'll stand erect,
feet on the socket of the mast; and let
the rope ends coil around the shaft itself;
and if I plead with you to set me free,
add still more ropes and knots most carefully.'

"So did I tell my crew all we might meet.
Meanwhile the stout ship, stirred by a fair breeze,
had reached the Sirens' island. Then the wind
fell off: a god had lulled the waves to sleep.
The calm was now complete. My crew stood up
and furled the sail and stowed it in the hold.
That done, they sat along the thwarts and beat
the water white with polished oars of fir.
But I, with my sharp blade, cut into bits
a great round cake of wax; I kneaded these
with my stout hands. The wax grew soft, gave way
before my force and Hélios' warm rays.
I sealed the ears of all my crew in turn.
That done, they bound my hands and feet, as I
stood upright on the mast box; and they tied
the ropes hard fast around the mast. They sat
and beat the gray sea with their oars. But once
we'd come in hailing distance of the Sirens,
though we were moving rapidly, they noticed
our swift ship and intoned their lucid song:

"'Remarkable Odysseus, halt and hear
the song we two sing out: Achǽan chief,
the gift our voices give is honey-sweet.
No man has passed our isle in his black ship
until he's heard the sweet song from our lips;
and when he leaves, the listener has received

delight and knowledge of so many things.
We know the Argives' and the Trojans' griefs:
their tribulations on the plain of Troy
because the gods had willed it so. We know
all things that come to pass on fruitful earth.'

"So did they chant with their entrancing voice.
My heart longed so to listen, and I asked
my men to set me free—it was my eyes
that signaled. But intent upon their oars,
they rowed ahead. Yet two of them were quick
to stand: Eurýlochus and Perimédës
bound me with more—and even tighter—bonds.
But when we'd passed beyond the Sirens' isle
and could no longer hear their voices chant,
my faithful men at once removed the wax
that shut their ears. They freed me from the mast.

"When we had left behind that isle, straightway
I sighted smoke and a disastrous wave
and heard a roar. My shipmates cringed; the oars
flew from their grip and dangled in the surge;
my mates had empty hands; the ship was stalled.
I went about the deck and spurred them all
with gentle words, approaching each in turn:

"'Dear friends, we've had our share of trials and tests;
and what has happened now is hardly worse
than when the Cyclops, with his brutal force,
imprisoned us in his deep cave; and just
as then my courage, stratagems, good sense
allowed us to escape, I know that we
will now survive and store in memory
these dangers, too. Come, follow what I say.
Retrieve your oars; despite the seething surge,
stay at the thwarts and strike the sea, for Zeus
may set us free, may let us flee this curse.
And you, the helmsman—since our hollow ship

Greek [189-217]

depends upon your grip—remember this:
Steer clear of smoke and fire; hug the cliff
that looms along this side, lest she swerve off
and crash, full force, against the facing rocks.'

"These were my words. My men did not delay.
Of Scylla I said nothing—after all,
we had no chance against her—lest my friends,
held fast by fear, desert their oars and cringe
down in the hold. At that point I forgot
the stern command of Círcë: I was not—
so she had said—to arm myself. Instead,
I put on my famed armor and advanced,
a long lance in each hand, to the foredeck:
from there I thought I'd first catch sight of Scylla
among the rocks, intent on killing us.
But though I peered and pored, my face bent toward
the misty cliff, my eyes grew weary—I
could not catch sight of her. We rowed, we wailed,
we sailed on up the strait. Along one side
lay Scylla; on the other side, divine
Charýbdis now was swallowing the brine.
And when she spewed it out again, she seethed
and swirled—a whirlpool—like a caldron set
above some holocaust; on high the spray
rained down upon the summits of the cliffs.
But when Charýbdis gulped the salty sea,
one saw her at the whirlpool's base, in frenzy;
her cliff roared terrifyingly; beneath
the sea, the earth's black sand lay bare; pale fear
held fast my crew; we feared the end and glued
our eyes upon Charýbdis. But just then,
Scylla seized six—the strongest—of my men;
she snatched them from the hollow ship; and when
I turned my eyes aside to seek my friends,
all I could see were feet and hands on high.
They called my name aloud for the last time
and shrieked in anguish. As a fisherman

Greek [218-250]

who, from a jutting rock, has cast his bits
of food as bait to snare small fish, lets down
into the sea his long rod tipped with horn,
and when he's made a catch will whip it back—
writhing; so were my men whirled through the air,
writhing, against the rocks. There, at the door
to her deep cavern, Scylla swallowed them
as, in their horrid struggle, my dear friends
stretched out to me their hands—the saddest sight
my eyes have ever seen in all that I
have suffered in my journeys on the sea.

"Once we'd escaped the cliffs of fierce Charýbdis
and Scylla, we sped on. Soon we had reached
the sun-god's lovely island: there he kept
his broad-browed cows and well-fed flocks of sheep.
Still out at sea, I heard those bleating sheep
and heard the cattle lowing as they reached
their stalls. And I recalled to mind the words
of that blind seer, Tirésias of Thebes,
and of Aeǽan Círcë, who had warned me
again, again, to shun the isle of him
who brings delight to mortals, Hélios.
With an uneasy heart, I told my men:

"'Friends, though your trials are harsh, hear what I say.
I must tell you Tirésias' prophecies
and those of the Aeǽan Círcë: they
warned me repeatedly to shun the land
of Hélios, who brings delight to men.
She said that here disaster waits for us.
No, row our black ship back; don't near this coast.'

"They heard what I had urged. Their dear hearts broke.
Eurýlochus replied with hateful words:
'Odysseus, your demands are merciless;
no man can match your courage, and your strength
will not relent. You surely must be made

Greek [251–279]

of iron if you do not let your friends—
worn-out, in need of sleep—set foot ashore,
where, on this seagirt land, we might once more
prepare a proper meal. You'd have us row
to nowhere through the swift night, men astray,
far from this island, on the shadowed sea.
At night malicious winds will rise—the kind
that batter ships. How can we flee the steep
descent to death if frenzied winds attack:
Notus or raging Zephyr—which, despite
the will of sovereign gods, can wreck a ship?
The night is far too dark: let us submit,
prepare our meal, and rest along the beach.
As soon as Dawn has come, we'll board again
and then row out and toward the open sea.'

"These were his words, and all the rest agreed.
Then I was sure that some dark god had schemed
disaster. And I countered with winged words:

"'Eurýlochus, I'm one against too many:
I am outmanned. But all of you must swear
a binding oath: If we should chance to see
a herd of cattle or a flock of sheep,
no one—through wanton arrogance—must kill
a single beast: you are to eat in peace
the food that we received from deathless Círcë.'

"These were my words. As I had urged, they vowed
at once; that done, we anchored our staunch ship
within a sheltered bay, close to a spring
that had fresh water for us. Once ashore,
my men had soon prepared a skillful supper.
Then, with our need for food and drink appeased,
my friends began to weep, remembering
their dear companions Scylla had devoured.
And sweet sleep came upon them as they wept.
. . .

Greek [280-311]

We reached the night's last watch, when stars turn course;
then Zeus, the gatherer of clouds, provoked
a terrifying tempest: storm clouds wrapped
both sea and land; night hurtled down from heaven.

"As soon as Dawn's rose fingers touched the sky,
we drew our ship into a sheltered place,
a grotto at the harbor's base—a cave
with seats for nymphs and ample dancing-space.
My shipmates gathered round me, and I said:

"'Friends, we have food and drink in our swift ship;
then, lest we meet disaster, do not touch
the cattle. They belong to a dread god,
to Hélios, who sees and hears all things.'

"These were my words. And their proud hearts agreed.
But then winds raged—they swept from south and east.
First, Notus, for a full month, without let;
then Eurus, too, attacked. Throughout that stretch,
with food and wine still theirs, my comrades left
the herds untouched; they did not wish for death.
But when we'd reached the end of all our stores,
my men were forced to prey along the shores.
Yet while they sought with curving hooks to snare
fish, birds, and anything that chance might bring—
such hunger gnawed their bellies—I instead
went inland; for I wanted most to pray
unto the gods, in hope that one of them
might offer me some stratagem. And when,
deeper inland, I'd left behind my friends
and found a place well shielded from the wind,
I washed my hands and called on all the gods
who hold Olympus as their home. But I
heard no reply. They cast sleep on my eyes.

"Meanwhile Eurýlochus provoked my men,
and what he offered was a fatal plan:

Greek [312–339]

'Friends, though your trials are harsh, hear what I say.
All deaths are dour; the fate of men is sad;
but there's no death more miserable than
the doom starvation sends. Come, let us take
Hypérion's best cows and sacrifice
to the undying gods, who rule the skies.
If we reach Ithaca, our fathers' land,
there we—at once—shall build for Hélios
an altar heaped with many glowing gifts.
And if our taking of his tall-horned cows
enrages Hélios, and he would wreck
our ship and has the other gods' consent,
I'd rather have my mouth drink brine and let
the waves kill me at once than meet slow death
by lingering on an island wilderness.'

"So did he speak, and all the rest agreed.
At once they chose the sun-god's finest cattle:
just then, those broad-browed cows with curving horns
were grazing near the dark-prowed ship; my men
surrounded them and prayed unto the gods;
since we, on board our ship, had no white barley,
they plucked the green leaves of a tall oak tree—
over their offering, they'd scatter these.
After they'd prayed and cut the throats and flayed
the cows, they sliced the thighs in chunks and laid
a double layer of fat across those chunks,
then spread raw flesh on top. They had no wine
to splash across the blazing sacrifice
but, using water for libations, roasted
all of the vitals on the fire. And when
the thighs were scorched and they had tasted all
the inner parts, they set the rest on spits.

"But now sweet sleep had left my eyes, and I
walked back to the swift ship at the seaside;
and when my steps drew close to our trim craft,
. . .

Greek [340-368]

I smelled the pungent fragrance of hot fat.
I groaned, then called upon the deathless gods:

"'You, father Zeus, and all the other blessed,
undying gods, you sent this wretchedness;
it's you who left me prey to senseless sleep;
you gulled me; I am ruined; now my men,
awaiting me, contrived this horrid plan.'

"Meanwhile Lampétië, the long-robed nymph,
had hurried off to tell lord Hélios
that we had killed his cows. Without delay,
before his fellow gods, he cried, enraged:

"'You, father Zeus, and all the other blessed
and deathless gods—you now must take revenge:
destroy the comrades of Laértës' son,
Odysseus; in their insolence they killed
the herds that I beheld with such delight
both when I climbed the starry sky and when
I wheeled and then returned to earth again.
If they're not made to pay a penalty
to match their sin, I shall descend to Hades
and shine among the dead.'

                         "In turn, Zeus said:
'Shine, Hélios, with light for the immortals;
and lighten, too, the lives of those who die
on earth, the giver of the gift of grain.
As for those sinners, I'll soon strike their ship
with blazing lightning—tearing her to bits
upon the winedark sea.'

                         "I heard all this
from the fair-haired Calypso after she
had heard it from the messenger Hermes.

□　□　□

Greek [369-390]

"I reached the ship and shore and—one by one—
denounced my men. But nothing could be done—
the herds lay dead. And soon the gods sent portents:
the flayed hides crawled along the ground; the flesh
upon the spits, both roast and raw, began
to bellow; we heard sounds of lowing cows.

"My faithful comrades feasted for six days
upon the finest beasts of Hélios.
But when Zeus, son of Cronos, brought to us
the seventh day, no longer fury-fed,
the wind died down. We boarded quickly, stepped
our mast and spread our sail, then drove ahead—
out toward the open sea.

                              "When we had left
that isle behind and saw no other land,
only the sky and sea, the son of Cronos
set a black cloud above our hollow ship;
below us waves grew dark. By now our run
was doomed; the howling Zephyr fell upon
our course; a wind amok, its fury cracked
the forestays of the mast. The mast fell back;
the sail and all the rigging crashed, collapsed
into the bilge. And at the stern, the mast
hit hard the helmsman's head; it crushed his skull;
and like a diver, from the deck he plunged
headlong; his sturdy spirit left his bones.
Zeus thundered as he hurled a lightning bolt.
He hit the hull: it filled with sulfurous smoke;
our ship whirled round full circle. All my men
pitched overboard; like sea crows they were borne
by waves around our black-bowed craft. A god
deprived them of the day of their return.

"I paced the ship until a comber ripped
the keel and hull apart. The naked keel
was carried by the surge, which also snapped

Greek [391-421]

the mast off from the hulk—but it still had
a backstay made of oxhide. This I grabbed.
That rope in hand, I lashed the keel and mast
together; hugging them, I then was driven
by the malicious winds. And after Zephyr
had slacked his storm's wild force, Notus at once
brought back the fear that I had known; for now
I'd have to cross Charýbdis once again.

"All through the night that wind did not relent.
The sun was rising when I spied the cliffs
of Scylla and the murderous Charýbdis,
who sucked in the salt waters of the sea;
she drew my mast and keel into her deeps.
But reaching up and toward the great fig tree,
I gripped it, clinging to it like a bat.
Yet I could find no foothold, could not climb
that tree, because its roots stretched far below;
nor could I ever reach its long, broad boughs—
so high, they wrapped Charýbdis in their shade.
I gripped that trunk; I would not yield until
she vomited again the mast and keel.
I waited long; at last they came. Just when
an elder who is called upon to judge
between the claims of young contenders, stands
and says the time for judgment's at an end
and leaves the marketplace to dine, so then—
such was the hour—Charýbdis spewed the mast
and keel. My hands and feet let go the trunk;
I fell into the water with a splash
next to the keel and mast; I mounted them;
and, with that vantage, soon my arms began
to row. The father of both gods and men
did not let Scylla's eyes spy me again.

"For nine days I was dragged; and on the tenth
the gods cast me upon Ogýgia's coast,
the island home of lovely-haired Calypso,

Greek [422–449]

the awesome goddess with a human voice,
who took me in and tended me. But why
do I retell this now? Just yesterday,
within this hall, I told that tale to you
and to your noble wife. I do not hold
with telling over what has been well told."

BOOK XIII

More gifts from the Phaeácians.

An evening departure from Schería;
a morning homecoming to Ithaca,
with Odysseus still asleep.

·

Poseidon's vengeance on the Phaeácians.

·

Athena's welcome of Odysseus to Ithaca;
her cunning counsel.

Preparation for revenge on the suitors:
Odysseus as an old and withered beggar.

Odysseus' tale was told. They all were still—
held in the darkened hall by some deep spell.
At last Alcínoüs found words—spoke out:

"Odysseus, after many griefs you've reached
my high-roofed house and threshold made of bronze;
that's cause enough for me to think you'll find
your native shore; you won't be thrust off course.
And now I'd urge each one of you fine lords
who always hear the harper in my halls
and drink the glowing wine that elders prize:
The clothing for our guest already lies
within the polished chest, together with
gold wrought with skill, and many other gifts
from the Phaeácian chiefs; let each of us
now add a caldron and a great tripod.
Our people can attend to that expense;
we'll be repaid by them for what we spend:
it would be far too hard for just one man
to give such gifts and get no recompense."

These were his words, and the Phaeácian chiefs
were pleased. Then each of them went home to sleep.
As soon as Dawn's rose fingers touched the sky,
they hurried to the ship, bearing their gifts
of bronze, which makes men strong. Alcínoüs,
with kingly force, went through the ship himself;
with care he stowed the gifts beneath the thwarts,
so that the oarsmen, when they stroked, might not
be blocked. Their gifts were given; now they all
assembled once again in his great hall.

Then, on behalf of them, Alcínoüs,
whose force was sacred, sacrificed a bull
to Zeus, the god of dark clouds, lord of all:
they offered up roast thighs, then with delight
they fell to feasting, even as divine
Demódocus, the harper men most prized,

Greek [1–28]

sang out. But while they banqueted, Odysseus
kept turning toward the glowing sun, most keen
to see it set: he could not wait to leave.
Just as, when day is done, a man who longs
for supper after tending two dark oxen
who've drawn his jointed plow through fallow fields
will greet with joy the setting of the sun
and—glad—at last head home to take his meal,
knees weary as he goes: so did Odysseus
welcome the setting of the sun. At once
he spoke to the Phaeácians, eager oarsmen,
and said—above all to Alcínoüs:

"Alcínoüs, the king whom all esteem,
as soon as you have poured wine offerings,
do send me off in peace. May you fare well.
All that my heart has wished is mine: the gifts
of friendship and an escort. May the gods
who rule high heaven bless these things for me,
and may I find my flawless wife unharmed,
at home with all the others I hold dear.
May you, remaining here, delight the wives
you've wed and all your children; may the gods
grant every good to you, and may your people
be proof against all evil."

So he said;
and all agreed and urged that he, their guest,
at last be taken home, for much good sense
informed his words. Then strong Alcínoüs
turned to his herald:

"Now, Pontónoüs,
mix wine within a bowl and see that all
within this hall are served, that we may pray
to father Zeus and send our guest away,
back to his native land."

▢ ▢ ▢

Greek [29–52]

These were his words.
The herald mixed the honeyed wine and gave
the bowl to all in turn; each man, in place,
poured out libations for the blessed gods.
But the divine Odysseus, standing up,
placed in Arété's hands the two-eared cup,
with these winged words:

     "O Queen, through all your years,
fare well until you meet old age and death,
just as all mortals must. And now I leave:
may you, within your house, find joy in these
your sons, your people, your Alcínoüs."

That said, divine Odysseus crossed the threshold.
To guide him to the swift ship and the shore,
Alcínoüs the mighty sent a herald.
Arété sent three women: one, to bear
his tunic and clean cloak; and one, the chest;
the third brought bread and wine. When they had reached
the ship and shore, his noble crew received
these things and stored them in the hollow hull.
They spread a blanket, spread a linen sheet
along the stern's half-deck, that he might sleep
in peace. He came aboard and quietly
lay down. The crew, in order, manned the thwarts;
and just as soon as they had loosed the hawser—
had freed it from a hole pierced through a stone—
the rowers bent, their oar blades beat the waters;
they churned the sea. Upon Odysseus' lids
there fell a sleep unbroken, deep, most sweet,
and much like death itself. As on a plain
four stallions yoked together feel the whip
and, leaping, gallop forward and complete
their journey, so did that stern leap and lift—
with foaming, roaring, frenzied waves behind it.
The ship coursed steady, sure: even the hawk,
fastest of birds, could not have matched her course.

Greek [53–87]

At that swift pace, she cleaved the surging sea,
bearing the man as cunning as the gods,
the man whose spirit suffered many trials,
warring with men and battling bitter seas.
But now he slept, at peace, forgetting griefs.
When that bright star glowed in the east, the one
that always heralds the firstlight of Dawn,
the ship approached dry land, its crossing done.

Along the coast of Ithaca there lies
a harbor dear to Phórcys, the old sea lord.
Two jutting headlands flank its mouth; seaward,
those cliffs are sheer, but on the sheltered side,
their slope is soft. The headland rocks keep out
the great surge raised by frenzied winds without;
within that gulf, stout ships can lie unbeached
as soon as they have reached their anchorage.
At harbor head there stands an olive tree
with slender leaves; nearby there lies a cave
that's dark and gracious, sacred to the nymphs
called Naiads. In that cave are mixing bowls
and amphoras of stone; there bees store honey.
There, too, long looms of rock allow the nymphs
to weave their cloth that glows like purple seas,
enchantingly. And never-failing streams
flow through that cave, which has two entryways:
the first lies north, and through that entrance men
descend; the other, facing south, is meant
to serve the gods—no mortals enter there;
it is the path of those who know no death.

The sailors knew that bay; they rowed straight in.
Thrust forward by the oarsmen's arms, the ship
was driven by such force and speed that she
ran hard—for half her length—onto the beach.
And when they went ashore from their benched craft,
lifting Odysseus, who was still asleep,
with his bright blanket and his linen sheet,

Greek [88-118]

they set him on the sands. Then to the beach
they brought the gifts Odysseus had received
from famed Phaeácians when he left for home—
Athena's gracious doing. And they heaped
these riches underneath the olive tree,
far from the road, so that no passerby
who reached that place before Odysseus woke
could steal his gifts. That done, they sailed for home.

But he who makes earth quake did not forget
the threats he'd hurled against the bright Odysseus,
and now Poseidon probed the plans of Zeus:

"Our father Zeus, the deathless gods cannot
pay honor to me if no mortal does—
not even those Phaeácians, who descend
from my own stock. I knew Odysseus was—
once he had suffered much—to reach his home:
in fact I did not try to block his course
once he'd received your promise and accord.
Yet these Phaeácians have carried him—
asleep—across the seas in their swift ship;
they set him down in Ithaca, with gifts
beyond all counting, bronze and gold and stores
of woven clothes, so many riches—more
than he could ever have brought back from Troy
had he returned unharmed with all his spoils."

Then Zeus, the shepherd of the clouds, replied:
"What have you, lord who shakes the earth, described?
You've never been dishonored or disprized
among the gods. Could any god deride
and scorn the oldest and the best of us,
the lord who rules a realm of such vast size?
And as for men, if any of them tries,
deluded by his power, to deny
the honor you deserve, you always can
. . .

take your revenge—that is, once he has sinned.
Your heart and will are free: do what you please."

Poseidon, lord who shakes the earth, replied:
"I'll do as you, god of dark clouds, advise
at once: I'm always ready to comply,
even as I am eager to avoid
your anger. The Phaeácians' handsome ship
is sailing homeward from its convoy trip;
and what I plan to do is shatter it,
so that they stop this traffic and desist
from serving men as guides. I mean to fling
a mighty mountain-mass around their city."

Zeus, shepherd of the clouds, then counseled him:
"Dear friend, I have a better stratagem:
When that returning ship is close to shore,
with all of the Phaeácians watching her,
transform her into stone, but in the shape
of their swift craft. They're sure to be amazed.
Then wrap their city in a mountain-mass."

That was enough. Poseidon hurried off: at once
he waited at the isle of the Phaeácians,
Schería, till the ship had neared the coast.
At that, the lord who shakes the earth approached
and turned her into stone. Then with a blow
of his great palm, he pressed her down; he set
that ship fast in the seabed. Then he left.

Now those Phaeácians, lovers of long oars,
men famed as master mariners, turned toward
their neighbors with winged words. And one would say,
sharing the stares of those who stood nearby:

"Who, even as our swift ship speeded home,
has chained her to the sea? For she had come
so close to shore; there's no mistaking her."   □ □ □

Greek [144-169]

These were their words—but they were baffled, still
bewildered by the scene they saw until
Alcínoüs explained:

                         "I can recall
an ancient prophecy, an oracle
my father told to me. He often said
that we would have to face Poseidon's wrath
since we, across his seas, gave safe escort
to all. Someday, when one of our fine ships
returned from convoy on the shadowed sea,
Poseidon would be sure to smash that craft
and wrap our city in a mountain-mass.
These were the words of my old father—now
all is fulfilled. But come, let everyone
do what I ask. When mortals reach our isle,
stop serving them as guides. To lord Poseidon
let's sacrifice twelve chosen bulls, so that
he may take pity on us and not wrap
our city in a mighty mountain-mass."

These were his words. In fear, they slaughtered bulls;
and all of the Phaeácian chiefs and elders
prayed to Poseidon as they ringed the altar.

But now Odysseus woke in his own land.
His sleep was done, but he had been too long
away; he did not know just where he was,
because Athena had enveloped him
in mist. She shielded him from prying eyes:
the goddess did not want him recognized—
not by the townsmen nor by his own wife—
until she'd counseled him and he'd contrived
a way to make those suitors pay the price
for all their crimes. So everything seemed strange
to one who was the ruler of this land:
the winding paths, the bays that sheltered ships,
the trees' rich foliage, the stalwart cliffs.

Greek [170-196]

He stood up, staring at his native land,
then sighed and struck his thighs with open hands.
In sorrow and lament, Odysseus said:

"What misery is mine? What mortals must
I meet in this new land that I now touch?
Are they unfeeling beings—wild, unjust?
Or do they welcome strangers? Does their thought
include fear of the gods? Where can I hide
the treasures I have brought? What way am I
to take? I should have left this wealth behind
in the Phaeácians' land and tried to find
another mighty king to welcome me
and offer escort for my homeward journey.
But now I do not know where I can stow
these gifts; I cannot leave them here, a prey
for any passerby who chanced this way.
They were not men of trust, not scrupulous,
that crew who left me on this unknown coast,
Phaeácian counselors and chieftains, those
who promised me my sunlit Ithaca
and then betrayed their word. May Zeus, the lord
of suppliants, who watches over all
and punishes men's faults, requite their sin.
But now I want to count my wealth, to see
if, when they sailed away in their lithe ship,
they did not plunder some of these rich gifts."

These were his words; and he began to count
the handsome tripods, caldrons, and the gold
and woven clothes. No thing was missing, yet
he wept for his own land; with long lament
he paced the shore beside the roaring surge.
Athena, taking on a young man's guise,
drew near: she seemed to be a shepherd—one
with gentle manners, like a chieftain's son.
She wore a well-wrought cloak in double folds
about her shoulders, and her shining feet

Greek [197-224]

were shod with sandals; in her hand she held
a lance. Odysseus saw her and was glad;
he went to meet her; with winged words he said:

"I greet you, friend: the first man I have met
on landing here. Don't be my enemy.
Save me and save my treasures. I beseech;
I clasp your knees as if you were a god.
And, too, I need to know the truth in full,
so tell me honestly: What land is this?
What men inhabit it? Is it an isle
lit by the sun? Or some peninsula
that juts out from the mainland with rich soil?"

Athena answered him: "You either are
a fool or else you come from very far:
you ask about a land that's known to all—
to men who live where Sun and Dawn first rise
and men who live behind the dark twilight.
This land is rough, not fit for chariots;
and though it is not spacious, it's not poor.
It has abundant wheat and wine and never
lacks rain or heavy dews. It has good pasture
for goats and cattle, and its woods are rich
with every sort of tree; its flowing streams
will never fail. And thus its fame has reached
to Troy itself, my friend, although they say
that Troy is far from these Achæan lands."

So went her words. The patient, bright Odysseus
was glad to find himself in his dear land,
rejoicing as he listened to the daughter
of aegis-bearing Zeus, Pallas Athena.
The words of his reply were winged, and yet
he did not tell the truth—he kept it back,
his heart forever churning stratagems:

□ □ □

Greek [225-255]

"Ah, even in broad Crete, far overseas,
I heard of Ithaca. Now I myself
have reached this island—bearing all this wealth.
And I have left behind as much again
to serve my children there. I fled that land
because I killed Idómeneus' dear son,
Orsílochus, a man who could outrun
all men who feed on grain in spacious Crete.
He'd tried to steal from me the spoils I'd won
at Troy, the wealth for which I paid with grief
in wars with men and quarrels with bitter seas:
he said that I'd refused to serve his father
at Troy and chose instead to take command
of my own men. My bronze spearhead in hand,
I waited on the road. I struck him as,
returning from the fields, he headed home:
none saw me or the comrade who had come
to help me—it was dark; I took his life
when skies were covered by the blackest night.
Once he had died beneath my pointed bronze,
I sought a ship at once; so I implored
some fine Phoenicians—and I paid them well—
to sail aboard their ship and then to land
at Pylos or at sunlit Elis where
Epeīans rule. But then, against their will,
a frenzied wind drove them off course (that crew
had no desire to cheat me). Thrust astray,
we reached this isle by night: with oars that strained,
we rowed into the bay. Though we had need
to eat, we did not even think of that;
as soon as we had beached, just as we were,
we stretched out on the shore. I was so weary
that sweet sleep took me quickly. Meanwhile they
had fetched my riches from the hollow ship
and set them near me on the sands. That done,
again embarked, they sailed toward gracious Sidon,
while I stayed here, in sorrow and confusion."

□ □ □

Greek [256-286]

These were his words. The gray-eyed goddess smiled
and stroked him with her hand: she'd taken on
the likeness of a woman tall and lovely,
whose hands can fashion work that glows with beauty.
And when she spoke to him, her words were winged:

"No one—not even if he were a god—
could hope to dodge the plots that you concoct,
unless he had consummate cunning, craft.
Tenacious, shameless, driven to deceive,
even in your own land you cannot leave
behind the tales and traps, the lies you love.
But come, enough of this. We're connoisseurs
of cunning: when it comes to words and wiles,
no mortal matches you; among the gods,
for guile and wisdom, I'm without a rival.
And yet you did not know me, did not see
that I was Pallas, born of Zeus, the one
who shields and shelters you in every trial,
who won for you the love of the Phaeácians.
Now I am here again to weave a plan:
we'll plot together—once we've hid the gifts
the fine Phaeácians, following my wish
and counsel, gave you when you left for home.
And, too, I want to tell you of the trials
that you will meet within your sturdy halls.
But use your strength to bear that sadness; lead
no one—no man, no woman—to suspect
that you, the man of wanderings, are back;
in silence suffer all your griefs; submit
to any violence that men inflict."

Odysseus, man of many wiles, replied:
"However keen his mind may be, it's hard
for any mortal man to know that he
is meeting you, Athena: you can take
so many shapes. But this I do know well:
You favored me in days gone by, through all

Greek [287–314]

the war that we Achæans waged at Troy.
But since the sack of Priam's citadel,
I've not seen you again; when we embarked
and Argive ships were scattered by a god,
I did not know that you, the child of Zeus,
had boarded my own ship to shelter me
from harm. And I have had to wander on,
a saddened heart within my breast, until
the gods delivered me from grief—until
your words, on the Phaeácians' splendid isle,
encouraged me: you led me to their city.
Now, in your father's name, I ask you this:
I don't believe I've reached my sunlit isle,
my Ithaca; and where I wander now
must be some other land: you would beguile
my wits—I think you mean to cheat my soul.
Tell me if I have truly reached my home."

Athena, gray-eyed goddess, then replied:
"Your native land is always in your thoughts;
and that is why I cannot give you up
to grief, for you are soft of speech, astute,
and prudent. Coming back from wanderings,
another man would—eagerly—have rushed
to see his wife and children in his house;
but you would wait to ask and learn; you'd first
test out your wedded wife, forever tried
by tears that have consumed her days and nights
as she, in sadness, stays in your old halls.
I never have despaired; my heart was sure
that, after losing all your comrades, you
would reach your home. And yet—this you must know—
I did not want to be Poseidon's foe;
for he, my father's brother, hated you
most bitterly: you blinded his dear son.
But come now, let me show you Ithaca,
so that you can be sure this is your land.
Here is the port of Phórcys, the old sea lord;

Greek [315–345]

at harbor head there stands the olive tree
with slender leaves; nearby there lies a cave
that's dark and gracious, sacred to the nymphs
called Naiads. And to them—within that broad
and vaulted grotto—you have often brought
your flawless hecatombs. Then see the woods
that clothe Mount Nériton."

As she said this,
the goddess freed Odysseus from his mist;
the land appeared, and he was cheered; happy
to see his Ithaca, he kissed the earth,
giver of grain. And he beseeched the nymphs
with his uplifted hands:

"You Naiad nymphs,
daughters of Zeus—you whom I never thought
to see again—accept my tender prayers.
As in the past, now, too, I'll give you gifts
if Zeus's daughter, goddess-guide of warriors,
should prove compassionate and let me live.
And may she bring to manhood my dear son."

Athena, gray-eyed goddess, then replied:
"Take heart: you need not fear such things. But now,
in the recess of that beguiling cave,
let's set your treasures: there they will be safe.
Then we'll devise the wisest course to take."

With this, she went into that shadowed space
to search for hiding places. And Odysseus
brought all of his Phaeácian treasures: gold,
tenacious bronze, and finely-woven clothes.
All these he stowed away with care. Athena,
daughter of aegis-bearing Zeus, closed off
the cave; she placed a stone before the door.
So, seated underneath the olive tree,
the two together plotted strategy,

Greek [346–372]

deving death for the outrageous suitors.
The gray-eyed goddess was the first to speak:

"Odysseus, man of many wiles, divine
son of Laértës, think of your attack
against the shameless suitors, men who act,
for three years now, like lords who own your house,
courting your godlike wife with wooers' gifts.
And she—sad longing always in her heart,
waiting for your return—gives hope to all:
she offers promises to every man;
she sends them messages. And yet her plans
are set on something else."

The man of wiles
replied: "Had I not heard your warning words,
within my halls I surely would have met
the squalid end of Agamemnon, son
of Átreus. Come, goddess, weave some plan
that lets me punish them. Stand at my side;
give me the gift of courage, as you did
when we tore loose Troy's gleaming diadem.
Were you, just as impetuous as then,
to stand beside me, gray-eyed goddess, I
could face even three hundred enemies:
I need your ready heart; I need your help."

Athena, gray-eyed goddess, then replied:
"I'll be beside you there; my watchful eyes
will not forget you when you start to act.
I'm sure that you will spatter the broad earth
with blood and brains of many who lay waste
your goods. But come, I'll see that you remain
unknown to all: I'll shrivel the fine skin
that sheathes your supple limbs; I'll rid your head
of its light hair, and dress you in such rags—
that men will shudder, seeing you so clad.
I'll dim your splendid eyes, and you will seem

Greek [373-401]

a mean and wretched thing to all the suitors
and to the wife and son you left behind
within your house. But now you must go off
to see the swineherd, keeper of your hogs;
he holds your son and wise Penelope
most dear. You'll find him with the sows that feed
beside the Raven's Rock, next to the spring
of Arethúsa, eating endless acorns
and drinking the dark water, for these add
abundant fat to hogs' rich flesh. Stay there
and, seated with the swineherd, do not fail
to ask him everything. And I, meanwhile,
will go to Sparta, land of lovely women,
to summon your dear son, Telémachus;
for he has gone to Meneláus' house
in spacious Lacedæmon. He would find
some tidings telling him you're still alive."

Odysseus, man of many wiles, replied:
"Why did you hide the truth from him? Your mind
knows everything. Or did you want him, too,
to suffer, wandering the restless sea
while other men lay waste his patrimony?"

Athena, gray-eyed goddess, then replied:
"That need not trouble you. It's I who sent
your son to Sparta; he can gain much fame
by venturing to see the son of Átreus.
And after all, among rich goods, fine feasts,
in Meneláus' house he sits in peace:
he has no troubles there. And though indeed
young men in a black ship now lie in wait,
most keen to kill your son before he can
return to his own land, I think their plan
will fail. It will be them instead—the suitors,
those who devour your goods—whom earth will cover."

□   □   □

Greek [402–428]

With this, Athena touched him with her wand.
She shriveled the smooth skin on his lithe limbs;
she took away the light hair from his head;
she sheathed his body with an old man's flesh;
she dimmed his eyes, the brightness of his glance;
she gave him ragged clothes, a squalid cloak
and tunic—tatters smirched with grime and smoke.
And over these she threw the giant hide
of a swift hind—worn thin and stripped of hair.
A staff, a battered pouch with its full share
of holes, slung by a cord—she had him wear
these relics, too.

          Their plan prepared, they parted.
The goddess left for lovely Lacedæmon;
she wanted to bring back Odysseus' son.

Greek [429-440]

BOOK XIV

Odysseus disguised:
his visit to Eumǽus, the loyal swineherd.

Eumǽus' account of the arrogant suitors;
Odysseus' fabricated tale of his identity and origin,
with news of Odysseus'
likely return.

A meal for the tattered guest.

Another fabricated tale to test Eumǽus.

Sleep.

Meanwhile Odysseus left the harbor, took
the rugged path that led him through the woods,
across the heights, to where Athena said
he'd find the swineherd, the most scrupulous
of all the servants bright Odysseus had—
the careful keeper of his master's goods.

Odysseus found him sitting at the gate,
before a courtyard in a sheltered place;
its circling walls were handsome, wide, and tall.
Confiding nothing to his mistress or
to old Laértës, he had built that court
to pen the herds of hogs his absent lord
had left behind. He'd hauled huge stones to gird
the yard, and he had topped the walls with thorns.
Around the court, to either side, he set
a row of pilings that were tough and thick,
oak trunks he'd stripped of their black bark; inside
the walls, to bed the sows, he built twelve sties
set side by side; and fenced within each pen,
some fifty brood sows lay along the ground.
But all the boars slept elsewhere. They were fewer
in number than the sows, because the suitors
were always calling for the fattest boars;
and now three hundred sixty head were left.
Beside the hogs, four watchdogs always slept—
as savage as wild beasts. It was Eumǽus
himself, a chief of men, who'd reared these hounds.

He now was fitting sandals to his feet;
his hands were busy as he shaped a piece
of finely-colored oxhide. All the young
herdsmen—the four who worked with him—were gone.
While three of them were roaming with their droves,
he had—begrudgingly—sent off the fourth
into the city, carrying a boar
for slaughter; it would serve the shameless feasts—
the suitors' gluttony. The dogs were quick

Greek [1–29]

to sight Odysseus; barking boisterously,
they rushed at him; he sat down prudently;
his staff fell from his hand. He'd have been bruised
on his own farm had not the swineherd dropped
his piece of hide and hurried through the gate:
with shouts and stones he drove those brutes away.

Then turning to his master, he said this:
"Old man, one moment more and they'd have mauled
and mangled you, and I'd have faced disgrace,
your bitter tirade—and I've had enough
of sorrows heaped upon me by the gods.
Here I lament and mourn a godlike lord;
I tend to these fat hogs for others now—
they'll feast upon these pigs, while he may be
in need, a hungry wanderer in cities
and lands of men whose speech is foreign—if
he's still alive and sees the sun's bright rays.
But come now; let us go into my hut:
that way, old man, once you have had enough
of food and wine, you then can tell me where
you come from and the griefs that were your share."

That said, the sturdy swineherd showed the way
and led him to a seat strewn with soft twigs;
across these he had spread a broad goatskin,
shaggy and black—his blanket when he slept.
Odysseus, glad to be a welcome guest,
responded to the swineherd with these words:

"Stranger, may Zeus and all the deathless gods,
since you have welcomed me so graciously,
fulfill your deepest wish."

                                And you, Eumǽus
the swineherd, then replied. These were your words:
"Dear guest, I'd never slight the least of strangers,
not even one more wretched than you are;

Greek [30-57]

for it is Zeus who sends to us all beggars
and strangers; and a gift, however small,
means much when given by a man like me,
for servants always must maintain their guard
when they have masters younger than themselves.
As for my own true lord, the gods have barred
his homeward path; he would have shown me love
and gifted me with everything: a house,
a bit of land, a wife whom many sought—
all that a gracious master gives a man
who works so hard and sees what he has done
win heaven's favor. And, because the work
in which I have persisted prospers, he,
my master, would have done so much for me,
had he lived here until old age; but he
is dead. And would that all of Helen's race,
brought to its knees, had died, even as she
herself had loosened many warriors' knees.
For he, too, in support of Agamemnon,
went off to Ílion, land of fine foals,
to fight against the Trojans."

                         Saying this,
he quickly bound his tunic with his belt
and hurried to the pigpens, picking out
a pair of younglings; and he butchered both,
and then he singed and sliced and skewered them.
And with the roasted meats still on the spit
and smoking hot, the swineherd served Odysseus,
sprinkling white barley meal upon the chunks.
Within a bowl of ivy-wood he mixed
sweet wine, then sat and faced his guest. He said:

"Now, stranger, eat what servants have to offer:
young pigs. The fattened hogs are for the suitors,
whose hearts have no restraint, no trace of pity.
The blessed gods do not love cruelty;
they honor justice and men's seemly deeds.

Greek [58-84]

Even the violent and vicious, when
they land on foreign soil and sack such spoils
as Zeus concedes to them—even such men,
who, when their ships are full, sail home again,
within their hearts are fearful of the gods.
But this band here has surely heard some word
from heaven saying that my lord has died
most miserably; so they will not woo
even as law and custom say they should.
And they will not go back to their own homes;
at ease and arrogant, they now consume—
not sparing anything—my master's goods.
With every day and night that comes from Zeus,
they do not sacrifice just one or two
fat swine; as for the wine they drink, they drain
our stores beyond all measure. For my lord
had untold riches, more than any lord
in Ithaca itself or on the dark
mainland—not even twenty men could match
his wealth. But let me tally it for you:
He has twelve herds of cattle on the mainland,
as many flocks of sheep, as many droves
of swine; as many ample herds of goats
are pastured for him there by Ithacans
and foreigners. And on this island's rim,
so many goats—eleven herds—are his,
watched over by his trusty guardians.
Each herdsman always drives one goat a day—
the fattest he can find—to serve the suitors.
I guard and watch these hogs and, after I
have chosen well, I send the finest boar."

These were his words. With gusto, eagerly,
Odysseus ate the meat and drank the wine
in silence while, maneuvering, his mind
was sowing seeds of sorrow for the suitors.
But once the visitor had been refreshed,
Eumæus filled his usual wine bowl

Greek [85-112]

brimful and handed it to his dear guest.
Odysseus took it, happy to accept;
then to his host he spoke with these winged words:

"Who was the man who bought you with his wealth,
the rich and mighty man of whom you spoke?
You say he died while helping Agamemnon.
Say more, for I may know of such a man.
Zeus and the other deathless gods know well
if I indeed have seen him and can tell
some news to you; I've wandered wide and far."

The swineherd answered him: "No wanderer
who claimed he'd heard about my master could
convince his wife and his beloved son.
For vagabonds have far more need of food
and shelter than of truth: they're quick to lie.
Whoever wanders here, onto this isle,
soon plies my mistress with his lying tales.
She greets and welcomes him and asks for all
details, and from her lids the sad tears fall;
so women are, when husbands die far off.
You, too, old man, would let your lying flourish
if someone gave you clothes—a cloak, a tunic.
By now the hounds and the swift birds have ripped
the marrow from my master's bones; his spirit
has fled from him; or fishes of the sea
have eaten him and left his bones on land,
along the shore, beneath the many sands.
Yes, he has died far off; and long lament
is all that's left for those who loved him so—
above all, me: I'll never find a master
as gentle as he was, no matter where
I go, not even if I should return
to my own father's and my mother's home,
where I was born—and where they nurtured me.
But I'm not heartsick for my family,
though I do want to see them and to be

Greek [113-142]

in my own land; it is for him I long—
Odysseus, distant one. Though he is gone,
dear guest, I hesitate to name him, for
he cherished me most lovingly. And I
call him my lord, although he is not here."

Then patient, bright Odysseus answered him:
"Dear friend, I know you have no taste for tidings;
you say he won't come back; your heart won't trust
my news; and yet I do not speak untruths
but under oath: Odysseus will return.
And let my good word be requited when
he reaches home again, for then you can
give me a tunic and a cloak—fine clothes.
But until then, despite my need, I'll not
take anything. For I despise a man,
however poor he is, who would descend
to idle tales: to me that is more hateful
than Hades' gates. Now let the gods be witness—
above all, Zeus—and, too, your cordial table
as well as good Odysseus' hearth, the place
where I now rest: It all will come to pass
as I have said. Odysseus will return
within this year, just when an old moon ends
and a new moon begins; he'll reach his home,
and there he'll take revenge on all of those
who prey upon his wife and splendid son."

And you, Eumæus, then replied to him:
"Old man, I'll not be called on to reward
good tidings: we won't see my lord's return.
But drink in peace; let's think of other things.
Do not remind me of his fate; my soul
grows sad within my breast when I am told
about my gentle lord. Forget your oath;
I simply long to see him in his country—
as do Penelope and old Laértës
and the godlike Telémachus. But now

Greek [143-173]

it is his son for whom I always worry.
The gods had nurtured him just like a sapling:
I thought that he, so sturdy and so comely,
would stand among all men as one no less
than his dear father. But some god or else
some human being jarred his senses, led
his mind astray; he's sailed away to sacred
Pylos to hear about his father, but
along his homeward path, the suitors wait
to ambush and destroy him, so that, nameless,
the line of the divine Arcēīsius
may vanish from the land of Ithaca.
But let that be; he either will fall prey
or else, with help from Cronos' son, escape—
Zeus may protect him yet. Instead, old friend,
come tell me now the sorrows you have met.
And tell me this, and tell it truthfully:
Who are you? Of what father were you born?
Where is your city, where your family?
On what ship did you sail? Why did that crew
bring you to Ithaca? And who were they?
For surely you did not come here on foot."

Odysseus, man of many wiles, replied:
"I'll tell you all; there's nothing I shall hide.
Yet even if we two had food enough
and sweet wine at our side within this hut
to eat and drink in peace as long as we
might want, and with no work to interrupt
our talk—with others to take care of that—
not even then, though I should spend a year,
could I tell all my tale of sufferings.
The gods have willed so many trials for me.

"I come from stock whose home is spacious Crete.
My father was a rich man; in his house
were many other sons born of his wife,
but my own mother was a concubine,

Greek [174-202]

bought as a slave. Yet Castor, son of Hylax—
whom I declare and swear my father—dealt
with me as if I were his lawful son.
The people honored him among the Cretans
as if he were a god, for his good fortune,
his wealth and noble sons. But then death called,
and fate took him away to Hades' halls.
His sons were arrogant and, casting lots,
divided the inheritance; to me
they left the least of portions, just a house.
And yet my prowess won for me a wife
whose parents owned much land: I was no coward
or blunderer. Now all my force is gone;
but looking at the stubble that you see,
I think that you can judge what was the wheat.
My many griefs have surely lessened me,
but once I had such devastating strength
and daring, gifts of Árës and Athena.
When I picked out the sturdiest of men
to join me as I ambushed enemies,
prepared to savage them, I had no fear
of death; my soul was sure; I was the first
to leap ahead, to drive my deadly lance
against the ranks I'd driven back. For war
was what I chose; I had no fondness for
working the land or caring for a house
or raising worthy children; I held dear
oared ships and battles, arrows, polished spears—
the deadly things that fill most men with fear.
Perhaps a god had made me fond of these:
what pleases one man need not please another.

"Before we sons of the Achǽans reached
the plain of Troy, nine times I'd led our men
and swift ships off to wars in foreign lands.
I'd won much booty: I had picked out all
I wanted as my spoils, and then by lot
I won still more. My house grew prosperous;

Greek [203-233]

I was a man the Cretans feared, revered.
And so, when Zeus the thunderer designed
the hateful voyage that would sap the knees
of many warriors, the Cretans asked
both brave Idómeneus and me to lead
their fleet to Ílion. The people's voice
insisted—hard and clear. We had no choice.

"We sons of the Achǽans fought at Troy
for nine years. In the tenth, when we'd destroyed
the citadel of Priam, we sailed off;
we headed home. But then a god contrived
to scatter the Achǽans far and wide.
And as for me, all-knowing Zeus devised
disaster. For no more than one month, I
delighted in my children, lawful wife,
and riches; but my spirit urged me on
to sail to Egypt with my godlike friends
as soon as I could fit out ships with care.

"I fitted out nine ships; the crews were quick
to gather. For six days they banqueted:
I did not stint; I offered many beasts
for sacrifices to the gods and feasts.
And on the seventh day, we went aboard
and sailed away from spacious Crete; as if
downstream, we ran at ease, a fine north wind
behind us. All our ships sped on, intact;
and none of us fell sick. All safe, we sat;
the wind and helmsmen kept our fleet on track.
In five days' time we reached the river Nile's
majestic waters; in that flow I moored
my agile ships. And these were my commands:
Most of my faithful men I asked to stand
beside the ships as watchmen; and I sent
a few to find a lookout, scout the land.
But reckless greed and fury gripped my crews;
nothing could check their frenzy; they began

Greek [234-262]

to ravage the fair fields, to carry off
the women and young children, kill the men.
The tumult reached the town at once. At dawn
all of the plain was filled with flashing bronze,
with men on foot and men on chariots.
Among my comrades, Zeus, the thunder lord,
cast fatal panic; no one dared to face
attack; on every side we met disgrace.
Their sharp shafts found and felled so many; those
who lived were carried back to work as slaves.
But it was Zeus himself who sent this thought
into my mind (though I'd have rather died,
have met my end in Egypt then, for I
was yet to face a swarm of miseries):
At once I freed my head from my stout casque
and freed my shoulders from my shield and cast
my lance away; and then I hurried toward
the chariot horses of the king. I clutched
and kissed his knees, and he delivered me
mercifully: he set me in his chariot
and led me, weeping, to his house. The crowd
was keen to kill me; many, angry, rushed
with ash-wood lances. But he held them off;
he feared the god of strangers, Zeus, the lord
whose wrath avenges every cruelty.

"I stayed there seven years, and there I gathered
much wealth. All the Egyptians gave me gifts.
But when, with turning time, the eighth year came,
I met a man of matchless greed and guile,
one who had cheated many; that Phoenician
convinced me, cunningly, to go with him
to his Phoenicia, where he had his goods
and houses. There I stayed for twelve full months.
But with the days and months of that year gone,
the round of seasons done, the new year come,
he had me board a ship bound out to Libya.
His pretext was this lie: He said that I

Greek [263–296]

could help him take his cargo there. In fact,
once we'd arrived he meant to sell my hide
for some huge price. Indeed I went aboard
with some misgivings, but I had no choice.
A swift and strong north wind behind us, we
coursed in mid-sea, beyond the isle of Crete—
but Zeus had something more malign in mind.
With Crete behind, no other land in sight,
only the sky and sea, the son of Cronos
hurled black storm clouds above our hollow ship;
below us, waves grew dark. At one same moment,
Zeus thundered and sent down a lightning bolt
against the hull; hit hard by that, our ship
whirled round full circle, filled with sulfurous smoke.
The crew were cast into the sea and carried
like sea crows by the surge round our black ship.
A god deprived them of their safe return.
But as for me, when I was most beset,
Zeus set the stout mast of the dark-prowed ship
into my hands, that I might once again
escape my death. I held that mast hard fast
and then was borne along by savage winds.

"For nine days I was dragged along; but on
the dark night of the tenth, a giant comber
thrust me, a tumbling body, on the shore
of the Thesprótians. Their lord and king,
Pheídon, who asked for nothing in return,
received me; I'd been found by his own son:
when I was weary, weak, and cold, he took
my hand and led me to his father's house
and clothed me in a tunic and a cloak.
I heard about Odysseus there. In fact
the king had welcomed him—a cherished guest—
when he had stopped along his homeward path.
And Pheídon showed me all the riches that
Odysseus had amassed: bronze, iron, gold
worked with painstaking craft. There were enough

Greek [297-324]

treasures that he had stored in the king's hold
to feed ten generations of his line.
The king said that Odysseus now had gone
to hear Dodóna's oracle, the tall
and sacred oak that speaks the will of Zeus;
and after he came back, Odysseus meant
to sail to Ithaca, his native land,
returning in the open or by stealth.
And in my presence, even as he poured
libations in his house, King Pheídon swore
that everything stood ready—ship and crew—
to take Odysseus back to his dear land.

"But I departed first: by chance a boat
of the Thesprótians was setting out
to reach Dulíchium, land rich with wheat.
He told them to conduct me there with care
to King Acástus; but that crew preferred
a vicious plan, that I might end my days
in utter misery. When we were far
from land, they tried to make a slave of me.
They stripped me of my tunic and my cloak
and gave me what you see: these squalid clothes—
these torn and tattered rags. At dusk they reached
the fields of Ithaca. Within their boat
they tied me fast and hard with twisted rope,
and then they went ashore; along the coast
they ate their supper quickly. But the gods
themselves undid the knots with ease; set free,
I wrapped my tattered clothes around my head;
and after sliding down the landing plank,
I let the sea reach to my chest, and then
I used my arms as oars; I swam and soon
touched land, but at a point far off from them.
I crept up to a spot with leafy thickets,
and there I waited, crouched. They searched about
on every side; their cries were loud; but when
a longer search seemed useless, they went back

Greek [325-356]

on board the hollow ship. It was the gods
who hid me easily, then led me here
into the fold of one who understands:
to let me live may be what fate has planned."

And you, Eumǽus, then replied to him:
"Ah, guest, harassed by griefs, my soul is stirred
as you retell your wanderings and trials.
Yet one thing leaves me unconvinced: I think
your tale about Odysseus is amiss.
And why, when it is useless, do you lie?
A man like you! I, too, know much about
my lord's return: I know that all the gods
so hated him that he was not allowed
to fall at Troy, nor did they let him die—
once he had wound up all the threads of war—
within the arms of his dear family.
Then all of the Achǽans would have heaped
a burial mound for him; he would have won
much glory for his son in time to come.
Instead, the storm-wind spirits—fiendish Harpies—
have swept him off; his death was without glory.

"I stay here with my swine, far from the city;
I only go there when Penelope—
wise woman—calls for me, when someone comes
with tidings. Everyone then crowds around
that man and questions him on every point—
both those who mourn my master, gone so long,
and those who take delight in wasting all
his wealth and never paying out. But I
don't care to probe and question since the time
I was beguiled by an Aetólian:
that man had murdered someone; after he
had wandered the wide earth, he came to me.
I took him in, received him graciously.
He said that he, in Crete, had seen Odysseus—
who had been welcomed by Idómeneus—

Greek [357–382]

mending his ships, the victims of a tempest.
He also said that by the early summer
or harvesttime, Odysseus would return
with godlike comrades, bringing back much wealth.
You, too, old man of many sorrows, since
it was a god who brought you to my door,
don't try to win my heart with false reports;
do not beguile me. It is not for this
that I shall show you kindness or respect,
but for my fear of Zeus, the god of guests—
and, too, I pity you in all of this."

Odysseus, man of many wiles, replied:
"The heart within your chest is slow to grant
belief, for even with an oath I can't
convince or move you. Come, let's make a pact;
in time to come, the gods who hold Olympus
will stand as witnesses for both of us.
If your dear lord returns to his own house,
then clothe me in a tunic and clean cloak
and send me to Dulíchium, the isle
I want to reach. But if your lord does not
return, if what I said is false, incite
your men to hurl me down from some great height,
so that all other beggars may think twice
before they dare to lie."

                    To this, the bright
swineherd replied: "Dear friend, indeed I might
win fame and fortune among men if I
who was your host within this hut, who cared
and shared, should kill you then, end your dear life—
and then go off and pray in peace to Zeus!
But now it's time to eat: I hope my friends
will soon be back again—we can prepare
a hearty supper all of us can share."

□   □   □

Greek [383–408]

Such were the words each heard the other urge.
Meanwhile the hogs and herdsmen had returned.
The men shut in the swine to sleep in sties;
once penned, the sows let loose tremendous cries.
The good swineherd asked this of all his men:

"Bring out your fattest boar for me to kill;
this stranger comes from far—a handsome meal
for him will serve us, too; for after all,
it takes long days to raise these white-tusked boars,
while others, spending nothing, eat our work."

That said, with cruel bronze he split stout logs;
and they brought in a five-year-old fat hog.
They set him near the hearth. The good swineherd
did not forget the deathless ones; his heart
was pious. First he cast into the fire
the hairs he'd plucked from that white-tusked boar's head
as he, beseeching all the gods, implored
return for dear Odysseus, his wise lord.
Then, rising to full height, he lifted up
a chunk of oak he'd saved for this: He struck
the beast. Life left the boar. The others cut
his throat and singed and sliced him quickly. Next,
the swineherd took raw flesh from all the limbs
and laid these bits on sacrificial fat,
then sprinkled them with barley meal and cast
that offering into the flames. The rest
was skewered, roasted carefully, then drawn
off from the spits. The platters were heaped high.
The swineherd stood and portioned out the boar
in seven proper shares. Now, with a prayer,
he set aside one portion for the nymphs
and Hermes, Maia's son. Then each received
his serving. To Odysseus, as an honor,
he gave the white-tusked boar's long chine—entire;
and this indeed delighted his dear master.
Odysseus, man of many wiles, gave thanks: ▢ ▢ ▢

Greek [409–439]

"Eumæus, may you be as dear to Zeus,
our father, as you are to me; you've given
to one as poor as I am, your best portion."

To this, Eumæus, you replied: "Whatever
we have is yours to share, afflicted stranger:
be happy with this supper. For the god
will give one thing and will withhold another
as pleases him, since all is in his power."

That said, the swineherd offered up the share
he'd set aside for the enduring gods
and, after pouring out libations, passed
the bright wine to Odysseus, who had sacked
great cities. Then it was Mesaūlius
who brought the bread, a servant whom Eumæus
had purchased from the Táphians on his own;
his lord was gone, and he'd not called upon
his mistress or the old Laértës—he
gave his own goods to get Mesaūlius.
Their fare was ready now; their hands reached out.
Then, when they'd had their fill of food and drink,
Mesaūlius took the bread away; and they,
sated with bread and meat, now wanted sleep.

That night was foul, the moon was hid, and Zeus
sent rain that never stopped; the west wind struck
with drenching gusts. Then shrewd Odysseus spoke.
He wanted to try out his swineherd host,
to see if he would strip off his own cloak—
or ask for one that his young men had on—
and give it to the guest for whom he cared:

"Hear me, Eumæus, and your other friends:
I mean to boast about an incident.
Wine can incite: even a cautious man
finds folly in his cups—he's spurred to dance
and aimless laughter, and set loose to chant

Greek [440-465]

and babble things that never should be said.
But since I have begun, I'll carry on.
Would I were young and with my strength intact,
enough to match my force when we attacked
beneath the walls of Troy, for we had planned
and set an ambush there. And in command
were Meneláus, son of Átreus,
Odysseus, and myself: we had three chiefs—
those two invited me along to lead.
When we reached Troy and its steep walls, we crouched
among dense thickets near the town, behind
the reeds and swampland—huddled under shields.
The north wind struck, the night was foul, and snow
flaked down and covered us like rime; the cold
was bitter; ice began to coat our shields.
The other men had brought along their cloaks:
they slept at ease, their shoulders under shields.
But I, when setting out—quite stupidly
forgetting that the cold might threaten me—
had left my cloak behind with friends; I brought
my shield and shining belt, and nothing else.
But when the night had reached its final third
and stars had crossed the zenith point, I turned
and nudged Odysseus with my elbow. He
was near me; he awoke; he heard me plead:
'Odysseus, man of many wiles, divine
son of Laértës, I shall die tonight.
I did not bring my cloak. Some demon trapped
and tricked me; I have nothing here to wrap
around my tunic. I have no escape.'
These were my words. Then he, adept at wiles
and war, devised a scheme. His voice was soft:
'Keep still; no one must hear you.' Then he propped
his head against his elbow and called out:
'Listen: While I was sleeping, some gods sent
a dream to me: my friends, it said that we
are too far from our ships and men; we need
more comrades here. Let someone hurry now

Greek [466–496]

to Agamemnon, shepherd of us all,
and ask for reinforcements from the shore.'
Thóas, Andræmon's son, got up at once
and rushed to reach our fleet. He had thrown off
his purple cloak; I gladly snatched it up
and wrapped myself in it; and then I slept
till Dawn, whose robe is cloth of gold, returned.
Would I were young and with my strength intact,
for then, out of respect for bravery,
some herdsman here would hand his cloak to me.
Instead, my wretched rags provoke their scorn."

And you, Eumæus, answered: "You have told
your story flawlessly, old man; you chose
your words with care; not one was wasted—so
you'll have a cloak and all else that is owed
to one who comes as sorry suppliant.
For now, that is. Tomorrow you must wear
your rags again: there's little here to spare;
each man has just one cloak—and nothing more.
But when the dear son of Odysseus comes,
he'll give you cloak and tunic—handsome clothes—
and send you on to where your heart would go."

That said, he rose and, near the fire, prepared
a place to serve Odysseus as a bed.
On this he laid the skins of sheep and goats,
and there Odysseus lay. The swineherd spread
a thick cloak over him, one kept at hand
to serve when storms had soaked his daily dress.

Odysseus rested there, and next to him
the young men slept. But that was hardly where
the swineherd meant to lie. He would not rest
far from the boars. He meant to go outdoors,
which made Odysseus glad: it meant that while
he was far off, his goods were closely watched.
Eumæus, making ready, slung his sharp

Greek [497-528]

sword over his stout shoulders; then, to fend
the wind, he wrapped himself in a thick cloak
and in the fleecy hide of a great goat.
He took a pointed javelin to keep
both men and dogs at bay. Then he went out
to sleep beside the white-tusked boars beneath
a hollow rock, out of the north wind's reach.

Greek [529-533]

BOOK XV

Telémachus urged homeward by Athena;
his departure from Sparta with handsome gifts
from Meneláus and Helen.

In Pylos, a befriended fugitive,
Theoclýmenus the seer.

Departure by sea for Ithaca.

.

Odysseus testing Eumǽus again.

Eumǽus' tale of his own life.

.

The safe arrival of Telémachus in Ithaca.

The omen of the hawk and dove.

The prophecy of Theoclýmenus.

.

Toward the farmstead.

Athena left for Sparta's spacious plains
to prod Odysseus' son: the time had come
for his return. She found the two young men
at rest in Meneláus' portico.
Sweet sleep held Nestor's son, but it had not
yet touched Telémachus; tenacious thoughts
about his father's fate kept him awake
throughout the deathless night. Beside him stood
Athena, gray-eyed goddess. And she said:

"Telémachus, don't wander from your house
too long when you have left behind your wealth,
with men so arrogant within your gates;
such men might well divide and then devour
your goods; your journey here would then prove useless.
But now be quick: convince lord Meneláus
to send you on your way, so that you may
still find your flawless mother in your house;
by now her father and her brothers urge
Penelope to wed Eurýmachus;
he's always offering suitor's gifts—more rich
than any gifts the other wooers give.
Take care, for she may try—against your will—
to carry off some treasures from your halls.
You know what sort of soul a woman's breast
may hold: she is so ready to forget
a husband who is gone; she never asks
about the children born of her first bed;
she would enrich the house of her new lord.
So when you have returned, be quick to choose
one handmaid, she who seems the worthiest:
into her care consign all you possess,
until the gods reveal the bride you'll wed.

"I also tell you this—keep it in mind:
Along the straits that separate rough Samos
from Ithaca, the strongest suitors wait
. . .

Greek [1-29]

for you; they're keen to kill; they want you dead
before you ever reach your own dear land.
But I don't think that is to be: before
that happens, many suitors, who devour
your wealth, will lie beneath the earth, well cloaked.
And yet take care: be sure your ship stays far
from island shores; and sail by night as well
as by daylight; a deathless god will send
a kindly wind astern, your guardian.
And when you've reached the nearest promontory
of Ithaca, let both your ship and crew
head for the town, while you go off at once
to seek your swineherd, he who tends your hogs,
a caring, kindly man. You can sleep there.
And send the swineherd off as messenger
down to the city: wise Penelope
must learn that you've come back from Pylos safely."

That said, Athena left for high Olympus.
Telémachus awakened Nestor's son
from sweet sleep; with his heel he nudged his friend
and said:

   "Peisístratus, we must be off;
get up; bring out the colts with eager hoofs
and yoke them to the chariot."

      To this,
Peisístratus replied: "Telémachus,
I know you're keen to leave, but we can't ride
through shadowed night. Since Dawn will soon arrive,
let's wait for Meneláus, famous spearman,
bright son of Átreus; he'll carry out
our gifts and load them on the chariot
and send us on our way with warm farewells.
A guest will keep in memory, held close,
the gift of friendship given by his host."
□ □ □

Greek [30–55]

These were his words. And Dawn, whose throne is gold,
came soon. And so came Meneláus, lord
of wild war-cries; he'd risen from the bed
he shared with fair-haired Helen. Seeing him,
Odysseus' dear son hurried: he threw on
his glowing tunic and, round his robust
shoulders, an ample cloak. Telémachus,
the dear son of divine Odysseus, went
to meet lord Meneláus, and he said:

"Zeus-nurtured Meneláus, son of Átreus,
captain of men, do send me home at once;
by now I long for my dear land, my house."

The lord of the wild war-cry then replied:
"Telémachus, I'd never hold you back
if you long for return; I'd look askance
at any man who keeps a guest too long
or too impatiently cuts short his stay.
All things are best when done without excess:
it is as wrong to hurry off a guest
who does not want to leave as to detain
a man who longs for home. Kind care for those
who stay—and warm farewells for those who go.
But now, do wait: I'll bring the precious gifts
and set them on your chariot; they all
will be arrayed, displayed; and I shall tell
my women to prepare a meal that draws
on my rich stores—and serve it in the hall.
First eat your fill and then attend to fame,
honor, and gain: the things that journeying
across the broad and boundless earth will bring.
And if you're keen to make your way through Argos
and Hellas, I'll yoke horses; at your side
I'll be your guide to cities men have built.
And those we visit will not be remiss:
they certainly will give us handsome gifts—
. . .

Greek [56-83]

at least a lovely brazen tripod or
a caldron, or two mules—or a gold cup."

Telémachus' reply was wise, precise:
"Zeus-nurtured Meneláus, son of Átreus,
captain of men, I'd rather hurry home;
I've left my goods without a guard. May I
myself not die or find that someone stole
some handsome treasure from my halls while I
was searching for my father."

Hearing that,
the lord of wild war-cries was quick to ask
his wife and maids to draw upon his stores
and serve the morning meal. Now Etëóneus,
Boéthus' son, who'd risen from his bed
and lived nearby, rushed in; the son of Átreus
asked him to light the fire and roast the meats.
He heard, and he obeyed. Then Meneláus
himself went down into his fragrant stores—
but not alone: beside him Helen went
and Megapénthës. When they reached the place
where precious treasures lay, the son of Átreus
took up a two-eared cup, while Megapénthës,
his son, when asked, was quick to carry off
a silver mixing bowl. And Helen stopped
before the chests that held embroidered robes,
those her own hands had woven. That fair woman
chose one, the largest and the loveliest
for its adornments. Like a star it glowed,
there where it lay beneath the other clothes.
Then they retraced their steps until they found
Telémachus. And Meneláus said:

"Telémachus, may Zeus, the thundering lord
of Hera, as your heart desires, grant
your safe return. Of all the gifts for guests
stored in my house—my precious treasures—I

Greek [84–113]

give you the handsomest and richest prize:
this crafted mixing bowl designed in silver,
with gold about the rim: Hephæstus' work.
Courageous Phædimus, the king of Sidon,
gave me this bowl when, on my homeward path,
I was his welcome guest. I want to give
this gift to you."

That said, the son of Átreus
gave to his guest the two-eared cup; and then
his son, the stalwart Megapénthës, offered
the splendid silver mixing bowl from Sidon.
Last, Helen of the lovely face drew near;
the robe was in her arms. She turned to him:

"Dear boy, I, too, would give a gift to you:
memento of the handiwork of Helen,
this robe is for your bride upon the day
of your glad wedding. Meanwhile let it wait
in your dear mother's care, in your own house.
And may you reach your native land in joy."

That said, she handed him the robe, which he
was happy to receive. Peisístratus
gazed at these gifts with wonder in his heart
and stowed them all within the chariot box.
Then fair-haired Meneláus led them both
into the house; the two young men sat down.
That they might wash their hands, a servant poured
fresh water from a lovely golden jug
into a silver basin; at their side
she placed a polished table. The old housewife
brought bread and ample meat from her rich stores.
Boéthus' son divided up the portions,
and famous Meneláus' son poured wine.
Their fare was ready now; their hands reached out.
Then, with their need for food and drink appeased,
Telémachus and Nestor's noted son

Greek [114–144]

were quick to yoke their horses and to mount
their painted chariot. Across the loud
courtyard and colonnade, they now rode out.
But fair-haired Meneláus, son of Átreus,
trailed after them; in his right hand he held
a golden cup of honeyed wine: a last
libation, to be poured before they left.
He stood before the horses as he pledged:

"Fair voyaging, young men; to Nestor, king
and shepherd of his people, take my greetings:
when we Achǽan sons made war at Troy,
he was most gentle with me—fatherly."

Telémachus' reply was thoughtful, wise:
"Be sure, o king whom Zeus has nurtured, we—
just as you ask us to—will tell him this
as soon as we reach Pylos. Would that I
on my return to Ithaca might find
Odysseus home again, that I might speak
to him of the warm welcome I received
from you—and of the many gifts I bring."

And even as he spoke, upon his right
a bird flew by: an eagle with a white,
enormous tame goose in his talons, one
he'd snatched up from the courtyard. And a crowd
of men and women followed him with shouts.
But then the eagle neared; off to the right
he veered and cut across the horses' path.
That sight delighted all of them; their hearts
rejoiced. The first to speak was Nestor's son:

"Captain of men, Zeus-nurtured Meneláus,
decipher what this sign sent by a god
might mean: was it designed for you or us?"

□ □ □

Greek [145-168]

And Meneláus, man of Árës, pondered:
he wondered what might be the right reply.
But in his stead, the long-robed Helen said:

"Listen, as deathless ones enlighten me,
I'll tell you what this prophecy must mean:
the things I think will come to pass. Just as
this eagle from the mountains—where he has
his birth, his brood, his nest—swooped down to snatch
the tame goose, so Odysseus, coming back
from many woes and wanderings, will take
revenge; or else he is already home
and setting snares that spell the suitors' doom."

Telémachus' reply was wise, precise:
"Should Hera's husband, Zeus the thunder lord,
grant that, I'll pray to you as to a god."

That said, he lashed the horses and they raced
across the city to the plain; all day
they shook the yoke that lay upon their necks.
The sun sank; all the roads were dark with shadows.
Telémachus and Nestor's son gained Phérae;
they spent the night as guests of Díoclës,
son of Alphéus' son, Ortílochus.

As soon as Dawn's rose fingers touched the sky,
they yoked their team of horses; quick to mount
their painted chariot, across the loud
courtyard and colonnade, they now rode out
and, as they lashed their horses, raced away.
They soon had reached the towering fortress-town
of Pylos. There, Telémachus insisted:

"Peisístratus, can I depend on you?
Will you fulfill my wish? We are old friends,
for we inherit friendship that descends
from fathers who were comrades. I am just

as old as you, and journeying together
brings deeper sympathy. Dear son of Nestor,
don't take me past the point where my ship waits,
but leave me there; for if I reach the gates
of your dear father, he will have me stay,
even against my will, as guest, but I
must reach my Ithaca without delay."

These were his words. The son of Nestor thought
of how to help his friend. This way seemed best:
He turned the horses toward the shore and ship
and, near the stern, unloaded all the gifts,
the clothes and gold that Meneláus gave;
and then he spurred his friend with these winged words:

"Be quick to board—both you and all your crew—
before I reach the house and break this news
to my dear father. For my heart is sure
of this: His will is so imperious—
he'll rush to see that you don't leave. And then
you'll stay: he won't go back with empty hands.
In any case, I'll have to face his wrath."

That said, he turned the foals with flowing manes
to Pylos, and he soon had reached the town.
Telémachus called to his men. He urged:
"Friends, set our gear in place on our black ship,
so we can board and finish up our trip."

These were his words. They heard, obeyed; at once
his comrades took their places at the thwarts.
The ship was ready and Telémachus
was praying, sacrificing to Athena
along the shore, astern, when there appeared
a stranger, fugitive from Argos, where
he'd killed a man. That stranger was a seer.
His forebear was Melámpus, famous prophet,
who long ago had lived in Pylos, land

Greek [198-226]

of ample herds; a man of wealth, he had
a splendid home. But when Melámpus left
his native land and went to Phýlacë,
strong Néleus, most renowned of living men,
seized all his wealth by force for one full year.
Meanwhile Melámpus was a prisoner:
for Phýlacus, the king of Phýlacë,
had chained him in the house of Íphiclës,
the king's own son. This was his punishment,
because Melámpus tried to carry home
the herd that Íphiclës had stolen from
great Néleus' mother, Tyro; and the man
who brought those cattle back would win the hand
of Pero, Néleus' daughter. And Melámpus,
infected with sad madness by the fierce
Erínys, dared to do this on behalf
of his dear brother, Bias—but was caught
and held in chains. Yet he avoided death
and then drove back the lowing herd to Pylos;
he punished Néleus for his act of force
and brought fair Pero back to Bias' house,
as wife for his dear brother. He himself
went to the land of other men, to Argos,
where horses pasture; he indeed was destined
to rule among the Argives as their king.
He took a wife and built a high-roofed house
and fathered two stout sons, Antíphatës
and Mántius. The first had Óiclës,
a great, stout-hearted son, and Óiclës
had as his son Amphiaráus, one
who spurred the ranks; although indeed much loved
by aegis-bearing Zeus and by Apollo,
he did not cross the threshold of old age;
he died at Thebes because his wife was bribed
by gifts. Alcmǽon and Amphílocus
were born of him. And Mántius fathered Clētus
and Polyphēīdës. Dawn, whose throne is gold,
snatched Clētus for herself—he was so handsome—

Greek [227-250]

that he might live among the deathless ones.
And when Amphiaráus died, Apollo
bestowed the gift of prophecy upon
the ardent Polyphēīdës; there was none
to match him as a prophet. When his father
had angered him, he went to Hyperésia;
and there he lived, an oracle for all.

It was his son, called Theoclýmenus,
who, just arrived, stood near Odysseus' son,
who then was pouring out wine offerings
and praying by his swift black ship. To him
the seer spoke these winged words:

                                    "I find you, friend,
offering sacrifices here; and I
beseech you—by your offerings, and by
the god, and by your own life and the lives
of those who follow you—to answer me
in full, concealing nothing: Who are you?
Where is your city, where your family?
Who are your parents?"

                                    And Telémachus'
reply was cautious, wise: "Most certainly,
my friend, I'll answer all you ask. I come
from Ithaca; my father is Odysseus,
who, though he lived, by now has died a death
most sad. And that is why I took my men
within this ship and went in search of word
about my father, who has long been gone."

Then godlike Theoclýmenus replied:
"I, too, am not in my own land, for I
have killed a man of my own clan; in Argos,
where horses pasture, he left many brothers
and dearest kin—his family has power.
I flee my death, the dark doom they'd inflict;

Greek [251–275]

it is my fate to be a wanderer.
But let me board your ship; this I beseech
as fugitive, for they may slaughter me;
in truth I think they follow in pursuit."

Telémachus' reply was wise, astute:
"You want to join us, and I'd not prevent
your sailing on my shapely ship. Come then
and share the goods we have in our own land."

With this he took the stranger's bronze-tipped shaft
and placed it on the deck of the lithe ship;
that done, he boarded, sat down at the stern,
and gave the seer a place next to his own.
He called upon the others to embark,
to loose the hawsers, and to man the thwarts.
Just then Athena blessed them with a fast
west wind to speed them on their salt sea paths.
At that, Telémachus spurred on his men:
their sail was needed now. He wanted them
to lift the fir-wood mast and step it in
the socket of the box. And this they did,
and then with sturdy forestays fastened it.
With twisted oxhide halyards, they hauled up
the white sail, and it swelled as they sailed off.
The surge was loud. They sailed ahead and passed
Crouni and Chalchis, land where fair streams flow.

The sun sank; all the sea roads now were shadowed.
Zeus sent a wind that sped them on; the ship
drew near to Phéae, then sailed past fair Elis,
where the Epēïans rule. Telémachus
then steered her toward the islands, wondering
if he'd escape or fall a prey to death.

Meanwhile Odysseus and the good Eumæus
were having supper in the hut, where all
the other men ate, too. But with their need

Greek [276–303]

for food and drink appeased, Odysseus thought
that he would test the swineherd, just to see
how courteous he'd be: if he'd invite
his guest to stay some time upon the farm
or send him into town. Odysseus said:

"Listen, Eumæus, and you others here.
At dawn tomorrow I'll head into town
to beg: I do not want to trouble you.
Give me your best advice, a knowing guide
to lead me there; once in the city I
will have to wander by myself; I hope
to cadge a cup of water and a loaf
from someone. If I get into the house
of the divine Odysseus, I may bring
my tidings to the wise Penelope
and even mingle with the bragging suitors;
they've endless stores for feasting—they may well
provide a meal. And I can serve their needs
at once. For I confess—hear this with care—
that Hermes holds me dear: the messenger,
the god who grants to all men's work its grace
and glory, willed that I be unsurpassed
by any mortal in the arts and tasks
of service. I can pile a proper fire
and split dry logs, carve, cook, and pour out wine:
all ways in which the poor man serves the fine."

You, swineherd, whom his words had moved, replied:
"Stranger, what made you conjure such a plan?
To mingle with the suitors means your end:
their violence and arrogance would vie
with iron heaven. And their serving men
are not like you: they're young, well clad with cloaks
and tunics, and their hair is oiled and sleek,
their features fair. And when the suitors feast,
smooth tables bend beneath much bread and meat.
Stay here: a welcome guest whom none of us—

Greek [304-335]

not I nor any of these men—begrudge.
And when Odysseus' cherished son arrives,
he'll give you cloak and tunic and provide
a passage out to any land your mind
and spirit seek."

                    To this, the patient, bright
Odysseus answered: "May you be as dear
to Zeus as you, Eumǽus, are to me:
you free me from atrocious misery
and wandering. Nothing's harder for a mortal
than roaming: for his dreary belly's sake,
the vagrant, tried and sorrowful, must bear
atrocious trials. But since you keep me here
and urge me to await Odysseus' son,
tell me about divine Odysseus' father
and mother, whom he left upon the threshold
of their old age: do they still live beneath
the sun, or are they dead, in Hades' halls?"

The swineherd, chief of men, then answered him:
"Stranger, I tell you this most honestly:
Though he is still alive, Laértës prays
always to Zeus: he pleads to have his soul
desert his body in his house. He mourns
incredibly for his departed son
and for his wedded wife, who was so wise:
it was her death that weighed so heavily,
that brought old age upon him prematurely.
And grieving for her son, who'd won such glory,
she died most miserably: I should hope
such death may never strike those who live close
to me as friends and show me sympathy.
But while she lived—though in such sorrow—I
found joy in asking after her, for she
raised me along with long-robed Ctímenë,
her worthy daughter—and her youngest child—
almost as if we both had shared one mother.

But when we reached the longed-for prime of youth,
they sent her as a bride to Samos; she
went off with countless bridal gifts, while I
was given cloak and tunic by her mother—
fine clothing—and got sandals for my feet
when I was sent to work the fields—and she
within her heart had still more love for me.
Though now I lack these things, the blessed gods
made prosperous the work I carried on.
That labor lets me eat and drink and offer
fit welcome to all strangers I would honor.
But from my mistress I cannot receive
a pleasant word or deed: calamity
has fallen on the house—a vicious crowd.
Yet those who serve my mistress long to hear
her words; they want to learn of everything,
to eat and drink in company and bring
some gift of hers back to the fields—such things
as always spell delight for servants' hearts."

Odysseus, man of many wiles, replied:
"How sad it is that you, swineherd Eumæus,
when still a boy, were taken from your parents
and native land. But tell me this—and truly:
Did armies sack your people's spacious city,
home of your father and your honored mother?
Or while you were alone with sheep and cattle,
did raiders snatch you up and sail away
and sell you to Laértës, one who paid
a proper price?"

                    The swineherd then replied:
"Stranger, since you insist on asking this,
be silent as I tell my tale; just sip
your wine and sit at ease. These are long nights:
there's time for sleep and time to take delight
in listening to tales; it is not right
to shut one's eyes too early: there's fatigue

Greek [366-394]

even in too much sleep. Yet if they need
to rest, the other men can go to bed;
at daybreak, they can eat and then attend
to our good master's sows. But you and I,
drinking and eating here within this hut,
will take delight as we bring back to mind
our times of trial. For one may even find
content in griefs that have gone by—not least
when one's known many woes and wanderings.
I'll answer what you ask so searchingly.

"There is an isle of which you may have heard:
its name is Syria; north of Ortýgia,
it lies where the sun rises at the solstice.
Although its men are few, its land is fine,
with many herds and flocks, much wheat and wine.
That island knows no dearth and does not suffer
the other ills that overwhelm sad mortals;
and when a generation there grows old,
then lord Apollo of the silver bow
arrives, and Ártemis is at his side:
he aims his gentle shafts—that's how they die.
There are two towns in Syria; they share
that isle between them. And my godlike father,
Ctésius, son of Órmenus, ruled both.
Then some Phoenicians reached that island: famed
as sailors, they were greedy, grasping knaves,
with countless gewgaws in their black ship's freight.

"Now, in my father's house there was a slave—
a woman from Phoenicia: she had grace,
fine stature, and her handiwork earned praise.
That woman was seduced by sly Phoenicians.
She'd gone to launder clothes along the shore
where they had moored; a sailor lay with her,
for fond caresses catch a woman's mind—
even the best of them can be beguiled.
And he began to question: Who was she?

Greek [394-423]

Where did she live? At once she pointed out
the tall room of my father's house. 'I'm proud
to have been born in Sidon, rich in bronze.
My father Árybas had endless wealth;
and pirates—men of Taphos—sought me out:
as I came from the fields they bore me off.
They brought me here and sold me to the lord
whose house you see; the price he paid was just.'
Her secret lover asked: 'Would you sail back
to your own land with us, to see them both—
your father and your mother—and their house?
For they're alive and said to have much wealth.'
The woman answered: 'I indeed may go
if you and all your shipmates pledge an oath
to bring me back unharmed to my own home.'
At that the sailors offered her their pledge.
But when they'd sworn, the woman spoke again:
'Now keep this secret! Let none of your crew
who meets me in the street or at the well
speak openly to me, lest people tell
the old man what they've chanced to see, and he—
suspicious—bind me in hard chains and scheme
to kill you all. Remember what you've sworn,
and barter quickly for the goods you need.
And after all is stowed within your ship,
send word to me at once in the great house;
for I shall also bring whatever gold
may lie at hand. And there is something else
I'll also give in payment for my passage.
Within my master's house I am the nurse
who tends his son, a child alert and keen,
who always follows me outdoors; I'll bring
that boy aboard. From any foreign lord
you'll get for him a price beyond all measure.'
That said, she went back to the handsome house.
And those Phoenicians stayed in Syria
for one full year, amassing many goods
within their hollow ship. But when their freight

Greek [423-457]

was stowed and they were ready to embark,
they sent a messenger to signal her.
A man of guile brought to my father's house
a golden necklace strung with amber beads.
While in the hall my mother and her maids
stared closely at that prize, caressing it
intently, offering him a price, he nodded
in silence to the woman from Phoenicia.
That done, he went back to the hollow ship.
She took my hand and led me from the house.
Crossing the outer hall, she found the cups
and tables of my father's counselors—
they had been banqueting and now were gone
to the assembly place, where we debate.
That woman hid three goblets in her dress
and bore them off; I followed in her steps.

"The sun sank; all the roads were dark with shadows.
We moved with speed and reached the famous port;
there the Phoenicians waited with their ship.
And after we were put aboard, the crew
embarked; so we began to sail across
the watery ways; kind wind was sent by Zeus.
For six days—day and night alike—we sailed.
But when Zeus, son of Cronos, brought to us
the seventh day, the archer Ártemis
struck down that woman; with a thud she fell
into the hold—just like a plunging gull.
They heaved her overboard—a meal they served
to seals and fish; now I was left alone,
despairing. Wind and water carried them
to Ithaca; here, with his wealth, Laértës
bought me—and so I came to see this land."

Odysseus, who was born of Zeus, replied:
"Eumǽus, you indeed have stirred my heart
in telling me so fully all the griefs
your soul has suffered. But besides the evil,

Greek [457-488]

Zeus also gave to you this good: You reached—
after a trial so harsh—the house of one
who's generous, and you can always count
upon his sympathy for food and drink,
and you live well; while I have only reached
this island after wandering through many
cities of mortals."

So they spoke; their sleep
was brief, not long; soon flowered Dawn had come.

Meanwhile, close into shore, Telémachus'
crew struck their sail and with dispatch took down
the mast, then rowed their ship to anchorage.
They cast out mooring stones and to the stern
tied fast the cables, landed, and along
the shore prepared their meal and mixed dark wine.
Then, with their need for food and drink appeased,
Telémachus spoke first—and cleverly:

"Now berth our black ship in the city's port;
while you row there, I'll seek my herdsmen out.
I'll not reach town until the sun has set,
after I've had a chance to see my lands.
Tomorrow, to reward you for this trip,
I want to offer you a worthy feast
with meats and sweet wine."

Theoclýmenus,
a godlike man, replied: "And I, dear boy—
where should I head? Which house am I to seek
among the homes of those who are the chiefs
of rugged Ithaca? Or shall I go
directly to your mother in your home?"

Telémachus' reply was tactful, wise:
"If things were different, I'd indeed invite
you, stranger, to my house, which can provide

Greek [488-514]

a proper welcome. But the time's awry,
for I won't be there and my mother stays
far from the suitors, at her loom upstairs:
you would not even see her—it is rare
for her to show herself. But there's one man
whom you can now approach: the notable
son of wise Pólybus, Eurýmachus;
the people now regard him as a god:
he is the noblest of the suitors, one
most keen to be the man my mother weds—
to gain the honor that Odysseus had.
But as to that, the heaven-dwelling Zeus,
the master of Olympus, knows the truth:
whether or not, before that wedding comes,
he'll strike the suitors with their fatal day."

As he said this, a bird flew to his right,
a hawk, who swiftly serves Apollo's wants;
he held a dove within his claws and plucked
her feathers, scattering them along the ground
between Telémachus and his black ship.
Then Theoclýmenus, drawing aside
Telémachus, gripped fast his hand and said:

"Telémachus, this bird flew on our right,
sent surely by some god—for I could see
he was a bird of omen. There will be
no house in Ithaca more kingly than
your own; your rule is sovereign in this land."

Telémachus' reply was keen and wise:
"Stranger, I would your words might be fulfilled.
You'd see my kindness then—so many gifts
that any man you met would say you're blessed."

Then to Peiræus, faithful friend, he said:
"Peiræus, son of Clýtius, of all
the friends who followed me to Pylos, you

Greek [514–541]

are he who's always heeded me the most;
so now do take this stranger to your house,
and welcome him with warmth till I return."

Peiræus, famous spearman, answered him:
"Telémachus, however long you stay
away, he'll be my guest: my house is his."

That said, Peiræus boarded and he asked
the others to embark and then cast off.
They came aboard at once and manned the thwarts,
while, fastening fine sandals to his feet,
Telémachus took from the deck his shaft
sharp-tipped with bronze—a massive spear. They slacked
the cables at the stern, then rowed toward town,
just as divine Odysseus' cherished son
had ordered them to do. But he himself
with rapid steps walked straight ahead, inland,
until he reached the farmstead. There he kept
his droves of countless swine; beside them slept
his master's loyal herdsman, good Eumæus.

BOOK XVI

Telémachus welcomed by Eumǽus.

Telémachus and the stranger.

Eumǽus' departure to bring the news to Penelope.

·

A visit from Athena.

Odysseus undisguised before his son:
a joyful reunion.

Planning revenge against the suitors.

·

The return of the foiled suitors to Ithaca.

Penelope and the suitors.

The deceitful Eurýmachus.

·

Eumǽus' return to the farm.

Meanwhile, at Dawn's firstlight, two in the hut—
Odysseus and the sturdy herdsman—stoked
the fire and cooked their morning meal. They'd sent
away the other men with hogs to tend.
And when Telémachus drew near, the hounds
fell still; they did not bark, but fawned around
the visitor. Odysseus caught the sound
of footsteps and the silence of the dogs.
At once he told the swineherd these winged words:

"Eumæus, this must be one of your men—
or else some other old, familiar friend—
the dogs don't bark, just fawn, and I hear steps. . . ."

His words were not yet done when his dear son
stood at the door. The startled swineherd rose;
he had been busy at the mixing bowls
for glowing wine—they clattered from his hands.
He went to greet his lord; he kissed his head
and both bright eyes and his two hands: he cried.
Just as a loving father greets his son
who, ten years after he had left, returns
from some far land—his only son, most dear,
whose absence brought more grief than one can bear—
so did the loyal swineherd now draw near
Telémachus; he clasped him fast and tight,
as one who is amazed to find alive
a son escaped from death. He spoke and wept:

"You're back, Telémachus, my eyes' sweet light.
I thought that you would never bless my sight
after you sailed to Pylos. Come, dear boy,
inside my hut; let me take full delight
in seeing you, just back from a far land.
In fact you're not a frequent visitor
to farms and herds; yes, you prefer the town—
you seem to find some joy in looking on
your mother's suitors, that malicious swarm."   □ □ □

Greek [1-29]

Telémachus' reply was thoughtful, wise:
"Well then, dear friend, it's for your sake that I
am here: I've come to see you with my eyes—
and, too, I want to know if I shall find
my mother waiting still. Or has she wed
another man and left Odysseus' bed
abandoned, full of dismal spider webs?"

Eumǽus, chief of herdsmen, answered him:
"Indeed, steadfast within your house she stays.
Her dreary nights and days are wept away."

That said, he took from him the bronze-tipped shaft.
Across the stone threshold, Telémachus
went in. As he drew near, Odysseus,
his father, rose up from his seat, made place;
but on his part Telémachus refused
the gesture, saying:

                    "Stranger, keep your seat;
this farm has other chairs that serve me well.
And here's the man who can attend to that."

That said, Odysseus took his place again.
And for Telémachus, the swineherd heaped
fresh brushwood; over this, he spread a fleece;
on that, Odysseus' dear son sat. Eumǽus
fetched trays of roast meat left from last night's meal
and baskets stacked with bread; within a bowl
of ivy-wood, he mixed the honeyed wine,
then sat down, facing the divine Odysseus.
Their fare was ready now; their hands reached out.
Then, with their need for food and drink appeased,
Telémachus turned to the good swineherd:

"Dear man, where does your guest come from? How did
a crew bring him to Ithaca? And who
were they? He surely did not come on foot." ▫ ▫ ▫

Greek [30–59]

And you, swineherd Eumæus, answered him:
"My son, I'll tell you everything in full.
He says that he was born in spacious Crete
and that he's roamed through many towns of mortals;
such is the fate a god has spun for him.
Just now, he's fled from some Thesprótians' ship
and reached my farm. I put him in your hands.
Do what you will: he is a suppliant."

Telémachus' reply was tactful, wise:
"Eumæus, what you ask lays bare my sadness.
How can I take a guest into my house?
I'm young: I lack the strength, the sure defiance,
to face with force those men who give offense;
meanwhile my mother's in a quandary—
she is not sure if she should stay with me
and tend my house, respect her husband's bed,
and heed the people's voice, or turn instead
to that Achæan suitor who is best
and offers the most gifts, as her new mate.
But since he's come to you, I'll clothe this guest
in cloak and tunic—handsome dress; I'll give
fine sandals and a two-edged sword as gifts
and send him on to where his heart would go.
So if you would, take care of him; he can
stay here with you, and it is here I'll send
both clothing and whatever food he'll need—
I'll not have you and yours face that expense.
But I'd not have him going into town
among the suitors—they are far too proud
and insolent. If they insulted him,
my grief would surely know no bounds. One man,
however strong, is hard pressed to defy
so many: that much force is more than mine."

The patient, bright Odysseus then replied:
"To answer you, my friend, is only right—
my heart is torn whenever you report

Greek [60-92]

that in your halls the wanton suitors work
their malice on a man as fine as you.
But tell me if you yielded willingly
or if, incited by a god, the people
of Ithaca became your enemies.
Or do you blame your brothers? For a man
can count on them to battle even when
he faces fearful odds. Would that I were
as young as you—my temper's always hot—
or were indeed another son of flawless
Odysseus, or Odysseus' very self:
for then a stranger might strike off my head
if I, on entering Odysseus' halls,
did not bring death and vengeance, killing all
that band of braggarts. Even if they won,
their numbers crushing one who was alone,
I'd rather die within my halls, cut down,
than have to watch such shameless acts, my own
guests mocked and men who drag my handmaids through
the handsome halls disgracefully, wine drawn
to waste and bread devoured by unchecked men
who prey in vain for ends they'll never gain."

Telémachus' reply was tactful, wise:
"Stranger, I'll tell you all that you would know.
The Ithacans at large are not my foes,
nor can I blame the brothers that a man
may count on in a battle even when
he faces fearful odds. In fact the son
of Cronos caused our family to run
in generations having just one son:
Arcēīsius fathered only one, Laértës;
and he had but one son, Odysseus; I,
the only son Odysseus had, was left
alone within his house—he was deprived
of fatherhood's delights. And that is why
so many enemies now crowd our house.
All lords with power in these isles—who rule

Greek [93-123]

Telémachus

Dulíchium and Samos and Zacýnthus,
the wooded isle, and those who now presume
to rule in rocky Ithaca—continue
to woo my mother and consume my goods.
She'll not reject the hateful wedding or
accept it. Meanwhile all their gluttony
lays waste my house; they soon will ruin me.
But these things rest upon the knees of gods.
Go quickly now, Eumǽus: tell the wise
Penelope I'm safely back from Pylos.
But I'll stay here and wait for your return.
Be sure that she's the only one to learn;
none of the others there must know I've come;
too many of those men want me undone."

And you, swineherd Eumǽus, then replied:
"I see; I understand. At your command
is one who has some sense. But tell me this
one thing, and tell me honestly: Am I—
along my way—to tell Laértës, too?
Sad man, though grieving for Odysseus, he
was able for a while to oversee
his fields and join his crew for drink and meals
within his house whenever he so pleased.
But since the day you sailed away to Pylos,
they say he never touches food or drink
and pays no visits to the fields; he sits
and sighs and mourns; the flesh thins on his bones."

Telémachus' reply was keen and wise:
"Such news is sad indeed; but though we grieve
for old Laértës, we must let him be.
For if a mortal could receive the gift
of having anything that he might wish,
the first thing that I should beseech is this:
the day of my dear father's coming home.
No, once Penelope has news of me,
come back: don't seek Laértës on his farm.

Greek [124–151]

Instead, just have my mother quickly send
her housewife to him secretly: she can
take news of my return to the old man."

His words urged on the swineherd. He picked up
his sandals, fastened them, and headed out
for town. Athena did not fail to see
he'd gone. She reached the farmhouse, taking on
the likeness of a woman, fair and tall,
one who's adept at glowing handiwork.
This was the guise in which she showed herself,
erect, within the doorway of the hut,
before Odysseus. But Telémachus
was unaware that she was there: the gods
do not appear directly to all men.
Odysseus saw her, and so did the hounds,
who did not bark but whimpered, taking off
across the yard. Athena, with her brows,
now signaled bright Odysseus. When he saw
that sign, he walked beyond the yard's huge wall.
He faced her. And Athena said to him:

"Odysseus, man of many wiles, divine
son of Laértës, speak now—it is time
to tell your son; there's no need here to hide.
And when you two have planned the suitors' doom
and death, then make your way into the town.
And I myself will not stay far behind
for long; I'm keen to fight."

                              Her words were done;
Athena touched him with her golden wand.
Then first of all, she cast around his chest
a well-washed cloak and tunic, then enhanced
his height and made him younger and more lithe;
his face grew bronzed again, his cheeks more full;
the beard upon his chin became blue-black.
That done, Athena left; but he went back

Greek [152-177]

into the hut. His son, astonished, turned
his eyes aside in fear, as if he'd seen
a god. And when he spoke, his words were winged:

"Stranger, you seem so changed from what you were
before: your clothes are different, and your skin
is not the same. You surely are a god,
a heaven-dweller. Be compassionate;
to you we'll offer pleasing sacrifice
and golden gifts, well wrought. But let us be."

The patient, bright Odysseus then replied:
"I am no god. What made you think I'm like
the deathless ones? I am the man for whom
you mourned so bitterly, for whom you bore
insult and injury: I am your father."

That said, he kissed his son and from his cheeks
now shed the tears that he'd held back before.
And yet Telémachus was still unsure:
in disbelief, he said insistently:

"You're not Odysseus; you are not my father:
you are a demon come to cast your spell,
that I may mourn and weep still more. No mortal
could ever have contrived such miracles
unless a god himself were at his side—
one who could make him young or old at will.
Before, you were an old man dressed in rags,
but now you're like the heaven-dwelling gods."

Odysseus, man of many wiles, replied:
"Telémachus, there is no need to wonder
or marvel much: I'm sure there is no other
Odysseus who'll appear before you here.
For I am he who, after long despair
and many wanderings, in the twentieth year
am here again, within my own dear land.

Greek [178-206]

Remember this: It was the goddess-guide
of warriors, Athena, who devised
my coming home. She gave me any guise
she pleased; she has that power: now I seemed
a beggar, now a young man richly dressed.
It's easy for the gods who rule high heaven
to glorify a man or cast him down."

That said, he sat. Telémachus, in tears,
embraced his dauntless father. In the hearts
of both the need to weep arose. Their cries
were piercing, louder even than the birds'—
sea eagles or those vultures with hooked claws—
when country fellows steal their nesting young.
The son and father let their sad tears fall.
The sun might well have set on still more tears,
had not Telémachus asked suddenly:

"Dear father, in what sort of ship were you
brought back to Ithaca? Who served as crew?
This much is sure: You did not come on foot."

The patient, bright Odysseus then replied:
"My son, I'll tell you everything in full:
It was Phaeácians, famous mariners,
who brought me here; they convoy any man
who seeks their help. And as they sailed I slept
aboard their ship until they set me down
in Ithaca; they gave me handsome gifts:
much bronze and gold and finely woven clothes.
Those treasures, with the help of gods, now lie
in caves. And as Athena had advised,
I reached this farm, where I can plan and plot
the slaughter of our enemies. Count off—
describe—the suitors, so that I may learn
how many and what sort of men they are.
As I deliberate in my stout heart
I then can see if just we two alone,

Greek [207–238]

with no one else beside us, are enough
to face their force, or if we must seek help."

Telémachus' reply was keen and wise:
"Father, I've always known of your great fame
as one with warrior's strength and cunning brain,
but what you now have urged is much too great.
I am amazed—two men can hardly face
a force so powerful, so numerous.
The suitors are not ten in number nor
twice that; their ranks can muster many more.
Now tally up the number that's exact.
Besides six servants, there are fifty-two
select young men come from Dulíchium;
from Samos there are twenty-four; Zacýnthus
sent twenty; and from Ithaca itself
there are a dozen men, and all of them
most noble—and they have the herald, Medon,
the godlike harper, and two servants skilled
at carving meats. Were we to face them all
within your halls, I fear that we would pay
a bitter and atrocious price to take
revenge when you come home. But why not seek
a helper—one unhesitating, keen?"

The patient, bright Odysseus then replied:
"First, listen carefully to what I say.
Consider: Is it not indeed enough
for us to have Athena and father Zeus
beside us? Or should I seek other help?"

Telémachus' reply was wise, astute:
"The two you've named are stalwart aids: in truth,
although they live on high among the clouds,
they dominate all men, all deathless gods."

The patient, bright Odysseus then replied:
"Those two will not be slow to join the fight

Greek [239-267]

when Árës' fury rages and decides
between us and the suitors in my house.
But now, as soon as we see Dawn's firstlight,
go home and stay with those outrageous men;
the swineherd then will guide me into town—
I'll seem to be an old and squalid beggar.
And if they should insult me in my halls,
submit to that; and even if I suffer
their scorn and spite as they apply raw force
to drag me by the feet out of the house
or batter me, do not protest, just watch.
But try with gentle speech to have them stop
their folly, though they will not change their course—
for now, in truth, their day of doom is close.
And there is one thing more your mind must store.
As soon as the ingenious Athena
alerts me, I shall nod my head; and when
you see that signal, gather up the weapons
of war within the house and store them all
inside the high-roofed room above the hall.
And if the suitors miss those arms and ask
why they are gone, just use this soft reply:
'I've had to place them out of reach of smoke:
the breath of fire had fouled with soot and grime
the look they had when they were left behind,
when long ago Odysseus left for Troy;
and, too, I had this greater fear (a god
had warned me): Wine incites. If brawls break out
when you are drunk, you might draw blood—and thus
drag feasts and courting rites into the dust.
For iron of itself can tempt a man.'
Just leave two spears and axes for ourselves,
together with a pair of oxhide shields;
for once we grip those arms in our defense,
the gods will stun the suitors into trance.
There is yet one thing more that I must add:
If you are my true son and share my blood,
let no one learn that I've returned—not even

Greek [268-301]

the servants, old Laértës, or the swineherd—
not even dear Penelope. But you
and I will test the temper of the maids;
and, too, we'll test our men, to see who fears
and honors us, and who neglects our goods
and lacks respect for one as young as you."

His splendid son replied: "You'll come to know
my spirit soon; meanwhile, you can be sure,
dear father, that my will won't waver. Yet
I think there's no advantage in your scheme.
I ask you to consider well: To test
the men who serve you means that you must waste
your time in single visits to your farms
while in your halls, unchecked, without a let,
the suitors sack your goods. But I urge this:
Try out the women servants; find out who
is mean and false—and who is loyal, true.
I have no taste for testing, farm by farm,
the temper of your men; that can be left
for later, if you know that you in truth
received a sign from aegis-bearing Zeus."

Such were the words the son and father shared.
The stout ship that had brought Telémachus
and all his friends from Ithaca to Pylos
now reached the sheltered inner port. They beached
their black ship on the shore, and their proud squires
bore off their armor; then, with no delay,
they brought the glowing gifts to Clýtius' house.
And to Odysseus' halls they then sent out
a messenger to tell Penelope
these tidings of Telémachus: that he
was home, but at the farm; and lest the queen
be anxious and in tears, most thoughtfully
her son had sent the ship straight to the city.

□   □   □

Greek [302-332]

And so the swineherd and the herald met,
both carrying the selfsame news to set
before Penelope. When they had reached
the palace of the godlike king, the herald,
who stood among the housemaids, said: "O Queen,
your son has just come home." The swineherd stood
close to Penelope and told her all
her son had ordered him to say. That done,
he hurried homeward to his hogs; he went
out from the house and yard. But now, downcast
and in distress, the suitors left the hall
and went out past the portico's great wall
and sat beyond the gates. The first to speak—
Eurýmachus, the son of Pólybus:

"My friends, Telémachus the insolent
was able to complete his task, a trip
so difficult that we were all convinced
he'd not complete it. Come, let's launch our best
black ship; call up the rowers now to reach
our comrades quickly, for our men must speed
back home. . . ."

Before he could complete his speech,
Amphínomus caught sight of their lithe ship;
seated, he looked around; he saw her reach
the inner harbor as the crew hauled down
the sail and held their oars in hand. He laughed
and jested as he said:

"There is no need
to send them any message now: they're back.
Some god has told them what had happened or
they saw his passing ship but missed their chance:
his craft was just too quick—it slipped their trap."

His words were done. The suitors left their seats,
went to the port. They saw the boat drawn up

Greek [333–359]

on shore, the proud squires carrying the gear.
And then they went to the assembly ground—
together, all of them—allowing none
to sit with them, no old man, and no young.
They heard Antínoüs, Eupēīthes' son:

"The gods have let that man escape his death!
By day, watch after watch, without a let,
our men sat on those windswept heights; and when
the sun sank down we did not sleep on land,
but on our black ship waited for the dawn
in ambush, keen to catch Telémachus
and kill him there. But some god brought him home.
Well then, let us contrive to kill him here.
He must not slip us; all that we have tried
will bear no fruit as long as he's alive.
He is alert and wise; we can't rely
upon the people's favor anymore.
But let us hurry now—before he calls
Achæans into council. I believe
he will not wait; his fury is too great.
He'll stand and tell the people that we'd planned
his steep descent to death but missed the mark;
and hearing that, they'll hardly be inclined
to praise our treachery. Indeed they might
use force, expel us from our lands—and we
would have to flee in search of some strange country.
Let us act first and seize him in the fields
far off from town or out upon the road;
then we can take his goods and land; we'd share
that wealth among us equally—we'd give
the palace to his mother and the man
she'd wed. But if you do not like this plan
and would prefer to see him live and keep
his father's riches, why then, let's not crowd
his halls and prey on his delightful goods;
let each of us, instead, present his suit
from his own house, attempt to win her hand

Greek [360-391]

with gifts; then she would wed whoever gives
the most—the man assigned to her by fate."

His words were done; they all were silent, still—
then one did speak: Amphínomus, bright son
of Nísus, and the grandson of Arétës.
He, from grain-rich Dulíchium, had led
some suitors, and his way of speaking pleased
Penelope—his heart was understanding.
And what he now would urge was wise and keen:

"Friends, I don't want to kill Telémachus—
not I. To kill a king's son is a thing
of horror: let us first consult the gods.
And if the oracles of mighty Zeus
approve, then I myself will kill him—and
encourage all the rest to lend a hand.
But if the gods discourage such an act,
then my advice is: Stop."

                         When that was said,
they all were pleased. At once the suitors left
to reach Odysseus' house. When they went in,
they sat on polished thrones.

                         Penelope
was bent, however, on another course:
She had decided to appear herself
before the suitors in their insolence;
for she had learned about the threat of death
her son faced in his halls. The herald, Medon,
had heard about that plot and told her all.
Her handmaids at her side, she reached the hall
but, where the suitors sat, came to a halt.
Beside a pillar that sustained the roof,
that lovely woman stood; before her face
she held a glowing shawl. And she denounced
Antínoüs:

Greek [392-417]

"You, arrogant and vicious
Antínoüs—your mind and speech are said
to be the most astute, most eloquent,
of all that Ithaca can show in men
as young as you. And yet you are a sham.
Madman, why do you scheme the death and doom
of my Telémachus? Can you ignore
the rights of hosts, those Zeus himself protects,
for he is guardian of both host and guest?
Conspiracy is an unholy act.
Can you be unaware that, once, your father
came to this house, a fugitive, in fear
of all the Ithacans? And they indeed
were furious with him, for he had leagued
with Táphian pirates who had preyed upon
our allies, the Thesprótians. For then
the people would have killed him, put an end
to all and swallowed up the goods and wealth
that gave him such delight. Yes, they were keen
to do just that. Odysseus held them back;
he stayed their rage. And now it is his house
on which you prey and then refuse to pay;
you court his wife, and you would kill his son,
and you bring me much grief. I say: Have done,
and tell your comrades, too—it's time to stop."

Eurýmachus, the son of Pólybus,
replied: "O daughter of Icárius,
you, wise Penelope, can set your fears
to rest; there is no need for such distress.
There's no man now nor will there ever be
a son of woman who can strike your son,
Telémachus, as long as I'm alive
and see the light on earth. For I say this,
and what I say is fixed: Whoever dares
to touch your son will see dark blood—his own—
splash on my spear; for he, the scourge of cities,
Odysseus, often held me on his knees

Greek [418-443]

and offered me roast meats and had me sip
red wine; therefore Telémachus means more
to me than any other man on earth.
I say to him that he need have no fear
of death at any suitor's hands—though there
is no escape from death the gods prepare."

His words encouraged her—yet he himself
was plotting death and doom for her dear son.
And so she climbed the stairs to her bright room
and wept for her dear husband, her Odysseus,
until Athena, gray-eyed goddess, cast
sweet sleep upon her lids.

                              Meanwhile, at dusk,
Odysseus and his son saw good Eumæus
return; and they were busy making ready
their supper—they had killed a year-old hog.
But standing near Laértës' son, Odysseus,
Athena touched him with her golden wand;
she turned him back into an older man
and gave him scrubby clothes to keep the swineherd
from recognizing him and rushing out
to tell the news to wise Penelope
instead of hiding it within his heart.

Telémachus was first to greet the swineherd:
"Eumæus, you've come back. What word runs round
the city? Have those suitors given up
their ambush and come home, or are they where
they were, still watching, hoping I will cross
their path so they can send me to my death?"

Then you, swineherd Eumæus, answered him:
"I was not so inclined to go about
the city, asking what was happening;
my heart said I must hurry back as soon
as I had told your mother all I should.

Greek [444-467]

But I did meet a herald from your crew,
a messenger whom they sent out as soon
as they had beached—the first to tell the news
to your dear mother. And I also know
another thing: I saw it with my eyes.
Above the city, as I made my way,
from Hermes' hill I saw a ship put in
to harbor; she was manned by a large crew
and carried shields and double-bladed spears.
I thought it was those men—but I'm not sure."

These were his words, and stout Telémachus,
while glancing at his father, smiled; but he
avoided looking at the swineherd's eyes.
And when their tasks were done and supper set,
they sat, began to eat—each man content
with what he had and shared so equally.
But with their need for food and drink appeased,
they thought of rest and took the gift of sleep.

BOOK XVII

Telémachus' and Odysseus'
separate travels to their palace.

Telémachus' conversation with Penelope.

His fetching of Theoclýmenus.

Theoclýmenus' prophecy to Penelope
of Odysseus' return and revenge.

·

Eumæus and Odysseus'
abrasive encounter with the goatherd Melánthius.

·

Argos, the faithful old hound;
his joy, his death.

·

Odysseus in beggar's guise before the suitors;
Odysseus struck with a footstool by Antínoüs.

·

Penelope and Eumæus.

The omen of the sneeze.

Eumæus' departure as the suitors feast.

As soon as Dawn's rose fingers touched the sky,
the dear son of divine Odysseus tied
fine sandals to his feet, then quick to clasp
his sturdy spear, well fitted to his grasp,
he hurried to the city. As he left,
Telémachus told this to his swineherd:

"My dear old man, I'm going into town
to let my mother see me; for I feel
that her lament and tears won't stop until
she sees me face-to-face. And you meanwhile
lead this unhappy stranger to the city;
there he can beg for food, and those who will
can give him bread and water as a meal.
I can't bear other burdens now: my heart
has too much sorrow. If he finds it hard
to swallow this, so much the worse for him.
I like plain talk: I never mince my words."

Odysseus, man of many wiles, replied:
"I, too, my friend, don't care to linger here;
a beggar has a better chance to grub
in town than in the country. What they give
I'll take. I'm far too old by now to stay
penned on a farm, a man who must obey
an overseer. No—be on your way.
Eumǽus here will do just as you say:
he'll guide me into town as soon as I
have let this fire warm me while I wait
until the sun has warmed the air. My clothes
are nothing more than rags; I am afraid
that morning frost may be too much for me—
you say the city lies quite far away."

These were his words. And now, with rapid strides,
Telémachus soon left the farm; his mind
was hatching his revenge—a deadly scheme.
But when he reached his seemly home, he leaned

Greek [1-28]

his spear against a pillar; he himself
then went inside, across the stone threshold.
The very first to see him was his nurse,
old Eurycleīa; and she dropped her work—
she had been draping their fine chairs with fleece.
She rushed, in tears, to meet him; then a crowd
of other women servants in the house
of firm Odysseus made his welcome warm:
they kissed his head and shoulders tenderly.
Now from her room the wise Penelope,
like Ártemis or golden Aphrodítë,
came down; she threw her arms around her son;
in tears, she kissed his head and handsome eyes;
then, even as she sobbed, she spoke winged words:

"You're back, Telémachus, my eyes' sweet light.
I thought that you would never bless my sight
once you had sailed to Pylos secretly—
not even asking my consent—to seek
some news of your dear father. Tell me then:
What did you find? Was there some trace of him?"

Telémachus' reply was tactful, wise:
"Dear mother, don't incite more sorrow; check
your tears; enough disquiet—let me rest;
I've just escaped the steep descent to death.
But you must bathe, put on fresh clothes, return
together with your women to your rooms,
and swear to bring unblemished hecatombs
to all the gods, that Zeus might strike, requite
the suitors for their sins. Meanwhile I'll go
to the assembly ground: I must invite
a stranger to our house, a man who sailed
from Pylos in my ship. Once here, I sent
ahead both him and all my godlike men;
I asked Peiræus to attend to him,
to make the stranger welcome, take him home,
until we meet at the assembly ground."   □ □ □

Greek [29-56]

These were his words, but hers were left unwinged.
Once she had bathed and changed her clothes, she swore
to offer up unblemished hecatombs
to all the gods, that Zeus might then requite
the suitors for their sins. Telémachus
went out and, as he crossed the hall, held fast
a lance; behind him two brisk hounds advanced.
Athena granted him a godlike grace,
and all the people marveled when he came
to the assembly place. There, the proud suitors
crowded around him; though their words were kind,
malicious schemes were hidden in their minds.
But he avoided them; he turned aside
to Mentor, Ántiphus, and Halithérses—
old friends of his dear father's house. He sat
beside them, and they questioned him. Peiræus
drew near; he'd led the stranger through the city
to the assembly place. Telémachus
did not hang back; he went to greet his guest.
Peiræus was the first to speak. He said:

"Telémachus, it's time for you to send
your women servants to my house to fetch
the gifts that you received from Meneláus."

Astute Telémachus replied: "Peiræus,
we do not know how all of this will end.
The suitors, in their insolence, intend
to kill me in my halls through treachery,
then share my father's wealth among themselves;
if that's to be, I'd rather have you keep
the gifts yourself, not save them for these thieves.
But if I sow their death and doom, you can—
most happily—bring home these gifts to me;
then I'll be glad to have them back."

                                          That said,
he led the luckless stranger to his house.

Greek [57-84]

When they had reached his handsome halls, they laid
their cloaks across the seats and high-backed chairs,
then went into the baths where handmaids washed
and smoothed them down with oil, and gave them soft
wool cloaks and tunics. Having left the baths,
the stranger sat beside Telémachus.
That they might wash their hands, a servant poured
fresh water from a lovely golden jug
into a silver basin; at their side,
she set a polished table. The old housewife
was generous: she drew on lavish stores,
and each of them was offered much and more.
Penelope sat opposite; her chair
was propped against a pillar as she wove
fine threads of wool. Their fare was ready now;
their hands reached out. But when they'd filled their need
for food and drink, the wise Penelope
spoke first:

   "Telémachus, I mean to go
up to my room and lie upon my bed—
that mourning bed of mine, forever damp
with tears since my Odysseus sailed away
with Átreus' sons to Ílion. And yet,
before the braggart suitors come again,
don't you feel some deep need to share with me
whatever word you heard about your father—
some news about his coming home again?"

Telémachus' reply was wise, astute:
"Now, Mother, I shall tell you all the truth.
We went to Nestor, shepherd of his people,
in Pylos; he received me cordially
in his tall house. Just as a father greets
a long-gone son who's come from far, so he
together with his fine sons welcomed me.
As to the brave Odysseus being dead
or still alive, he said he'd heard no word

Greek [85–115]

from any man. He sent me on instead
with horses and a sturdy chariot
to Meneláus, master spearman, son
of Átreus. There I saw the Argive Helen,
for whom—such was the will of gods—the Trojans
and Argives suffered such long grief. At once
the lord of the loud war-cry, Meneláus,
asked me why I had come to Lacedǽmon:
what was I looking for. I told him all.
Then he replied to me: 'How cowardly
they are! So keen to occupy the bed
of such a stalwart man. As, when a deer
has placed her pair of newborn, suckling fawns
to sleep within a mighty lion's lair
and gone to roam and graze the mountain spurs
and grassy glens, the lion then returns
to find that pair of fawns within his den,
and slaughters them ferociously—so will
Odysseus kill the suitors savagely.
O father Zeus, Athena, and Apollo,
would that Odysseus might confront the suitors
with that same might he showed when long ago
in well-built Lesbos, in a wrestling match,
he faced Philomelēïdes, throwing him
with force: how all Achǽans then rejoiced!
Could he regain that strength, his foes would meet
swift death and bitter wooing. What you need
to know, I'll tell you now; I won't deceive—
I won't use shifty or evasive speech.
I heard about your father from the Old
Man of the Sea, who speaks unerringly.
I'll not hide anything he told to me.
He said that he had seen him on an island,
within Calypso's house, in bitter grief:
he has no ships with oars, he has no friends
to sail with him across the sea's broad back.'
So Meneláus, master spearman, son
of Átreus, spoke to me. When that was done,

Greek [116–147]

I sailed for home; blessed by the deathless ones,
I had fair wind; I soon saw my dear land."

His words encouraged her. And now she heard
from Theoclýmenus, the godlike augur:
"Odysseus' honored wife, because the news
that Meneláus gathered was confused,
hear what I have to say; this is the truth—
I tell you everything—all is revealed.
May Zeus, the god of gods, now be my witness,
and, too, the cordial board and hearth of lord
Odysseus, where I am a guest: I say—
he's here already; in his own dear land,
Odysseus either moves about or stays
in one place, learning of the suitors' base
misdeeds; he's plotting vengeance. This I learned
as I sat in the shapely ship and watched
the passage of a bird of augury.
And then I told it to Telémachus."

This was the wise Penelope's reply:
"I would your words might be fulfilled. My guest,
you'd see my kindness then—so many gifts
that any man you met would say you're blessed."

Such were the words they spoke and heard. Meanwhile,
outside Odysseus' house, the suitors played:
as in the past, with all their arrogance
they threw the discus, tossed the javelin
across the leveled open space. But when
the time for feasting came and flocks came in,
led from the fields by the familiar herdsmen,
Medon, the herald they liked most, the one
who always joined their banquet table, said:

"Young men, your need for sport is now appeased.
My lords, come now into the halls; to eat
from time to time is hardly cause for grief."   □ □ □

Greek [148-176]

The suitors did as he had urged. They went
back to the handsome house; they draped their cloaks
across the seats and tall chairs; for their feast,
they butchered these: fat goats and swine, huge sheep,
a heifer from the herd.

                    Meanwhile Eumǽus
was hurrying to leave the farm. He said:
"Stranger, I see you're keen to reach the town
today—my master said that's what you'd want.
I'd have preferred to see you stay and guard
the farm, but I respect and fear him; if
you stayed he would have chided me. It's hard
to hear a master offer a rebuke.
Come, then; the better part of day is over;
and when night falls, you'll find it's even colder."

Odysseus, man of many wiles, replied:
"I hear; I understand. Now lead the way.
But since you say the road is slippery, if
you've cut and saved a stick, I'd lean on it . . ."

That said, he flung his miserable sack,
in tatters, round his shoulders, with a strap.
Eumǽus handed him the welcome staff.
So they went off together; to protect
the farm, they left the herdsmen and the hounds.
Along the road to town, Eumǽus led;
his master, dressed in rags, seemed but a sad
old beggar as he leaned upon his staff.
But when along that rugged path they reached
the outskirts of the city, they could see
a fountain wrought in stone; its lovely stream
served Ithacans with its fresh water. Three
had built it: Íthacus and Néritus
together with Polýctor. Round that fountain ranged
a grove of poplars fond of such damp soil;
the water flowing down the rock was cool;

Greek [177-210]

on top there stood an altar to the Nymphs
where all the passersby made offerings.
Beside that spring they met Melánthius,
the son of Dólius, with the goats he drove,
the best of all his herds—fated to serve
the suitors' feast. Two helpers followed him.
And when he saw the beggar and the swineherd,
his mouth reproached them with indecent words
that left Odysseus' heart distraught, disturbed:

"Ah, yes, it takes a filthy wretch to lead
a filthy wretch: a god has made this match,
where like has met his like. Watcher of swine,
where are you taking this repugnant pest
who, when the feast is done, licks what is left?
At any doorpost he can lean against,
he'll rub his shoulders out, begging for scraps—
he's hardly one to ask for kingly gifts.
Just hand this fellow over to me: he
could watch my farm, could sweep out stalls and feed
green fodder to the kids; and he himself
could fatten out his thighs by drinking whey.
But then again, he's learned the worst of ways:
that laggard will not want to work; to scrounge
and lounge—that's all his avid belly wants.
But this I say—and do be sure it's true:
If he intrudes on good Odysseus' house,
those stools the suitors fling around his head
will suffer damage from his dodging ribs;
he'll be a target pelted through the halls."

The stupid goatherd spat these words, then kicked
Odysseus on the hip. But he stood fast
along the path: he thought he might attack
and bludgeon him to death with his stout staff,
or grab him round the waist and dash his head
against the ground. But then he checked himself;
his rage did not erupt. The swineherd stared

Greek [211-238]

Melánthius in the face; then lifting up
his hands, he damned him with this fervent prayer:

"Daughters of Zeus, Nymphs of this fountain, if
Odysseus ever burned upon your altar
roast thighs of sheep and kids wrapped in rich fat,
do grant what I beseech: See that this man,
led by a god who guides, comes home again.
Your brash and braggart vaunts would be undone,
Melánthius; he'd end the taunts and scorn
you scatter as you strut about the town
while, on the farm, your men neglect their goats."

Melánthius the goatherd then replied:
"Just listen to this cunning dog. But I
will hustle him away some day; I'll pack
this fellow on a black and well-oared ship
and take him far from here—I'll surely win
a pretty profit from the sale of him.
And may Apollo of the silver bow
strike down Telémachus within his house
this day—or may the suitors kill him—just
as surely as Odysseus has lost,
in some far place, the day of his return."

That said, he left those two behind: their pace
was slow. Soon he had reached Odysseus' halls.
He entered quickly, scurried to his place
among the suitors, on a seat that faced
Eurýmachus—whose darling he'd become.
The servants offered him a share of meat;
the old housekeeper brought him bread to eat.

By then Odysseus and the good swineherd
had reached the house. They stopped outside; they heard
the hollow harp resound; for Phémius,
as prelude to his song, had struck some chords.
Odysseus clasped the swineherd's hand and said: □ □ □

Greek [239-263]

"Eumǽus, this must be the handsome house
of lord Odysseus. Anyone would see
this house among a thousand: it stands out.
Each part respects the other; and the court
is ringed by walls and cornices; the doors
are double, built to stand; no one could force
his way inside. I see there is a feast
with many guests to feed; above the house,
smoke rises from roast meats; I hear the harp—
the gift of gods that graces feasts—resound."

And you, swineherd Eumǽus, then replied:
"You're quick indeed to notice things—you're shrewd
in many ways. But let us now decide.
You can go first into the house to join
the suitors, leaving me behind, or else
I'll forge ahead and you can wait outside.
But if you wait, don't linger long; they might
catch sight of you and let things fly or try
to beat and bludgeon you. Keep that in mind."

The patient, bright Odysseus then replied:
"I know; I see. There's good sense left in me.
You enter first, and I'll wait here. I'm not
a novice when it comes to being struck
and pelted. I am patient: I've had much
distress among the waves and wars; I'll add
this trouble to the other trials I've had.
You can't conceal the cravings of the belly,
that cursed cause of many griefs; for it,
we mortals even ready well-oared ships
and, sailing over restless seas, inflict
disaster on our enemies."

        These words
were spoken by the beggar and the swineherd.
Just then a dog that lay there raised his head,
pricked up his ears—a hound that he himself,

Greek [264-292]

the brave Odysseus, long ago had bred,
but never had enjoyed, for he had left
for Ílion too soon. That dog was Argos.
When he was grown, young men would take that hound
to track wild goats and deer and hares; but now,
his master long since gone, he lay unwanted
in the deep dung of mules and oxen heaped
outside the doors, until Odysseus' servants
removed those piles to fatten his wide fields.
There Argos, flea-infested, lay. And when
he saw Odysseus standing near, he wagged
his tail and dropped his ears. But when he tried
to move, he lacked the strength—it was no use.
Odysseus saw it all. He turned aside
and wiped a salt tear from his eyes: to hide
that gesture from the swineherd was not hard.
That done, he asked at once:

                              "I wonder why
this dog was left to lie on heaps of dung.
His shape is fine, but I can't tell if he
had speed of foot to match his handsome body,
or was he like those table dogs men keep
only for show, dogs bred for luxury?"

Swineherd Eumæus, this was your reply:
"He is indeed the dog of one who died
far from his own dear land. If you could see
this hound with all the strength and grace that he
once had—when lord Odysseus left for Troy—
you'd be astonished by his force and speed.
When he was chasing game, there was no beast
within the deep woods' dens who could escape;
he never lost the scent of those he tracked.
But now he's set aside; his lord has died
so far away; the women here don't tend
or care for him. When no one can command,
· · ·

Greek [293-320]

when they're without a master, servants lose
the will to work. The lord of thunder, Zeus,
takes half the worth of any man away
as soon as he's reduced to servitude."

That said, he went into the handsome house;
he joined the noble suitors in the hall.
But Argos, just as soon as he had seen
his master after nineteen years, fell prey
to death's dark fate.

          Now, as the swineherd paced
across the hall, the first to see him was
the tall Telémachus. With a quick nod,
he called Eumǽus to his side. The swineherd
looked round and took a stool that lay at hand,
the one the carver sat on when he sliced
the suitors' slabs of meat. He slipped this stool
beside the table of Telémachus
and, facing him, sat down. The herald brought
both meat and bread, and soon the swineherd ate.
Odysseus did not linger: he was quick
to join the swineherd; leaning on his staff,
he seemed a sad old beggar, dressed in rags.
Along the ash-wood threshold—there he sat
within the doorway as he leaned against
the post a carpenter had planed with craft
from cypress-wood, a plank cut true and straight—
work done long years ago. Telémachus
took from a handsome basket one whole loaf
and as much meat as his two hands could hold,
then called the swineherd over with these words:

"Take this to feed the stranger. Tell him that
he can approach each suitor now and beg:
for any man in need, shame is no friend."

□ □ □

Greek [321–347]

Eumæus heard and hurried: he was quick
to reach Odysseus. These winged words were his:
"O stranger, this is from Telémachus;
he also says that you are now to beg
from each and every suitor; he's convinced
that beggary and bashfulness don't mix."

Odysseus, man of many wiles, replied:
"May you, lord Zeus, bestow your blessings on
Telémachus; may all his heart might want
be granted to him."

      Saying that, he took
the food and set it on his tattered sack,
there at his feet. He then began to eat
and ate until the singer's chant was done.
As soon as he had finished with his meal—
when, too, the singer's sounding harp fell still—
the suitors' clamor filled the hall. Athena
stood by Laértës' son; she urged him on
to beg for bits of bread among the suitors,
to learn which men were just and which were wanton,
though she was hardly set on saving any—
not even those who gave. Odysseus started
upon his right and, as he moved, stretched out
his hand to every side, as though he'd been
a beggar for so long. And out of pity,
they gave and wondered as they gazed at him;
they asked each other who he was and where
he'd come from. And the goatherd also spoke:

"Hear me, you suitors of our splendid queen:
I know this stranger; I indeed have seen
this man before. The swineherd led him here,
but I don't know just who he claims to be."

At that, Antínoüs denounced Eumæus:
"You, cursed swineherd, why did you bring such

a man to town? We surely have enough
beggars and pests and vagabonds who scrounge
at all our feasts. So many of them come
to waste your master's wealth, consume his stores—
don't they suffice? Why then invite one more?"

Swineherd Eumǽus, this was your reply:
"Antínoüs, your words are not designed
to match your worth. You know no one invites
a stranger from another land unless
that stranger is a master of some craft:
a prophet or a healer of disease,
a master carpenter or else a man
who brings delight when he's inspired to chant.
Across the earth, all men invite such guests.
Yet there is none who'd willingly accept
the burden of a beggar in his house.
But in the way you treat Odysseus' slaves
and, most of all, in your mistreating me,
you always show more harsh discourtesy
than any other suitor. Let that be—
as long as I can count on both the wise
Penelope and her dear son, godlike
Telémachus, as keepers of this house."

Telémachus' reply was keen and terse:
"Be silent; do not lavish many words
on answering Antínoüs; he stands
forever ready to provoke one's wrath
with bitter jibes; and he encourages
the others, too, to join in his abuse."

Then with winged words he turned to him: "Indeed,
Antínoüs, you take good care of me,
as would a father shield a son: you'd have
my brusque words drive this stranger from the hall.
May no god let me utter such commands.
Take from your meal and give to him; in fact,

Greek [376-400]

your food is mine, but I would not object,
nor would my mother—whom you so respect—
or any of divine Odysseus' servants
prevent your act. But in your heart, in truth,
you will not choose to give him food: you'd rather
glut your own gut than give to some poor beggar."

This was the answer of Antínoüs:
"Telémachus, you reckless orator,
what have you dared to say? If all the suitors
would only hand this beggar just as much
as I shall give, you'd surely hold him off,
far from your banquets, for a full three months."

That said, he grabbed the stool he always used
to prop his smooth, oiled feet when he would feast;
that stool stood ready there, beneath the table.
But all the others gave Odysseus bits
of bread and meat; his sack was filled with gifts,
and he was just about to take his place
again along the threshold, where he'd taste
the gifts of these Achæans, when he stopped
along the way, to ask Antínoüs:

"Come, friend, and give me something; for you seem
to be no lowly man among the Greeks,
but their most noble lord—indeed a chief.
So you should offer more than others can—
I'd make you famous then in endless lands.
I, too, was once a man of means; my house
was rich; I often gave to vagabonds,
whoever they might be, who came in need.
There I had countless slaves and all those things
that grace a man whom men consider blessed.
But Zeus, the son of Cronos, then was pleased
to ruin me: he had me fit out ships
and sail away with pirate crews to Egypt—
that journey was to be the end of me.

Greek [401-426]

I moored my agile ships along the Nile,
and these were my commands: Most of my men
would stay beside the ships in constant watch;
a few must find a lookout, serve as scouts.
But reckless greed and fury gripped my crews:
nothing could check their frenzy; they began
to ravage the fair fields, to carry off
the women and young children, kill the men.
The tumult reached the town at once; at dawn,
all of the plain was filled with flashing bronze,
with men on foot and men in chariots.
Among my comrades, Zeus, the thunder lord,
cast fatal panic: no one dared to face
attack; on every side we met disgrace.
Their sharp bronze found and felled so many; those
who lived were carried back to work as slaves.
But I was given to a visitor
who happened to be there in Egypt: Dmétor,
the son of Íasus. He ruled in Cyprus;
and it's from Cyprus that I have come here—
though only after many misadventures."

This was Antínoüs' reply: "What god
has sent this pest to foul our feast! Stand off,
far from my table, lest—and soon enough—
you find a still more savage Egypt or
an even harsher Cyprus. You are just
a brash and brazen beggar; you approach
each man in turn, and they, without a thought,
hand food to you. They've no regrets, no scruples;
they're glad to share—those goods that are not theirs;
for at his side, each man has ample fare."

Astute Odysseus said as he drew back:
"Yes, you are handsome, but your wits don't match
your beauty. When it touches what's your own,
you would not even give a grain of salt
to any suppliant—you had no heart,

Greek [427–455]

while seated at another's board, to part
with bits of bread you could have broken off;
yet there at hand you surely have enough."

When he heard this, Antínoüs was spurred
to fury. As he glared, he spoke winged words:
"Your farewell from this hall won't be polite:
you speak abuse as if it were your right."

That said, he grabbed the stool and threw it at
Odysseus; and it hit him in the back,
just under his right shoulder blade. When struck,
he did not budge; he stood, firm as a rock;
he only shook his head; within his heart,
in silence, he devised a deadly plot.
He went back to the threshold; there he sat;
and once he had laid down his bulging sack,
he told the suitors:

                         "Listen, you who court
the splendid queen; I speak what my heart says
I must. A man does not feel pain or grief
if he is struck while fighting for his goods,
his cattle or white sheep. But it was just
my paltry, lowly belly that provoked
Antínoüs' assault: that cursed cause
of so much human misery—the paunch.
But if there are indeed some gods who care
or Furies who will answer beggars' prayers,
may death's dark fate attack and take his life
before Antínoüs has found a wife."

Antínoüs, Eupēïthes' son, replied:
"Now, stranger, sit and eat in peace, or else
go elsewhere, lest they drag you through the house
by hand or foot until your skin's stripped off."

□ □ □

Greek [456-480]

But when they heard Antínoüs, the rest
were furious with him. One proud young man
protested:

"This is scandalous: you struck
a wretched vagabond. Antínoüs,
you're doomed if he is one who comes from heaven.
For gods may wear the guise of strangers come
from far-off lands; they take on many forms
and roam about the cities; they would see
if men live justly or outrageously."

So did the suitors speak. Antínoüs
ignored them. Though Telémachus was grieved
to see his father struck, he did not let
one tear fall to the ground. He shook his head
in silence—but he plotted dark revenge.

When word of what had happened in the hall
reached wise Penelope, when she learned how
the stranger was attacked, she said aloud,
with all her servingwomen ranged about:
"May you who struck the stranger suffer now
an arrow shot from lord Apollo's bow."

Eurýnomë, the housewife, added: "Should
our prayers be answered, of those braggarts none
would live to see the golden throne of Dawn."

This was the wise Penelope's reply:
"Nurse, all of them are men of malice—I
despise them all; and yet Antínoüs
is like dark death itself; he is the worst.
A wretched stranger wanders through the house;
driven by need, he begs; and all the rest
fill up his sack and give him gifts—except
Antínoüs, who throws a stool that hits
the beggar at his shoulder on the right."   □ □ □

Greek [481–504]

Such were the words she spoke as, in her room,
she sat among her maids, while in the hall
the good Odysseus ate. And then she called
the faithful swineherd to her side and said:

"Go, good Eumǽus, bring the stranger here.
I want to greet him and to hear if he
has news of brave Odysseus or has seen
my lord with his own eyes; he seems to be
a man who's wandered far, to many lands."

Swineherd Eumǽus, this was your reply:
"Ah, Queen, if those Achǽans in the hall
would just fall silent now. That stranger tells
enchanting tales; they'd captivate your heart.
When he'd escaped the ship that touched our shore,
I took him in as guest within my hut,
and for three days and nights, I heard him talk;
but even that was hardly long enough
for him to tell me all of his ordeals.
Just as a man will stare in wonder when
a bard the gods have taught begins to chant—
his song brings mortals such delight that men,
in longing, hope that it will never end—
so did this stranger charm me as he sat
beside me in my shed. He said Odysseus
was once his father's guest and friend; his place
of birth was Crete, the land of Minos' clan.
Now he has landed here, a man much tried
and buffeted; he's wandered far and wide.
And he insists Odysseus is alive
and will bring many treasures home with him.
He heard this news from the Thesprótians,
those men whose rich lands lie so close at hand."

This was the wise Penelope's reply:
"Go, call the stranger here; I'd have him speak
to me directly. Since the suitors need

to sport, they can stay in the hall or else
outside—and so enjoy themselves. They keep
their own goods—food and sweet wine—safe at home,
untouched by any but their servants. So
each day they crowd into our house. They slaughter
oxen and rams and fat goats; here they guzzle
our glowing wine: their stupid rite, their revel.
They waste our wealth away; there's no defense.
But if Odysseus were to reach his land,
both he and his dear son would be avenged;
he'd put quick end to their brutalities."

And just as she said that, Telémachus,
down in the great hall, sneezed—a thunderous
and awesome sneeze that echoed through the house.
She laughed, then told the swineherd these winged words:

"Go, call the stranger to me: don't you see
that at my very word my dear son sneezed?
That is the sign that death will overtake
the suitors one and all: none will escape.
I also tell you this—keep it in mind:
If what he says is true, if I'm convinced,
I'll give him cloak and tunic—handsome gifts."

That said, the swineherd hurried to obey.
Beside the stranger, he had this to say:
"Old stranger, wise Penelope has called
for you; the mother of Telémachus
says that her heart, though she has suffered much,
now urges her to ask for news about
her husband. And if you would speak the truth
in all you say, then she will offer you
a tunic and a cloak, things you need most.
As for your belly, beg throughout the land—
and any man who wants to feed you, can."

☐ ☐ ☐

Greek [531–559]

The patient, bright Odysseus then replied:
"I'll soon confide to wise Penelope,
the daughter of Icárius, all I know—
concealing nothing. I have news of him—
and he and I have suffered harsh affliction.
But now, Eumæus, I'm afraid of these
crude suitors, men whose force and savagery
can reach the iron heaven. Even now,
as I went—innocently—through the hall,
a suitor struck and hurt me; he was stopped
by no one—not Telémachus and not
a single other man among that crowd.
So tell Penelope, though she's impatient,
to wait within her room until nightfall.
Then she can ask me all she wants to know
about her husband and his coming home.
But let me sit beside the fire—for warmth.
My clothes are ragged, thin; you saw that's so—
you were the first to help me: that we know."

The swineherd, hearing this, went off. He crossed
her threshold. Seeing him alone, she asked:
"Eumæus, why have you not brought him back?
What does he mean by this retreat? Is he
afraid of someone here, though needlessly,
or is he just uneasy in this house?"

Swineherd Eumæus, this was your reply:
"But there is much good sense in what he says;
he would avoid those braggarts' insolence.
He asked for you to wait until nightfall.
Indeed, o Queen, it's more appropriate
for you to speak to him and hear his words
when you're alone."

                    The wise Penelope
replied: "Indeed he does not lack good sense;
this stranger fears what might well come to pass.

Greek [560-586]

There are no mortal men so wanton as
to match these suitors' savage stratagems."

That said, the splendid swineherd answered her in full,
then left to join the suitors in the hall.
That others might not hear, he bent his head
over Telémachus. His winged words said:

"Dear friend, I'm going back to tend the swine
and everything that's there: both yours and mine.
But you take care of all that's here—and watch
your own self first: these men mean harm. May Zeus
destroy them well before they ruin us."

Telémachus' reply was keen and wise:
"Old man, I'll do just as you say. Now eat,
then leave. But do come back tomorrow morning;
and don't forget—fine beasts for butchering.
But all the rest—whatever happens here—
with the immortals' help, is in my care."

That said, Eumæus took his polished seat,
then, with his need for food and drink appeased,
went off to tend his swine. He left behind
the courtyard and the suitors at their feast,
the crowd inside the hall. In dance and song,
they took delight, for evening now had come.

Greek [587-606]

BOOK XVIII

The boxing match between two beggars:
the insulting Irus and Odysseus in disguise.

Odysseus' warning to Amphínomus.

·

Penelope in the great hall;
her censure of Telémachus
for allowing the beggar's mistreatment.

The suitors enamored of beguiling Penelope;
their gifts to her.

·

The shameless handmaids.

Odysseus taunted by Melántho and the suitors.

Another footstool flung at Odysseus.

Telémachus' brave words.

·

Day's end.

And then a beggar came, a tramp well known
in Ithaca: he scrounged throughout the town.
His belly called for glutting, so he ate
and drank without a break. He had no guts
or force, but he did not lack bulk. Arnæus—
his mother called him that when he was born—
was Irus now, the nickname he had earned
by running any errand you might want.
He came; he tried at once to drive away
Odysseus from his own house. Now he spat
his rough and rude attacks—his words were shafts:

"Old man, give way to me or—soon enough—
I'll grab your foot and drag you from the door.
They're winking at me now—they mean to say
they'd like to have me haul you off. I'd hate
to take that way. Come; move along, before
my words grow into blows."

                                    Beneath his brows
Odysseus' gaze was grim. He said: "Wild man,
no word or deed of mine would bring you grief.
If you are offered more than I receive,
you'd see no envy in me. There is place
for both of us within this entranceway.
There's no need to begrudge what others have:
I'd say you were a beggar—so am I—
and it's the gods on whom we must rely.
But don't provoke my fists; do not incite;
however old I am, if we should fight,
your chest and lips would run with blood; that done,
tomorrow we'd be spared another ruckus—
I doubt that you'd be visiting with us
again—here in the halls of lord Odysseus."

Enraged, the vagrant Irus cried: "Hear this!
How glib he is—this wretch; he gabs as if
he were a clacking, oven-tending hag.

Greek [1-27]

But I'll take care of him; I'll bash with both
my fists; I'll spill his teeth across the ground,
as though he were a hog who's raided corn.
Tuck in your clothes; we'll fight in sight of all.
But can you stand against a younger man?"

So did those two incite each other's rage
before the entrance, on the smooth doorsill.
Robust Antínoüs could hear them bicker
and, breaking into laughter, told the suitors:

"Friends, we can see what no one's seen before
within this house: some god has sent new sport.
For Irus and the stranger are at odds;
come, let us spur them on—they want to box."

That said, they all got up and gathered round
the ragged beggars. And Eupeīthes' son,
Antínoüs, announced:

                              "Listen to me,
you proud contenders, for I tell you this:
Goats' bellies plump with blood and fat are set
upon the fire: fare for us to sup.
Whoever is the victor when you box
can choose whichever fat paunch he might want.
And he, the victor, is to feast with us
forever; he alone has begging rights
in here—and no one else must cross our sight."

So said Antínoüs; they liked his speech.
At this, bent on a stratagem, Odysseus,
the man of many wiles, spoke out:

                              "My friends,
it's surely hard enough for an old man,
whom bitter days have battered, to contend
with one who's younger. But, insidious,

Greek [28-53]

my belly urges me; I shall be mauled
and fall. May all of you at least swear this
great oath: that none of those who side with Irus
will use his fist to bludgeon me and so
force me to crumple under some foul blow."

That said, they all swore, just as he had asked.
And after all their oaths had been declared,
Telémachus, with regal power, said:

"Stranger, if your proud heart and soul insist,
and you would face this fellow, do not fear
any of the Achæans: for if one
should strike you, many more would take your part.
This house is mine; I am your host; and men
of judgment will accord with me—both lord
Antínoüs and lord Eurýmachus."

These were his words, and all of them agreed.
Then, gathering his rags around his loins,
Odysseus showed his firm and robust thighs.
They saw his massive shoulders and his chest,
his brawny arms. Athena, drawing close,
gave vigor to his limbs. The suitors stared;
and glancing at his neighbors, someone said:

"Irus, or What-Was-Irus, soon will get
the battering he asked for; look at that
thigh bulging there beneath the old man's rags."

Such words were said, and Irus' heart was wretched.
But even so the servants girded him,
and then they pushed him on—a man in fear—
to fight. His flesh was trembling on his limbs.
Antínoüs rebuked him, saying this:

"Buffoon, it would be better for you now
if you were not alive or still unborn—

Greek [54–79]

if you quake so before a man so old
and so beset by sorrows: you should know—
I'll ship you to the mainland in the hold,
and there King Échethus, the master maimer
of all men, will slice off your nose and ears
with ruthless bronze, hack off your private parts
and serve them to his hounds to swallow raw."

That said, the limbs of Irus quaked still more.
They led him to the center; both contenders
put up their hands. Then patient, bright Odysseus
was undecided: whether then and there
to smash him, so that as he fell life left,
or to deliver a light blow, to stretch
the beggar on the ground. And as he thought,
the light blow seemed to be the better course—
lest the Achæans find out who he was.

Both men had cocked their hands; now Irus jabbed
at his right shoulder, but Odysseus punched
straight to the neck beneath the ear and crushed
the bones; red blood at once gushed from his mouth;
and groaning, Irus crumpled to the dust,
gnashing his teeth and kicking with his feet
against the ground. And throwing up their hands,
the young lords laughed. At that Odysseus grabbed
the beggar's foot; he dragged him through the porch
across the courtyard to the outer door,
then, propping him against the courtyard wall,
stuck Irus' staff into his hands and said:

"Now squat there, scaring off the hogs and dogs;
don't try to lord it over foreigners
and beggars: squalid as you are, you might
be forced to face a still more foul disgrace."

That said, Odysseus tossed his tattered pouch,
riddled with holes, held by a worn-out strap,

about his shoulders. He went back, reclaimed
his place along the threshold. When he sat,
the suitors greeted him with boisterous laughs:

"Stranger, may Zeus and other deathless gods
grant what you want the most, the wish that is
the deepest, dearest in your heart. You've rid
this island of that guzzling vagabond—
we'll freight him to the mainland soon, a gift
for Échethus, the king who maims all men."

These were their words. The radiant Odysseus
was glad to hear them speak that augury.
And then Antínoüs set out before him
a goat's great belly stuffed with blood and fat.
Amphínomus picked out two loaves; this bread
he set before the stranger. Then he pledged
his health; he lifted up a golden cup:

"Accept my greeting, stranger: may you know
good fortune in the days to come, although
you are besieged by many sorrows now."

Odysseus, man of many wiles, replied:
"Amphínomus, you seem a prudent man;
your father, too, was such, for in my time
I heard of his fair name—the bravery
and wealth of Nísus of Dulíchium.
They say you are his son, and one whose words
seem courteous. Then hear what I now say:
Of all the things that move and breathe on earth,
earth nurtures nothing frailer than a man.
As long as gods bestow prosperity
and he can move about with agile knees,
he thinks the future holds no misery;
but when, against his will, the blessed gods
allot his share of griefs, he yields to these
with patient heart. And so indeed it shifts—

Greek [109-136]

the mind of man on earth: it changes with
the changes in the days sent by the father
of men and gods. I, too, might once have ruled,
but stupidly beguiled by power and pride,
misused my strength—I acted wantonly;
I trusted in my father and my brothers.
Thus, let no man—and at no time—be lawless;
whatever gifts the gods have given him,
let him guard these in silence. Now I see
the suitors on a reckless path, wasting
the riches and dishonoring the wife
of one who, I assure you, will not be
forever distant from his friends and country;
for he is near indeed. But may some god
guide you away from here, back to your home:
may you not meet the day of his return.
I don't believe his coming back will be
without bloodstains beneath this roof when he
and those who woo his wife part company."

That said, he poured libations, drank the honey-
sweet wine, and gave the cup back to that lord
who now, his mind foreseeing bitter trials,
head bowed, his heart dejected, crossed the hall.
But that was not enough to set him free
from fate; he, too, would face Athena's trap:
it was Telémachus, with hand and lance,
who would attack and kill Amphínomus,
who now sat down upon the chair he'd left.

And then Athena, gray-eyed goddess, sought
to have the wise Penelope entrance
her suitors' hearts and, too, win more respect:
she had the queen decide to show herself
before the suitors. So Penelope,
forcing a laugh, turned to her nurse and said:

□ □ □

Greek [137-164]

"Eurýnomë, my heart inclines me now,
though this desire is new to me, to go
before the suitors—yet I hate them so.
And, too, I want to tell this useful word
to my dear son: He should not spend much time
with men so arrogant; their words are fine,
but they have sordid minds."

Eurýnomë
replied: "Dear child, what you have said is right.
Go tell your son just that—no need to hide.
But first, do bathe your body and anoint
your cheeks; your face is stained with tears—it's wrong
to show yourself as one who always mourns.
Consider, too, your son. Your deepest prayer
to the undying gods has been—for years—
to see him grown and bearded: now he is."

To this the wise Penelope replied:
"Eurýnomë, don't let your love for me
urge me to bathe my body and anoint
myself with oil. For since the day my lord
sailed off in hollow ships, Olympus' gods
quenched all the loveliness I may have had.
But I would have Hippodamēıa and
Autónoë beside me when I stand
within the hall: I am ashamed to go
among so many men when I'm alone."

That said, the old nurse left the room; she went
to gather up the women needed now.

But then Athena added to her plan
this stratagem. The gray-eyed goddess shed
sweet sleep upon Penelope, who leaned
back on her couch, with all her limbs at ease.
And to the sleeping queen, the goddess gave
. . .

Greek [165-191]

immortals' beauty, that she might amaze
the suitors. First she cleansed her lovely face
with the ambrosial balm that Cytheréa
the fair-haired uses to anoint herself
when, in entrancing dance, she joins the Graces;
then, too, she made her taller and more stately,
and made her skin more white than new-sawn ivory.
When that was done, the lovely goddess left.

Now, from the hall, the white-armed handmaids came.
Their chatter woke the queen from her sweet sleep;
and as her hands rubbed her fair cheeks she said:

"What tender drowsiness had wrapped me round
despite my misery! If Ártemis
the chaste would only offer me sweet death,
so that I might not waste my life away
in mourning, longing for the excellences—
so various—of my dear husband, one
with gifts that no Achǽan could surpass."

That said, she left her handsome room upstairs—
but not alone; two handmaids walked beside her.
And when that lovely woman reached the hall,
beside a pillar that sustained the roof,
she stopped—a glowing shawl before her face,
and, to each side, there stood a faithful maid.
Love struck the suitors' hearts, made weak their knees—
each prayed that he might lie beside that lady.
She turned to her dear son, Telémachus:

"Telémachus, your mind and thoughts have lost
their force. You had more judgment in your soul
when you were still a child. Now you have grown;
you've reached your manhood, so that anyone
who came from far away and saw you—handsome
and tall—might say you were indeed the son
of some rich man. But now your wits are gone.

Greek [192-222]

How could you let the stranger face insult
within this house? And if, in that assault,
he suffered harm, then you would bear that fault:
dishonor and disgrace would be your lot."

Telémachus reply was tactful, wise:
"I don't resent your anger in this matter:
Mother, I do take care; I note the good
and evil in our acts—my childhood's passed.
But I can't tend all things judiciously;
these men harass me with malicious schemes;
they hem me in: I've no one here to help me.
And, after all, the fight between this man
and Irus brought no comfort to the suitors:
it was the stranger who—by far—was stronger.
And—father Zeus, Athena, and Apollo—
I would that even now that wooing crowd
out in the courtyard or inside this hall
had crumpled heads and battered limbs to match
sad Irus huddled at the outer gate—
his head befuddled, wobbly as a drunk's—
not able now to stand or make his way
back home, a beaten heap of fat and bones."

These were the words that they exchanged, and then
Eurýmachus turned to Penelope:
"Penelope, wise daughter of Icárius,
if all the Argives in Iásian Argos
could see you now, tomorrow they would crowd—
as suitors here—to banquet in your house;
among all other women, none can find
the likes of you in grace, in height, in mind."

To this, astute Penelope replied:
"Eurýmachus, although they once were prized,
my form and grace are gone; they were undone
by the immortals on the day my husband
Odysseus and the Argives sailed to Troy.

Greek [223-254]

Were he returned to be my life's dear lord,
my name would be more fair, my fame assured.
But now I grieve: some god has sent such trials
against me! At the very moment when
Odysseus left his homeland, he held fast
my right wrist, saying: 'Wife, I can't believe
that all the strong-greaved Argives will return
intact from Troy: they say the Trojans, too,
are worthy—sturdy spearmen, skillful archers—
with horses that are swift, the odds that can
decide a quick result when equal ranks
confront each other. So I do not know
whether the god will spare me or I'll meet
my death at Troy: I charge you then, take care
of all things here. When I am far away
be mindful of the welfare of my father
and mother in this house—as you now are,
but even more attentively. But when
you see our son a bearded man, you can
wed whom you would and leave your house.' These were
his words, and all he said has come to pass.
That night will fall when I, unhappy—one
whom Zeus deprived of every good—will face
a hateful wedding. And my heart and soul
are torn by bitter sorrow; for the way
you suitors now behave is not the way
that wooers are to take when they would vie
in courting one who is a noblewoman,
a rich man's daughter: it is *their* plump sheep
and oxen they should offer up as feasts
for all her guests, and bring to her fine gifts—
and not devour her goods unrecompensed."

These were her words. The patient, bright Odysseus
was glad to see her seek the suitors' gifts,
beguiling them with suasive words while she
had other things in mind.

□ □ □

Greek [255–284]

Antínoüs,
Eupēïthes' son, then spoke: "As for these gifts,
o wise Penelope, Icárius' daughter,
let each Achǽan bring what he sees fit;
and what each brings, may you accept, for it
is scarcely proper to refuse a gift.
But as for our returning to our fields
or leaving here for elsewhere, do be sure
we won't do that until you choose the best
of the Achǽans as the man you'll wed."

So spoke Antínoüs. His words pleased all.
And each man sent a herald out to fetch
his gifts. The herald of Antínoüs
brought back with him a fair embroidered robe
with twelve gold brooches fitted with curved clasps.
And for Eurýmachus another herald
was quick to bring a richly crafted torque
of gold adorned with sun-bright amber beads.
And to Eurýdamas his herald brought
a pair of earrings, each of them with three
mulberry pearls that glittered gracefully.
And from the storerooms of Polýctor's son,
Peisánder, came the fairest jewel, a necklace
his herald had brought out. And so it was
that each Achǽan offered up his gift,
even as all the other suitors did.
Then she, fairest of women, climbed the stairs
to her own rooms; behind her, handmaids bore
the splendid offerings. But the suitors turned
to dance and pleasant songs, and as they reveled
they waited for the night. Then darkness fell.
And now, to light the hall, they had at once
set up three braziers and, around these, tough,
well-seasoned faggots that had just been split.
They mixed that wood with pine knots; then in turn
the handmaids of steadfast Odysseus stirred
· · ·

Greek [285-311]

the fire. That's when the man of many wiles,
the Ithacan whom Zeus had nurtured, spoke:

"You, servants of the long-since absent lord,
go find the rooms that house your stately queen;
and there, beside her, card or spin your wool
and give her joy; I can take care of all
the men within this hall—I'll give them light.
And if they want to wait throughout this night,
till Dawn has come upon her golden throne,
their patience never will outlast my own."

The handmaids heard his words. Exchanging glances,
they jested. Lovely-cheeked Melántho—shameless—
began to mock him; although born of Dólius,
it was Penelope who brought her up
as if she were her own dear child; she gave
Melántho every gift a girl might crave.
And yet Melántho's heart refused to grieve
for sad Penelope; Melántho loved
Eurýmachus and shared his bed. Now she
rebuked Odysseus with these fleering words:

"You, scrubby foreigner, your battered wits
won't let you find a forge where you can sleep
or any other place where vagrants meet:
brash, unabashed, you babble here instead
among your betters. Are you wild with wine
or do you always blab with muddled mind?
You whipped a tramp like Irus, but take care—
remember who you are, lest one more fit
than Irus pound your skull with sturdy fists
and ship you, fouled with blood, away from here."

The man of many wiles replied, incensed:
"Bitch, if you want to talk that way, I'll fetch
Telémachus, who'll hack you into bits."
□ □ □

Greek [312-340]

His words scared off the women. Down the hall
they rushed, limbs quivering with fear: they thought
he would in truth do that. But he stood fast
within the light the glowing braziers cast;
he looked at all the men. Meanwhile he wished
for things that soon would not be unaccomplished.

Athena did not let the suitors stay
the course of their outrage; she wanted pain
to fill Odysseus' heart more deeply still.
Among them, then, the son of Pólybus,
Eurýmachus, began to taunt Odysseus
with jeering words that made the suitors laugh:

"Hear me, you wooers of the splendid queen;
I want to tell you words my heart impels:
This man who's come into Odysseus' house
was sent by gods: I surely see the glow
of torchlight round his head, a sudden halo—
for he is bald—a head where no hair grows."

Then for Odysseus, ravager of cities,
he added this: "You—would you be inclined
to serve as my day laborer if I
should hire you to work a far-off farm,
to gather stones for walls and plant tall trees?
Be sure, you would be paid sufficiently.
I'd give you food through all the year, and clothes,
and see that you had sandals for your feet.
But since you've learned nothing but shabby deeds,
you will not care to work. No need to worry
when you can cadge your way throughout this country
and grub enough to feed your greedy belly."

Odysseus, man of many wiles, replied:
"Eurýmachus, I wish that you and I
might vie at labor when the spring arrives
with longer days: my hands with one curved scythe

while you held fast another, in a test
of mowing hay—both fasting until dusk,
and each with grass enough to try our force.
Or else there might be oxen we could yoke—
a pair that were the best that are, each large
and tawny, both well fed with fodder, both
well matched in age and firm force under yoke—
and us with a four-acre field to plow,
with soil that gives way as the colter drives,
then you would see how straight a furrow I
could trace from start to finish. Or allow
that on this very day the son of Cronos—
from anywhere he would—brought war to us,
and I'd a shield, two spears, a casque of bronze,
tight fitting at my temples; then you'd see
how I could battle in the foremost ranks;
and if you spoke at all, it wouldn't be
to mock me, blaming me for this poor paunch.
But you're too arrogant; your wits are coarse:
you think that you are great, a man of force,
since you're among few men, of little worth.
But if Odysseus found his own dear land,
then, though those doors are wide, they soon would prove
too narrow to allow escape for you."

That said, Eurýmachus, his heart inflamed,
scowled as he cast these words of winged disdain:
"Wretch, I'll be quick to thrash you now for all
you say—brash, unabashed—within this hall
among your betters. Are you wild with wine
or do you always blab with muddled mind?
You only whipped a tramp—that's what he was."

That said, he grabbed a footstool; but Odysseus
foresaw that throw; he dodged it, ducking low
beside the knees of lord Amphínomus.
The stool hit the right hand of the cupbearer;
his wine jug clattered as it struck the ground;

Greek [370-398]

the bearer groaned and fell back in the dust.
The suitors' clamor filled the shadowed hall—
and turning to his neighbor, one man bawled:

"Would that this wanderer had died elsewhere
before he reached us! He could not have stirred
such bedlam then. We're bickering over beggars,
and this fine feast no longer gives us pleasure:
all that is low has gained the upper hand."

At this, Telémachus the strong spoke up:
"Mistaken men, you're mad; you can't conceal
how well you've feasted and how much you've swilled.
It surely is some god who spurs you on.
The feast was fine, and now, when you so choose,
go home to sleep—though I'll not hurry you."

His words were done. All bit their lips, amazed
to hear Telémachus speak words so brave.
The one who answered was Amphínomus,
Arétës' grandson, son of noble Nísus:

"Friends, no one in reply to words so seemly
can answer sharply or contentiously.
Do not abuse this stranger here or any
who serve within divine Odysseus' halls.
Come, let the bearer pour into our cups
the drops for our libations: once we've poured
our offerings, we can go home to rest.
As for this stranger, he is here as guest
beneath Odysseus' roof: Telémachus
will tend to one who visits in his house."

These were his words; his plan pleased all of them.
And then a herald from Dulíchium,
Amphínomus' retainer, Múliüs,
mixed wine and served them all. When they had poured
libations to the blessed gods, they drank

Greek [399–426]

the wine as sweet as honey—just as much
as each one willed. That done, they went to rest;
each suitor left for his own house, his bed.

BOOK XIX

Odysseus and Telémachus
preparing for their final revenge.

.

Odysseus and Penelope beside the fire:
her questions and predicament;
Odysseus' fabricated tales.

.

The washing of Odysseus' feet.

The tale of the white-tusked boar and Odysseus' scar.

Euryclēia's discovery of the scar—
and of his identity.

Her joyful welcome hushed.

.

Penelope's dream;
the gates of horn and ivory.

Penelope's plan: the archery test.

Odysseus stayed behind within the hall,
devising—with Athena—ways to kill
the suitors. Soon his winged words spurred his son:

"Telémachus, it's time to take all arms
of war out of this hall: store them inside.
And if the suitors miss those arms and ask
why they were taken, use this soft reply:
'I've had to place them out of reach of smoke;
the breath of fire has fouled with soot and grime
the look they had when they were left behind—
when, long ago, Odysseus left for Troy.
And, too, I had this greater fear (a god
had warned me): Wine incites. If brawls break out
when you are drunk, you might draw blood—and thus
drag feasts and courting rites into the dust.
For iron of itself can tempt a man.'"

He heard what his dear father urged; at once
Telémachus obeyed: he called his nurse;
when Euryclēa came, these were his words:

"Nurse, come now, keep the women in their rooms
until I've laid away my father's arms
within the storeroom, out of reach of soot.
For many years these weapons were neglected:
he left when I was still a child; his arms
have lost their luster in the grime and fumes
of hearth fires in this hall."

                    The dear nurse answered:
"My child, would that your mind were set at last
on caring for this house and all it has!
But come, someone must light the way for you—
a thing you'll hardly ask the maids to do."

Telémachus' reply was tactful, wise:
"This stranger here can serve for that: a man

who gets his daily quart of grain from me
must earn it, though he comes from far-off lands."

These were his words, but hers were left unwinged.
The two—Odysseus and his noble son—
sprang up to gather helmets, shields embossed,
and spears with beech-wood shafts. Then they went off;
Athena lit the way. She held up high
a golden lamp: she shed entrancing light.

At that, Telémachus cried suddenly:
"My eyes, dear father, see a prodigy:
the walls, the handsome panels, fir crossbeams,
the towering pillars are so bright—they seem
as if they had been lit by blazing flames.
Some god—of those who rule high heaven—must
have come to us."

                      Odysseus stopped his son:
"Be silent; curb your thoughts; do not ask questions.
This is the work of the Olympians.
Go, take your rest; I'll stay behind to find
just what your mother and her women think:
in tears, she'll have me tell her everything."

These were his words. As blazing torches lit
his way across the hall, Telémachus
went to the room where he had often found
the solace of sweet sleep. There he lay down,
awaiting Dawn's firstlight. But bright Odysseus
stayed in the hall, where, with Athena's help,
he schemed the suitors' day of reckoning.

Down from her room came wise Penelope—
like Ártemis or golden Aphrodíte.
Her women set her customary chair—
inlaid with silvered loops of ivory—
beside the fire. Icmálius' skill and craft

Stored Armor

long years ago had built it and attached—
to form one piece—a footrest underneath;
and over this they threw an ample fleece.
That chair now served Penelope as seat.
Her white-armed women cleared away the feast,
the rich leftovers and the stained wine cups
from which the overbearing lords had drunk.
They cleared the braziers, raking dying coals
onto the floor, and now, for light and warmth,
piled high fresh wood. But once again Odysseus
had to endure Melántho's coarse abuse:

"Stranger, night through, must we still suffer you?
Will you roam through this house and ogle women?
Be off, you oaf; be glad you've grabbed a meal—
or else we'll fling a torch to clear you out."

Odysseus, man of many wiles, just scowled:
"Poor thing, why are you sick with scorn and spite?
Because I'm filthy or am dressed in rags
and beg throughout the town? This is the fate
that vagabonds and beggars can't escape.
I, too, once lived—a rich man—in my house
of wealth, where wanderers received my help
for any need, whoever they might be.
My slaves could not be counted; and I had
all other things with which a man is blessed
and said to be most prosperous. But Zeus,
the son of Cronos, ended all of that:
such was his wish. Thus, woman, do beware,
lest you in turn lose all the pride of place
that lets you lord it over other slaves.
Your mistress might yet turn and spurn you, or
Odysseus might return—there's hope of that.
And even if he's dead and won't come back,
by now his son is like Odysseus' self:
Telémachus, Apollo's favorite.
If any of the women in this house

Greek [57-87]

gives way to wantonness, he'll notice it:
he's not the child he was."

These were his words—
and wise Penelope rebuked her maid:
"Arrogant slut, I am not ignorant
of your indecency—for which you'll pay.
You knew what I desired; you'd heard me say
that I was always anxious, much in need
of talking to this foreigner, to glean
some word about my husband."

So she spoke,
then told the old housewife, Eurýnomë:
"Set out a chair and cover it with fleece
so that this stranger, seated here, can speak
and hear me out: I need to question him."

That said, Eurýnomë was quick to bring
a polished chair and cover it with fleece:
it served as patient, bright Odysseus' seat.
The first to speak was wise Penelope:
"Stranger, I must begin by asking this:
Who are you? What's your family, your city?"

Odysseus, man of many wiles, replied:
"Woman, no mortal on the boundless earth
could find a fault or flaw in you; your fame
ascends to heaven's heights, as does the name
a blameless king can claim: a righteous lord
who governs mighty men, who fears the gods;
he's bent on justice, and his land's black soil
is rich with wheat and barley; all the trees
are fruitful, flocks are always fertile, seas
bring fish as bounty—such prosperity
blesses his people, since he governs well.
So ask me—in your halls—about all else,
but not about my land and family;

Greek [88-116]

recalling them my heart would fill with grief:
I've suffered many trials. It is not just
to moan and weep within another's house;
unending talk of sorrow only brings
more pain; I'd not have you or your handmaids
so vexed that you would scorn me as a man
awash with tears—his mind weighed down by wine."

This was the wise Penelope's reply:
"Stranger, my form and grace are gone—undone
by the immortals on the day my husband,
Odysseus, and the Argives sailed to Troy.
But were he to return, to watch with care
my life, my fame would surely be more fair
and more widespread; instead I live in grief—
in sorrow that some god inflicts on me.
For all the lords who rule these isles—from Samos,
Dulíchium, and forest-clad Zacýnthus,
and even sunlit Ithaca itself—
want me, against my will, as wife: these men
lay waste my house. So I distrust all strangers
and suppliants and even hold at bay
all heralds, men who ply a public trade:
my heart is sunk in sorrow as I think
of my Odysseus. While the suitors seek
a wedding, I weave schemes. At the beginning,
within my room I set a spacious loom.
The web was wide, the threads were fine, and I
assured them all—unhesitatingly:
'Young men, since bright Odysseus now is dead,
be patient; though you're keen to marry me,
wait till this cloth is done, so that no thread
unravels. This is lord Laértës' shroud—
the robe he'll wear when dark death strikes him down.
I weave it now, lest some Achæan women
condemn me for neglect, for having let
a man who'd won such wealth lie at his death
without a shroud.' These were my words; and they,

Greek [117–148]

with manly hearts, agreed. So I would weave
that mighty web by day; but then by night,
by torchlight, I undid what I had done.
I hoodwinked all of them for three long years;
but when, as spring returned, the fourth was here,
some of my shameless bitches, well aware
of all my stratagems, revealed the plot.
The suitors caught me in the act, just as
I was unraveling my lovely cloth.
I had no choice but to complete my work.
Now I cannot escape my wedding: I
can call upon no other stratagem.
My parents pressure me to take a husband:
my son despairs as men devour his goods;
he understands—by now he is a man
most fit to guard his house, a man to whom
Zeus gives much wealth. But though my state is sad,
tell me what is your land, your family:
you surely were not born of stone or trees—
the sort of thing of which old fables sing."

This was the man-of-many-wiles' reply:
"O woman cherished by Laértës' son,
Odysseus, you keep after me with questions
about my family. Well then, I'll answer—
though you will only make my sorrows harsher:
such is the rule of grief for men kept far
from their own land for many years, who are
like me—the prey of long adversity,
a wanderer through many mortals' cities.
So be it. I shall set your mind at rest.

"Along the winedark sea, by water ringed,
there lies a land both fair and fertile: Crete,
the home of countless men, of ninety cities.
Some speak in one, some in another fashion—
an isle of mingled tongues. There are Achæans
and—men most generous—the native Cretans,

Greek [149-176]

Cydónians, three tribes of Dórians,
and fine Pelásgians. Their greatest city
is Cnóssus; there for nine years Minos ruled:
he had the confidence of mighty Zeus
and was the father of my father, good
Deucálion, who had as sons both me
and Prince Idómeneus. In his curved ship,
together with the sons of Átreus,
Idómeneus sailed off to Ílion.
My famous name is Æthon. I'm the younger;
my brother was the elder and the stronger.
I saw Odysseus there; he was my guest;
for as he made for Troy a great wind forced
your husband off his course, beyond Maléa;
and he, too, came to Crete. His fleet laid anchor
in the rough waters of Amnísus' harbor,
where Eīleīthyīa's cavern stands; at last—
but barely—he'd escaped a tempest's path.
He went up to the city and at once
sought out Idómeneus; he said that they
were friends, that he had been my brother's host.
But since the day my older brother left
for Troy, he had already seen his tenth
or his eleventh dawn. So it was I
who led Odysseus to my house, a guest
to whom I offered every care and kindness.
And to his followers, from public stores
I offered barley and dark wine and bulls
for sacrifice—to satisfy them all.
The good Achæans stayed twelve days in Crete,
penned in by mighty Bórëas: his gusts
must have been stirred by some ferocious god—
even on land, no man could stand their force.
But on the thirteenth day, he stopped. They left."

So, telling many lies, he mimed the truth.
She, hearing him, shed tears that bathed her cheeks.
Just as snows melt upon the steepest peaks—

Greek [177-204]

the snows the west wind heaped and south wind frees—
and with the melting snows, the rivers swell;
so did her lovely cheeks melt as she wept,
lamenting for her husband—he who sat
beside her. Though his heart felt pity for
his grieving wife, Odysseus' eyes held fast,
like horn or iron, staring, motionless,
beneath his brows; astute—he did not weep.

Then, with her need to moan and weep appeased,
again she spoke: "Consider carefully,
stranger; I mean to test you now, to see
if what you tell is true, if you indeed
welcomed my husband and his men to Crete
in your own house: tell me what clothes he wore
and how he seemed and who his comrades were."

Odysseus, man of many wiles, replied:
"Lady, how hard it is to speak when I
have been so distant for so long a time;
for this year is the twentieth since I
sailed off and left my native land behind.
But I shall tell you what my heart recalls.
The bright Odysseus wore a purple cloak
of wool with double folds; its brooch was gold
and had two clasps. The brooch displayed a hound
that held a speckled stag in his forepaws
and watched his writhing prey. All were amazed
to see how, though in gold, the hound that choked
the stag stared hard and how his victim pawed
the air in vain, to flee. I also saw
his tunic, which around his body glowed
like some dry onion skin; it was so thin,
so fragile—like the sun itself it shone.
And many women marveled at his clothes.
Yet you had better keep this, too, in mind:
I do not know if when he left your home
Odysseus was already dressed like this

or if he got these clothes much later, gifts
from one of the companions on his ship
or from some gracious guest, for he was friend
to many; the Achæans had few men
to match Odysseus. I myself gave him
a sword of bronze, a handsome purple cloak
with double folds, a tunic that was fringed,
and, to his ship, with every honor, then
escorted your Odysseus. There, behind him,
a herald followed, somewhat older than
your husband. And I can describe him, too.
He had hunched shoulders, curly hair, dark skin.
His name: Eurýbatës. Odysseus showed
respect for him beyond the measure known
by any other of his men, because
this herald's thoughts were like Odysseus' own."

These were the words she heard; her tears were stirred;
the signs Odysseus had revealed were sure.
But with her need to weep and grieve appeased,
Penelope again began to speak:

"Now, stranger, you who've been so wretched here
will be an honored presence, one held dear
within my house. The clothes of which you speak
are things that I myself had given him,
folded and taken from the room we share;
to these I'd added on the glowing brooch—
a fond adornment for him. But I can
not hope to see him in these halls again,
returned to his own house and dearest land.
So, on his hollow ship, black destiny
sent my Odysseus off, that he might see
the land of malediction, Troy-the-ugly."

Odysseus, man of many wiles, replied:
"O woman whom Laértës' son, Odysseus,
has honored, do not mar your loveliness

Greek [238-263]

or sap your spirit with unending sadness,
with tears for your dear husband. I indeed
don't blame you: anyone who's lost a man
with whom, at one in love, she had a child,
would mourn him, even if he could not match
Odysseus, who—they say—was like the gods.
But stop your tears and hear what I now say.
Without deceit, concealing nothing, I
must tell you that I have already heard
about Odysseus coming home; I learned
in the Thesprótians' rich land—so close
to Ithaca—that he is still alive
and that he'll bring back many precious things
he's gathered in that land. His faithful men
and hollow ship, upon the winedark sea,
while crossing from Thrinácia, were lost—
he'd roused the wrath of Zeus and Hélios,
whose herds his men had slaughtered. They all died
along rough seas. And he alone survived,
left clinging to the keel of his wrecked ship;
a comber cast him on the coast of men
who claim the gods as kin: Phaeácians.
They honored him as if he were a god;
they gave him many gifts and would have brought
your brave Odysseus home as his escort.
Indeed he'd have been back by now, but he
decided he'd gain more by gathering
much wealth while wandering through many lands.
Odysseus knows so many stratagems:
no other man can match his cunning plans.
Now Pheīdon, king of the Thesprótians,
told me and—as he poured libations—swore
that ship and crew stood ready to escort
Odysseus home; but I left first—by chance
a ship was sailing to Dulíchium,
land rich in wheat. Before I went aboard,
King Pheīdon showed me all the precious hoard
Odysseus had amassed: indeed your lord

Greek [264–293]

had stored enough rich goods in the king's hold
to serve ten generations of his line.
The king said that Odysseus now had gone
to hear Dodóna's oracle, the tall
and sacred oak that speaks the will of Zeus;
and after he came back, Odysseus meant
to sail to Ithaca, his own dear land,
returning in the open or by stealth.
Thus he is safe, and he is soon to come:
he'll not delay return to his dear ones,
his fathers' land: for you, I'll swear to this.
May Zeus, the greatest god, be my first witness,
just as I call upon the cordial hearth
of good Odysseus as my witness now:
all is to happen just as I avow;
Odysseus will return within the year—
just when, at old moon's end, the new begins."

This was the wise Penelope's reply:
"I would your words might be fulfilled. My guest,
you'd see my kindness then—so many gifts
that any man you met would say you're blessed.
Yet this is what my soul foresees—and this
is what shall be: Odysseus won't return,
and you will get no ship to see you home;
for in this house there are no masters now
to match Odysseus—most hospitable
of men, whose cordial welcomes and farewells,
as surely as he lived, graced honored guests.
But now, my women, wash this stranger's feet;
prepare his bed with blankets of bright fleece
and cloaks to keep him warm until he meets
Dawn on her throne of gold. Then early on
tomorrow bathe him and anoint him, so
that he can sit beside Telémachus
in the great hall and think of banqueting.
And any of those men who would oppress
the soul of this man act in vain: their wrath

Greek [294-324]

and blustering are empty things. Dear guest,
how can you judge my keenness and good sense
and see how I indeed surpass the rest
of womankind if you are dressed in rags
when you sit down to meals within these halls?
The days of men are brief. For one who is
malign, whose mind is harsh, all mortals wish
that he be cursed with sorrow while he lives;
and once he's died, all men despise his name.
But he whose heart and acts are kind finds fame
among all men, a name borne far and wide
by strangers—many call him excellent."

Odysseus, man of many wiles, replied:
"O woman honored by Laértës' son,
Odysseus, I've indeed disliked bright fleece
and blankets since I left the snowcapped peaks
of Crete and made my way across the seas
in long-oared boats. No, I prefer to lie
as I have often lain through sleepless nights.
For I, on many nights, have rested on
a battered bed, awaiting Dawn's bright throne.
So, too, there is no need to bathe my feet:
my heart would not be pleased if that were done
by any servingwoman in these halls—
unless there is an old and faithful one
whose soul has suffered sorrows like my own;
I would let such a woman touch my feet."

This was the wise Penelope's reply:
"Dear guest, among the foreigners who've come
into this house no one has been as welcome
as you are now: your words show such good sense.
Among my women, one is old and wise:
fond nurse of the unfortunate Odysseus,
just after he was born, she took him from
his mother's arms. Though age has left her weak,
it's she who'll bathe your feet. Wise Euryclēia,

Greek [325-357]

come now and wash the feet of one as old
as your own master is: by now perhaps
Odysseus' hands and feet are like our guest's,
for men much tried grow old before their time."

These were her words. At this, the old nurse hid
her face within her hands and shed hot tears,
while uttering these words of deep despair:

"I weep for you, my child, but can do nothing;
Zeus hated you above all other men,
although your spirit always feared the gods—
no man has roasted more fat thighs or more
choice hecatombs for Zeus the thunder lord
than you have offered him while praying for
serene old age and time to see your son
grow into glory. But to you alone
has Zeus denied the day of coming home.
Stranger, I think that even as you are
derided by these shameless bitches here,
so he, within a distant land, was mocked
by women when he reached some splendid house.
Now you, in order to avoid their taunts
and insults, shun their touch; you do not want
these sluts to bathe you. Wise Penelope,
the daughter of Icárius, has thus
asked me—and I respond most willingly.
I'll wash your feet to please Penelope
and you; my soul is stirred by grief and pity.
But hear what I declare: Though many strangers,
sore-tried, have landed here, I say that I
have never seen a man so like Odysseus
as you are—in your form, your voice, your feet."

Odysseus, man of many wiles, replied:
"Old woman, all who've seen the two of us
find we're alike—just as your keen sense must."
□ □ □

Greek [358–385]

That said, the old nurse brought the burnished tub
she'd need to wash his feet; in this she poured
cold water first, and then she added warm.
But at his seat, set well back from the hearth,
Odysseus quickly turned; he faced the dark;
he had the sudden fear within his heart
that, touching him, his nurse would note his scar
and so discover who this stranger was.

This was the wound dealt by a boar's white tusk.
Long years ago he'd visited Parnassus.
Autólycus, his mother's noble father,
lived there together with his sons—a man
whose cunning oaths and thefts no mortal matched.
It was a god who'd given him such craft—
Hermes himself, for whom Autólycus
would often roast the thighs of kids and lambs;
so he could count on Hermes as a friend.
Now, when he came to Ithaca's rich land,
Autólycus had found a newborn babe,
his daughter's son. And Eurycleīa placed
that child upon his lap; and when the meal
was done, she turned to him:

"Autólycus,
do find a name to suit your child's dear child,
the dear grandson for whom you've always longed."

To this Autólycus replied: "The name
I now declare must be the name that you,
my son-in-law and daughter, are to use:
Because I come as one who, on his ways
across the fertile earth, has been enraged
by many men and women, let his name
now be Odysseus, 'son of wrath and pain.'
And for my part, I shall not stint when he
becomes a man and visits our great house,
the palace of his mother's family,

Greek [386–410]

where I store all my riches, there beneath
Parnassus' peak. I'll see that he receives
fine gifts: he will return to you, content."

And so, to gain such glowing gifts, Odysseus
came to Parnassus and received the warm
words and embraces of Autólycus
and all his sons. Odysseus' mother's mother,
Amphíthëa, hugged him, and she kissed his head
and handsome eyes. Autólycus urged on
his noble sons: the time to feast had come.
At once they brought and butchered there a stout
five-year-old ox; they flayed and dressed it, cut
its limbs with skill and skewered it; with care
they roasted it, then gave each man his share.
They feasted till the day was done—and none
was slighted; shares were fair. Then, when the sun
sank down and darkness won, they took their rest;
the gift of sleep was welcome. But as soon
as Dawn's rose fingers touched the sky, they left
to hunt: the hounds and all Autólycus'
dear sons and good Odysseus. On the steeps
and slopes of Mount Parnassus, they soon reached
windswept ravines. There, risen from the deep
of Ocean's gliding flow, the sun now beat
upon the fields; the forward trackers reached
a forest glen; along the trail of scent
the hounds advanced; behind the trackers went
Autólycus' fine sons and good Odysseus,
who brandished his long lance. Deep in the copse,
a great boar lay—his den so densely hid
that it was proof against the strong, wet wind,
and sun could never pierce it with bright rays;
rain never poured or seeped into that den:
around it, fallen leaves lay high and thick.
Then, as the hunters pressed ahead, the boar
made out the tread of men and dogs; he burst—
his back erect and bristling—from his den;

Greek [411-445]

his eyes ablaze, he stopped at bay before them.
Odysseus was the first to make his rush;
eager to kill, he lifted his long lance
with sturdy hands. The boar, too quick, attacked;
he charged aslant; his tusk tore one long gash
above the knee, but left the bone intact.
Odysseus hit; the point of his bright shaft
drove through the boar's right shoulder. With a shriek,
the beast fell back into the dust; his breath
took flight. Autólycus' dear sons bound up
Odysseus' wound with skill; then they intoned
a spell to check the flow of his dark blood
and hurried back to their dear father's house.
And there Autólycus and all his sons,
once they had healed Odysseus, gave him such
impressive gifts that, when they saw him off
to his own Ithaca, he went in joy.

At his return, his father and good mother
rejoiced and asked to hear in full the tale
of how he got his wound. He told them all
the truth, how he had joined Autólycus'
fine sons on Mount Parnassus; in that hunt,
he had been wounded by a boar's white tusk.

The old nurse held his leg within her palms;
she felt the scar. Touch was enough; she let
his foot fall. When it dropped, the basin's bronze
rang out; the basin tilted; water spilled
upon the ground. Both joy and sorrow filled
her heart; tears filled her eyes; her firm voice choked.
She reached up, touched Odysseus' chin, and sobbed:

"Dear child, you surely are Odysseus, yet
I did not recognize you till my hands
had touched the very flesh of my dear lord."

□ □ □

Greek [446–475]

These were her words, and then her eyes turned toward
Penelope; she wanted her to know
that this was her dear husband—here, come home.
That look was lost upon Penelope:
her mistress noticed nothing—she had been
distracted by Athena. And Odysseus
reached for his nurse's throat; with his right hand
he clutched it; with his left he pulled her close,
and said:

      "Nurse, do you mean to ruin me?
You nursed me at your breast; now after trials
and sorrows, after more than nineteen years,
I've come back to my land. You've found me out;
a god let you discover me; but keep
this secret to yourself—you must not speak
of this to anyone within these halls,
for if you babble and I then subdue,
with some god's help, these noble suitors, you
can count on this: Though you're my nurse, I shall
not spare you when, within this house, I kill
the other servingwomen."

                        Eurycleīa,
wise nurse, replied: "My child, what words escape
the barrier of your teeth! You know my will—
its strength and stubbornness: I shall be still
as solid stone or iron. But I'll tell
another thing to you—and note it well:
If you, with some god's help, subdue that band,
I'll tell you who among these women here
dishonored you, and who were faultless, true."

Odysseus, man of many wiles, replied:
"Nurse, there's no need for you to speak of them;
I'll note and know how each maidservant acts.
Keep silent; let the gods command events."
□　□　□

Greek [476–502]

These were his words. The old nurse left the room
to fetch fresh water for his feet, for all
had spilled. She bathed and then, with ample oil,
she smoothed him down; that done, Odysseus moved
his seat back toward the fire—he wanted warmth;
and with his rags he covered up the scar.

Then wise Penelope was first to speak:
"Stranger, there's one slight thing I've still to ask—
a question to be answered briefly, for
the hour of gentle rest will soon be here,
at least for those who can, despite their cares,
receive sweet sleep. But, given by a god,
my sorrow has no bounds: by day I find
release in grief and mourning as I tend
to household tasks, my women's work, my own;
but when night falls and sleep takes all, I lie
upon my bed with my afflicted heart,
besieged by tears so stubborn and so sharp
that, even as I mourn, tear me apart.
Just as the daughter of Pandáreüs,
the nightingale of the greenwood, while perched
among the clustered leaves when spring returns,
sings sweetly, often varying her song
with shifting accents as she mourns her son,
her Ítylus, lord Zéthus' child, whom she
in madness—long ago—had killed with bronze;
so does my soul shift, thrust, now here, now there,
not knowing whether I should stay beside
my son and keep all things intact—my goods,
my servingwomen, and this high-roofed house—
and so respect both my dear husband's bed
and what our people want, or if I should
not wed that man who proves to be the best
of the Achæans, one who, wooing me
within this house, would offer countless gifts.
My son, as long as he was still a child—
too young to judge with sense—held that I must

Greek [503-530]

not marry, not desert my husband's house.
But now that he is grown, a man in full,
appalled as the Achæans waste his wealth,
he even prays that I may leave these halls.

"But come now, hear the dream that I have dreamt
and tell me what it means. We always keep
some twenty geese: I love to watch them feed—
here, at our water trough, they peck at wheat.
But in my dream, down from the mountain peak
a giant eagle swooped with crooked beak;
he broke the necks of all; I saw them heaped
within this hall. My twenty geese had died—
and he flew off into the glowing sky.
Still in my dream, I wept and wailed. Meanwhile
Achæan women, all with lovely hair,
surrounded me as I mourned bitterly
the eagle's slaughtering my geese. But he
flew back and perched upon the jutting eaves;
from there, with mortal voice, he checked my grief:
'Daughter of great Icárius, take heart;
this is no dream but something you have seen
with eyes awake—foretelling what will be.
The geese are those who woo you; just as I,
who was the eagle, am your husband now,
come home again, about to strike the crowd
of suitors with dark death.' These were his words.
Freed from sweet sleep, I looked about and saw
my geese within the halls, still feeding from
their trough—just as those geese have always done."

Odysseus, man of many wiles, replied:
"Lady, you cannot thrust this dream aside:
Odysseus' very self made plain its sense,
disclosing what, in truth, will come to pass.
The suitors' doom is plain—for all to see;
none can escape that death, that destiny."

□ □ □

Greek [531-558]

This was the wise Penelope's reply:
"Dear guest, dreams are ambiguous and sly—
not all that men may see in them will be.
There are two gates of disembodied dreams:
the gate of horn and gate of ivory.
Those dreams that reach us through carved ivory
bring words that damage us, for they delude;
they promise, but they never will fulfill.
But dreams that take the gate of polished horn,
when they are seen by mortals, do foretell
what is in truth to come. Yet my strange dream
did not—I think—come through the gate of horn;
for if it had, it would have made my son
and me rejoice. But there is something else
which I must tell you now—and mark it well.
I hate the day that soon will dawn—the day
that will divide me from Odysseus' house.
For I today will call a test to try
the prowess of the suitors: I'll align
the axheads that Odysseus used to set—
all twelve of them—like wedges for a ship;
then, from far off, with just one shaft, he'd shoot
through all the socket hollows. And this test
will try the suitors' craft: the man most deft,
whose hands can string the bow, then shoot through all
those axheads with one arrow—he will be
the one with whom I'll go, abandoning
the house in which I led my wedded life—
these halls so fair, so filled with treasures, halls
that I'll remember, even in my dreams."

Odysseus, man of many wiles, replied:
"O lady honored by Laértës' son,
Odysseus, don't delay this competition
within these halls. The man of many wiles
will have returned before these men have strung
the polished bow and shot a shaft through iron."
□ □ □

Greek [559–587]

This was the wise Penelope's reply:
"Stranger, would you, consoling me, might sit
beside me in these halls—were that your wish,
sleep never would descend upon my lids.
Yet mortals cannot be forever sleepless;
upon all things, the deathless ones set limits
for those who dwell on earth, giver of grain.
So now I want to go back to my rooms,
to lie upon my bed of sorrow, stained
with tears since dear Odysseus left to see
Ill-Ílion, abominable country,
best left unnamed. I'll lie within my room;
you rest within this hall—upon the floor,
where you can lay your bedding out, or else
upon a bed my maids will quickly fetch."

That said, she made her way to her fine rooms,
but not alone: her women went along.
There she began to weep for her dear husband;
she wept for her Odysseus till gray-eyed
Athena shed sweet sleep upon her lids.

Greek [588-604]

BOOK XX

Sleepless Odysseus.

The faithless handmaids.

Odysseus' forebearance—for now.

.

The feast of the suitors:
Apollo's festival.

Melánthius, the treacherous goatherd;
Philœtius, the faithful cowherd.

Odysseus avoiding the ox hoof.

The suitors' strange fit:
a sign of their doom for Theoclýmenus the seer.

The rudeness of the suitors.

Meanwhile the bright Odysseus tried to rest
within the entrance hall. There he had stretched
an untanned oxhide; over this he'd heaped
the fleeces left from many suitors' feasts—
from all those slaughtered sheep. As soon as he
had settled down, the kind Eurýnomë
was quick to bring a cloak to cover him.
But he lay sleepless, sifting scheme on scheme
to crush his enemies. The women came
out from the hall—those women who, long since,
had served the suitors as their sluts; carefree,
that band of handmaids bantered boisterously.
His heart was hot with fury; mind and will
debated: Should he rush to kill them all
or should he let them leave now, go to lie
with those proud suitors—for this one last time?
His spirit growled within him. Like a bitch
who, guarding her defenseless pups, is quick
to snarl and keen to fight on catching sight
of any stranger, so Odysseus growled
within, disgusted by those shameless tarts.
But then he struck his chest, rebuked his heart:

"Be still, my heart. You've suffered greater shame:
the Cyclops' ruthless frenzy when he ate
your sturdy friends; you found the strength to wait—
although you thought you'd die—within his cave
until your cunning led to your escape."

He held in check the heart within his breast;
obedient now, his pride submitted; yet
Odysseus' own self thrashed this way and that.
Just as a man before a blazing fire
who's skewered a paunch that's stuffed with blood and fat
will swiftly turn the spit this way and that,
eager to have it roasted fast, so did
Odysseus toss from side to side; he thought
of traps in which the suitors could be caught,

Greek [1-29]

though he was one alone and they a crowd.
Then, in the likeness of a mortal woman,
Athena came from heaven; over him
she stood, saying:

            "Why are you sleepless now?
It's true that you have suffered greater sorrow
than any man; but here at last you've come
to your own house, which holds your wife and son—
the kind of son that any man would welcome."

Odysseus, man of many wiles, replied:
"Yes, goddess, all that you have said is right,
and yet there is this question in my mind:
How can one man alone assault this crowd?
They always are together in my house.
And, too, I'm troubled by a greater doubt:
Even if I, with your and Zeus's help,
can kill them, how am I to find escape
from their avenging kin? Consider that."

Athena, gray-eyed goddess, then replied:
"You, stubborn one! Most mortals trust a friend,
yet you are ready to distrust a goddess
who always cares for you in your distress.
But I'll speak plainly: Though we were besieged
by fifty squads of mortals, all most keen
to butcher us in battle, you'd succeed
in capturing their cattle and plump sheep.
But now, give way to sleep. For you to keep
an all-night watch is, too, a harsh ordeal.
You soon will see the end of all your trials."

That said, Athena shed sleep on his lids;
then she, bright goddess, left for high Olympus.

When sleep had overtaken him, had eased
his limbs and freed his heart from care and fret,

Greek [30-57]

his ever-loyal wife awoke; she sat
on her soft bed and wept. But with her need
for tears appeased, the fair Penelope
asked this of Ártemis:

               "I would that you,
great goddess, Ártemis, daughter of Zeus,
might rid me of my life at once, might send
your shaft to pierce my breast; or if not that,
may storm winds snatch me up and bear me off
on foggy paths and thrust me to the mouth
of Ocean's backward flow, even as once
storm winds bore off the daughters of Pandáreüs.
For when the gods had killed their parents, all
those girls were nurtured by fair Aphrodítë
on cheese, sweet honey, and delicious wine;
and Hera gave them loveliness and wit—
surpassing any other women's gifts;
their stately stature came from Ártemis;
Athena taught them craft in fashioning
consummate handiwork. Then Aphrodítë
went up to high Olympus to implore
from Zeus a happy wedding for those girls
(since Zeus, the lord of thunderbolts, foresees
all gladness and all griefs that mortals meet).
But when the goddess left, the storm winds swept
those girls away and gave them to the Furies
to serve as slaves. As the Olympians
effaced those orphans, may they ruin me—
or else permit the shafts of Ártemis
to strike and send me down below grim earth
as I think on my lost Odysseus and
am not compelled to please some lesser man.
Grief still is bearable if one must weep
with troubled heart by day but then can sleep
by night, a sleep that can enfold the lids
and bring forgetfulness of all that is—
the good, the evil. I instead must live

Greek [58-87]

with the malicious dreams a god inflicts:
this very night beside me lay a man
who wore the likeness of Odysseus when
he sailed away with the Achæan ranks;
my heart was glad; mistaking it as fact,
I thought it was no dream."

Her words were done.
Dawn came at once upon her golden throne.
But good Odysseus heard his wife's lament;
and in his reverie, his heart now seemed
to see her stand beside—and recognize—him.
He gathered up the sheepskins and the cloak
in which he had been sleeping; these he stowed
upon a chair inside the hall, then took
his oxhide out of doors and set it down.
He lifted up his hands and prayed to Zeus:

"O father Zeus, if I who have so long
been tried by gods, at last am favored now,
if over land and sea they've brought me back
to my own home, do show two signs to me:
Let one of those who now, inside the halls,
are waking, speak some word of augury
while, out of doors, you send another sign."

This was his prayer. Wise Zeus had heard; straightway
he thundered on Olympus' glowing heights,
out from the sky. Laértës' son rejoiced.
Then from within the house a woman spoke
a word of augury. She sat before
the millstones of her lord and king, Odysseus.
Twelve women were assigned to these to grind
barley and wheat—the marrow of mankind.
The rest had finished with that task—and slept.
But one of them, the weakest, still not done,
sat on alone. She stopped her mill and spoke
these words to serve as omen for her lord: □ □ □

Greek [87-111]

"You, father Zeus, master of gods and men,
indeed have thundered loud from your starred heaven,
and yet there is no cloud; you surely meant
to send a sign to someone here below.
Now, too, for me—I am in misery—
fulfill what I beseech: Let this day be
the last of days in which the suitors eat
within Odysseus' house; my knees are weak
from turning mills for them—this grinding swink.
May this day see the suitors' final feast."

Her words were done. Odysseus was glad
to hear her omen and the thunderclap
of Zeus; he now was sure he'd win revenge
against the suitors' savage insolence.

And now, within Odysseus' handsome house,
the other servingwomen woke; they lit
unwearied fire upon the hearth. Godlike
Telémachus rose from his bed and dressed.
He slung his sharp sword round his shoulder, bound
his handsome sandals to his feet, took up
his warrior's spear, sharp-tipped with bronze, then went
and stood upon the threshold, saying this
to Eurycléïa:

                    "Dearest nurse, did you
provide the stranger with a bed and food,
or did you let him lie as no man should?
My mother has good sense, but she is given
to taking splendid care of lesser men,
while sending off the best of visitors."

Wise Eurycléïa answered: "In this matter,
dear boy, your mother's blameless: do not fault her.
Our guest sat here and drank his fill of wine,
but when she offered food to him, declined:
he had no appetite. And when he'd turned

Greek [112–138]

his thoughts to rest and sleep, she asked her maids
to set and strew a seemly bed; and yet,
as one whom dismal fortune has beset,
he stretched out in the entrance hall to rest
on an undressed oxhide and fleece of sheep;
and we threw down a cloak to warm our guest."

These were her words. Telémachus went off,
across the room, with spear in hand—swift dogs
beside him—pacing to the council place
of the Achæans, men with sturdy greaves.

Meanwhile good Euryclēīa—daughter born
of Ops, Peisénor's son—called to her maids:
"Come now, be quick to sweep and damp the hall;
throw purple fabrics on the shapely chairs;
let others of you sponge the tables, scour
the vessels and two-handled cups, while some
fetch water from the well. It won't be long
before the suitors come. For everyone
this is a sacred day—they'll be here early."

These were her words. They heard; they went to work.
While twenty went outdoors to the dark well,
the rest worked carefully within the halls.
Then sturdy servingmen came in; well skilled,
they split the logs. The women soon returned
with water from the well; and on their heels,
the swineherd drove in three plump hogs—his best.
These he left free to feed in the fair yard,
while to Odysseus he spoke gentle words:

"Do the Achæans show you any more
respect, my friend, or do they—as before—
offend you in these halls?"

                          Odysseus answered:
"Eumæus, may the gods avenge this outrage:

Greek [139–169]

these men, who know no shame, would perpetrate
their obscene scheming in another's house."

While they exchanged these words, Melánthius,
the goatherd, leading in his finest goats
to serve the suitors for their feast, approached,
two other herdsmen at his side. He tied
his goats beneath the echoing portico
and, turning to Odysseus, taunted so:

"Stranger, are you still scrounging—still a plague?
Can't we be rid of you? It's clear you'll taste
my fists before we part; there's little grace
in all your begging ways. You need a meal?
Then find Achæan feasts in other halls."

Such were his words. But there was no response:
astute Odysseus simply shook his head,
his silent heart intent on stratagems.

After the swineherd and Melánthius,
the third to enter was Philœtius,
captain of men: he drove a barren heifer
and fat goats for the banquet of the suitors.
He had been ferried over from the mainland
by those who also convoy other men,
whoever asks for passage. First he tethered
his beasts within the echoing portico,
and then he asked the swineherd, drawing close:

"Swineherd, who is the stranger newly come
into this house? Can he claim noble stock?
Where is his family, his native land?
Sad man! He has the likeness of a king;
yet gods, when they weave webs of misery,
cast even kings into drear wandering."

□ □ □

Greek [170-196]

Then, drawing near and offering his right hand,
the cowherd welcomed him with these winged words:
"I greet you, I respect you, stranger: may
fair fortune be your fate in future days,
though it is sorrows that assail you now.
O father Zeus, no other god is more
unpitying than you: for you yourself
bring men to birth, but then to them allot
pain, gall, and misery. When I saw you,
dear guest, I felt my body sweat, my eyes
were damp with tears: I thought upon Odysseus.
He, too, in tatters like your own, may be
a wanderer in foreign lands if he
is still alive, still sees the light of day.
But if he's dead by now, in Hades' house,
then I indeed must mourn for my dear lord.
When I was still a boy, he gave to me
the care of all his cattle on the mainland;
those herds are countless now; no broad-browed cows
could offer better yield to mortal men.
But he is gone; and upstarts order me
to drive this herd—which they themselves will eat:
these men ignore the young man of the house:
they're eager to divide among themselves
the riches of our long-gone king. My heart
is often troubled by this thought: As long
as my lord's son still lives, it would be wrong
to take these cattle to a new, strange land
and keep them safely there; but it is hard
to stay in sorrow here and guard these herds
for that marauding band. Yes, I'd have left
long since, have fled elsewhere to some strong king—
what happens here is just too much to bear—
did I not always hope that my sad lord
might yet return and cast the suitors out."

Odysseus, man of many wiles, replied:
"Cowherd, you do not seem to be a fool

Greek [197–227]

or faithless—I myself can see that you
are one who understands; so I'll speak out
and swear a great oath to support my words.
May Zeus, the greatest god, attest this truth
together with the hospitable hearth
and friendly table of the good Odysseus:
Our master will return with you still here;
and if you will, you'll see with your own eyes
the slaughter of the overbearing suitors."

The keeper of his cattle answered him:
"Ah, stranger, how I hope that Cronos' son
brings this to pass! If that were done, then you
would learn just what my sturdy hands can do."

And then, in that same way, Eumæus prayed
to all the gods for his wise lord's return.

Such were the words they shared. Meanwhile the suitors
contrived a plot to kill Telémachus.
But on their left a bird of omen flew,
an eagle, there on high; within its claws
it clutched a timid dove. Amphínomus
said this to all those lords:

                              "My friends, the plot
won't work; we cannot kill Telémachus.
Let's think of feasting."

                    So Amphínomus
advised, and what he said won their assent.
On entering divine Odysseus' house,
they placed their cloaks upon the chairs and thrones,
then started slaughtering great sheep, fat goats,
plump hogs, and, too, a heifer from the herds.
They roasted innards, serving them around,
and mixed the wine in bowls. The swineherd brought
each man his cup; and then Philœtius,

Greek [228-254]

captain of men, brought bread in handsome baskets;
it was Melánthius who brimmed the cups.
Their fare was ready now. Their hands reached out.

But, cunningly, Telémachus had set
Odysseus close beside the stone doorsill:
his stool was rickety, his table puny.
Beside him he placed portions of the entrails,
poured wine into a cup of gold, and said:

"Sit here to eat and drink among the lords;
and I myself will shield you from the blows
and taunts of all the suitors, for this house
is not a public place—it is Odysseus',
and I'm his son. And as for all you suitors,
curb any urge you have to strike or threaten:
let no bad blood or quarrels disturb this hall."

His words were done. All bit their lips, amazed
to hear Telémachus speak words so brave.
Antínoüs, Eupeīthes' son, then said:

"Achæans, it is hard, but let's accept
Telémachus' request—despite his threats.
For Zeus, the son of Cronos, blocked our plan;
had it succeeded, we'd have silenced him,
however loud and clear his oratory."

Antínoüs was done. Telémachus
ignored his words. Meanwhile the heralds led
the holy hecatomb into the town
as offering for the gods. Long-haired Achæans
now gathered in Apollo's shadowed grove.
And when the celebrants had finished roasting
the backs and flanks and drawn them off the spits,
each took his share: they feasted splendidly.
And for Odysseus, those who served set out
a portion like the share they had themselves;

Greek [255-282]

such were the orders of Telémachus,
dear son of the divine Odysseus.

But now Athena would not let that pack
turn back from harsh outrage; she'd have disdain
sink deeper still into Odysseus' heart.
Among the suitors was a lawless man:
Ctesíppus was his name; he came from Samos.
He, trusting in his father's countless wealth,
was courting the long-gone Odysseus' wife.
And now Ctesíppus offered this harangue:

"Proud suitors, hear me now. I tell you this:
This stranger—as is proper—has long had
an equal portion; it's not fine or just
to scant the rights of one who visits us
as lord Telémachus' dear guest. Come now—
I, too, will offer him a cordial gift,
which he, in turn, can offer to the slave
who pours the water for his bath, or else
to any other servant in the house
of the divine Odysseus."

                    That was said;
and having snatched up with his sturdy hand
an ox hoof lying in a basket, he
hurled it; that hoof just missed Odysseus—quick,
he bent his head—instead it hit the wall.
Odysseus smiled a grim, sardonic smile.
Telémachus rebuked the man from Samos:

"You missed the mark, Ctesíppus, and our guest
himself was able to avoid the hit.
That is the best result you could have asked:
had it been otherwise, I would have sent
my sharp spear through your midriff; and instead
of being busy with a wedding feast,
your father would be called upon to tend

Greek [283-307]

a funeral within this land. Be warned:
Within this house, let no man flaunt or strut;
I note and understand all that is done—
both good and evil; I'm a child no more.
Yet we endure the sight of such transgressions:
the slaughtered sheep, the swilled wine, feast on feast—
it's hard for just one man to curb a crowd.
Come now—enough of rancor, spleen, and spite;
though if you mean to murder me with bronze,
I should choose that; it's better far to die
than to let acts of shame offend one's eyes
forever: guests insulted and the sight
of servingwomen dragged through these fine halls."

That said, they all were still. Then Ageláus,
Damástor's son, spoke up; he told the suitors:
"My friends, no man would answer such good sense
with bickering and wrath. We've had enough:
do not abuse the stranger anymore
or any of the servants in the halls
of the divine Odysseus. But I give
this cordial counsel to Telémachus
and to his mother; may it please them both.
As long as in your heart you stored the hope
that wise Odysseus would come home, why none
could fault your waiting or your need to curb
the suitors here: that was the better course,
if he indeed came back to his own house.
But now it's certain that he can't return.
Then come, sit by your mother, tell her this:
Wed the best man—the giver of most gifts.
Then you, at peace, can guard your father's wealth—
eat, drink, while she rules in another's halls."

Telémachus' reply was tactful, wise:
"May Zeus and, too, the sufferings of my father—
who, so far off from Ithaca, is dead
or wandering—now attest the truths I say:
O Ageláus, I shall not delay

Greek [308–341]

my mother's marriage—not in any way.
I bid her wed whatever man she would;
I'll give her countless gifts when she does leave.
But I'm ashamed to drive her from this house
against her will, with menaces and threats.
And may the gods not bring such things to pass."

These were his words. But then Athena stirred
a fit of unchecked laughter in the suitors:
their wits were dazed, adrift. Their laughing lips
and jaws were skewed and strange; the flesh they ate
was stained with blood; their eyes shed tears, a flood;
their spirits wanted to lament. At this,
the suitors heard from Theoclýmenus:

"Poor men, what has afflicted you? A shroud
of darkness wraps your faces, heads, your knees;
your sobs erupt, and tears have soaked your cheeks;
the walls and stout crossbeams are dabbed with blood,
and phantoms crowd the colonnade and court;
they rush toward Érebus—they seek the dark;
the sun is blotted from the sky; a fog
of fetid evil sweeps across all things."

These were his words, but they—their fit had passed—
just laughed. It was the son of Pólybus,
Eurýmachus, who spoke:

                              "He must be mad—
this stranger who's just come from foreign lands.
Be quick, young men; escort him from this house;
he'll be more pleased with the assembly ground,
since here he seems to find it far too dark."

The godlike Theoclýmenus replied:
"Eurýmachus, I do not need a guide.
I have my eyes, my ears, and my two feet;
my mind is firm and sound, by no means weak:
with these I leave this hall, because I see

Greek [341-367]

disaster overtaking you—which none
among you can escape or can repel—
you suitors, who in good Odysseus' halls
are free with insults and unholy plots."

That said, he left those handsome halls; he went
into Peiræus' house—a welcome guest.

Then, trying to provoke Telémachus,
the suitors, glancing at each other, laughed
at those he chose to shield. One young lord said:

"No man is more unfortunate than you,
Telémachus, in picking guests. Witness:
You found this filthy vagabond, a man
who scrounges bread and wine, who is unfit
for work or war, a deadweight on this earth;
and then that other fellow, who got up
to prophesy. But you'd be better off
if you'd just mind my words: Let us throw out
these strangers, pack them on a ship with oars,
and hie them off to the Sicilians—
you'd gain a tidy profit from my plan."

So spoke the suitors, but Telémachus
ignored their words. He waited silently—
his eyes upon his father—for the signal
for their assault against the shameless band.

But from her chair, which faced the corridor,
Penelope, Icárius' wise daughter,
could hear the words of each man in the hall.
The suitors, laughing, had prepared a feast
most sweet and ample—butchering many beasts.
But there could be no meal more bitter than
the feast the gray-eyed goddess and fierce man
were soon to set before them. After all,
the suitors' shameless selves deserved to fall.

Greek [369-394]

BOOK XXI

Odysseus' bow and shafts fetched by Penelope.

The archery test.

Telémachus' attempt.

Some suitors' attempts.

·

Odysseus revealing himself
to Eumǽus and Philœtius.

All gates barred.

The servingwomen behind locked doors.

·

The failure of Eurýmachus.

Antínoüs' suggestion—to postpone the contest
in honor of Apollo's festival.

Penelope and Telémachus
encouraging the stranger's attempt.

Odysseus' success.

Athena, gray-eyed goddess, set this scheme
into the heart of wise Penelope,
the daughter of Icárius: to bring
before the suitors in Odysseus' house
his bow and gray axheads—and once the test
was done, that bow would be the tool of death.
She climbed the high stairs to her room and took
within her steady hand the curving key
of bronze—its handle was of ivory.
Then she, together with her women, reached
the far-off room that stored her lord's rich trove:
his battle gear in iron, bronze, and gold,
all worked with care. There lay the pliant bow,
and there, within their quiver, many shafts,
the messengers of death.

       These friendly gifts
Odysseus had received from Íphitus—
the son of Eurytus—a godlike man.
They'd met as guests of wise Ortílochus
near Sparta, in Messénë. What had led
Odysseus to that city was a debt
he'd come to claim for all the Ithacans:
for in their well-oared ships, Messénë's men
had sailed away from Ithaca with some
three hundred sheep—and shepherds, too. Though young,
Odysseus had been chosen for that mission
by both his father and the other chieftains;
to press that claim he'd had to journey long.
And, on his part, the son of Eurytus
had come in search of twelve brood mares he'd lost—
all twelve were nursing sturdy mules. (These mares
soon brought poor Íphitus to doom and death,
when he met Héraclës—the dauntless son
of Zeus—who perpetrated monstrous wrongs:
though Héraclës had welcomed him as guest,
in his own house he murdered Íphitus,
a ruthless killing—he had no regard

Greek [1-28]

for gods or for the table he had set
before his guest. And Héraclës then kept
for his own self—now Íphitus was dead—
the stout-hoofed mares that he had coveted.)
While searching for his brood mares, Íphitus
had met Odysseus, and to him he gave
this gift: the bow that mighty Ēurytus
of old had borne and at his death had left
to his dear son in their tall house. Odysseus,
as token of a friendship he held dear,
in turn gave Íphitus a sturdy spear
and sharp-edged sword. And yet they never had
a chance to share a meal as host and guest;
for Héraclës—before that came to pass—
had murdered Íphitus, the godlike man,
from whom Odysseus had that bow as gift.
This bow Odysseus never took with him
when he sailed off to wars in his black ship;
he kept that bow at home as a memento
of his beloved friend; in Ithaca
alone, Odysseus used to bear that bow.

And now the fair Penelope had reached
the storeroom, stepping on the oaken sill
the carpenter—long since—had planed with skill
and laid true to the line, before he shaped
and planted posts and placed the gleaming doors.
She quickly freed the handle from its thong,
thrust in the key, then aiming straight, she shot
the bolts back. As a bull will bellow when
he grazes in a meadow, even so
the fair doors, as the key struck, bellowed now.
And they were quick to open. She stepped up
and gained the platform where the storage chests
for scented clothes were kept. From there she stretched
her hand out, and she took down from a peg
the handsome case that held the bow. She sat
and laid the case upon her lap; she wept

Greek [29-55]

and then took out the bow of her dear lord.
But when her need for tears had been appeased,
she started toward the hall, to face the suitors.
She brought the pliant bow, the many shafts
within their quiver—messengers of death.
Her maids, beside her, carried out a chest
with bronze and iron gear her lord had left—
and with the axheads needed for the test.
And when that lovely woman reached the hall,
beside a pillar that sustained the roof,
she stood—a glowing shawl before her face;
and to each side, there stood a faithful maid.
These were her words:

    "Proud suitors, hear: I say
that you, to eat and drink without an end
or pause, harass the house of one long gone.
And you give only this as your pretext:
to take me as a wife, to see me wed.
Come, suitors, stand—for you can win your prize.
You see divine Odysseus' mighty bow;
whoever strings this bow with greatest ease
will be the man I follow. I shall leave
this house where I was bride and wife—so rich,
so fair a house: I shall remember it
even in dreams."

    These were her words, and now
she asked Eumǽus to set out before
the suitors both the axheads and the bow.
In tears, the faithful swineherd took them out
and set them down. And where he stood, the cowherd
sobbed when he saw the bow of his dear lord.
Antínoüs, rebuking both, spat out:

"You oafs, you only know what plows can furrow!
Why do you boors shed tears and vex the heart
within a woman's breast? She's had enough

Greek [56-87]

of pain, in any case: her husband's lost.
No, sit and eat in silence, or go out
and whine elsewhere. Just leave behind the bow;
this suitors' test is crucial—and I feel
that stringing this smooth bow is not that simple.
There's no man here who is Odysseus' equal—
for I myself saw him; I can recall."

These were his words, but in his heart he hoped
to string the bow and shoot the iron through.
Instead he was to be the first to taste
an arrow from the hands of great Odysseus,
within whose house he had trespassed, just as
he had incited others' wantonness.

To them the strong Telémachus said this:
"Zeus must have muddled me: I've lost my wits.
My dear, dear mother, one with much good sense,
informs me that she'll join another man
and leave this house—and I, like some poor lout,
laugh and am glad. Then stand, you suitors; now
your prize is close at hand: you will not find
her like in all of the Achæan lands—
in Pylos, holy Argos, or Mycénë,
in our own Ithaca or on the dark
mainland. But you know well that she is priceless;
there is no need for me to sing her praises.
Don't use excuses to delay; don't wait
too long before you show us how you shoot.
I, too, shall try this feat. If I succeed,
why then, I should not grieve were she to leave
this house and wed another: I'd be left
behind, but then at least I would have tried
my strength at arms my father laid aside."

At this, he threw away his crimson cloak
and stood erect, and from his shoulders took
and put aside his sharpened sword. He dug

Greek [88-119]

for all the axheads one long trench and set
the blades in one true row; he fixed them fast
by heaping dirt around them, which he stamped.
All were amazed to see how he had traced
so straight a line on which to place twelve blades,
though he had never seen that done before.
Then, crossing to the threshold, standing there,
he tried to draw the bow. Three times it quivered—
he was that eager; each time he fell slack,
though in his heart he hoped to draw it taut.
He would have strung it at his fourth attempt,
had not Odysseus signaled him to stop;
though keen to show his force, he had to halt.
To them the strong Telémachus then said:

"Even in days to come—what misery!—
I'm doomed to be inept and weak. Or else
I'm still too young and cannot trust my strength
to ward off anyone who gives offense.
But come, you men with power I can't match:
try out the bow; let's finish with this test."

That said, he set the bow upon the ground,
leaned it against the smooth and sturdy door,
and, on the handsome bow tip, propped the shaft,
then sat again upon the chair he'd left.

Eupēīthes' son, Antínoüs, spoke next:
"Rise up, my friends, one at a time, from left
to right, beginning with the one most close
to where the wine is poured."

                              His words pleased all.
The first to rise was Œnops' son, the augur
Leīódës. There he always set his chair
well back, beside the handsome mixing bowl,
for he alone among the suitors scorned
depravity—they all had felt his wrath.

Greek [120-147]

The first to face that task, he took his stand
upon the threshold. There he tried to bend
and string the bow. He failed. Too delicate
and too unused to work like that, his hands
fell slack. He told the suitors:

                                   "Friends—I can't.
Let someone else attempt. This bow will sap
the zeal and strength of many stalwart men;
it is indeed far better to be dead
than to live on and never reach the goal
for which we gather here day after day
expectantly. Now, many in their hearts
have hoped and longed to wed Odysseus' wife.
But once one feels what this bow's like, he'll try
with gifts to woo and win another bride
among the long-robed women of the Argives.
As for Penelope, just have her wed
the man whom fate has blessed—the wealthiest."

That said, he set the bow far off, against
the smooth and sturdy doors, and propped the shaft
upon the handsome bow tip; then he sat
again upon the chair that he had left.
And now he heard Antínoüs' rebuke:

"Leīódes, can you let such words pass through
the barrier of your teeth—words of defeat!
I am incensed to hear you prate of how
men will be stripped of spirit by this bow—
and just because your own self was too weak.
Your honored mother failed to give her son
the force for bow and arrow at your birth.
But other suitors—men who can command—
will soon succeed."

                        When that was said, he called
the goatherd: "Light a fire in this hall,

Greek [148-176]

Melánthius; beside that fire set
a bench with fleeces on it; then go fetch—
out from the stores—an ample cake of fat,
so we young men can heat and grease the bow,
and try again—and end this test at last."

These were his words. Melánthius was quick
to kindle the unweary fire; he fetched
an ample cake of fat out from the stores;
it melted, and the young men greased the bow.
Then they all tried to string it, but their force
fell short; just two—godlike Eurýmachus
together with Antínoüs—persisted.

But both Odysseus' swineherd and his cowherd
had gone outside the hall. Odysseus followed.
And when they'd left behind the gates and court,
he turned to them and spoke these gentle words:

"Cowherd and swineherd, shall I speak, or keep
my question to myself? No—my heart tells
my tongue to ask. How would you act if he—
Odysseus—needed help, if suddenly
some god had brought him back from some far land?
Would you be on the suitors' side or his?"

The cowherd answered him: "Grant us this wish,
o father Zeus! Allow him to return
with some god as his guide. Then you would learn
what strength I have, how much my hands can do."

And then, in that same way, Eumǽus prayed
to all the gods for his wise lord's return.
But once he knew these two were loyal men,
Odysseus answered, speaking out again:

"I am at home. It's I. My trials were long,
but in the twentieth year at last I've come

Greek [177-208]

to my own land. But of my servants none
has yearned for my return, except for you;
among the rest I've heard no others ask
to have me back. So I tell you this truth—
just as it is to be: If I subdue
the suitors through the help a god provides,
I promise each of you a wife and goods,
together with a house close to my own;
and in the future, you—for me—will be
the friends and brothers of Telémachus.
But now I also want to show you this:
a sign so clear that you will be convinced—
the wound inflicted by the boar's white tusk
when I, together with Autólycus'
stout sons, went out to hunt on Mount Parnassus."

As he said that, he drew aside his rags
and showed them his great scar. When they saw that
and looked at it with care, the two men wept.
They threw their arms around the wise Odysseus;
in loving welcome they embraced his head
and shoulders; and in turn he kissed their hands
and heads. And now the sun might well have set
with them still weeping, if Odysseus' words
had not restrained their tears. For now he urged:

"Enough of tears and moans, lest anyone—
come from the hall—might see and then report
to those inside. Let's go back one by one,
not all together; I'll be first, then you.
And let this be the signal: All that crowd
will be at one in their denying me
the bow and shaft. But, good Eumǽus, as
you bear the bow across the halls, just hand
that bow to me; and have the women lock
the fitted doors; if, in their rooms, they hear
men's groans and cries that echo from in here,
they're not to hurry out, but stay inside

Greek [209-238]

in silence, at their work. This is your charge,
Philœtius: First bar the courtyard gate,
and round that bolt be quick to knot a cord."

That said, he went into the shapely house
and took his place upon the stool he'd left.
Then his two herdsmen entered in their turn.

By now Eurýmachus had bow in hand:
by firelight, on this side and on that,
he warmed it; even so, he could not bend
the bow; he groaned within his sturdy heart;
then, vexed, incensed, he turned and cried aloud:

"What drear defeat for me—for all of us!
It's not that I have lost a bride—though I
do grieve for that—for after all there are
so many other women in Achǽa,
some here in seagirt Ithaca itself,
and some in other cities; but I mourn
our falling so far short of what he was:
we cannot match that man so like the gods,
Odysseus; we're too weak to string his bow.
In time to come, who hears our name will know
our shame."

        Eupeīthes' son, Antínoüs,
replied: "That won't be so, Eurýmachus!
And you yourself are well aware of that.
This day is dedicated to Apollo—
a sacred day. Who then may bend a bow?
Delay this test; be calm. Don't touch the axheads;
just leave them here; I'm sure no one will come
into the great hall of Laértës' son,
Odysseus, to disturb them. Now let's call
upon the bearers to prepare our cups,
for only after we have poured libations
are we to set aside the bow. Tomorrow

at dawn Melánthius must bring the best
she-goats in all his herds; when we have offered
roast thighs to the great archer-god, Apollo,
we'll try the bow again and end this test."

So said Antínoüs; they all were pleased.
They washed their hands with water pages poured;
boys brimmed the mixing bowls, then served the wine;
and each man's cup received libation portions.
But when those lords had poured the offerings
and drunk as much as one might wish, Odysseus,
the man of many wiles, spoke cunningly:

"Hear me, contenders for the splendid queen;
I speak just as my spirit urges me.
Above all I beseech Eurýmachus
and, too, godlike Antínoüs, for he
spoke justly when he asked you to delay
your archery today—instead to leave
the verdict with the gods; the victory
will be assigned by them to whom they please—
tomorrow. Let me simply try it now—
the polished bow—that I, before you, show
what strength my hands still have. Do I possess
the force that once informed my supple limbs,
or am I weak from wandering and neglect?"

His words aroused their fear that he might string
the polished bow—and fear can lead to wrath.
Antínoüs assaulted him; he spat:

"You, wretched wanderer, have lost your wits.
Do you need more than this? You share the feasts
of men most eminent; you hear our speech
and words—no other scrounging stranger can
lay claim to things so fine. It must be wine
that wounds your mind—wine, honey-sweet, when swigged
in endless gulps, indeed infects a man.

Greek [265-294]

Even Eurýtion—that far-famed centaur—
when he was visiting Peiríthoüs,
the Lapiths' lord, a king most generous,
was driven wild by wine; it dazed his mind;
depraved, he raped within that royal realm.
Incensed, the Lapiths then attacked; they dragged
the centaur through the gate, hacked off his ears
and nose with ruthless bronze. In frenzy he
went on his way, his heart astray, his mind
still blinded by the price of pain he'd paid.
So did the war between mankind and centaurs
begin; yet he himself had been the first
who—spurred by wine—had suffered such a hurt.
And I predict that you would be hurt, too,
were you to string this bow; indeed you'd get
no sympathy from any of our men;
we'd send you off straightway on our black ship
to one who slaughters men: King Échethus,
from whom you'd not escape. Why risk that fate?
Drink quietly, don't challenge younger men."

This was the wise Penelope's reply:
"It's neither right nor seemly to offend
a guest invited by Telémachus.
And even if that stranger, summoning
whatever force he has, at last should string
the great bow of Odysseus, do you think
he'd lead me to his house, make me his wife?
That's surely not his hope. It hardly suits
to spoil your feast with fears so far from truth."

Eurýmachus replied: "Penelope,
wise daughter of Icárius, indeed
it's not that we believe he'd lead you off—
that would be too improper; it's the talk
of men and women that we fear; in days
to come, some spiteful tongues—much to our shame—
might scorn us, saying: 'See how lesser men

Greek [295-325]

would woo the wife of one most excellent—
and they can't even string his polished bow.
Meanwhile a beggar, one who wandered here,
has strung the bow with ease, and shot the shaft
through iron.' Men will surely babble that—
and we would be disgraced."

                    Penelope
replied with words most wise: "Eurýmachus,
there surely cannot be much good repute
within this land for you who have consumed
with scorn a noble's livelihood. Are you
to chide or to rebuke? This stranger's tall
and sturdy, and he says that he was born
of one who was a lord. Come, let us see:
give him the polished bow. This I affirm,
and this will surely be: If with the gift
Apollo grants, this man can string the bow,
I'll give him cloak and tunic, handsome clothes,
and, too, a pointed pike to fend off dogs
and men, a two-edged sword, and sandals for
his feet, and help him sail to any shore
his heart and mind desire."

                    Telémachus'
reply was keen and wise: "Dear mother, I
alone among Achæans can deny
or give this bow to any man I will.
Of those who rule in rugged Ithaca
or in the isles that face the grazing land
where horses pasture, Elis, no one can
obstruct my will by force, not even if
I wished to give the stranger as my gift
this bow—to carry off, forever his.
But go now to your room; tend to your tasks,
the distaff and the loom; your women can
complete the work that they began. Leave speech
. . .

Greek [326-352]

to men: to all those here and—most—to me;
within this house I have authority."

Amazed, while going to her room, she laid
to heart her son's wise words. Then, with her maids,
she reached the upper floor and wept and wept
for her dear husband, her Odysseus,
until Athena, gray-eyed goddess, shed
sweet sleep upon her lids.

                              The good swineherd
had in the meantime lifted up the bow
and carried it. The suitors' shouts were loud;
one, young and strutting, bawled:

                              "You swineherd wretch,
have you gone mad? Where are you taking that?
For if Apollo and the other gods
should favor us, you'll soon be food for dogs:
alone, far off from men, far from your swine,
it's you on whom the hounds you reared will dine."

Such words, the clamor in the hall, the crowd
of suitors' brouhaha dismayed the swineherd;
dead in his tracks he stopped, set down the bow.
But on the other side Telémachus
cried out by way of menace:

                              "Do not stop,
my friend, unless you want to feel regret
at having heeded all this crowd: unless
you lift that bow again, I'll pelt you out
with stones across the fields. I may be young,
but I've more force than you—would that I had
the same odds when my sinews and my strength
are matched against the suitors. Were that so,
that plotting pack would have to scurry out,
a sorry lot evicted from this house."   □ □ □

Greek [353–375]

These were his words. The suitors were amused;
they set aside the spleen and spite they'd stored
against Telémachus. The swineherd walked
across the hall with bow in hand; he brought
the bow to wise Odysseus. Then he called
the old nurse to his side:

                    "Wise Eurycleīa,
Telémachus commands you now to shut
the doors between the women's rooms and us;
and should your women, in their chambers, hear
men's groans and outcries echo from this hall,
they're not to hurry out but stay inside
in silence, at their work."

                         These were his words.
Meanwhile Philœtius slipped out; he barred
the well-fenced courtyard's gate. That done, he found
a rope twined from papyrus strands; once meant
to serve a stately ship, that rope now lay
beneath the portico. With this he tied
the gate tight, fast. Then he went back and sat
again upon the stool he had just left.
His eyes upon Odysseus, he could see
his lord, bow now in hand, intent upon
its sides, its every part: he turned it round
and round, again, again—afraid that when
he, master of the bow, was far from home,
worms might have worked their mischief on the horns.
One suitor, glancing at his neighbor, mused:

"This fellow's shrewd—a connoisseur of bows.
Perhaps he has one like it stored at home,
or else that vagabond, that lord of nuisance,
intends to carve one for himself—and thus,
he turns it in his hands, this way and that."

□ □ □

Greek [376–400]

And still another suitor added this:
"I hope this beggar has as little luck
in life as in the stringing of this bow."

So did the suitors babble. But the man
of many wiles, Odysseus, now had scanned
the bow on every side; and just as one
expert in song and harping works with ease
when he is called upon to stretch a string
around new pegs and so at either end
makes fast the twisted gut—just so, Odysseus'
stringing of that great bow was effortless.
Then he took up the bow; with his right hand,
he tried the string; it sang as clearly as
a swallow's note. The suitors were dismayed;
they all turned pale. Zeus sent a thunderclap
as omen; and it gladdened patient, bright
Odysseus—he was waiting for some sign
from cunning Cronos' son. At that, he snatched—
it lay upon his table—one lone shaft
(the rest, which the Achæans soon would taste,
within their hollow quiver lay in wait).
Then, even as he sat upon the stool,
he laid that arrow on the bridge, then drew
the bowstring and notched shaft. His aim was true:
he shot clean through each axhead in that row;
not one was missed; through every socket hollow
the shaft had passed—the heavy, bronze-tipped arrow.
Then to his son he said:

                    "You see this guest
has not dishonored you, Telémachus:
I did not miss the mark nor did I strain.
Although the taunting suitors said my strength
was gone, I have it yet. And now it's time—
there's still daylight—to see that all is ready
for the Achæans' feast; and then to add

. . .

Greek [401-428]

still other pleasures, those of harp and chant—
at banquets these are pleasing ornaments."

That said, he gave the signal with his brows.
Telémachus, dear son of bright Odysseus,
strapped on his sharp sword, clasped his spear, and stood
beside his father, armed with gleaming bronze.

BOOK XXII

The start of the slaughter of the suitors.

Armor from the storeroom.

Melánthius in the storeroom.

Athena as Mentor.

The final attack.

·

Telémachus' plea for Phémius and Medon;
their lives spared.

·

Odysseus' instructions to Eurycleīa.

The fate of the twelve handmaids.

The mutilation of Melánthius.

Sulfur and fire:
the cleansing of Odysseus' hall.

Astute Odysseus now threw off his rags.
He leaped onto the great threshold; he grasped
the bow; he grasped the quiver full of shafts.
He cried out to the suitors:

                    "Now at last
the crucial test is at an end, and yet
there is another mark, one that no man
has ever struck before. But I've a chance
to reach it—if Apollo is my friend."

That said, he shot a bitter shaft straight at
Antínoüs, who then was lifting up
a handsome, double-handled, golden cup;
he'd tipped it to his lips that he might drink
the wine; no thought of death had crossed his mind.
And who among the feasters could have guessed
that one, however strong, who faced a crowd
would dare an act so sure to bring revenge—
dark death and destiny—upon himself?
But taking aim, Odysseus hit his mark;
the point passed through and out the tender neck.
He sank back as the shaft struck; from his hand
the cup fell; mortal blood gushed from his nostrils—
a thick stream; and his feet, in frenzy, kicked
aside the table; remnants of the feast
spilled on the floor; the bread and roasted meats
were fouled with blood. The suitors saw him fall;
dismayed, they shouted, leaped up; through the halls
they rushed; their eyes were searching all around
the sturdy walls for weapons, but they found
no shield, no stalwart spear—no arms to grip.
Their anger and abuse assailed Odysseus:

"Stranger, if it is men your arrows seek,
this is your final test: you're sure to meet
the steep descent to death. The one you killed
. . .

Greek [1–29]

was Ithaca's most noble youth: you will
be food for vultures."

So they cried; all thought
that he had hit that man by chance; those fools
were not aware that now they all were snared,
that death cords lashed them fast. Odysseus scowled:

"You thought I never would return from Troy;
and so—you dogs—you sacked my house, you forced
my women servants to your will and wooed
my wife in secret while I was alive.
You had no fear of the undying gods,
whose home is spacious heaven, and no fear
of men's revenge, your fate in days to come.
Now all of you are trapped in death's tight thongs."

Pale fear clutched all of them; their eyes sought out
some place of refuge from death's steep abyss.
The only one to speak—Eurýmachus:

"If now indeed you have come back, Odysseus
of Ithaca, then all that you ascribe
to the Achæans is most justified:
their many acts of outrage in your house
and many in your fields. But he who now
lies dead—he caused it all: Antínoüs.
And in inciting us, he was not bent
so much on marriage as on other plans
that Cronos' son did not fulfill for him:
He wanted to be king in this rich land
of Ithaca; he laid the snare to catch
and kill your son. That schemer now has come
to his just end, and you can pardon us—
your people. Then we'll gather through the land
your recompense for all that we have drunk
and eaten in your halls; to that we'll add—
from each of us—a grant of gold and bronze

Greek [30–58]

worth twenty oxen, to appease your heart.
Until now, who could fault the rage you felt?"

The man of wiles and cunning scowled and said:
"Eurýmachus, were you to shower me
with all the riches you inherited—
and add whatever other goods you can—
not even then would I restrain my hands
from slaughter till you've paid the price in full
for all your arrogance. The choice is yours:
to fight me face-to-face, or else to flee—
though I do not believe that any can
escape that steep descent."

His words were done.
Their knees, their hearts, went weak. Eurýmachus
again spoke up:

"My friends, he will not stop;
within his overpowering hands he holds
the quiver and the polished bow; he'll shoot
from that smooth threshold till he kills us all.
We have to think of battle. Draw your swords;
let's wield these tables as a shield against
the arrows of swift death; let's all, compact,
press on, dislodge him from the door, rush out
and hurry through the city, shout alarm;
with that, he'd soon have shot his final shaft."

That said, he drew his sharp bronze blade, two-edged,
and with a savage roar, rushed on against
the bowman. But the bright Odysseus shot
a bitter shaft that struck him in the chest,
below the nipple; and its sharp tip pierced
straight to his liver. Now the suitor's sword
fell clattering to the ground; he shuddered, slumped,
then crashed across the table, body bent,
and spilled his food and his two-handled cup

Greek [59–85]

across the floor. His forehead struck the ground
in agony; his two legs kicked the chair;
it teetered; darkness fell across his eyes.

Amphínomus, with sharp drawn sword, then rushed
against Odysseus, hoping he could thrust
that bowman from the door. Telémachus
was quick; he cast his bronze-tipped spear and caught
the suitor from behind, right at the spine;
and then he drove the spearhead through his chest.
His body thudded down; his forehead struck
the ground full flush. At that, Telémachus
recoiled, with his long-shadowed spear still fixed
within the corpse that was Amphínomus—
afraid that if he tried to tug it out,
some one of the Achæans might well rush
at him as he bent down beside the corpse.
Instead he ran to reach his father's side;
and standing there, he spoke these winged words:

                                  "Father,
a shield, two spears, a tight bronze helmet—these
are what you need: I'll fetch them now with speed;
and I'll return with armor for myself
and weapons for Eumæus and the cowherd—
we're better off with battle gear."

                        To this,
the man of many wiles replied: "Be quick.
The shafts I have to fend them off will finish.
I don't want them to thrust me from this door
because I'm left alone."

                    Telémachus
had heard Odysseus' words; and at once he left
to reach the room where splendid arms were kept.
From there he carried out four shields, eight spears,
and four bronze helmets plumed with thick horsehair.

Greek [86-111]

He quickly brought them back to his dear father.
Then first he girt himself in bronze; and when
the herdsmen, too, put on their handsome arms,
three stood beside the dexterous, wise Odysseus.
But he, as long as he had shafts to spend,
kept aiming: every shot brought down a man
within his house; there, one by one, they fell.
But when that lord had no more shafts, he leaned
his bow against the doorpost of the hall;
it stood upright against the gleaming wall.
He strapped his shoulders with a four-ply shield,
and on his sturdy head he set a casque
with horsehair plumage, waving, ominous;
he gripped two stalwart spears, both tipped with bronze.

Inside the walls there stood a postern door
raised somewhat from the floor; a passageway
led from the far end of the great hall's gate,
right to that private door. That way was shut
by outer panels fitted tight. Odysseus
had told the good swineherd to watch with care
the entrance to that corridor, to stand
close by the only way to that far door.

Then Ageláus spoke to all the suitors:
"Friends, can't we send one man to reach that door,
alert the people, sound the loud alarm;
then we could see the last of these attacks."

Melánthius the goatherd answered him:
"Zeus-nurtured Ageláus, that can't be:
the entrance to that corridor is much
too near the handsome door; it's hard to pass
that narrow entranceway; one man's enough
to keep us all in check—if he is tough.
Instead, I'll fetch you weapons from the stores;
for it is there, I think, and nowhere else

. . .

Greek [112-140]

that arms were hidden by Odysseus
and his famed son.”

That said, Melánthius
the goatherd sought Odysseus’ inner rooms.
He took twelve helmets with their horsehair plumes,
twelve shields, as many spears; these he brought back
to serve as suitors’ gear when they attacked.
And when Odysseus saw them gird their arms
and brandish long spears with their hands, his heart
and knees went weak: he faced a monstrous task.
Now with winged words he spurred Telémachus:
“Telémachus, some woman in this house
has hatched this plot—or else Melánthius.”

Telémachus’ reply was wise, astute:
“Father, it’s I myself who am at fault:
no other bears the blame; it’s I who left
the storeroom door ajar; it seems their guard
was more alert than I. My good Eumǽus,
rush now to seal that door, and do find out
who’s opened it: one of the women or—
as I suspect—the son of Dólius,
Melánthius.”

So son and father spoke.
Meanwhile Melánthius the goatherd went
off to the storeroom once again, to fetch
more weapons—but he caught Eumǽus’ eye.
The swineherd asked Odysseus at his side:

“Astute Odysseus, son of Zeus, that man
whom we suspect has left the hall again:
another storeroom-raid. But if I prove
the stronger of the two, what should I do:
am I to kill him there or haul him here
to pay for all his fetid plots and snares?”
▢ ▢ ▢

Greek [141-169]

Odysseus, man of many wiles, replied:
"Telémachus and I will stay the rush
of suitors in this hall, however harsh
their fury; meanwhile—with Philœtius
to help you—twist that traitor's feet and arms
back to his spine; and once he's trapped inside
the storeroom, bind him to a board and take
a length of twisted rope and tug that thing
along a towering pillar to the rafters,
that he may live—and suffer—somewhat longer."

Those two were quick to do what he had urged.
They reached the storeroom door; each took his place:
unseen, they flanked the entrance, lay in wait.
Melánthius, to gather arms, had gone
into the farthest corner of the room.
And then the goatherd came out carrying
a handsome helmet in one hand; the other
held fast a rust-flecked shield that had been borne
by brave Laértës when he was a boy—
the stitching on its strap was long since torn.
Those two were quick to grab him; by his hair
they dragged him back inside the room and threw
that quaking felon on the floor; they used
a ruthless rope to tie his hands and feet,
to twist them back, bound fast, to meet his spine—
as patient, bright Odysseus had asked.
Then with a plaited cord, which they attached,
they hoisted him along a towering pillar
up to the rafters. You, Eumæus, said—
to mock the goatherd, hanging overhead:

"Now you, Melánthius, can watch night through
on your soft bed, the sort that's rightly yours;
you won't miss Dawn's firstlight, her golden throne;
you'll see her rising from the Ocean's flow—
just when you used to drive your plump she-goats
to serve the suitors' revels in these halls." □ □ □

Greek [170-199]

They left him there, well stretched by their fierce ropes,
put on their armor, shut the polished door,
and then rejoined their wise and cunning lord.
But now the rival ranks stood face-to-face,
arrayed in rage: upon the threshold, four;
and stalwart, in the hall, so many more.

But now, beside those four, Athena stood:
Zeus' daughter, in her voice and aspect, took
the guise of Mentor. At the sight of her,
Odysseus' heart was glad. He pleaded:

                                    "Mentor,
I am your friend: we shared fond years together.
I favored you. Now help me foil disaster."

Despite his words, he recognized Athena,
who rouses warriors. But facing them,
the suitors' shouts were loud. First, Ageláus,
Damástor's son, rebuked Odysseus' friend:

"Don't let his honeyed words persuade you, Mentor,
to join his side, to fight against these men.
For this is how our plan will come to pass:
Once we have killed the father and the son,
then we shall kill you, too; for all you want
to do within these halls, your head will pay.
And when our bronze has stripped you of your force,
we'll add those goods that you possess—your house
and land—to everything Odysseus owns
and take it all; and we'll forbid your sons
to live within your halls, and not allow
your daughters and dear wife to move about
this city, Ithaca."

                    On hearing that,
Athena, now incensed, with words of wrath,
stormed at Odysseus:

Greek [200-225]

              "You have surely lost
the fury and tenacious force that once
were yours when, for those nine long years, you fought
for white-armed Helen; in those wild assaults,
you killed so many; and it was your plot
that brought the city of wide roads, the Troy
of Priam, to its end. Why is it, then,
that, with your house and goods again at hand,
you weep and wail? And all of this just when
your force should crush those men. Instead, my friend,
come closer, at my side take up your stand;
just see what I can do when I contend
with enemies. The son of Álcimus—
I, Mentor—can repay your kindnesses."

These were Athena's words, but she did not
give him the strength he'd need to win at once;
the goddess still was bent on trying out
the power to resist and to assault
of both Odysseus and his sturdy son.
Then she herself flew upward, taking on
the likeness of a swallow as she perched
upon a rafter in the murky hall.

These men now led the suitors: Ageláus,
Damástor's son; Amphímedon; Peisánder,
Polýctor's son; and Demoptólemus,
Eurýnomus, and cunning Pólybus—
by far the best of all the suitors left
alive and fighting to avoid their death;
the bow, the flow of shafts, had felled the rest.
And Ageláus urged on all his comrades:

"Friends, this resistless man has tired at last.
Mentor—whose braggart words you heard—ran off;
they are alone now at the outer doors.
So do not cast your long spears all at once.
You six throw first, in hope that Zeus allows

Greek [226-252]

Odysseus to be struck—a prize for us.
And once he's fallen, do not fear the rest."

These were his words. Then those six suitors cast
their shafts with eager force, as he had asked.
But each shot missed its mark—Athena's work.
One hit the sturdy doorpost of the hall;
and one, the tightly fitted door itself.
The other ash-wood shafts just struck the wall.
So did all four escape the suitors' spears;
and seeing that, Odysseus spurred his men:

"The time has come for us in turn to cast
our shafts against their ranks; my friends, don't let
that crew, to all their wrongs, now add our death."

That said, with deadly aim all hurled their shafts.
Odysseus' spear downed Demoptólemus;
Telémachus struck down Euryadës;
the swineherd's shaft caught Élatus; the cowherd's,
Peisánder. Those four bit the spacious floor.
The other suitors fell back in the hall;
at that, Odysseus and his men moved up
and stripped the dead men's bodies of their bronze.

Again six suitors cast their shafts with force;
but each shot missed its mark—Athena's work.
One spearhead struck the sturdy hall's doorpost,
and one, the tightly fitted door itself;
two other ash-wood shafts, tipped with stout bronze,
just struck the wall. And though two shafts drew close,
they leveled nothing more than glancing blows;
Amphímedon's spear reached Telémachus,
but its bronze spearhead only grazed his wrist.
Ctesíppus' crossed above Eumæus' shield
but only scratched his shoulder, then flew on
and thudded to the ground. Now, once again,
the stout, astute Odysseus and his band

Greek [253–281]

heaved hard their shafts against the suitors' ranks.
Odysseus, ravager of cities, struck
Eurýdamas; it was Telémachus
who downed Amphímedon; the swineherd's shaft
felled Pólybus. The cowherd heaved his spear
into Ctesíppus' chest, and then he jeered:

"You, taunting, fleering son of Polythérsës,
forget your folly and fanfaronades
forever; it's for gods alone to speak
the final word: their will exceeds our reach.
This spearhead is the gift that will requite
the ox-hoof gift you gave to the godlike
Odysseus when he begged within this house."

But now Odysseus and his men attacked
close in; Odysseus' massive spear struck down
Damástor's son; and once Telémachus
had wounded in the waist Leócritus,
Evénor's son, he drove his spear clean through;
the suitor crashed headlong, face to the ground.
Then from above, close to the roof, Athena
held high her aegis, sign of death for mortals.
And terror took the suitors; through the hall
they fled like cattle when the gadfly darts
to sting the herd, in spring, when days grow long.
And just as vultures with their crooked beaks
and talons, swooping from the mountains, seek
to snatch the smaller birds (in panic, these
fly toward the plain, beneath the clouds, and yet
the vultures pounce upon and kill them—no
device and no defense can help—and men
enjoy that chase), so did Odysseus' band
hunt down the suitors to this side and that,
through the vast hall. As heads were struck the groans
were horrid; all the pavement streamed with blood.
But rushing out to clasp Odysseus' knees,
Leīódës, with winged words, now made this plea: □ □ □

Greek [282-311]

"Odysseus, as your suppliant I ask
for your regard and mercy. This I can
assure you: Nothing I have said or done
has ever wronged the women of your house;
indeed, I tried to curb the wanton course
of others—they ignored what I had urged.
A squalid fate repays their unjust ways.
Yet I, an augur, one who did no wrong,
will die as they have died. Can this be true:
Those who do good will gain no gratitude?"

Odysseus, man of many wiles, just scowled:
"If you indeed declare yourself to be
their augur, then you often made this plea
within my halls: that I might be denied
a sweet return. You would have had my wife
choose you and bear your brats. And that is why
you won't escape a death that terrifies."

That said, his sturdy hand picked up the sword
that Ageláus, as he died, let fall
upon the ground. He struck Leīódës' neck—
a clean slice. As the augur tried to speak,
his head fell in the dust.

                              But Phémius
the singer, son of Térpius, still sought
escape from darkest fate; he had been forced
to sing at suitors' feasts. With harp in hand,
close to the postern door, he stood; two thoughts
debated in his mind: Was he to leave
the spacious hall and sit beside the altar
of Zeus, the god of courts and yards, for whom
Laértës and Odysseus sacrificed
their oxen, burning many fatted thighs;
or must he rush to clasp Odysseus' knees
and make his plea? This plan seemed best: He set
his hollow harp between the mixing bowl

Greek [312–341]

and silver-studded chair, then rushed ahead
to clasp Odysseus' knees as he beseeched
with these winged words:

                   "I am a suppliant,
Odysseus; I implore—grant me regard
and pity. If you were to kill a bard,
a man like me who sings to men and gods,
you'd feel remorse. My chanting is self-taught;
it is the gods who planted every sort
of song within my heart. I am as fit
to sing to you as to a deity.
Then do not be so keen to cut my throat.
My witness is Telémachus, your son:
I did not come through my own will or zeal
to sing at suitors' feasts within your halls.
Their force was far too much: I was compelled."

These were his words. Telémachus the strong
had heard and, turning to his father, urged:
"Stop. Do not kill a man who has no guilt.
And let us save the life of Medon, too:
that herald always cared for me when I
was still a boy, within our house—unless
by now the swineherd or Philœtius
has done him in, or he's met death beneath
your sword as you raced raging through the house."

These were his words, and prudent Medon heard:
he'd crouched beneath a chair; there—to escape
his fate—he wore an oxhide newly-flayed.
But he was quick to rush out. Throwing off
the oxhide, straight away he hurried toward
Telémachus to clasp his knees. And now
the herald made his plea with these winged words:

"Friend, here I am. Do stay your hand and ask
your father to relent: my fear is that

Greek [342-368]

his sovereign force might kill me in his wrath
against the suitors, who consumed his goods
and did not honor you—for they were fools."

Astute Odysseus, as he answered, smiled:
"Take heart. My son has won: he saved your life
that you may know and tell to others, too,
that goodness gains far more than malice can.
But now, do leave these halls and sit outside;
stay in the courtyard, far from blood and strife—
you and the singer of such varied songs—
but I'll stay here—to finish up my work."

These were his words; the two men left the hall.
Beside the altar of great Zeus, they sat,
looking from side to side, still fearing death.

Odysseus' eyes searched round his house, to see
if any, to escape dark destiny,
were still alive and hiding. But he saw
that all were fallen in the blood and dust—
so many, like the fish that fishermen
draw from the gray sea in their fine-meshed nets
onto the curving beach: they lie in heaps
along the sands—the fish that long to reach
the waves, but stay beneath the bright sun's rays
and die. So did the suitors now lie heaped
one on another. Then astute Odysseus
said to his son:

                    "Go now, Telémachus,
and call your old nurse, Euryclēia: I
must tell her what I have in mind."

                                    That said,
Telémachus obeyed. He shook the door
and called to his old nurse:

□ □ □

Greek [369-394]

"Come, Eurycleīa,
be quick: my father wants to speak to you,
the guardian of all our women servants."

These were his words, but hers remained unwinged;
she simply came in silence, opening
the door, and stepped into the handsome hall,
led by Telémachus. She found Odysseus
standing among the bodies of the dead.
There he, befouled with blood and filth, was like
a lion who has torn apart an ox
along the plain and, having gorged, moves off,
blood staining all his chest and both his jaws—
the sight of him strikes fear; just so, blood smeared
Odysseus' feet and hands. And when she saw
the corpses and the countless streams of blood,
she felt the need to shout with joy—so great
a task was now complete. But she was checked:
with these winged words, Odysseus held her back:

"Old woman, check yourself; you must restrain
your joy—don't shout aloud. It is profane
to let your voice exult when men are slain.
These men were struck down by a god-sent fate
and by their wanton acts; for they, in truth,
had no respect for any man on earth—
not only evil men, but even those
we deem most good and fair, whoever was
unfortunate enough to cross their path.
Their insolence has earned this squalid end.
But come now, tally for me all the women
within these halls: which ones dishonored me
and which deserve no blame."

                    Then Eurycleīa,
his dear nurse, answered him: "I shall indeed
tell you, my son, the truth. Within this house
you have some fifty women servants: these

Greek [395-421]

we've trained to do their work—to card the wool
and to be chaste in every way. In all,
just twelve have given way to wantonness,
with no respect for me or even for
Penelope. As for Telémachus,
he's only reached his manhood recently:
his mother's given him no right to rule
the women of the house. But it is time
for me to climb up to her lovely rooms
and tell your wife all that has happened here;
she's steeped in the deep sleep some god has sent."

Odysseus, man of many wiles, replied:
"This is no time to wake her; go instead
to fetch the faithless women—bring them here."

That said, the old nurse left, her task was clear.
Meanwhile, with these winged words, Odysseus urged
Telémachus, the cowherd, and the swineherd:

"Start hauling off the dead, and have the women
assist you. Then wash down and sponge with water
the handsome seats and tables. Once you've set
the house in order, lead the women out.
Place them between the round tower and the court's
stout wall; then, with the suitors' long sharp swords,
strike—strike until those sluts have lost their lives
and can't remember how their loving plied
the suitors, when they dallied at their sides."

These were his words. With terrifying cries
and many tears, the crowd of women came.
First, then, they carried off the dead. They placed
each corpse beneath the courtyard's colonnade,
each body propped against another—and
Odysseus urged them on with his commands;
they had no choice—they did all that he asked.
When that was done, the women washed and sponged

Greek [422-452]

the handsome chairs and tables, while with hoes,
Telémachus, the cowherd, and the swineherd
went through the sturdy house and scraped the floors.
The women took those scrapings out of doors.

The hall was now in order. And they led
the women out into the court—like cows—
between the round tower and the sturdy wall—
into a narrow space, with no escape.
The first to speak was wise Telémachus:

"I would not strip these women of their lives
by way of some clean death; they have defied
my mother and her son; they've slept beside
the suitors."

      That was said, and then he bound
the cable of a dark-prowed ship around
a sturdy pillar of the portico,
then ran it to the round tower, stretched it high,
so that no woman's feet might reach the ground.
Just as when doves or thrushes, wings outstretched,
head for their nests but fall into a net
that's set within a thicket, finding death
and not the place where they had hoped to rest,
so were those women's heads, aligned, caught tight
within a noose, that each of them might die
a dismal death. Their feet twitched for a while—
but not for long.

      That done, Melánthius
was led outside the door into the court;
with savage bronze they hacked off both his ears
and nose, cut off his genitals—a raw
meal for the dogs—and then, with frenzied hearts,
hacked off his hands and feet. Their work complete,
as soon as they had washed their hands and feet,
. . .

Greek [453–478]

again they joined Odysseus in the house.
But he urged Eurycleīa, the dear nurse:

"Old nurse, bring sulfur now and cleansing fire
to purify these rooms. Then go and fetch
Penelope with all her maids at hand,
and ask the other servingwomen, too,
to gather here."

       Old Eurycleīa answered:
"Your words, my child, were all indeed well said.
But come now, let me fetch more seemly clothes,
a cloak and tunic, so that you'll not stand
here in your hall, your broad back wrapped in rags—
such tatters hardly suit."

       And the astute
Odysseus answered her: "But first of all,
let fire be readied for me in this hall."

These were his words. She did not disobey.
She fetched the sulfur and the fire; with these
Odysseus cleansed the hall, the house, the court.
Meanwhile the old nurse hurried to alert
the loyal servingwomen. Crowding round
Odysseus, they embraced him: faithful, fond,
they kissed his head and shoulders and his hands.
Sweet need to weep and wail seized him within
his heart, for he had recognized them all.

Greek [479-501]

BOOK XXIII

Penelope's obdurate doubt
of Odysseus' return.

Her test, the secret sign, and her belief:
their tearful reunion.

Athena delaying dawn.

The prophecy of Tirésias retold.

The joys of love, the joys of talk.

Odysseus' summary of his trials.

At dawn, Odysseus off to see Laértës.

The old nurse, jubilant, went up the stairs
to reach her mistress' rooms, to let her know
that her dear husband had indeed come home.
Her knees were agile and her feet were quick.
She stood beside her mistress' bed—said this:

"Penelope, dear child, awake; you may
see what your eyes have longed for every day.
Odysseus now is here; he has returned;
his absence has been long, but he has killed
the bragging suitors who have sacked his wealth,
defied Telémachus, and plagued this house."

This was the wise Penelope's reply:
"Dear nurse, your words are wild; the gods can drive
the wisest mortal mad, or even guide
a fool to wisdom. Yes, you once were wise,
but now the gods have led your wits astray.
Why do you mock me so when my heart grieves?
Why speak wild words that wake me from a sleep
that held my eyes in sweet embrace, more deep
than any sleep that I have known since he—
my dear Odysseus—sailed to Troy-the-ugly.
Now go away—back to the women's hall.
Had any of my other women dared
to wake me with such tidings, I'd have sent
her off straightway; she would have felt my wrath;
but you are old—you benefit from that."

The faithful Eurycleīa did not budge:
"I am not mocking you, dear child: in truth
Odysseus—as I said—is here; he's home;
he is the stranger whom they all reviled
in your great hall. For some time now your son
has known that he was here, but wisely kept
secret his father's plans, until revenge
could end the outrage of those bragging men."
□ □ □

Greek [1-31]

She said no more. With joy, Penelope
leaped from her bed, hugged the old nurse, and said—
even as tears fell from her lids—winged words:

"Come now, dear nurse, do tell me all the truth:
how did he—he was one alone—attack
those braggarts—many men, a crowded pack?"

The dear nurse answered her: "I did not see;
I only heard the groans of those who died.
Behind tight doors we women, terrified,
crouched at the farthest corner of our room.
I did not budge until I heard your son,
Telémachus, call me into the hall,
just as his father ordered him to do.
You'd have rejoiced to see Odysseus like
a lion, blood-flecked, fouled. The dead were piled
before the doorway to the portico
as he, once he had kindled mighty fires,
purged his fair hall with sulfur, while he called
on me to fetch you. Come—I'll lead you both
to joy that follows many trials. You've yearned
so long; at last he's home; he's reached his hearth
alive; he has found you and found his son;
against the suitors' malice, he has won
revenge within this house."

                                This was the wise
Penelope's reply: "Do not delight
as yet. You know how welcome he would be
to all within these halls, especially
to me and to our son, Telémachus.
Yet in your news I place but little trust.
One of the gods struck down that lordly band,
a god whom their foul crimes and arrogance
incensed; for they, in fact, had no respect
for any man on earth—whether he was
evil or excellent. Their insolence

Greek [32–66]

has earned this squalid end. As for Odysseus,
far from Achæa he has lost the path
of his return, and he himself is gone."

Then Eurycleīa answered: "My dear child,
how can the barrier of your teeth permit
such speech to cross your lips? How can you say
that your Odysseus never will return
when he is in this house, at his own hearth?
You've always had an unbelieving heart.
But there's another certain sign that I
must share with you: the wound that long ago
the white-tusked boar inflicted on Odysseus.
I saw this when I washed his feet; I should
have told you this, but it was he himself
who laid his hand upon my mouth; he would
not let me speak—yes, he is keen, astute.
But follow me; I stake my life—if I
have tricked you, I am forfeit, I must die."

Then wise Penelope replied: "Dear nurse,
however wise one is, it still is hard
to read the counsels of the deathless gods.
But let us hurry to my son, that I
may see the slaughtered and their slaughterer."

That said, she left behind her upper rooms.
Her heart was still unsure: Was she to probe
her husband from afar or, drawing close,
to kiss his head and hands? She crossed the sill
of stone and took a seat within the hall,
facing Odysseus as he sat beside
the far wall in the firelight. His eyes
cast down, he leaned against a pillar, waiting
to see if, when she saw him there, his wife
would speak to him. But she sat long in silence,
her heart assailed by wonder; now her eyes
stared full upon his face, and once again

Greek [67-94]

she failed to recognize him—he was dressed
so miserably. But Telémachus
rebuked her:

           "Mother, you are hard of heart:
why do you stay so far away from my
dear father? Were you at his side, you might
ask question after question. Yes, your heart
is stubborn—surely there's no other woman
who'd keep her distance from her own dear husband
who, after he has suffered many trials
in more than nineteen years away, returns
to her, in his dear land. Not even stone
is harder than the hardness your heart shows."

This was the wise Penelope's reply:
"My son, the soul within my breast is struck
with wonder; I've no words; I cannot ask;
I cannot even look him in the face.
If what I see in truth is my Odysseus
come home to me, we two shall certainly
know one another without questioning:
we've secret signs, unknown to all but us."

That said, the patient, bright Odysseus smiled.
He turned to his dear son with these winged words:
"Telémachus, be patient: let your mother
test me within these halls; she soon will find
the way in which I can be recognized.
Now, since I'm dressed in tattered rags and filth,
she scorns me—won't admit that I am he.
Meanwhile the two of us can make our plans.
Even if a slain man has left few friends
who'd seek revenge, the killer flees that land—
he's exiled from his city and his clan.
But we have killed the pillars of this town,
the noblest youths of Ithaca: I ask
that you reflect most carefully on that."   □ □ □

Greek [95-122]

Penelope

Telémachus' reply was keen and wise:
"Dear father, you yourself can see to this.
They say that you're the most astute of men—
no mortal can contrive more cunning plans.
We three will follow where you choose to lead;
whatever strength we have is yours to spend."

Odysseus, man of many wiles, replied:
"Then I shall tell you what seems best to me.
Once you have bathed yourselves, I'd have you dress
in tunics; let the women wear their best.
The godly singer is to take his harp
and lead us in a glad and varied dance,
so those who live nearby or those who chance
to pass along the road will say that we
are in the middle of a wedding feast.
Then rumors will not spread throughout the town:
no one will hear about the suitors' deaths
until we've left for our well-wooded farm.
Once we are there, we can devise a scheme—
whatever plan Olympus will concede."

His words were done. They heard, and they obeyed.
They bathed, and then they dressed; in fine array
the women gathered; and the godly singer
took up his hollow harp and spurred them on:
they longed for seemly dance and gracious song.
Out from the great house echoed loud the tread
of men who danced and women finely dressed.
And those who heard those sounds outside now said:

"Someone has surely wed the queen at last—
the woman whom they wanted so. That bitch
no longer guards the great house of her own
true husband, waiting—firm—for his return."

So some did say, but none knew what had passed.
Meanwhile Eurýnomë, the housewife, bathed

Greek [123-153]

in his own halls the resolute Odysseus,
then smoothed his body down with oil and cast
a tunic round his back. That done, Athena,
the gray-eyed goddess, made him more robust
and taller, and she gave him thicker hair,
which flowed down from his head in curls and clusters
that seemed much like the hyacinth in flower.
Just as a craftsman who has learned his secrets
from both the gray-eyed goddess and Hephǽstus
frames silver with fine gold and thus creates
a work with greater plenitude and grace,
so did the goddess now enhance the face
and head and shoulders of Odysseus.
When he came from the bath and reached the hall,
his form was like the form of the immortals.
Again he took the chair from which he'd risen,
facing his wife. He said:

                "Perplexing woman!
To you the gods who hold Olympus gave
a heart more obdurate than any they
have ever given other—weaker—women.
What other woman has a heart so stubborn
as to deny herself her own dear husband,
who's suffered trial on trial and, after more
than nineteen years, returns to his own shores!
Come, nurse, I need to rest; prepare a couch,
that I, though all alone, may lay me down:
within her breast she has a heart of iron."

This was the wise Penelope's reply:
"Wild man! I am not proud, I do not taunt,
nor am I stupefied—I know full well
how you appeared when, in your long-oared ship,
you left your Ithaca. Yes, Eurycleı̄a,
prepare the sturdy bedstead for him now
outside the solid bridal room that he

. . .

Greek [154-178]

himself constructed; carry out the bed,
and over it throw cloaks, bright blankets, fleece."

These words of hers were meant to test Odysseus.
Incensed, her husband cried to his keen wife:
"Woman, your words have wounded me. Who tore
my bedstead from its base? For it would take
a god—if he so pleased—to shift its place.
No man alive, however young and strong,
with mortal force alone could hope to budge
that bed without great strain, for it contains
a secret in its making. No one else
contrived that bed: I fashioned it myself.
Within our court a long-leaved olive trunk
stood stout and vigorous, just like a pillar.
Around that trunk I built our bridal room.
I finished it with close-set stones and laid
a sturdy roof above; I added doors
that fitted faultlessly. Then I lopped off
the olive's long-leaved limbs; and so I thinned
the trunk, up from its base; with my bronze adze,
I smoothed it down with craft and care; I made
that wood run true and straight, and it became
my bedpost. Once I'd bored it with an auger,
I, starting with that part, began to shape
my frame and, with that job well done, inlaid
my work with silver, ivory, and gold.
Inside the frame I stretched taut oxhide thongs;
their crimson shone. My secret sign is told.
Woman, I do not know if my bed stands
where it once stood or if by now some man
has sawed the bedstead from the trunk and set
my bed elsewhere."

　　　　　　These were his words; her knees
and heart went weak; the secret signs that he
revealed were certain proof. She ran to greet
. . .

Greek [179-207]

Odysseus, threw her arms around his neck,
and kissed his head and said:

                       "Dear heart, don't rage:
Odysseus, let the wisdom you've displayed
in all else show here now. It is the gods
who destined us to sorrow; they begrudged
our staying side by side—the two of us—
enjoying youth and coming to the start
of our old age together. Do not be
indignant if at first I did not greet
or welcome you as I do now: the heart
within my breast has always been afraid
that there might be some stranger who would come
to trick me with his blabber; many plot
with cunning malice. Even Argive Helen,
Zeus' daughter, never would have lain in love
beside a stranger had she known that sons
of the Achæans were to wage a war
to bring her back again to her own land.
It surely was a god who spurred her act
of wantonness, who blinded her so that
she could not see what fate had brought to pass;
our sorrows, too, were born of her blindness.
But now you've listed clear, unerring signs
of our dear bed; no mortal's ever seen
that bed except for you and me and one
lone servant, Actor's child, the girl my father
had given me when I first journeyed here
to Ithaca—the maid who kept the doors
of our stout bridal chamber; and with this,
my heart, which was so stubborn, is convinced."

These were her words; they spurred his need to cry;
in tears Odysseus clasped his dear, wise wife.
And as the sight of land is welcomed by
the only shipwrecked sailors to survive
when whiplash winds and crashing combers sent

Greek [208-233]

by lord Poseidon have destroyed their ship;
in flight from the gray sea, they swim toward shore,
their bodies caked with brine, and now at last
set foot upon the beach; their grief is past:
so at the sight of him, there was delight
in her; she twined her white arms round his neck.

And Dawn with her rose fingers would have found
those two still tearful had the gray-eyed goddess,
Athena, not devised this stratagem:
She slowed the night, delayed its journey's end;
and then she held back Dawn, whose throne is gold;
she did not let her yoke the racing foals
that carry light to men—the colts of Dawn,
Lampus and Pháethon. Odysseus said:

"Dear wife, we've not yet reached the end of all
our toils; in days to come, I'll face a test
so long and hard—so measureless—and yet
there is no part of it I can neglect.
So did the spirit of Tirésias
foresee; of this he told me on that day
when I went down to Hades' house to ask
about my comrades' and my journey back.
But come, wife, it is time for us to see
our bed, our joys, our rest, wrapped in sweet sleep."

This was the wise Penelope's reply:
"Now that the gods have brought you back again
to your own house and native land, your bed
stands fully ready any time you wish.
But since you called to mind that trial—it is
some god who made you think of that—speak out:
I'll have to hear of it at some time soon,
and now is just as good a time as then."

Odysseus, man of many wiles, replied:
"Strange woman! Why do you incite me so

Greek [234-264]

to speak? And yet I'll tell you all I know
without disguise, though there is no delight
for you—and none for me—in hearing this
just as I heard it from Tirésias.
He said that I, with shapely oar in hand,
must visit many cities till I reach
a land where men know nothing of the sea
and don't use salt to season what they eat;
they're ignorant of boats with purple cheeks
and shapely oars that are the wings of ships.
He told me this clear sign, which I won't keep
from you: When on the road a man meets me
and says that what I'm carrying must be
a fan for winnowing, I can be sure:
that is the place where I must plant my oar
and offer lord Poseidon handsome gifts—
a ram, a bull, a boar that mates with sows.
Then, once I have returned to Ithaca,
I am to offer holy hecatombs
to the undying gods, wide heaven's lords—
to each in turn. I shall not die at sea:
the death that reaches me will be serene.
I shall grow old—a man of wealth and ease—
surrounded by a people rich, at peace.
All this, he said, will surely come to be."

The wise Penelope had this to say:
"Yet if the gods, at least in your old age,
allow you better days, you may escape
at last from trials and wars. So we can hope."

Such were the things they shared with one another.
Meanwhile, by bright torchlight, old Eurycleia
had joined Eurýnomë, and both were busy
wrapping the sturdy bedstead in soft blankets.
The old nurse then went back to her own room.
Eurýnomë, the keeper of their chamber,
led them across the court by firelight

Greek [265-294]

and then went back again. And he and she
delighted in the sight of their old couch.

Telémachus, the cowherd, and the swineherd
meanwhile had stayed their feet; they danced no more;
and once they'd stopped the women, they themselves
lay down to sleep within the shadowed halls.

But when Odysseus and Penelope
had had their fill of love's delights, the joys
of talk were theirs, the telling one another
of all their trials. She told him of her grief
as she—fair woman—watched the vicious suitors,
that crowd who, in their wooing her, had butchered
so many beasts—both cattle and plump sheep—
as well as drawing wine beyond all measure.
Odysseus, born of Zeus, in turn rehearsed
the sorrows he'd inflicted and endured;
he spared her nothing. His dear wife felt deep
delight in listening, and no sweet sleep
touched her until his telling was complete.

His story started with his victory
against the Cíconës, and how he reached
the fertile land of men who feed on lotus.
He touched on all the malice of the Cyclops,
and how he'd made that monster pay his due
for having mercilessly eaten some
of his stout crew. King Æolus came next,
the lord who welcomed him, then sent him off,
though fate denied him passage to his home:
a storm wind snatched him up, thrust him across
the fish-rich sea as he groaned heavily.
And then his tale took in Telépylus,
the city of the Laestrygónians,
who wrecked his ship and killed his well-greaved men.
He also told of Círcë's wiles and craft
and how, upon a ship with many oars,

Greek [295–322]

he came to Hades' somber house to meet
the spirit of Tirésias of Thebes;
there he saw all his comrades and his mother,
she who had borne and reared him. Then he told
how he had heard the never-ending song
the Sirens sing; and how he reached the rocks
they call the Wanderers, and grim Charýbdis,
and Scylla, she from whom no man has yet
escaped intact; and how his comrades killed
the herds of Hélios—and Zeus, the lord
of thunder, struck his swift ship with a bolt
of smoking lightning; all his comrades died,
and he alone escaped death's heartless Fates.
His coming to Calypso's isle, Ogýgia,
was next: that nymph had kept him in her caves;
she wanted him as husband; tending him,
she thought to make him deathless, ever young;
but she could not convince the heart within
his breast. So after many trials, he came
to the Phaeácians, who, most eagerly,
paid him the honors men bestow on gods
and, after they had given him much gold
and bronze and many clothes, escorted him
back to his own dear land on their swift ship.
This was the end of what he had to tell;
now sleep assaulted him, sweet sleep that can
loosen the limbs and soothe the griefs of men.

And now Athena had another scheme.
When she was sure his heart had filled its need
for love and bed and sleep, at once she roused,
from Ocean's flow, Dawn on her throne of gold
to carry light to men. From his soft bed
Odysseus rose; and to his wife, he said:

"By now we both have had our fill of trials.
You here, dear wife, were mourning over my
harassed and slow return; while on my part,

Greek [323-351]

Zeus and the other gods combined to thwart
my longing for my native land. But now
that we have found the bed for which we yearned,
stay here, watch over all that I still own;
I shall replace the herds the braggart dead
consumed; I'll take much booty—do be sure—
and what I still may miss, Achæans must
give me, until my every stall is full.
But now I leave the city; I must see
my father on our wooded farm—he grieves
for me. May you, dear wife—so wise—do this:
At sunrise, word of what I've done will spread;
men soon will know about the suitors' deaths;
so, with your women, go and stay inside
your room upstairs. See no one; ask no questions."

That said, he shouldered his fine armor, woke
Telémachus, the cowherd, and the swineherd,
and asked all three to wear their weaponry.
They did as he had asked: they took their arms
of bronze and, opening the doors, went out.
Odysseus led the way. Though light had touched
the earth by now, Athena cloaked those four
in night; she led them quickly from the city.

Greek [352-372]

BOOK XXIV

Hermes guiding the suitors' shades to Hades.

The encounter of
Achilles and Agamemnon.

Amphímedon's account of the fate of the suitors.

·

The visit to Laértës in his orchard.

Odysseus' fabricated tale.

The joys of recognition.

·

Rumor through Ithaca.

The burial of the suitors;
their kin and partisans
in assembly, seeking vengeance.

The beginning of a battle;
Athena's parting of the factions.

Odysseus bent on more bloodshed—
halted by Zeus' thunderbolt.

The pact; the peace.

Now Hermes of Cyllénë summoned all
the spirits of the suitors. In his hand
he held the fair gold wand that can enchant
the eyes of men with sleep or, when he wants,
wake men at rest. He led; they followed him.
As in an eerie cavern's deep recess,
if one among a cluster of the bats
that hang down from a rock should fall, the rest
flit round with their thin shrieks; so here, those souls,
as they advanced along dank paths behind
their guide and helper, Hermes, voiced thin cries.

They passed the Ocean's flow and the White Rock;
they passed the gates of Sun and land of Dreams;
and soon they reached the Field of Asphodels,
home of the helpless dead—of faded souls.
They found the shades of Péleus' son, Achilles,
and, in his close-knit company, Patróclus,
flawless Antílochus, and Ajax—he
whose form and stature outdid all the Greeks
except for the incomparable Achilles.

But then the grieving soul of Agamemnon,
the son of Átreus, approached the band
of souls around Achilles. In his wake
came all the shades of those who met dark fate
and died beside him in Aegísthus' house.

Achilles' spirit was the first to speak:
"O son of Átreus, we were sure that you
would be the favorite of thundering Zeus,
his dearest warrior, through all your days;
for you in Troy, where we Acháeans suffered,
commanded men of might. But then, in truth,
before your time, at your side, too, there stood
dark death, the fate that none who's born escapes.
Ah, had you died in Troy, the honors due
a master warrior would have been yours!

Greek [1-31]

All the Achǽan army would have heaped
a towering tomb for you; and, too, your son
would have won greater fame in days to come.
Instead it was decreed: You were to fall
a victim of the saddest death of all."

The soul of Átreus' son replied: "Godlike
Achilles, son of Péleus, you were blessed:
you died in distant Troy and not in Argos.
Around you, battling for your body, fell
the Trojans' and Achǽans' finest sons,
as you lay in the whirling cloud of dust,
forgetful of the clash of chariots:
a man of might within his mightiness.
We fought the Trojans all day long: we'd not
have stopped had Zeus not stayed us with a storm.
Then from the battlefield we brought you back
into our camp. We set you on a bier
and cleansed your handsome body with warm water
and unguents; mourning you, the Dánaans wept
hot tears and cropped their hair. As soon as word
reached her, your mother rose up from the sea
together with the deathless Néreïds;
unearthly wailing swept across the deep,
a shudder shook the army of the Greeks.
They would have hurried then to man our ships
if one most wise in many ancient things
had not prevented that; his counseling
before this had proved best; with keen good sense
old Nestor spoke to the Achǽan ranks:
'This is no time to sail away! Young Greeks,
look now! His mother's coming from the deep
together with the deathless nymphs, to see
her dead son.' So did Nestor urge. Heartstrong,
all the Achǽans halted at his words.
The daughters of the Old Man of the Sea
surrounded you; in all their misery,
they wailed; they wrapped you in immortal cloaks.

Greek [32-59]

With their sweet voices, all the Muses—nine—
intoned your dirge; and you would not have seen
one Argive there who did not weep: such was
the power of the Muse's limpid song.
We wept—we deathless gods and mortal men—
without a let, by day and night alike,
for seventeen full days. The eighteenth came,
and then we gave your body to the flames.
Around your pyre we slaughtered many sheep
and many oxen with their curving horns.
Dressed in the garments of the gods, you burned,
your body steeped in unguents and sweet honey.
There, hurrying to join the wheeling dance
of men in arms, the Argives, rank on rank,
on foot and riding chariots, advanced;
around your pyre the tumult was immense.
But when Hephæstus' flames had done their work
and morning came, we gathered your white bones;
the wine in which we steeped them was unmixed;
the unguents that we brought were ample, rich.
Your mother gave a double-handled urn
of gold—the famed Hephæstus fashioned it,
she said—and this was Dionysus' gift.
Your bones now lie within it, bright Achilles;
they mingle with the bones of dead Patróclus,
Menœtius' son; but set apart lie those
of one who, after strong Patróclus' death,
you held more dear than any comrade left:
Antílochus. Above that urn, we strong
Achæan spearmen heaped a handsome cairn
upon a headland jutting out along
the spacious Héllespont, that from the sea,
no matter how far off, it might be seen
by men alive today and those to come.
Your mother asked the gods for handsome trophies
and set them in the middle of the field
for those who were the finest of the Greeks.
You've seen so many solemn games for chiefs

Greek [60-87]

and heroes—at the funerals of kings,
young Dánaans getting ready to compete;
but wonder would have struck you had you seen
the splendid gifts that silver-footed Thetis,
your goddess mother, offered in your name.
The gods held you most dear; so after death
you did not lose your fame; among all men,
Achilles, you will be forever named.
But what delight was mine to claim when I
wound up the skein of war? For Zeus devised
a horrid death for me at my return:
Aegísthus and my foul wife struck me down."

Such were the words those warriors exchanged.
The guide and helper, Hermes, led the shades
of suitors whom Odysseus had slain
still closer now. Both heroes were amazed
to see that company; without delay
they greeted them. The soul of Agamemnon
was quick to recognize Amphímedon—
for Mélaneus' dear son had been his host
when Agamemnon, years ago, had come
to Ithaca. Now Átreus' son spoke first:

"Amphímedon, what sorry destiny
has led you—all of one age, all so princely—
to this dark land? Were one to choose a town's
best men, he'd have to pick your splendid band.
Was it Poseidon's waves and wild storm winds
that struck your ships? Or did you die on land,
undone by enemies—a deadly clash—
when you were raiding handsome sheep and oxen
or warring for a city's wealth and women?
Do answer me, for I have been your guest.
Don't you remember that? With Meneláus
I came to Ithaca to urge Odysseus
to join us as we sailed to Ílion
in sturdy ships. Between our journey out

Greek [88-117]

and back, and our long stay within your house,
we spent one month: it was that hard to get
Odysseus, scourge of cities, to agree."

The spirit of Amphímedon replied:
"O Agamemnon, Átreus' famous son,
Zeus-nurtured king of men, all you describe
I can recall. There's nothing I shall hide—
I'll tell you fully how we came to die.
When he had been away so long, we tried
to win Odysseus' wife; though she despised
a second marriage, she did not refuse
our suit, did not accept it: she devised
death and dark fate for us. And she contrived
this wile within her heart: Within her room,
she wove a fine broad web upon the loom.
The web was wide, the threads were fine, and she
assured us all—unhesitatingly:
'Young men, since bright Odysseus now is dead,
be patient; though you're keen to marry me,
wait till this cloth is done, lest any thread
unravel. This is lord Laértës' shroud—
the robe he'll wear when dark death strikes him down.
I weave it now, lest some Achǽan women
condemn me for neglect, for having let
a man who'd won such wealth lie at his death
without a shroud.' These were her words; and we,
with manly hearts, agreed. So she would weave
that mighty web by day; but then by night,
by torchlight, she undid what she had done.
She hoodwinked all of us for three long years;
but when, as spring returned, the fourth was here,
one of her women servants, well aware
of all her stratagems, revealed the plot.
We suitors caught her in the act, as she
alone unraveled that consummate cloth.
She had no choice but to complete her work.
▢ ▢ ▢

Greek [118-146]

"No sooner had she woven that great cloth
and washed and showed it to us, as it shone
like sun or moon, than some malicious god
brought back Odysseus to his farmlands' edge,
the swineherd's house. Divine Odysseus' son,
his dear Telémachus, had also come
to that same house—he'd made his way back home
from Pylos' sandy shores in his black ship.
A savage plan was plotted by that pair,
to kill the suitors. With their scheme prepared,
they headed for the famous city: first
Telémachus, and then Odysseus—dressed
in rags and tatters, stooping on a stick,
much like a blind, old, squalid beggar—led
by his own swineherd. And not one of us—
even the oldest suitors—knew it was
Odysseus: he had come so suddenly.
We battered him with words of insult, and
we pelted him with anything at hand.
With patient heart he stood it for a while—
insult and injury in his own halls.
But when the will of aegis-bearing Zeus
spurred him at last, with his Telémachus
he took his arms and, hiding them within
the storeroom, shot the bolts. Then he convinced
his wife to carry out this cunning plan:
to set his bow and axheads of gray iron
before the suitors. This would be a test—
then with that bow he'd start to slaughter us.
Not one of us could stretch that great bow's string;
that test found every one of us too weak.
Yet when the great bow reached Odysseus' hands,
we all cried out, we menaced, shouted threats;
however much he might insist, we asked
that he not have a chance. Telémachus,
alone now, spurred him on: he was to try.
So patient, bright Odysseus grasped the bow;
he strung it easily, then shot the shaft

Greek [147-177]

straight through the socket hollow of each ax.
That done, he stood upon the threshold, glared
ferociously, then shot his rapid shaft;
and lord Antínoüs was struck. Again,
again, he shot still other fatal barbs
against the rest of us; his aim was sure.
We fell in heaps. His ally—it was clear—
must be some god; for even as they ran
amok, they slaughtered every man they caught
within those halls, upon all sides. Those struck
cried out in horror, and the pavement smoked
with blood. O Agamemnon, that is how
we died. Our bodies lie there even now,
unburied in Odysseus' house; and none
among our kin has heard what happened, none
can mourn us, laying out our bodies, once
they've washed away the black blood of our wounds:
that much is surely every dead man's due."

The soul of Agamemnon answered: "You,
Odysseus, man of many wiles, are blessed:
the wife you won has every excellence.
Her mind has understanding: she, unmatched
Penelope, did not forget the man
she wed. The daughter of Icárius
will never lose the fame that she has won;
for your Penelope the deathless ones
will shape a song to bring delight among
all men on earth. The daughter of Tyndáreus
was unlike that: her deeds were dark; she killed
the man whom she had wed; a song of hate—
such is to be the chant that shapes her name
among all men; the fame of womankind—
even the chaste—is blemished by her name."

Meanwhile Odysseus' men had left the town.
They reached the fields of lord Laértës' farm;
he'd tilled and tended them with his own hands,

Greek [178-206]

long labor spent on what became rich land.
His house was there; and round about stood sheds
where bondsmen, men who worked at what he asked,
would eat and sleep when they were done with tasks.
There, too, an old Sicilian woman stayed:
her care and kindness eased Laértës' days—
an old man on a farm far off from town.

Odysseus told the servants and his son:
"Go now into that sturdy house and butcher
straightway the finest hog you find, for supper;
and I shall test my father, see if he
knows me on sight or fails to recognize
a son who has been gone so long a time."

That said, he gave his weapons to the herdsmen,
who then ran quickly to the house. Odysseus,
still searching for his father, reached the orchard.
But in that spacious section, rich with fruit,
he could not find the guardian, Dólius,
or any servant who worked under him;
the sons of Dólius were also gone,
for they had hurried off to gather stones
to shape the garden wall—and as their guide,
old Dólius had left with them. But he
did find his father there; he saw Laértës:
alone, he spaded soil around a sapling;
his clothes were miserable, filthy, patched;
to shield his shins from scratches, he had wrapped
two greaves of stitched cowhide and, on his hands,
wore gloves to fend off thorns; a goatskin cap
was on his head. He held his sadness fast.
So did the patient, bright Odysseus see
his father, worn with age, his heart in grief.

Odysseus, underneath a pear tree, wept.
His mind and heart debated: Should he clasp
and kiss his father here and tell him all,

Greek [207-236]

how he had now come back to his own land;
or should he probe and question—try him out?
But as he thought, this seemed the better course:
to urge him on with words that could provoke.
With that in mind, the bright Odysseus went
straight to his father, who—his head now bent—
was digging round the tree. Odysseus said:

"Old man, there is no lack of mastery
in all that you have done to tend these trees.
There's nothing you've neglected: not one plant,
no vine, no tree—no olive, fig, or pear.
Yet I must also say—and don't be angry—
that you've not taken care of your own self:
you bear a sad old age; you're black with filth
and dressed in squalid rags. You are not lazy—
your master can't neglect you, charging sloth;
and there is nothing in your face or stature
to say that you're a slave; indeed you seem
a king—a man who after bath and food
might well expect to sleep on a soft bed;
old men deserve such things. But tell me this,
and tell it frankly: Who's the man you serve?
Who owns the fields you tend? And tell me, too,
in honesty, so that I can be sure,
have I indeed arrived in Ithaca?
A man whose path I crossed while coming here
just told me that, but he was not too kind;
he did not hear me out, not take the time
to answer fully when I asked about
an Ithacan who'd been a guest of mine:
I needed to find out if he's alive,
or dead and in the halls of Hades. I
must tell you this, and listen carefully.

"In my own land, I once had been the host
to one who, when he visited our house,
was such a guest as none before had matched;

no stranger come from distant lands was ever
as welcome as that man. He said his stock
was Ithacan; his father was Laértës,
Arceīsius' son. I did not stint; that guest
received my every kindness; I was rich—
I gave him friendly, just, and lovely gifts:
I gave him, when he left us, seven talents
of well-wrought gold, a silver mixing bowl
embossed with flowers, twelve cloaks with single folds,
and just as many rugs and handsome blankets,
and linen tunics, too—and, furthermore,
four graceful women, skilled in handiwork:
he wanted to pick out these four himself."

On hearing that, his father wept and said:
"Stranger, you've reached indeed the land you seek;
but reckless, wanton men oppress it now.
Those lavish gifts you gave were all in vain.
Had you found him alive in Ithaca,
he'd have requited you with many gifts,
warm welcome, and a generous farewell;
you had been first with kindness—it's your due.
But tell me this—and speak with honesty:
How many years have passed since you received
that man as guest, that luckless man, the one
of whom I now must say, he *was* my son.
Far from his home, his friends, beset by griefs,
he's been devoured by fishes of the sea
or fallen prey on land to birds and beasts.
His mother had no chance to shroud his corpse,
to weep beside his body, nor did I—
for we, his parents, were denied that right.
Nor could his wise Penelope, the wife
whom he had wooed with many bridal gifts,
lament beside his bier or close his eyes
in death, although the dead deserve that rite.
But tell me, too, that I may hear the truth:
Who are you? Of what family? What city?

Greek [268-298]

Where did you moor the ship that brought you here
together with your crew of godlike friends?
Or did you reach us as a passenger
on someone else's ship, which then was quick
to sail away once you had gone ashore?"

Odysseus, man of many wiles, replied:
"I'll tell you—and there's nothing I shall hide.
I come from Álybas. A splendid house
is mine. My father is Apheīdas, son
of Polypémon. I'm Epéritus.
I sailed out from Sicánia, but thrust
far off my course by some god, I was forced
to find my landing here. My ship is close—
moored near the open fields, and far from town.
More than four years have passed since that sad man,
Odysseus, sailed away from my dear land.
Yet when he left, the signs were surely bright:
the birds that flew past flew upon his right.
How glad we were to see that omen—both
the man who left and he who stayed could hope
that we would meet again as guest and host,
exchanging glowing gifts."

                         These were his words.
A dark, a sudden cloud of sorrow caught
Laértës; sobbing, he scooped up black dust
and scattered it on his gray head. Odysseus
saw his beloved father, and his heart
was stirred; his nostrils felt a pang—most sharp.
He sprang up, kissed and clasped Laértës, cried:

"Dear father, it is I; you see the man
you asked about; he stands just where I stand.
Now, after nineteen years, at last I'm here
in my own land. Enough of grief and tears;
we must be quick—yet I can tell you all

. . .

in brief: I've killed the suitors in our halls;
their acts were foul—I've made them pay in full."

Laértës answered: "If you are indeed
Odysseus, my returning son, I must
be sure: give me a sign I can't refute."

Astute Odysseus said: "First mark this scar;
you see the wound inflicted by a boar,
the one whose white tusks gored me on Parnassus,
where I'd been sent by you and my dear mother
to visit lord Autólycus, her father,
to claim the gifts that he had promised me
when he came here. And I should also speak
about the tree that you once gave to me
within this ordered orchard; I, a child,
trailed you along these paths; you taught me each
tree's name. To me you gave thirteen pear trees,
ten apple trees, and forty trees of figs;
you promised me some fifty rows of vines,
each bearing different grapes—so many kinds—
that ripened, each in turn and in its time,
as Zeus sent down his seasons from on high."

But when he heard Odysseus' words, his knees
and heart went weak; he recognized the signs
his son revealed; they could not be denied.
He threw his arms around the son he loved.
And as his father fainted, patient, bright
Odysseus held him close. When he revived,
his soul returning to his breast, he cried:

"O father Zeus, the gods still rule on high
Olympus if in truth the suitors paid
the price for all their arrogant abuse!
Yet I have this uncanny dread: I fear
the Ithacans will mass against us here

. . .

Greek [325-353]

and send out messengers alerting all
the cities of the Cephallénians."

Odysseus, man of many wiles, replied:
"Take heart. Forget such fears. Your house lies near
the orchard; and I've taken care to send
Telémachus, the cowherd, and the swineherd
to set a meal for us. It's all prepared."

These were their words. They hurried to the house.
They found the herdsmen and Telémachus
slicing great slabs of meat and mixing wine.
When the Sicilian woman, in his house,
had bathed and then anointed brave Laértës,
she dressed him in a handsome cloak. Athena
drew near and gave new vigor to his limbs:
she made his body taller, more robust.
He came out from the bath; his dear son stared,
amazed to see him now so like the gods.
To him Odysseus offered these winged words:

"Dear father, this must surely be the work
of one of the enduring gods: he's made
your features and your stature young again."

These were his words. Then wise Laértës prayed:
"O father Zeus, Athena, and Apollo,
would that I could reclaim the force I had
when I, the Cephallénians' captain, led
the sack of Néricus, that noble fortress
along the mainland shore. For then, arrayed
in armor there beside you yesterday,
my son, I would have smashed the suitors, left
the knees of many weak within our halls.
That would have made you glad."

                              So did the son
and father speak. But now the rest had done

Greek [354–383]

their tasks: the meal was ready; all sat down.
They were about to eat, when suddenly
old Dólius and his sons returned, worn out
from hard work in the fields; it was their mother,
the old Sicilian woman, who had called
her husband and her sons back to the house;
she tended to their needs and took fond care
of Dólius—he was well along in years.

They saw him in the house; they knew it was
Odysseus; and amazed, they did not budge.
But then he spoke these calm and gentle words:

"Old man, sit down to dinner now; forget
your wonder; we have been expecting you;
we waited long, and now we want to start."

When that was said, old Dólius rushed ahead,
reached out his arms: he clasped Odysseus' wrist,
then kissed his hand, with winged words saying this:

"Dear master, how we longed to have you back,
though we had lost all hope of seeing that!
But now the gods themselves brought this to pass:
you're here, we greet and welcome you, and may
the gods give you this gift—untroubled days.
But tell me this—that I may know the truth:
Has wise Penelope already heard
you're here? Or should we send a messenger?"

Astute Odysseus answered: "Do not fret:
old man, my wife has heard that I am back."

So Dólius sat down. As he had done,
crowding around their famous lord, the sons
spoke words of welcome, clasped his hands. In order,
each took his proper place beside his father.
□ □ □

Greek [384–411]

But even as they busied with their meal,
Rumor, the messenger, was rushing through
the city, telling everyone the news:
the suitors' horrid death and doom. At once
from here, from there, around Odysseus' house
men swarmed. They wept. They mourned. And each one bore
his own kin from the house and buried him.
As for the dead who'd come from other towns,
they were assigned to seamen; rapid ships
then sailed each dead man back to his own kin.

That done, all went to the assembly ground
in grief. And when they'd congregated there,
Eupēīthes rose to speak: unending tears
weighed on his heart; he mourned Antínoüs,
his son, the one Odysseus slaughtered first.
Eupēīthes, weeping for him, said:

        "My friends,
this man has done great harm to the Achæans.
He sailed away with many stalwart men
and lost his hollow ships and lost his comrades
and, on return, has slaughtered—not a few—
the finest Cephallénians we had.
Come then, before he can escape to Pylos
or sunlit Elis, where Epēīans rule:
attack him now, or be disgraced forever.
If we don't punish those who killed our sons
and brothers, then in time on time to come
our name will live in long contempt and scorn.
For me, life would indeed lose its sweet taste;
I'd rather join the dead at once. Don't wait;
don't let them cross the sea: block their escape."

Such were his words, his tears. Achæan hearts
were touched by pity. But astonishment
took everyone when they saw Medon come
together with the godlike singer from

Greek [412-439]

Odysseus' house to the assembly ground—
those two had not awakened until then.
And Medon, man of understanding, said:

"Now listen to me, Ithacans: Odysseus
did not devise his plot without the help
of the undying gods. For I myself
saw an immortal standing at his side,
a god who showed himself in Mentor's guise,
a god who now appeared in front to guide
and spur Odysseus, then at other times
raged through the great hall, hunting down the suitors;
in dread they fled from him; they fell in heaps."

These were his words. Pale fear took all who heard.
Then old lord Halithérses, Mastor's son,
the Ithacans' lone augur, one who saw
the past and times to come, now spoke with wisdom:

"Listen, you Ithacans, to what I say:
My friends, it is your cowardice that brought
these things to pass. We warned—but you did not
heed me or Mentor, shepherd of his flock:
you did not stop your sons' stupidities.
Their insolence and malice wrought great harm,
wasting the wealth of one so notable,
insulting his dear wife; they thought that he
would not return. But now, do hear my plea:
Do not defy him: all you'll reap is grief."

His words were done. Though others did not budge,
now more than half—with heated shouts—leaped up:
they could not stomach what the augur urged.
And these, Eupeīthes' partisans, rushed off
to arm themselves; then, with their bodies clothed
in gleaming bronze, they gathered at a spot
before the spacious town. And at their head,
in all his folly, marched Eupeīthes: he

Greek [440-469]

thought he'd avenge the killing of his son,
but he himself was never to return;
instead, right there, he was to meet death's doom.

Meanwhile Athena said to Cronos' son:
"Our father, lord of lords, tell me what plan
lies hidden in your mind? Will you prolong
this bitter war, this battle's savage roar?
Or would you rather reconcile these clans?"

Zeus, summoner of clouds, replied: "My child,
why ask me this? Odysseus' taking vengeance
upon the suitors once he had returned—
was this not something you yourself had urged?
Do as you will, but this way is the best:
The suitors have been punished; bright Odysseus
has his revenge; and now let both the factions
conclude a solemn treaty; let Odysseus
rule over Ithaca for all his days,
and we'll persuade them to forget the slaughter
of sons and brothers. Let them live as once
they did: as friends, men blessed with peace and wealth."

Athena was already keen, but now
his words stirred her still more: she darted down
from high Olympus.

                    In Laértës' house
the meal, meanwhile, was done. They'd had their fill
of sweet food. Patient, bright Odysseus spoke:
"Let someone go to see if they've drawn close."

That said, the son of Dólius did as told
but, seeing enemies, stopped on the threshold.
At once he warned Odysseus with winged words:
"They're near already: let's be quick to gird."

☐ ☐ ☐

Greek [470-495]

That said, they rushed to put their armor on:
Odysseus' band of four—three and himself—
and all of Dólius' six sons. Laértës
and Dólius, though both were old and gray,
dressed, too, in armor—for in such a fray
they would be needed. With their bodies clothed
in gleaming bronze, they opened wide the doors;
Odysseus led the way as they rushed out.

Then, taking on the form and voice of Mentor,
Athena, Zeus's daughter, drew still closer.
The patient, bright Odysseus, seeing her,
was glad. He did not wait to tell his son:

"Telémachus, you'll learn this soon enough
when, in the thick of battle, you confront
the test that tries the bravest: Bring no shame
upon your father's house, for we are famed
on all this earth as men both strong and brave."

Telémachus' reply was keen and wise:
"If you so please, dear father, you will see
my courage: I shall not disgrace your house."

When he heard that, Laértës cried with joy:
"Dear gods, how great a day you've given me!
Indeed I'm happy now: a man who sees
his son and grandson vie in bravery!"

Gray-eyed Athena, at his side, then said:
"Arceīsius' son, most dear of all my friends,
first call upon the gray-eyed virgin and
our father Zeus, then do not wait to cast—
once you have balanced it—your long lance shaft."

She spoke—and gifted him with stalwart force.
He called upon the daughter of great Zeus,
then, quick to brandish his long shaft, he cast

Greek [496-522]

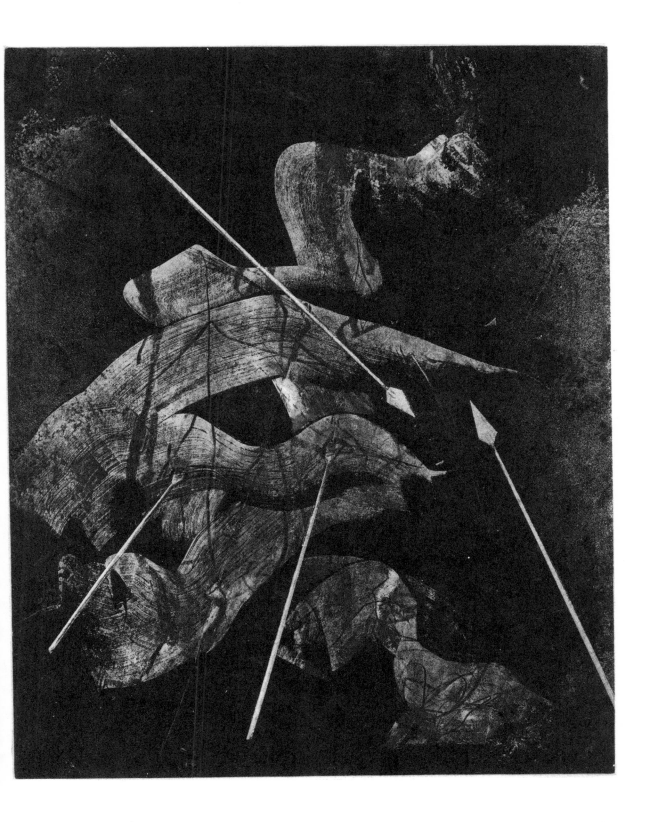

The Final Battle

his lance; he struck Eupeïthes in his casque's
bronze cheeks. That spearhead did not stop; it pierced
straight through. He thudded down, his armor clanged.
Odysseus and his stout son fell upon
the forward ranks; with swords and two-edged spears,
they thrust and would have killed them all, cut off
all chance of their returning home, had not
Athena, daughter of aegis-bearing Zeus,
cried out. She checked the crowd of warriors:

"This gruesome war has lasted long enough.
Stop now, shed no more blood, and stand apart."

These were Athena's words. The townsmen heard;
and pale with fear, they lost their weapons: spears
and swords flew from their hands, dropped to the ground—
the goddess' voice had terrifying force.
They wheeled back, toward the city, keen to live.

Then patient, bright Odysseus' battle cry
was savage; like an eagle from on high,
he gathered force and swooped in fierce pursuit.
But now the son of Cronos cast a bolt
of blazing thunder, and it fell before
the daughter of the mighty lord of lords.
At that, Athena, gray-eyed goddess, warned:

"Laértës' son, Odysseus, sprung from Zeus,
o man of many wiles, this is too much.
Halt now; have done with this relentless war,
lest you provoke the wrath of Zeus, the lord
of thunder, he whose voice is carried far."

He heard Athena's words and, glad at heart,
obeyed. A pact was sworn between the parts,
a treaty for all time: Athena's work
when she, the daughter of aegis-bearing Zeus,
had taken on lord Mentor's form and voice.

Greek [523-548]

Translation exacts and invites much micro-labor, many days in the burrows. (Though the frequency of controversy in questions Homeric often makes the burrows seem like trenches.) Emerging at work's end, one hopes the labyrinthine time will, in its result, be informed by—and shed—light. One blinks—and feels compelled to chart the works that accompanied the burrowing.

The apparatus on which I have been most dependent, the one that allowed me the most comforting and often enlightening conversation with alternatives, was the Valla Foundation six-volume edition of the *Odyssey*, published by Arnoldo Mondadori Editore between 1981 and 1986. The detailed commentary in Volume I (Books I–IV) is by Stephanie West; in Volume II (Books V–VIII) by J. B. Hainsworth; in Volume III (Books IX–XII) by Alfred Heubeck; in Volume IV (Books XIII–XVI) by Arie Hoekstra; in Volume V (Books XVII–XX) by Joseph Russo; in Volume VI (Books XXI–XXIV) by Manuel Fernández-Galiano and Heubeck. That apparatus does allow some above-ground vision within the notes themselves and, above all, in Heubeck's "Interpretazione dell'*Odissea*" that prefaces Volume I, and in each volume-editor's introductory essay to his or her volume. (In the case of Volume VI, Fernández-Galiano writes the introduction to Books XXI–XXII and Heubeck to Books XXIII–XXIV.) The Clarendon Press has a revised version of the Valla edition in course of publication in English; the completion of that English edition will only reinforce what the Italian edition already made clear: this is the state-of-the-art commentary on the *Odyssey*, and it will probably not be matched for a substantial stretch of time.

The Valla bibliographies are especially complete and led me to many follow-up aids, even as my use of that edition—coincident with the work of translation—was preceded by a range of works that were the shared fare of Homerists over these last decades. W. B. Stanford in his two-volume edition of the *Odyssey* (with editions, additions, and reprints from 1947-1948 on) characterizes the range of that shared fare since 1795, the date of the appearance of F. A. Wolf's *Prologomena ad Homerum*, as "severely critical of the form and contents of the *Iliad* and *Odyssey*." Perhaps that is an understatement of the dismembering frenzy sanctioned by the school of Analysts: their search for anomalies and incoherences has indeed been relentless.

Stanford offered an ecumenical hope of reconciliation between the dismemberers and the "'unitarian' view that both *Odyssey* and *Iliad* were almost entirely composed by one poet." Seeing Milman Parry's work on oral techniques as mediating between antagonistic schools, Stanford opined: "Unitarians now believe that much of Homer's material was prefabricated, and analysts concede that many anomalies may be due to the conditions of oral composition."

Stanford's ecumenical hope is perhaps less on target than Howard Clarke's skepticism in "Homer Analyzed," the fourth chapter of his *Homer's Readers: A Historical Introduction to the* Iliad *and the* Odyssey (a work with much anecdotal exuberance and a keen sense of the wens, warts, and blebs on the body of scholarly controversy): "It would be pleasant to be able to report that now the war is over and the combatants have settled their differences. . . . They have not and cannot, for . . . analysts and unitarians . . . have always operated on different wavelengths. . . . The analyst assumes that diverse sources forced Homer, or someone, into anomalous constructions, the unitarian assumes that good reasons persuaded Homer to construct the poems as he did. . . . So there has been no synthesis of approaches."

But Stanford's conclusion is certainly to the point: "But how the controversy will go in the future is *unpredictable* (my italics)." And just as the future of exegesis may be unpredictable, so the reconstruction of the past in questions Homeric is so often conjectural:

One Homer composing two books: the *Iliad* and the *Odyssey?*
Two separate poets, each composing his book (or her book—in
the case of Samuel Butler's wild but charming assertion that
we owe the *Odyssey* to an "authoress," a woman from Sicilian
Trapani)? A long tradition spanning the flowering of Mycenaean civilization, its downfall, illiterate Dark Ages, and then a
time of literacy regained? Strata of diverse creative oral compo-
sitions, then compiled under the aegis of a unitary will by a
creative redactor? By a less creative compiler? Strata of essen-
tially reproductive performances welded into oneness by a unitary will—and perhaps dictated by that will at the point when
literacy followed the introduction of the Phoenician alphabet
in the eighth century B.C.?

However Unitarian my sympathies (as Clarke notes, "transla-
tors tend to smooth over the stylistic unevennesses alleged by
the analysts"), some verses in what is called the Peisistratean
Recension, the one that held sway in antiquity, though considered "canonical," were, early on, athetized by the Alexan-
drines—that is, marked as interpolated, spurious. These lines can
be bracketed; or combining early exegetes, Byzantine exegetes,
and the labors of the Analysts (though the Analysts themselves
often disagree with each other), one might even conjure something like the chromatically marked strata in a Passover Hagga-
dah I have. In as long a text as the *Odyssey*, this last, color-coded
solution would be both typographically arduous-expensive and
hardly inviting to general readers. This list of lines I have omitted is a quick but practical substitute. And one can see from the
very small number of lines that I have been rather unexcising,
rather conservative. Omissions include: I 148; II 393 and 407;
III 78, 308, and 493; IV 57-58, 303, 432, and 783; IX 483; X 265,
430, and 482; XI 631; and XXIII 320. All of these except for five
(IV 432; X 430 and 482; XI 631; and XXIII 320) are repeated—and
translated—elsewhere in the *Odyssey*.

For the climate in which these omission decisions must be
made, it may be useful to general readers to note that Aristar-
chus would not only have omitted XI 568-627, in what we can

call middle-level excision (59 lines), but gave rise to a view of the *Odyssey* as originally concluding at XXIII 296 (in my English: "And he and she / delighted in the sight of their old couch"), while some extend the "original" *Odyssey* to XXIII 344 (in my English: "This was the end of what he had to tell; / now sleep assaulted him, sweet sleep that can / loosen the limbs and soothe the griefs of men").

But leaving aside such major surgery, which would exclude all of Book XXIV of the *Odyssey*, and instead coming closer to typical gritty decisions, one might cite Book X 364-372, where each of the nine lines is repeated elsewhere in the *Odyssey* (respectively: at III 466; VIII 455; X 314 and 315; while the last five lines are repeated four times, in Book I 136-140; VII 172-176; XV 135-139; and XVII 191-195). In the case of these lines, repetition seems to me to involve effective motif-fixing not only in oral contexts but in written contexts that invite aurality—and invite the translator to adhere to the resonances repetition can evoke. (Joseph Russo's "Is 'Oral' or 'Aural' Composition the Cause of Homer's Formulaic Style"—in *Oral Literature and the Formula*, ed. by Benjamin A. Stolz and Richard S. Shannon, III, Ann Arbor, 1976, pp. 31-54, with a discussion on pp. 55-71—may leave post-Parry theorists somewhat discontent, but it seems to suit, with appropriate fit, a verse translator working on an astutely constructed text.)

But in XII 137-152, one does not have a compact set-piece but a mosaic made up of tesserae that have appeared in four earlier books, with only one "new" line. This is the kind of passage where the Analysts are only too ready to see interpolation, and the translator must bear the burden of decision. Here, again, I suppose that Russo's later formulation (this time, on page XVI of his Valla volume) comes closest to my sense of the best practical-poetic guide: "I do not doubt that our text contains interpolated lines, but I do not share with former editors their confidence that we can identify those lines with reasonable probability."

Before and beyond the burrows, there was vitality for me in some sections of Wace and Stubbings, and in the work of Lloyd-Jones (not only his *Justice of Zeus*, but his essay on "Pindar and the After-Life"), Jasper Griffin, W. J. Woodhouse, Bernard Fenik, Norman Austin, M. N. Nagler, Johannes Th. Kakrides—and others. And well before the burrows, there were always Hegel's *Esthetics*, Lukács, Auerbach, and Horkheimer and Adorno—but with many more correctives to them than I could have divined three decades ago. But correctives do not impugn the "essayistic" hold (even, at times, pathos) of those antecedents, just as they do not lessen the cultural energy involved in Greece's own massive "mythologization" of Homer, his long Neo-Platonic afterlife, detailed so well in Félix Buffière's work and, more recently, in Mark Lamberton's. If Clarke calls the Analysts' labors Talmudic, the Neo-Platonists may be called Midrashic (even as are the sons of Hegel—and in their own, other ways, the Joyce of *Ulysses*, and Simone Weil).

Buffière concludes: "Greek thought, in effect, never abandoned Homer . . . and in the last centuries of its existence . . . reached the point where it could reconcile the two great geniuses of Greece, uniting both in the same cult: it brought the philosophy of Plato into the poetry of Homer." Against that reconciliation stand—most recently—Walter Burkert's labors on Greek religion. I've been nourished by both—contradictory—currents. But it is the last that has weighed more as I worked on this translation, trying to render both Homer's musicality and his thought, which I have never felt as anything but subtle, determined, measured, canny, and as committed to mortality as is his homesick Ithacan. (Though the words of Arnaldo Momigliano do always cast a shadow: "It is imprudent to pose questions about the Greek gods that the Greeks themselves would never have understood. The styles in treating the Greek gods have often changed—from symbolism to theology, from naturist to racial explanations, from esthetic interpretation to existentialist. But what has remained constant is the fear of being caught—in a moment of weakness—confessing: 'What do I understand about Greek religion?'")

·

All of the above with—as noted—my special indebtedness to the Valla edition, could not substitute for what the verse translator needs most. For one who is intent on the poetic line as instigator of the voice and ear, readers-hearers are indispensable. Three have read the earlier drafts of this translation line by line: Raymond Prier, who was completing his *Thauma Idesthai: The Phenomenology of Sight and Archaic Greek,* as I worked on this translation; John Bernard, who had taught the *Odyssey* some dozen times before reading my draft; and Daniel Feldman, painter by now, who has long since been a close reader of my own verse and my translation of the *Comedy,* where he collaborated on the notes-apparatus of the Bantam edition.

At the draft before the last, Robert D. Richardson and Steven Zwicker read the first three books; and Henry Weinfield, even as he worked on what should be the best Mallarmé translations we have had, read those three books and has always been available for decisions on variants. And at a time when I was still obsessed by final revisions on the poetic text, Nancy Diessner not only helped in copy-editing decisions, but compiled the basic draft of the glossary.

Having Wake Forest University as main work-site in this final stretch made all the easier my calling on James Hans for a quick but telling look at some problems in decision. With drafts on his desk for a book of his that deals "somewhat" with the gods (Hesiod's, for instance), Homer was hardly that distant from him. This volume is dedicated to his and Hilma Hans' daughter and to my grandson—both born about the time when I began work on this translation.

Barry Moser's gifts have graced five of my labors in this last decade; and with this *Odyssey,* Marialuisa de Romans' incisive images have graced four. I asked—and they indeed answered.

Even as she was throughout four previous volumes, Toni Burbank has been tutelary editor-nurturer for this work on the *Odyssey.* Athena takes many guises.

GLOSSARY

The number at the end of each entry in this glossary refers to the page number of the first and/or principal occurrence of the name in this translation.

·

"Valla" refers to the apparatus in the six volumes of the Valla Foundation edition of the *Odyssey*, and "Stanford" refers to W. B. Stanford's two-volume edition (for both of these editions and the volume editors of the Valla edition—Stephanie West and others—see my Afterword).

·

In transliterating names, Greek *kappa* is usually treated here as "c" and *chi* as "ch"; "os" is altered to "us" (with some exceptions, such as "Cronos"), and "ai" to "ae" (thus, "Aegísthus" not "Aigísthos"); and sometimes "oi" appears as "oe."

·

Some very familiar names are left unmarked; so, too, are names that, though less familiar, are simply monosyllabic ("Thon") or unequivocally bisyllabic—with the stress on the first syllable (as in "Pero").

For all other names, the following practices apply with "reasonable" consistency:

The acute accent marks the vowel in the syllable that bears the principal stress in a word (except for "Pýriphlégethon" and "Anabásinéus," where the accent appears twice).

Where not a single-letter vowel but a diphthong bears stress, accent is marked by a macron in the case of "ei," "oi," "au," and "eu"; but these diphthongs do not bear a macron in unstressed position—thus, "ei"

has a macron in "Clēītus," but not in "Peisánder." (But see "Ēīlēīthȳía.")

The other diphthongs, "ae" and "oe," appear with ligature in stressed position, with the normal accent overhead at the midpoint of the ligature ("Achǽans"); where "ae" does not bear stress, it is not bonded by a ligature (thus, "ae" has ligature in "Ǽolus," but is without it in "Aeólia"), while "oe" sometimes appears with ligature even in unstressed position—as in "Bœótia".

The diaresis is used to mark clearly a vowel forming part of a separate syllable—when that separateness in not already made clear by a normal accent mark on the preceding or following vowel (thus, in "Amphiaráus," the accent on the "a" before the "u" already precludes reading "au" as a diphthong).

But the unmarked "eu" of "Odysseus" and of "Átreus," variously treated in various standard English dictionaries, are variously treated here, too: I have sometimes called on "Odysseus" to fill three metrical positions and sometimes four, and on "Átreus" to fill two and sometimes three. The prosodic context leaves no doubt for the ear.

·

It is impossible to know precisely what the poet of the *Odyssey* can count on as known to his readers or hearers, but we do have indications within the *Odyssey* that he is counting on *some* things as known (as in the reference to Jason in Book XII, p. 245). Even the minimal size of the entries here in this glossary may stretch to elements that were not in the reference haversack of Homer's contemporaries. But most of what in drawn on here did probably form part of that haversack's contents.

The most convenient key to those contents is the Loeb Classics volume, *Hesiod, The Homeric Hymns, and Homerica*, tr. by H. G. Evelyn-White, even though that volume in made up of post-Homeric materials. See especially pages 3-17 of Hesiod's *Works and Days*, and his *Theogony*, pages 79-155. Then browse the brief pages (481-535) devoted to what has been called the Epic Cycle, narrative poems very possibly written between 750 and 550 B.C., but later lost; they may have given way before the overwhelming excellence of the *Iliad* and *Odyssey* (on which see Chapter 23 of Aristotle's *Poetics*). What we have now are snatches of snatches—scrawny abridgements by Photius, a 9th-century Byzantine, of the 2nd- or 5th-century Proclus' extracts. But however late the *Iliad* and *Odyssey* appear after Mycenaean civilization and the Trojan War, they are too early for us to search for literary antecedents that unequivocally precede them in their tradition. Some of what is somewhat helpful in understanding the *Odyssey* must be found in later texts—in Hesiod and in the rag-tag remnants of the Epic Cycle.

□ □ □

Acástus: lord of the isle of Dulíchium. 292

Acháea: region in the northern Peloponnese. Its name is used by Homer to refer to all of Greece. 222

Acháeans: a collective term for all Greeks, just as are "Argives" and "Dánaans." 14

Ácheron: ("the stream of grief") one of the three rivers that intersected near the entrance to Hades, at the place where Odysseus digs his pit to call forth the dead. 211

Achilles: a son of Péleus and the sea-goddess Thetis, father of Neoptólemus. He was one of the greatest heroes of the Trojan War, and the principal hero of the *Iliad*. He was killed by an arrow shot by Paris and guided by Apollo in one of the final battles of the war. He descended to Hades, where Odysseus encountered him in the Field of Asphodels. 46

Acronéus: ("top ship") a young Phaeácian lord. 153

Actor: the father of Eurýnomë, a young girl given to Penelope by Icárius to serve as her maid. But for some—not followed in this translation—the Greek "Actoris" is not a patronymic for Eurýnomë, but in itself the name of a long-dead handmaid of Penelope. 473

Adrástë: a handmaid of Helen. 69

Æacus: grandfather of Achilles, father of Péleus, and son of Zeus and Aegína. 232

Aeæa: the wooded island home of Círcë. 174

Aeétës: brother of Círcë, son of Hélios and Pérsë. 199

Ægae: possibly an island off Eubœa or an Acháean city on the north coast of the Peloponnese, known for its worship of Poseidon. 110

Aegísthus: son of Thyéstës, and lover of Clytemnéstra. When Agamemnon left for Troy, Aegísthus seduced Agamemnon's wife, Clytemnéstra, and with her plotted the murder of Agamemnon. After the war ended and Agamemnon returned home, Aegísthus slew him and his comrades. Aegísthus carried out this wickedness despite Hermes' warnings against such deeds. Eight years after the murder of Agamemnon, his son Oréstes avenged his death by killing both his mother Clytemnéstra and Aegísthus. 6

Aegýptius: father of the suitor Eurýnomus, and wise elder of Ithaca. 25

Aeólia: ("shifting place") isolated floating island surrounded by a bronze wall where Æolus lived in splendor with his large family. 195

Æolus: ("changeful" or "shifting one")
1. the mortal appointed by the gods as a guardian and controller of the winds, which were kept in a cave on his island but could be released at his bidding. 195
2. father of Crétheus. 224

Aeson: son of Tyro and Crétheus, and father of Jason. 225

Aethon: the name that Odysseus assumed when he returned to his palace in the guise of a beggar and was questioned by Penelope. 394

Aetólian: of Aetólia, a region in central Greece. 293

Agamemnon: son of Átreus, brother of Meneláus, husband of Clytemnéstra, and king of Mycénae. He was elected commander in chief of the Greeks in the Trojan War. When the war was over he sailed home without incident, but soon after stepping ashore in his homeland, he and his comrades were invited to Aegísthus' palace where they were all murdered by Aegísthus and Clytemnéstra. Odysseus speaks with his spirit in Hades. 6

Ageláus: a suitor, son of Damástor. 422

Ajax: ("Ajax" is used in this translation for the less familiar "Aias")

1. son of Télamon. Next to Achilles, he was considered the strongest and handsomest of the Greeks fighting at Troy. The suicide of Ajax, son of Télamon, resulted from his failure to win the arms of the dead Achilles. Thetis had promised them to the most valorous of the Greeks—and then awarded them to Odysseus. That suicide (XI, 543) is told in the *Little Iliad*, part of the Epic Cycle. West: "The poet can presume that the episode was familiar to his readers, even if not a particular poetic version." 47

2. son of Oíleus, and leader of the Locrians in the Trojan War. For some reason—later writers say, because he had defiled her shrine after the war, raping Cassandra there—he was hated by Athena, who had throughout the war been the Greeks' guardian. After the war, on his way home from Troy, he was drowned by Poseidon for his boasting in the face of the gods. 81

Alcándrë: a woman of Egyptian Thebes, wife of Pólybus. 69

Álcimus: father of Mentor. 453

Alcínoüs: (Stanford: "brave mind" or "minded to help") king of ·the Phaeácians, husband of Arétë, father of Nausícaa. 117

Alcíppë: a handmaid of Helen. 69

Alcmǽon: son of Amphiaráus the seer and Eriphýlë. (See "Amphiaráus.") 311

Alcménë: mother of Héraclës by Zeus, wife of Amphítryon. 29

Aléctor: a Spartan whose daughter was betrothed to Megapénthës. 65

Alœus: husband of Iphimedéïa, and putative father of his wife's children by Poseidon, huge Otus and Ephiáltës. 227

Alphéus: the god of the large river Alphéus, which rises in Arcadia and flows through Elis, and father of Ortílochus. 61

Álybas: (probably related to a stem meaning "wander") a fictional city that Odysseus invents as his homeland when speaking with Laértës. 491

Amnísus: main port of Cnóssus in northern Crete. 394

Amphíalus: ("double-sea") a young Phaeácian lord, winner of the jumping contest. 153

Amphiaráus: an Argive seer and hero. Descendant of Melámpus, he was a son of Oïcles, a relative of Theoclýmenus, and husband of Eriphýlë. Although he knew that none would survive the campaign of the Seven against Thebes other than Adrástus, his brother-in-law, he was tricked into joining the campaign by the advice of his wife, who had been bribed to accomplish just that. He was loved by Apollo and Zeus, who allowed him to be swallowed up by the earth rather than struck in the back with a spear. His son Alcmǽon eventually avenged his father's death on the Thebans and his mother, Eriphýlë. 311

Amphílochus: a son of the seer Amphiaráus and Eriphýlë. 311

Amphímedon: a suitor. After his death, his shade is recognized by Agamemnon in the Field of Asphodels; and Amphímedon tells him of the plight and massacre of the suitors. 453

Amphínomus: son of Nísus of Dulíchium. He was the suitor most pleasing to Penelope and the most righteous, perhaps the only righteous, of them all. However, he does not heed the warnings of the disguised Odysseus and is slaughtered with the rest of the suitors. 337

Calypso: ("she who conceals") nymph-goddess, daughter of Atlas. She was enamored of Odysseus and kept him with her on her island, Ogýgia, for seven years, promising him eternal youth and immortality if he would agree to stay with her and be her husband. She plays no mythological role outside the *Odyssey*. 5

Cassandra: the fairest of Priam's twelve daughters. She was gifted with prophetic powers; but when she resisted Apollo's advances, he caused her prophecies to suffer this fate: no one believed them. When the Greeks sacked Troy at the end of the Trojan War, she was taken by Agamemnon as his concubine, and soon after their ship put ashore in Greece, she was murdered by Clytemnéstra while Aegísthus killed Agamemnon and his comrades. 231

Castor:

1. a son of Leda and Tyndáreüs, twin brother of Polydeūces, brother of Clytemnéstra, and half-brother of Helen (see "Leda"). The twins were honored by Zeus after their death by both being given partial immortality: each of them lived and died on alternate days. Castor was known for his skill as a horse-tamer and charioteer. 227

2. the name of a fictitious father used by Odysseus in speaking to Eumǽus. 288

Caucónians: the tribe southwest of Pylos whom Athena visited after she left Telémachus on Pylos. 56

Cephallénians: the collective name for the subjects of Odysseus on the mainland. 493

Cetēīans: people of Mysia, a region near Troy; comrades of Eurýpylus. 235

Chalchis: a city on the west coast of Eubœa. 313

Charýbdis: ("wide-swallower") a monster beneath the trees across the narrow channel from Scylla. Three times a day Charýbdis gulped tremendous quantities of water and belched them out again, causing a teeming maelstrom, treacherous for sailors. 246

Chios: hilly and rocky island in the Aegean Sea, off the western coast of Asia Minor. 49

Chlóris: wife of Néleus, mother of Nestor, Chrómius, Periclýmenus, and Pero. 226

Chrómius: son of Néleus and Chlóris, and brother of Nestor. 226

Cíconës: a people of southern Thrace who lived on the coast of the Aegean Sea. They were allies of Troy during the Trojan War and their city, Ísmarus, was raided by Odysseus and his crew on their way home after the war. 174

Cimmérians: for Homer (unlike Hesiod), a legendary people who lived in a dark and misty land near the entrance to Hades. 217

Círcë: goddess and enchantress proficient in the use of herbs and drugs. She was the daughter of Hélios and Pérsë, and lived on the island of Aeǽa. 165

Cleītus: the very handsome son of Mántius whom Dawn fell in love with and carried away to live among the gods. 311

Cyménë: a heroine Odysseus sees in Hades. 228

Clýmenus: father of Eurýdicë. 60

Clytemnéstra: daughter of Tyndáreüs and Leda, wife of Agamemnon, and half-sister of Helen (who was fathered by Zeus). While Agamemnon was away at Troy, she took Aegísthus as a lover and plotted with him to kill her husband on his return from the war. She was ultimately killed by her son Oréstes, who was avenging his father's murder. 52

Clýtius: father of Peirǽus. 321

Clytonéus: a son of Alcínoüs, and winner of the footrace contest. 153

Cnóssus: principal city in Crete. 394

Cocýtus: ("river of lament") a tributary of the river Styx. Cocýtus intersected two other rivers near the entrance to Hades. 211

Cratǽis: ("mighty woman") mother of Scylla. It was only by invoking her that Scylla could be restrained from attacking a second time. 248

Creon: the father of Mégara and ruler of Thebes. 225

Cretans: inhabitants of Crete. 288

Crete: large island in the Mediterranean Sea southeast of Greece. 53

Crétheus: son of Ǽolus (2) and Enarétë, husband of Tyro, and founder and ruler of Iólcus. He raised Tyro's two sons by Poseidon, Pélias and Néleus, and fathered by her Æson, Phérës, and Amytháon. 224

Cronos: a Titan, youngest son of Gǽa and Uranus, and the father of Zeus, Poseidon, Hades, Hera, and Deméter—among others. He castrated and dethroned his father and, in turn, was overthrown by his own son Zeus. 6

Crouni: city on the west coast of Greece. 313

Ctesíppus: son of Polythérsës, and a nasty and unruly suitor from Samos who throws an ox hoof at Odysseus. 421

Ctésius: father of Eumǽus. He was king of the Aegean island of Syria. 317

Ctímenë: sister of Odysseus, who is an only son, but not an only child. 315

Cyclops: (used in this translation as both plural and singular) a race of uncivilized, man-eating giants with one eye in the center of their foreheads who lived in mountaintop caves and tended sheep. Odysseus encountered the Cyclops Polyphémus. 7

Cydónian: people of Cydónia, a seaport on the northern coast of Crete. 53

Cyllénë: mountain in Arcadia, birthplace of Hermes. 481

Cyprus: island near the northeastern end of the Mediterranean Sea. 67

Cythéra: an island lying off the southern tip of the Peloponnese. 175

Cytheréa: name for Aphrodítë, referring to one of the principal centers of her worship, Cythéra. 159

Damástor: father of Ageláus. 422

Dánaans: like "Achǽans" and "Argives," a collective term for all Greeks. 18

Dawn: also known by her Greek name "Eos," goddess of the dawn. Each day she drove her golden chariot across the sky, heralding the day and the coming of her brother Hélios. She had many mortal loves: the Trojan Tithónus (her husband), Oríon, and Cleïtus. 25

Dëïphobus: son of Priam and Hecuba. After Paris died, he was awarded Helen for his valor in the war. When the Greeks sacked Troy, Meneláus and Odysseus forced their way into his palace, and Meneláus killed him. 74

Delos: a small island in the Aegean Sea, later the center of the cult of Apollo and Ártemis. Homer is the only one to speak of a visit there by Odysseus. It was here that Ártemis shot Oríon. 102

Deméter: the goddess of harvests, particularly that of corn, and the fertility of the earth. (See "Persephone.") 102

Demódocus: ("welcomed by the people") blind bard of the Phaeácians. 150

Demoptólemus: a suitor. 453

Deucálion: son of Minos and father of Idómeneus. 394

Día: an island in the Aegean, where Ariádnë was abandoned and killed by Ártemis. 228

Díoclës: son of Ortílochus, and lord of Phérae. He gives lodging to Telémachus and Peisístratus on their way to the palace of Meneláus. 61

Diomédës: son of Týdeus, and a great Greek warrior in the Trojan War. 48

Dionýsus: god of wine, fertility, and joy. He is hardly central in the *Odyssey*; Homer mentions him only tangentially. 228

Dmétor: son of Íasus, and king of Cyprus. 360

Dodóna: town in northwestern Greece, center for the worship of Zeus and noted for its oracles, which were interpreted from the rustlings of the leaves of oak trees. 292

Dólius: faithful servant given to Penelope by her father when she married Odysseus. In old age he worked with Laértës on his farmstead. He was the father of several sons who were loyal to him and to Odysseus and his family, and was also the father of Melánthius and Melántho, who aligned themselves with the suitors. But, to serve in all these roles, there may be two or three men with the same name. 89

Dórians: a conquering race of northern invaders, some of whom lived in Crete. 394

Dulíchium: island in the Ionian Sea near Ithaca, and part of Odysseus' kingdom. Some of Penelope's suitors came from this island. (See "Ithaca"). 14

Dymas: a Phaeácian, the father of Nausícaa's best friend. 117

Echéphron: son of Nestor. 58

Echenéus: venerable Phaeácian elder respected for his learning and wise counsel. 138

Échethus: (perhaps "holder"—restrainer, jailer) mythical Sicilian king, a connoisseur of cruelties. 372

Eidóthëa: sea-goddess who took pity on the stranded Meneláus and told him how to overpower her father, Próteus. 77

Eileīthȳïa: (with "yi" to be pronounced like the English "we") goddess of childbirth. 394

Élatreus: ("paddleman") a young Phaeácian lord, winner of the discus contest. 153

Élatus: a suitor. 454

Elis: a fertile region in northwestern Peloponnese, lying just southeast of Ithaca. 86

Elpénor: youngest member of Odysseus' crew. The morning of their departure from Círcë's island, he falls from the goddess's rooftop, where he went to sleep the night before, and breaks his neck. Odysseus meets his soul in Hades. 212

Elysian Fields: plain somewhere near the end of the earth where the souls of those who had led exemplary lives dwelled, blessed with immortality by the gods. 83

Enípeus: god of the river Enípeus in Thessaly, with whom Tyro fell in love. 224

Epeīans: inhabitants of the region of Elis. 272

Epeīus: with the help of Athena, he built the wooden horse inside of which the Greeks clandestinely passed through the gates of Troy to their final victory. 166

Epéritus: ("the chosen one") the fictitious name Odysseus assumes when in speaking with Laértës. 491

Ephiáltës: enormous son of Iphimedeīa and Poseidon, twin brother of Otus. The two brothers intended to overthrow the gods, reaching the realm of the divine ones in the sky by stacking one mountain atop another, but their plan was never enacted because of their early deaths at the hand of Apollo. 227

Éphyrë: the home of Ílus. The location of this place is uncertain; it is believed to have been somewhere in western Greece, perhaps in Elis or in Thesprótia. 15

Epicástë: (name used by Homer for the more familiar "Jocasta" or, as in Sophocles, "Iocaste") the mother and wife of Oedipus. In her ignorance she married her own son after he had murdered the man he did not know was his father. When she became aware of what she had done, she hung herself. 225

Érebus: ("the dark place"—perhaps related to the Hebrew *erev*, "evening") another name for Hades, the land of the dead. 212

Eréctheus: mythical king of Athens, reared by Athena. 135

Erémbians: a people encountered by Meneláus during his wanderings after leaving Troy. They are very variously identified by ancient and modern exegetes. Strabo's suggestion—Arabs—will do as well as any. 67

Erétmus: ("rower") a young Phaeácian lord. 153

Erínys: singular for Erínyës. See "Furies." 311

Eriphýlë: wife of the seer Amphiaráus. Polyneīces bribed her with a beautiful necklace to urge her husband, who was at the mercy of her decision because of an earlier pact between them, to join Adrástus in the war of Seven against Thebes. See "Amphiaráus." 228

Erymánthus: mountain in northwestern Peloponnese sacred to Ártemis. 120

Etëóneus: a chamberlain of Meneláus. 65

Ethiopians: (probably means "those with sun-burnt faces," though Homer does not allude to their color) inhabitants of Ethiopia, a distant land on the shore of Ocean. Their king was Memnon. 5

Eubœa: large island in the eastern Aegean Sea. 49

Eumǽus: faithful swineherd of Odysseus. 281

Eumélus: husband of Penelope's sister, Iphthímë. 92

Eupeīthes: ("persuasive") father of Antínoüs. He incites revenge against Odysseus for the massacre of the suitors. 19

Eurus: personification of the east wind. 107

Euryádës: a suitor. 454

Euryalus: ("wide-sea") a young Phaeácian lord, winner of the wrestling contest, who rudely challenges Odysseus. 153

Eurybatës: a herald of Odysseus who went with him to Troy. 396

Eurycleīa: ("wide-fame") daughter of Ops. While a young girl, she was bought by Laértës and became Odysseus' nurse. She later became the nurse and attendant of Telémachus. 21

Eurydamas: a suitor. 379

Eurydicë: wife of Nestor, daughter of Clýmenus. 60

Eurylochus: a relative (by marriage) and comrade of Odysseus on the voyage home from Troy. 201

Eurymachus: one of the two leaders of the suitors, who throws a footstool at Odysseus, disguised as a beggar, after insulting him. 20

Eurymedon: ("wide-ruling") ruler of the Giants and father of Peribœa. 134

Eurymedúsa: ("wide-ruling") an old nurse of Nausícaa. 133

Eurymus: father of the seer Télemus. 190

Eurynomë: old devoted housewife of Penelope. 262

Eurynomus: a suitor. 25

Eurypylus: handsome commander of the Cetēians during the Trojan War, killed by Achilles' son, Neoptólemus. 235

Eurytion: a drunken centaur who attacked the bride of Peiríthoüs (at the wedding feast), and was then mutilated by the Lapiths. These acts began the war between the Lapiths and the centaurs. 437

Eurytus: father of Íphitus, and king of Oechalía. His skill as an archer led him to challenge Apollo to a contest, but the god, infuriated by his presumption, killed him. 157

Evánthës: father of Maron. 180

Evénor: father of Leócritus. 33

Field of Asphodels: the meadow-region covered with the gray plant asphodel, over which most of the spirits in Hades wandered. 238

Furies (also Erínyës and Avengers): goddesses or spirits who inflicted curses and punished crimes, primarily those within families. They paid particular attention to avenging crimes by children against their mothers. 361

Gǽa: earth goddess, mother of Títyus. 144

Gerǽstus: promontory on the south of Eubœa, with an important altar of Poseidon. 49

Gerénia: possibly a city in Laconia where Nestor once lived. 46

Giants: mythical savage race, enormous in size and possessing great strength. Eurymedon was once their ruler, but they were destroyed in the war they waged on the Olympian gods. 135

Gorgon: a monster with a red tongue and horrible face framed by serpents writhing around its head. The sight of the creature was so hideous that it could turn a person to stone. 239

Gortyn: city in southern Crete. 53

Graces: goddesses of grace, beauty, and charm. Attendants of Aphrodítë. 117

Great Bear: a prominent constellation in the northern sky, also called the Wain. 106

Gýrae: the cliff in the Aegean Sea against which Poseidon smashed the ships of Ajax (2), and with a part of which he then drowned him. 81

Hades: god of the underworld, one of the sons of Cronos. The name also refers to his domain, the underworld itself, where the dead well. 58

Halithérses: elderly seer of Ithaca, friend to Odysseus. 30

Hálius: son of Alcínoüs, an accomplished dancer. 153

Harpies: the spirit-winds, supernatural beings in form and substance like spirits and wind, who were dedicated to snatching and carrying off people. Pandáreüs' daughters were snatched away from Aphrodítë by these spirit-winds and given to the Furies. 14

Hébë: daughter of Zeus and Hera. She was given to Héraclës as wife after his death and apotheosis. 237

Helen: daughter of Zeus and Leda. She was the beautiful wife of Meneláus whose abduction by Paris was the cause of the Trojan War. 65

Hélios: sun-god. In Hesiod—and probably for Homer—son of the two Titans Hypérion and Théa. He was also the god of herds and flocks; he kept his own sacred cattle on Thrinácia, an island given to him by Zeus. 5

Hellas: region in Thessaly, part of the territory ruled by Péleus, father of Achilles; also used in the *Odyssey* as a name for all of northern Greece, coupled with Argos for Greece south of the Isthmus of Corinth. (Later, Hesiod will use Hellas for all of Greece. Stanford cites Herodotus for its first use including Greek settlements overseas.) 18

Héllespont: narrow straits near Troy, now called the Dardanelles. 483

Hephǽstus: lame god of fire and metalworking, and master of the arts associated with it. He made many magical objects used by the gods and by mortals. In the *Odyssey* he is the wily husband of Aphrodítë. 85

Hera: queen of the gods, second in power to her husband and brother, Zeus. 82

Héraclës: son of Alcménë and Zeus, raised by Amphítryon. Famous for his courage and strength and his ability as an archer. He was told by the Delphic oracle that he had to go to King Eurýstheus, a weakling king, and agree to perform the labors he demanded; if he passed all of those trials successfully, he would be granted immortality. One of these labors consisted of his bringing Cerberus, the hound with numerous heads, up from his guard post in Hades. Héraclës also unjustly murdered Íphitus, who was innocently seeking his lost cattle. Later, the Roman Hercules probably derives from—or is absorbed by—Heracles. 157

Hermes: son of Zeus and Maia, messenger of the gods and guide for the souls of the dead on their way to Hades. 6

Hermíonë: daughter of Meneláus and Helen, given in marriage to Achilles' son Neoptólemus. 65

Hippodameīa: a handmaid of Penelope. 375

Híppotas: ("horseman") father of Ǽolus (1). 195

Hylax: father of Castor (2). 288

Hypereīa: ("the land beyond") an invented name for the distant, former homeland of the Phaeácians, before they settled on the island of Schería. 117

Hyperésia: city in Achǽa. 312

Hypérion: (Valla: "etymology uncertain, but may be equivalent to the Latin *superior*") an epithet for the sun-god Hélios, very possibly a patronymic naming his father, the Titan Hypérion. 5

Iardánus: river in Crete. 53

Iásian: epithet for Argos, used in one place alone in Homer. Stanford doubts its linguistic and historical connection with "Ionic"; Valla leans toward that connection. 377

Iásion: son of Zeus and Electra, Deméter's lover who was killed by Zeus for his audacity in lying with a goddess. 102

Íasus:
1. father of Amphíon (2). 226
2. father of Dmétor. 360

Icárius: father of Penelope. 17

Icmálius: craftsman of Ithaca who made Penelope's chair. 388

Idómeneus: valiant leader of warriors from Crete in the Trojan War, despite his old age. 49

Ílion: another name for Troy, referring to its founder Ílus, not to be confused with the son of Mérmerus. 25

Ílus: the son of Mérmerus who continued his family's art of making poisons, an art that was practiced by his great-grandmother Medea. 15

Ino: daughter of Cadmus and Harmonia. Zeus saved her when she was near death—because she had, as a girl, protected Dionysus from Hera's wrath—and then transformed her into a sea-goddess, known thereafter as Leucóthëa. 109

Iólcus: port city in Thessaly (the modern Volo). From there, Jason sailed in search of the Golden Fleece. 225

Íphiclës: son of Phýlacus, the king of Phýlacë. Melámpus the seer was imprisoned in his house for trying to steal back the cattle Íphiclës had stolen from Tyro. 226

Iphimedeīa: wife of Alœus, mother by Poseidon of Otus and Ephiáltes. 227

Íphitus: son of Ēurytus. He gave Odysseus the bow that is later used by the suitors in a contest, and then is used by Odysseus to slaughter them. Íphitus was cruelly murdered by Héraclēs, in revenge for an offense Ēurytus, Íphitus' father, had previously given to the hero. 427

Iphthímē: sister of Penelope, whose form is taken by the phantom that Athena sent to counsel Penelope in a dream. 92

Irus: (a masculine form comically derived from "Iris," the messenger goddess) nickname of the beggar Arnǣus. 369

Ísmarus: city of the Cíconēs in southern Thrace. 174

Ithaca: rocky island off the west coast of Greece, homeland of Odysseus. To clarify the location of Ithaca and the other islands, the most common solution historically has been to identify Ithaca with modern Thiaki; Zacýnthus with the modern isle of that name; Samos, or Sámē, with Cephallenia; and Dulíchium with Leucas, which is now separated from the mainland by a shallow channel. Alternatively, Ithaca has also been identified with Leucas, Dulíchium with Cephallenia, and Samos with Thiaki. 7

Ithacans: the people of Ithaca. 8

Íthacus: co-builder with Néritus and Polýctor of the fountain on Ithaca. 351

Ítylus: son of Zéthus and Áedon. His mother, Áedon—"the nightingale of the green wood"—accidentally killed him when intending to stab the son of Níobē, her sister-in-law. She was then transformed into a nightingale whose song forever mourned her son. Stanford—with much good humor—notes Homer's "flagrant error in natural history: the female nightingale does not sing." 405

Jason: son of Áeson, leader of the Argonauts. Together with his followers, the Argonauts, he sailed off to seize the Golden Fleece, which would allow him to reclaim his family's right to rule Iólcus, a right that had been usurped by Áeson's half-brother Pélias. 245

Lacedǣmon: southeasternmost region of the Peloponnese, which had Sparta as its principal city and was the kingdom of Meneláus. I have used Sparta and Lacedǣmon somewhat interchangeably in this translation. 54

Laércēs: goldsmith in Pylos who gilds the sacrificial heifer's horns. 59

Laértēs: father of Odysseus and son of Arcēīsius. 12

Laestrygónians: monstrous cannibal giants who lived in Telépylus. They destroy all of Odysseus' fleet except his own ship and eat all of his men except his crew. 197

Lampétiē: ("the radiant one") a daughter of Hélios. She tended her father's cattle on the island of Thrinácia. 248

Lampus: ("shiner") one of the two colts that drive Dawn's chariot across the sky, beginning each day from the shores of Ocean. 474

Lamus: founder of the Laestrygónian city of Telépylus. 197

Laódamas: favorite son of Alcínoüs, and a talented boxer and dancer. 138

Lapiths: a people of northern Thessaly, famous for their battle with the centaurs. 437

Latóna: Roman name for Leto. 120

Leda: wife of Tyndáreüs and, in Homer, mother of Castor and Polydēūces (and, presumably, Clytemnéstra) by her husband, and—by Zeus—of Helen. (Hesiod, however, also attributed to Zeus the paternity of Castor and Polydēūces, reserving to Tyndáreüs the paternity of three daughters, one of whom was Clytemnéstra.) 227

Lemnos: island in the northwestern Aegean Sea, near Troy, settled by the Síntians, a people from Thrace. 158

Leócritus: a suitor. 33

Leīódēs: (probably "soft") a suitor. 431

Lesbos: island off the western coast of Asia Minor, where Odysseus wrestled Philomeleīdes. 49

Leto: a Titaness, daughter of the Titans Cǣus and Phǣbē, and mother of Apollo and Ártemis by Zeus. Títyus once assaulted her and was severely punished by Zeus. 227

Minos: son of Zeus and Europa, a king of Cnossos in Crete for nine years. After his death he delivered judgments among the dead in Hades. 227

Mínyae: people of Bœótia, specifically in the area surrounding and including Orchómenus, and of Iólcus in Thessaly. 226

Múliüs: attendant of Amphínomus from Dulíchium. 383

Muses: daughters of Zeus and Mnemosyne, goddesses of the fine arts, who provided particular inspiration to those gifted in the arts of poetry and music. The *Odyssey* refers to the Muses as nine in number in Book XXIV, p. 483, and—with Hesiod—that number becomes traditional. At the beginning of the *Odyssey*, the singular is used, just as it is used a few lines later in the passage in Book XXIV—a somewhat puzzling use, which I was tempted to regularize but did not. 5

Mycénae: a city in Argolis, the region of Argos, ruled by Agamemnon. 54

Mycéné: a legendary heroine, daughter of Ínachus. Mycénae is named after her. 29

Mýrmidons: a people from southern Thessaly ruled by Péleus, Achilles' father; Achilles led their contingent into battle at Troy. After his death, his son Neoptólemus became their leader. 49

Naiads: nymphs of flowing bodies of water—springs, rivers, brooks, and fountains. (See "Nymphs.") 266

Naūbolus: ("ship-launcher") father of Eurýalus. 153

Nausícaa: the lovely and discreet daughter of Alcínoüs and Arétë. 117

Nausíthoüs: a son of Poseidon and Peribœa, father of Alcínoüs and Rhexénor. He was the leader of the Phaeácian people who brought them to the safety and peace of Schería and established their home there. 117

Naūteus: ("sea-going") a young Phaeácian lord. 153

Neaéra: (Stanford: "perhaps 'new, fresh'"—with reference to the newly dawning day) a nymph, the mother of Lampétië and Phaëthúsa by Hélios. 248

Néion, Mount: a ridge projecting from Mount Nériton in Ithaca. 12

Néleus: son of Poseidon and Tyro, twin brother of Pélias, husband of Chlóris, and father of Nestor, Chrómius, Periclýmenus, and Pero. He became king of Pylos by expelling the founder of the city, and the city prospered under his rule. 43

Neoptólemus: the valiant son of Achilles and Déidameía who fought in the Trojan War after his father's death. 65

Néreïds: nymphs of the sea, daughters of Néreus and Doris, who were led by Thetis. 482

Néricus: a town on the west coast of Greece (possibly on today's island of Leucas, which was originally joined to the mainland as a peninsula), across the water from Ithaca. It was sacked by Laértës in his younger days. 493

Nériton, Mount: a prominent, densely forested mountain on Ithaca. 173

Néritus: co-builder with Íthacus and Polýctor of a fountain on Ithaca. 351

Nestor: son of Néleus and Chlóris; king of Pylos. He was a bold fighter in the Trojan War despite his old age, and was a respected, somewhat garrulous advisor during the war. 16

Nísus: king of Dulíchium, father of Amphínomus. 339

Noémon: ("thoughtful one") an Ithacan inspired by Athena to lend Telémachus his ship. 38

No-one: name Odysseus calls himself to trick the befuddled Polyphémus. 185

Notus: personification of the south wind, regarded as a wind of mist and fog. 107

Nymphs: minor female divinities who were guardians of places or specific objects, whose existence was intimately interwoven with the place or thing with which they were identified. (See also "Naiads"and "Néreïds.") 352

Ocean: both the god of the Ocean and the Ocean itself, conceived of as a swiftly flowing river that issued from Hades and flowed in a circle back into itself around the flat platter surface of the earth. All rivers and seas arose and flowed out from the encircling body of Ocean. 84

Ocýalus: ("swift sea") a young Phaeácian lord. 153

Odysseus: son of Laértës and Anticlēīa, husband of Penelope, father of Telémachus. A cunning, shrewd, and eloquent hero. During the Trojan War Odysseus' battle strategy was indispensable; and near the end of that war, he was the commander of the Greeks inside the wooden horse, which passed through the gates of Troy and brought victory to the Greeks. 5

Œchalía: kingdom of Ēūrytus, possibly the town of that name in Messénë—though there are other Œchalías. 157

Oedipus: son of Laius and Epicástë. He unwittingly killed his own father and then married his mother. When the facts of his situation came to light, his mother hung herself and he gouged his eyes. According to Homer, but not Sophocles, Oedipus remained in Thebes after these events but was plagued by hardships resulting from his crimes. 225

Oénops: ("wine-face") father of Leiódës. 431

Ogýgia: mythical island home of Calypso, situated in the very center of the sea, isolated and distant from all other islands. 8

Oïcles: son of Antíphatës, grandson of Melámpus, and father of Amphiaráus. 311

Old Man of the Sea: used to refer to both Próteus and Néreus. 76

Olympians: gods and goddesses, whose abode was Mount Olympus. 141

Olympus, Mount: a high mountain located in northern Thessaly, whose summit was seen as the home of the gods. The area inhabited by the gods was free from the inclemencies of weather, and the gods lived there in blissful perfection. 6

Onétor: ("benefactor") father of Phróntis. 53

Ops: father of Euryclēīa, son of Peisénor (1). 21

Orchómenus: city in Bœótia, principal city of the Mínyae, and dominant city in the area until the rise of Thebes. 226

Oréstes: son of Agamemnon and Clytemnéstra. He had been in exile when his father was murdered, but after eight years he returned in secret to Mycénae and avenged his father's murder by killing his mother and her lover, Aegísthus. 6

Oríon: a great hunter of great size and great beauty, loved by Dawn. For the offense Dawn's love of Oríon gave to the other gods, Ártemis was urged to kill Oríon. Odysseus saw Oríon's spirit hunting on the Field of Asphodels when he descended to Hades, and navigated by his constellation in the sky. 101

Órmenus: father of Ctésius, and grandfather of Eumǽus. 317

Orsílochus: son of Idómeneus. In one of his crafty tales, Odysseus tells Athena, who is disguised as a shepherd, that he killed Orsílochus because he tried to rob him of his spoils from Troy. 272

Ortílochus: father of Díoclës, and son of Alphéus. It was in his home in Messénë that Odysseus met Íphitus. 61

Ortýgia: an island not clearly identified (it may be Delos—and I have used Delos for it on page 102), lying south of Syria. 317

Ossa, Mount: peak in northern Thessaly. Otus and Ephiáltës planned to stack it atop Mount Olympus and Mount Pélion to reach the gods' domain. 227

Otus: enormous son of Poseidon and Iphimedēīa, twin brother of Ephiáltës. (See "Ephiáltës.") 227

Pǽon: ("healer") god of medicine. 72

Pallas: epithet—of uncertain derivation—of Athena. The epithet is explained by the ancients as from pallō, i.e. she who "brandishes" the spear and aegis. 15

Pandáreüs: a king of Miletas in Crete. He stole a golden dog from the temple of Zeus in Crete, a transgression for which he and his wife were killed by the god. Their daughters were spared and two of them were raised by Aphrodítë, but were ultimately abducted by the spiritwinds, the Harpies, in Aphrodítë's absence. For the third daughter, Aédon, see "Ítylus." 405

Pánopeus: a city in Phocis. 237

Páphos: a city in Cyprus, and important center for the worship of Aphrodítë; she was believed to have arisen from the waves near its coast. 161

Parnassus, Mount: mountain northwest of Athens in the region of Phocis. The caves and grottoes in the mountain were considered principal dwelling places for Apollo and the Muses, and it was a sacred place of music and poetry. On its southern slope was the oracle of Apollo at Delphi. The mountain was also the home of Autólycus and his sons. 401

Patróclus: Menœtius' son, dear companion of Achilles. He was killed by Hector during the Trojan War when he entered the battle carrying Achilles' arms. Achilles mourned his death deeply and refused to bury him or take any food before he had avenged himself on the Trojans. After Achilles' death their ashes were mixed together and placed in the same urn. 47

Peiræus: a son of Clýtius, and trusted friend of Telémachus. 321

Peiríthoüs: king of the Lapiths. It was at his palace, during his wedding festivities, that the centaur Eurýtion became drunk and unruly (and attempted to abduct the bride), beginning the war between the Lapiths and the centaurs. He also fought in the Trojan War. 437

Peisánder: a suitor, son of Polýctor. 379

Peisénor:

1. father of Ops. 21

2. a herald in Ithaca. 26

Peisístratus: (Stanford: "persuader of the host," after his father's powers of persuasion) Nestor's youngest son, who befriends Telémachus when he lands on the shore of Pylos, and accompanies him to Sparta. 44

Pelásgians: a people of uncertain origin. Some are described by Homer as living on Crete and, in the *Iliad,* as being allies of the Trojans. 394

Péleus: father of Achilles by the sea-goddess Thetis, and king of the Mýrmidons in Thessaly. He was too old to fight in the Trojan War, but he gave his weapons to his son. 108

Pélias: son of Tyro and Poseidon, and twin brother of Néleus. He became king of Iólcus by imprisoning his half-brother Æson, legitimate heir to the throne, and banishing his brother Néleus from the city. 225

Pélion, Mount: a wooded mountain in Thessaly. It was one of the three mountains that the giant twins Otus and Ephiáltës planned to stack in order to reach heaven. 227

Penelope: (There is no certain etymology for the name. But of the ancient suggestions, deriving it from *pene,* "thread," or *penelop,* a varicolored duck, the second has much appeal for recent scrutinists, who note the monogamous fidelity of the duck, and the express presence of the duck as symbol of conjugal fidelity, at least in other literatures—but not in Greek.) daughter of Icárius and the naiad Períbœa, faithful and devoted wife of Odysseus, mother of Telémachus. 13

Períbœa: daughter of Eurýmedon, and mother by Poseidon of Nausíthoüs. 134

Periclýmenus: the eldest son of Néleus and Chlóris. 226

Perimédës: a comrade of Odysseus on the journey from Troy. 217

Pero: only daughter of Chlóris and Néleus. She was very beautiful and was sought by many men, but her father would only give her to the man who could bring back the cattle stolen by Íphiclës from Néleus' mother, Tyro. (The task was successfully completed by Melámpus for his brother Bias, who became Pero's husband.) 226

Pérsë: daughter of Ocean, and mother by Hélios of Círcë and Aéetës. 119

Perséphonë: daughter of Deméter and Zeus, wife of Hades, and queen of his kingdom of the dead. She had been abducted by Hades and taken to the underworld, but her mother's intense grief over her loss resulted in a withering of the crops of the earth and desolation in the fields. To amend the situation, Zeus allowed Perséphonë to rise from Hades each spring and join her mother, and return to the underworld each autumn. 210

Pérseus: a son of Nestor. 58

Phaeácians: a people loved by the gods and often visited by them. They lived on the island of Schería and were ruled by Alcínoüs. They were descendants of Poseidon and were unparalleled in their seafaring abilities. Their crews could count on ships that traveled across seas on their own, without the help of navigator or helmsman. 98

Phǽdimus: king of the Sidónians, and friend of Menelǎus. 85

Phǽdra: daughter of Pasíphaë and Minos, and wife of Théseus. She fell in love with her husband's son, Hippólytus, by Antíopë the Amazon. Her love was unrequited, and she hung herself. 227

Phǽstus: city on the south side of the island of Crete. 53

Pháethon: ("bright") one of the two colts that were harnessed to Dawn's chariot and carried it from Ocean's shore, across the sky. 474

Phaëthúsa: ("the light-giving one") a daughter of Hélios and Neǽra who tended with her sister, Lampétië, their father's cattle on the island of Thrinácia. 248

Pharos: an island at the mouth of the Nile, lying opposite Alexandria. It was the home of the sea-god Próteus and his herd of seals. 76

Phéae: a city in Elis, on the west coast of the Peloponnese. 313

Pheīdon: ("he who spares") king of the Thesprótians in Odysseus' fictive tale to Eumǽus. 291

Phémius: ("he who praises") an Ithacan bard, son of Térpius. Forced by the suitors to entertain them, but at heart faithful to Odysseus, he is spared in the final battle. 11

Phérae:
1. The home of Díoclës, perhaps the modern Calamata in Messénë. 61
2. A city in Thessaly, home of Iphthímë and Eumélus. 92

Phérës: son of Crétheus and Tyro. 225

Philoctétës: son of Poīas, and a great archer and hero of the Trojan War. 49

Philœtius: ("desirable fate") cowherd who remained faithful to Odysseus in his absence. 417

Philomeleīdes: a wrestler of Lesbos. He invariably won, until Odysseus wrestled with—and defeated—him. 76

Phoebus: ("the bright") epithet of Apollo, reflecting the identification of him with the sun. 53

Phoenicia: a long, narrow country on the coast of the Mediterranean Sea in Syria. 67

Phoenicians: inhabitants of Phoenicia. They were known for their skill as craftsmen and seafaring traders. 272

Phórcys: a sea-god, father of Thöósa, and grandfather of the Cyclops. 7

Phrónius: ("man of keen mind") father of Noémon. 38

Phróntis: ("prudent") son of Onétor, and skilled helmsman of Menelǎus' ship. 53

Phthía: city in southern Thessaly, part of the territory ruled by Péleus, father of Achilles. (See "Mýrmidons.") 234

Phýlacë: city in Thessaly ruled by Phýlacus. 226

Phýlacus: king of Phýlacë, and father of Íphiclës. 311

Phylo: handmaid of Helen. 69

Piéria: region north of Thessaly, on the northern side of Mount Olympus. 98

Pleiades: a constellation of seven stars, which were originally seven sisters, daughters of Atlas and Pleíonë. Various legends account for their being placed in the sky. 106

Plowman: a northern constellation, also known by its Greek name, Boótës. 106

Poīas: father of Philoctétës. 49

Polítës: a close comrade of Odysseus. 202

Pólybus: ("many oxen")
1. father of Eurýmachus. 20
2. man in Egyptian Thebes whom Menelǎus and Helen visited, and from whom they received several precious gifts. 69
3. a craftsman who made the crimson ball that the two Phaeácian youths, Laódamas and Hálius, use in a dance. 162
4. a suitor. 453

Polycástë: youngest daughter of Nestor. It is she who bathes Telémachus. 60

Polýctor:
1. co-builder with Íthacus and Néritus of a fountain on Ithaca. 351
2. father of Peisánder. 379

Polydámna: an Egyptian woman, wife of Thon. She taught Helen the medicinal properties of various herbs and gave her the drug she serves to Telémachus and Peisístratus to dispel all grief and sadness. 72

Polydeūces: (the Latin "Pollux") son of Leda and Tyndáreus, twin brother of Castor; he was noted for his skill as a boxer. (See "Castor.") 227

Polynéus: ("many-ships") father of Amphíalus. 153

Polypémon: ("much woe" or—more suited to this context—"much wealth") the fictitious grandfather Odysseus creates in the false genealogy he relates to Laértës. 491

Polypheīdes: ("much thrift") the father of Theoclýmenus, son of Mántius, and grandson of Melámpus. He was a great seer of his generation, second only to Amphiaráus, his relative. 311

Polyphémus: a Cyclops, son of Poseidon and Thöósa. When Odysseus and his comrades are trapped in his cave, Polyphémus dines on some of the crew members before Odysseus intoxicates him and impales his single eye, and then successfully escapes. Polyphémus then prays to his father Poseidon to avenge this wrong-doing on Odysseus. 7

Polythérsës: ("of much brashness") father of Ctesíppus. 455

Pónteus: ("deep-sea") a young Phaeácian lord. 153

Pontónoüs: herald of Alcínoüs. 139

Poseidon: god of the sea, the "earth-shaker," son of Cronos and Rhea, brother of Zeus and Hades. During the Trojan War he aided the Greeks whenever possible, but turned against Odysseus after the war and made his homeward course difficult and dangerous because he had blinded the god's son Polyphémus. 5

Prámnos: a city or region of unknown location from which the wine used by Círcë originated. 202

Priam: king of Troy, son of Laómedon and Strymo, and husband of Hecuba. He was father of fifty sons and twelve daughters. After seeing nearly all of his sons die in the Trojan War, he was slain by Neoptólemus as the city fell. 46

Procris: a daughter of Eréchtheus, king of Athens, and wife of Céphalus, who accidentally killed her while he was hunting. 227

Próreus: ("lookout") a young Phaeácian lord. 153

Próteus: a sea-god, son of Ocean and Tethys, and father of Eidóthëa. He had the power of assuming as many different forms as he liked, but, if caught and held through several transformations, was compelled to answer the questions of his captor. He took a daily nap with his seals on Pharos. Like Nereus, he is called by Homer the Old Man of the Sea. 77

Prýmneus: ("poop-man") a young Phaeácian lord. 153

Psýria: a small island west of Chios. 49

Pylos: city on the southwest coast of the Peloponnese, developed by Néleus and ultimately inherited by his son Nestor. Of the three cities in the Peleponnese bearing this name, one is in Elis, one (less well-known) in Messenia, and one in Triphylia. This last has—early (Strabo) and late (Stanford)—been offered as the most probable candidate. But the contents of Homer's own gazetteer are often inscrutable. 8

Pýriphlégethon: ("aflame with fire") one of the three rivers that intersected near the entrance to Hades. 211

Pytho: old name for Apollo's oracle at Delphi on Mount Parnassus. The name originated from the serpent, Pytho (Python), who at one time guarded the oracle, but was killed by Apollo. 151

Rhadamánthus: a son of Europa and Zeus, brother of Minos. A wise and just ruler during his life, after death he was immortalized and lived in the Elysian Fields as judge of the dead. Only Homer refers to a visit of his to Títyus. 83

Rhēīthron: a harbor on Ithaca, near the foot of Mount Néion. 12

Rhexénor: Nausíthoüs' eldest son, brother of Alcínoüs, and the father of Arétë. He was the natural heir to the kingdom of the Phaeácians, but was killed while still young by Apollo. His brother Alcínoüs inherited the kingdom and married Arétë. 135

Rumor: personified as a messenger, spreading news throughout Ithaca. 495

Salmóneus: son of Æolus (2) and father of Tyro. 224

Samos: a large island west of Ithaca. Today it is known as Cephallénia (but see "Ithaca"). 14

Schería: fertile island of the Phaeácians, where they lived a peaceful life and were frequently visited by the gods. 98

Scylla: a hideous and dangerous creature, across the channel from Charýbdis. 245

Scyros: island in the Aegean Sea. It was here that Achilles was hidden to prevent him from going to the Trojan War and here that his son Neoptólemus was born and raised. After Achilles' death, Odysseus came to the island and took Neoptólemus with him back to Troy to fight. 235

Sicánia: for Herodotus and Thucydides, an ancient name for Sicily. 491

Sicilians: the people of Sicánia, particularly those people who dealt in the slave trade, but also referring to the Sicilian woman servant of Laértës. 424

Sidon: a city on the coast of Phoenicia, and principal city of the Phoenicians. 272

Sidónians: inhabitants of Sidon. 67

Síntians: a people from Thrace who settled on Lemnos. They nurtured Hephæstus after he was hurled from Olympus and fell on their island. 159

Sirens: these creatures (Homer does not describe them physically) were known for their alluring, sweet song. When ships approached their island, which lay near Scylla and Charýbdis, the sailors heard the song of the Sirens and were so transfixed that they forgot their homeland, landed, and died on the Sirens' shores, unable and unwilling to tear themselves away from the songs. 244

Sísyphus: son of Æolus, and king of Corinth; a "legendary sufferer" in Hades who was forever compelled to push a huge stone up a hill—once it reached the top it would slide back down again. As in the case of Tántalus, Homer does not specify the transgression for which he has been made to suffer. 237

Sólymi: a people in or near Lycia, a small region in the south of Asia Minor, characterized as brave, mountain-dwelling warriors. 107

Sparta: the principal city in the southwest Peleponnese, situated on the Eurotas River. It was the city most loved by Hera and was the home of Meneláus and Helen. 8

Strátius: a son of Nestor. 58

Styx: ("the abhorrent") one of the rivers that flowed near Hades. It was invoked by the gods when uttering the most solemn oaths. 104

Súnium: high promontory at the southernmost tip of Attica. 53

Syria: an island—not clearly identified—in the Aegean Sea, one of the Cyclades. It was Eumæus' birthplace. 317

Tántalus: mythical king of Phrygia, father of Pelops and Níobë. Odysseus encounters him in Hades where, because of (variously narrated) crimes against the gods, he was compelled to suffer everlasting torment: the fruit and water that hovered near his lips would always somehow slip beyond his reach when he tried to satisfy his eternal thirst and hunger. 237

Táphians: inhabitants of Taphos, ruled by Méntës. They were primarily a seafaring people, though some mention is made of their piracy. 8

Taphos: a place variously located near the western coast of Greece. 21

Taÿgetus: the highest mountain range in the Peloponnese, located in the westernmost part of Laconia. 120

Tecton: ("shipwright") father of Polynéus, and grandfather of Amphíalus. 153

Télamon: father of Ajax (1). 236

Telémachus: (possibly "he who fights from afar"—with reference to his father's prowess with the bow [VIII, page 156]—or "he who fights in places far away"—again with reference to Odysseus) son of Odysseus and Penelope. He was just an infant when Odysseus left home to fight the Trojan War. 10

Télemus: a seer who had lived among the Cyclops and had warned Polyphémus that a visitor called Odysseus would grind out his eye. 190

Télephus: father of Eurýpylus. 235

Telépylus: fortress city of the Laestrygónians. 197

Témesë: the city, perhaps fictional, toward which Athena, disguised as Méntës, tells Telémachus she is heading. 12

Ténedos: a small island in the Aegean Sea off the northwest coast of Asia Minor, near Troy. 48

Térpius: ("delight") father of Phémius. 456

Thebes:
  1. a city in Egypt, straddling the Nile. 69
  2. city in Bœótia. 311

Themis: goddess of justice and order, who presides over human customs and social behavior. Hesiod already speaks of her as Zeus' second wife. 27

Theoclýmenus: ("god-famed") a prophetic son of the seer Polyphēīdes and descendant of the seer Melámpus. He had killed a man in Argos and is a fugitive when Telémachus takes him aboard his ship and carries him to Ithaca. 312

Théseus: son of Ægeus, and a hero of Athens. He went to the court of Minos in Crete to slay the Minotaur. The king's daughter Ariádnë fell in love with him and gave him a thread to escape the labyrinth once he had killed the Minotaur. Together they fled to Athens on a ship. (See "Ariádnë.") 227

Thesprótians: the inhabitants of a region in northwestern Greece. 291

Thetis: sea-goddess, mother of Achilles by Péleus. 484

Thóas: son of Andrǽmon, and leader of the Aetólians in the Trojan War. 298

Thon: an Egyptian, husband of Polydámna. 72

Thóön: ("swift one") a young Phaeácian lord. 153

Thóösa: ("swift, agile," evoking the movement of the sea) a nymph, daughter of Phórcys, and mother of Polyphémus by Poseidon. 7

Thrace: a region northeast of Greece, east of Macedonia. Its people worshipped a war-god whom the Greeks identified with Árës. 161

Thrasymédës: son of Nestor. 44

Thrinácia: (probably "isle of the trident"—Poseidon's implement or sign) a mythical island where Hélios' herds of cattle were pastured and tended by his two daughters. Later identified with Sicily. 220

Thyéstës: father of Aegísthus and brother of Átreus. 82

Tirésias: a blind Theban seer. Stanford notes: "most famous prophet of the Heroic Age, belongs not to the epoch of the Trojan War but to the earlier Theban cycle of legends, with Cadmus, Oedipus, Creon, Polynēīces." He was said to have lived through many generations, and after death he retained, as a gift from Perséphonë, his divining powers and his intellect, undiminished, in Hades. 210

Tithónus: son of Laómedon, brother of Priam, and husband of Dawn. He was a beautiful youth whom Dawn fell in love with and carried off to be her husband. 97

Títyus: giant son of Gǽa. It was his audacity in attacking Leto that led to his being killed by her children Ártemis and Apollo and eternally tormented in Hades, where two vultures tore at his liver, the organ that was believed to be the seat of desire. 144

Tritogenía: epithet of Athena of uncertain significance, but of the varied suggestions, "third-born"—that is, after Apollo and Ártemis—is somewhat persuasive. 56

Trojans: inhabitants of Troy, ruled by Priam. The Greeks overcame them in the Trojan War. 46

Troy: city in northwestern Asia Minor, domain of Priam and the site at which the war between the Greeks and the Trojans over Paris' abduction of Helen was fought. 5

Týdeus: father of Diomédës. 74

Tyndáreüs: husband of Leda and father of Castor, Polydeūces, and Clytemnéstra, and the putative father of Helen. (See "Leda.") 227

Tyro: a beautiful daughter of Salmóneus. She fell in love with Enípeus the river-god, but was tricked into lying with Poseidon when he took on Enípeus' shape. From that union she bore Pélias and Néleus. By her husband Crétheus she was the mother of Æson, Amytháon, and Phérës. 224